Windows

Millennium Me

Windows

Millennium Me

simple to understand

easy to use

informative

Authorised issue 2001 for Mixing GmbH, 74172 Neckarsulm

The publisher has taken the utmost care in ensuring the accuracy of the information published. However, the publisher and the company cannot accept liability of any kind for the use of this information.

Windows (TM) is a registered trademark of the Microsoft Corporation Inc. Further trade names used in this book including software and hardware descriptions are subject to the general trademark or patent protection laws and protected accordingly. The naming of products is purely for information purposes and does not constitute any infringement.
This book is not an original document from the Microsoft company concerning its products.

Printed in Germany.

Contents

Chapter 1
Introduction to Windows Me

Chapter 2
Windows Help

Chapter 3
Programs and documents

Chapter 4
Desktop, taskbar and the *Start* menu

Chapter 5
My Computer and *Windows Explorer*

Chapter 6
The *Recycle Bin*

Chapter 7
Windows Search Functions

Chapter 8
The Control Panel

Chapter 9
System Tools

Chapter 10
Multimedia Applications

Chapter 11
Online Applications

Chapter 12
The Drawing Program *Paint*

Chapter 13
WordPad Word Processor

Windows Glossary

1. Introduction to Windows Me

The first chapter illustrates the essential features of the *Windows Me* operating system with graphic interface. It describes first of all how to start and close *Windows*. It then goes on to indicate how to set the start-up mode or the *MS-DOS Prompt* according to one's requirements. In addition, the chapter describes how to use the mouse properly in *Windows Me* and the functions associated with the right mouse button.

Starting *Windows Me*

Windows Me is the review, published in 2000, of the Windows 98 32-bit operating system, brought on to the market in 1998, not requiring any knowledge of *MS-DOS* (*Microsoft Disk Operating System*) by the user. This means that no further commands are needed to call up the *Windows Me* graphic interface.

Switch on the computer

BIOS

To start *Windows Me*, you must first switch on the computer and, if necessary, the monitor. After it is switched on, the computer undergoes an operating check. The *BIOS* (*Basic Input Output System*) checks that the computer recognizes all the devices present, such as the hard disk units, the floppy disk and CD-ROM units, the working memory and the graphic card, so that it can use them properly. In most computers, this process may be followed on the screen in the first messages displayed.

Loading

A few seconds after these messages disappear, the starting screen with the *Windows Me* logo is displayed. During this process, the hard disk is in fully activity because it has to load hundreds of system files, documents and drivers, and the starting programs.

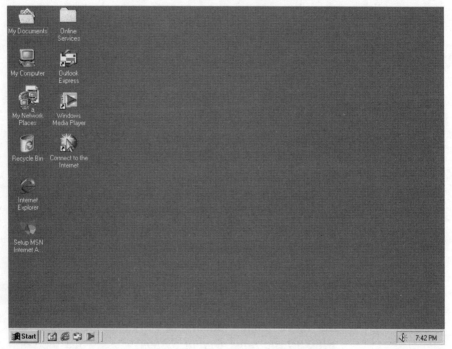

Figure 1.1   Windows Me Desktop after the computer is switched on

Windows Me
network

In a *Windows Me* network or with the user administration activated, the *Network Password* dialog window (Figure 1.2) is displayed after a short time (the *Windows Me* startup time has been greatly reduced with respect to the earlier versions). Type your name in the field *User name* and under *Password* the password established at installation. Then press the key ⏎ or click on the *OK* button.

14

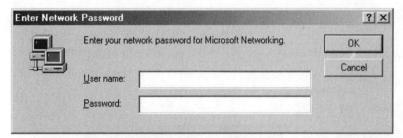

Figure 1.2   This dialog window provides user notification in *Windows Me* networks

After this "logon" the desktop is displayed, this is the zone of reference for working in *Windows Me*.

Closing *Windows Me*

After finishing work with *Windows Me,* a user inevitably faces the question of switching the computer off. At this point, the procedure described below should be applied, straight away the first time.

When *Windows* starts, hundreds of files are loaded. While the different software applications are in use, the computer loads a lot of information invisible to the user on to the hard disk and in the working memory. Before shutting the PC down, this information must be stored or deleted properly. Therefore the computer must not be switched off by its main power switch. Data losses or computer malfunctions could result from such an action.

Shutting down
Windows Me

To shut down *Windows Me*, a circular vision of the procedures must be acquired: just as the *Start* menu represents the graphic interface operating system's control panel, so the *Start* button must also be pressed in order to exit from the system. Click on the *Start* button and select the command *Shut Down...* on the *Start* menu.

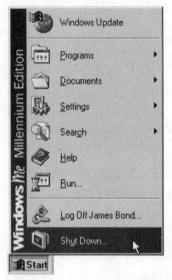
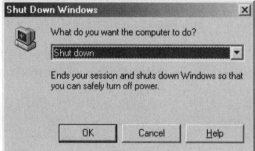

Figure 1.3   From the *Start* menu, the *Shut down Windows* dialog window is opened

At this point, the system behaves differently depending on whether all open documents have been saved or not. If this has already been done, the desktop darkens and the *Shut down Windows* dialog window illustrated in Figure 1.3 (on the right) is displayed. Then select the *Shut down* option and press ⏎ or click on *OK*.

Documents not saved

If there are still unsaved documents open in the *Windows* applications when you select *Shut down*, a message is displayed that enables you to save your data. If you do not want to save changes, click on *No* in the dialog window displayed.

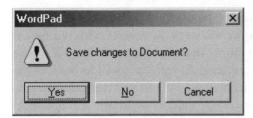

Figure 1.4   During the system shutdown, Windows Me reports that there are documents which have not been saved

**System shutdown
in progress**

At this point, *Windows Me* proceeds to automatic shutdown of all open applications. The system is then stopped. Shortly afterwards, the screen darkens out and the message "It is now safe to switch off your computer" appears in the centre. Only after completing the above operations should you press the power switch to switch your computer off. Modern PC's now switch off automatically after a few seconds.

Working with the mouse in *Windows Me*

At the beginning, those who have never used a graphic interface could be intimidated by this "electronic rodent". Beginners in fact often have the impression that the pointer moves across the screen faster than their hand on the mouse.

**Hints on using the
mouse**

However, it is not difficult to learn how to use this mouse. In no time at all, you become attached to it and cannot do without it. In addition to basic notions on how to handle and move the mouse, the main commands must also be learnt.

Graphic interface

Throughout this manual reference is made constantly to the actions that have to be performed with the mouse. This is the great advantage of a graphic surface. You can do everything in *Windows Me* using the mouse. Put your hand on the mouse without exerting pressure, so that the ball underneath the mouse is in contact with the mouse pad. Your index finger must be resting on the left mouse button, without pressing. As reference will be made in the following to concepts (and operations) that are based on precise assumptions, a unique definition of the main mouse commands must be established.

Mouse pointer

After Windows starts, a small arrow like this ⌖ is displayed on the screen. This is the *mouse pointer*, also called simply *pointer*. If you cannot see the pointer on the screen, move the mouse a little on its pad to display it.

The mouse pointer follows on the screen

As you can see, the mouse pointer responds to the user commands promptly and swiftly. When the mouse moves, the pointer follows on the screen with precision the movements made. If the mouse is moved up, the arrow ⌖ also moves up. If the mouse is moved to the left, the pointer also moves in the same direction.

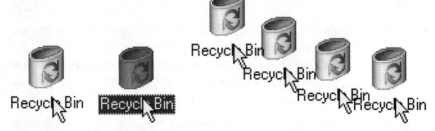

Figure 1.5   Mouse actions: pointing, clicking and dragging

"Ballistic" principle

The faster the movement of the mouse, the greater the distance travelled by the pointer on the screen. If the mouse moves slowly, the pointer only makes short displacements, and slowly.

This "ballistic" principle is highly important. In fact, before performing any action or a command with the mouse, you must first move the pointer into a well determined position.

Operations with the mouse: *pointing*

This operation is called simply *pointing*. Move the mouse in such a way that the pointer is on the *Recycle Bin* icon on the desktop. The mere action of *pointing* does not result in any reaction from the computer.

Recycle Bin

Figure 1.6   Setting the mouse pointer on an icon

Operations with the mouse: *clicking*

Pressing the left mouse button once only, the *Recycle Bin* icon is displayed, and the operation of pressing slightly is called *clicking*. The left mouse button lets you perform most operations. The right mouse button, on the other hand, lets you call up what is called the *contextual menu*. Except where expressly instructed to use the right mouse button, reference in this text is always taken to be to the left button.

Recycle Bin

Figure 1.7   The icons you click on are highlighted

Operations with the mouse: *dragging*

At this point set the pointer on the *Recycle Bin* selected, press the left mouse button and hold it down. Move the mouse a little to the right; this action is called *dragging*.

As you can see, the *Recycle Bin* icon is "stuck" to the mouse pointer. When the mouse button is released, the icon is found in its new position. The combination of the two mouse operations is called: *Drag & Drop*.

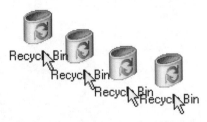

Figure 1.8   Dragging an icon holding down the mouse button

Text fields

The operation of dragging with the mouse is also used in the text fields of dialog windows or when processing text with *Word*, for example in *Wordpad*. *Dragging* is a useful way of selecting text blocks for formatting in a special way, overtyping, deleting or copying. For this purpose, set the cursor in front of the first sign you wish to select, then drag your selection holding the mouse button down until the last sign required.

Operations with the mouse: *double-clicking*

At this point set the pointer again on the *Recycle Bin* icon. To do this, beginners will need a certain amount of concentration: press the left mouse button briefly twice in succession. This is known as *double-clicking* and lets you open folders and document, start programs or carry out certain commands faster.

Too long a pause

If the window depicted in Figure 1.9 is displayed, this means that all the necessary operations have been carried out correctly. If nothing happens, this means that there was too long a pause between the two clicks. In this case, try again. As you will discover, with a bit of exercise, even the double click becomes child's play.

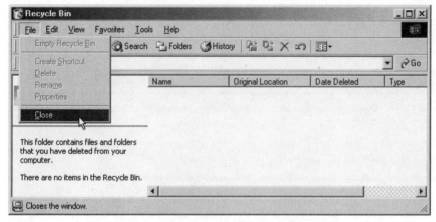

Figure 1.9   With a double click the Recycle Bin is opened

To conclude, let us summarize the most important mouse commands, again taking the *Recycle Bin* icon for reference:

Set the pointer on the *File* menu and click on it to open it. Set the pointer on the *Close* command – this selects it – and click to close the dialog window.

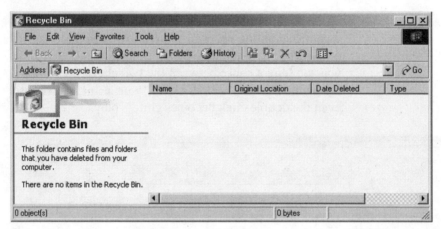

Figure 1.10   Open menus by clicking, point to the commands and execute them with a click

Function of the right mouse button

If you have already worked with a previous version of *Windows Me*, e.g. *Windows 3.x*, you will probably be wondering why the mouse has a second button. It was in fact useless in some programs as it was not associated with any function. However, *Windows Me* and above all the *Windows* applications have revolutionized use of the mouse.

Now, in *Windows Me* and in all the modern Windows applications, a precise function has been assigned to the second mouse button: it lets you call up contextual menus for almost all of the screen elements or sectors and their components.

Contextual menus   Displayed local to the mouse pointer, these menus are called "contextual menus" because the options they contain depend on the position of the pointer.

Right mouse button Let's try displaying some of these menus: if you click with the right button on almost any free point of the desktop, a contextual menu is displayed with the commands for arranging the icons or to create new folders.

Figure 1.11   The desktop contextual menu

The shortest way These commands are the ones used most frequently with the desktop. As the desktop does not have a menu bar, the contextual menu is the fastest way, and sometimes the only way, of performing certain operations.

By clicking with the left mouse button on an element, it is selected. A click on a free point or $\boxed{\text{Esc}}$ results in the contextual menu being closed. Other contextual menus are then displayed regarding the desktop icons, the applications bar or the *Start* button.

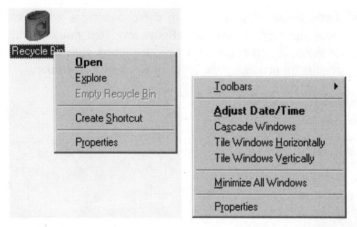

Figure 1.12   Contextual menu of the *Recycle Bin* and of the *applications bar*

Windows lets you change the mouse properties by way of the *Control Panel*. If you are left-handed and you change key layout from the standard configuration *Right-handed* to *Left-handed*, the functions of the mouse keys are inverted. In this case, to display the contextual menu, press the left mouse button. In the procedures described in the text, reference is always made to the standard configuration. For further information on the mouse properties, see Chapter 8.

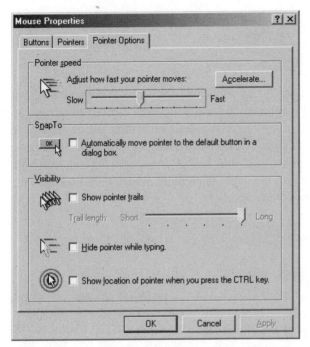

Figure 1.13   *Mouse* comfort functions in the *Control Panel*

Using the menus

In *Windows*, the commands are grouped into menus. The windows of folders and applications have been assigned a *menu bar* under the title bar, containing the names of menus. Each menu contains a list of *commands* arranged by topic and with which you can perform specific operations.

Control menus

A particular menu, containing commands for dimensioning and positioning windows, is the *control menu*. For folders and programs, it is displayed with the box of the control menu in the form of the relative icon of the application or folder ⬜ in the top left corner of the title bar.

Figure 1.14 Different icons of the *control menu*

Menus

All the document windows in which the contents of folders are displayed and the windows of program groups in the *Start* menu have the same structure: inside they have the *File, Edit, View, Favorites, Tools* and *Help* menus. The number and function of the menu options available depends on the type of element selected and on the current operating conditions.

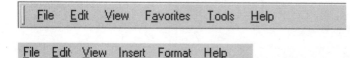

Figure 1.15 Folders menu bar (top) and applications bar (*Wordpad*, bottom)

Menu bar

The menu bar of an applications always contains menus with the characteristic commands of that program. Irrespective of the type of menu or the commands available in it, the control items are used in the same way. This also applies to selection of the commands.

Using the menus with the mouse

To open a menu, set the mouse pointer on the name and click. The menu you open in this way contains a series of options arranged vertically. After opening a menu, simply move the mouse pointer on to the adjacent menu to open it.

Pull-down menus

Among the menu commands, there are some that include a pull-down submenu, which can be displayed simply by setting the pointer on the command in question. Pull-down menus are available, when a small black triangle ▶ can be seen on the right of a menu item.

Selecting a command

To select one of the items displayed in a menu, simply click on the required item. Depending on what conventions are established for a menu, the command may be run directly, or *Windows Me* opens other configuration elements. Further details will be provided later.

Control menu box

The application and document windows also have a *control menu*. This type of menu is opened when you click on the control menu box, which is always in the top left corner of the title bar. It is displayed with the icon of the application or of the folder or of a group of programs.

Figure 1.16   Control menu of a folders window

Resizing

The six items on the system menu (Figure 1.16) are always the same and are used solely to redimension or move the program or document window.

***Close* command**

The *Close* command lets you close a document or application window.

A menu opened by mistake can be closed by clicking again on the menu name. A mistake can be corrected – but not always – with *Edit/Undo Typing* which restores matters as they were before.

Use of the menus with the keyboard

In *Windows*, menus and commands are not selected with the mouse only, though this is the most usual way. This preference is due simply to the fact that people tend to use a graphic user interface. In this section, we will see how to select menus and commands using the keyboard.

Keys ⎡Alt⎤
or ⎡F10⎤

With the keyboard, activate the menu bar by pressing the keys ⎡Alt⎤ or ⎡F10⎤. *Windows* indicates that a menu is selected by showing in 3-D the name of the first *File* menu.

To next menu

Then press key ⎡→⎤ to move to the adjacent menu on the right. With the ⎡←⎤ key you go back, selecting one menu name at a time. To open a selected menu, press ⎡↵⎤ or the ⎡↓⎤ key. Then select the required command with the keys ⎡↓⎤, ⎡↑⎤ and finally press ⎡↵⎤.

To the main menu

If the command includes a pull-down menu, use the cursor keys ⎡→⎤ and ⎡←⎤ to move into the submenu or return to the main menu.

Key combinations

The underlined letter in the name of a menu indicates a key combination with which to open the menu: press the key ⎡Alt⎤ and hold it down. Then press the letter underlined in the name of the menu.

To open the *Edit* menu of a folders window, press for example the shortcut key ⎡Alt⎤ + ⎡M⎤. To call up other menus press the ⎡Alt⎤ key again and then the letters underlined in the menu name.

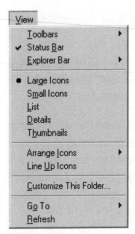

Figure 1.17   *View* menu open with commands and settings

Alternatives

Alternatively, it is also possible to move from an open menu to the adjacent one using the ← or → keys. To close a menu using the keyboard, press key Alt or F10.

You can also use the Esc key. In this way, you close the menu, but the menu bar stays active; this lets you select another menu. The menu selected last on the menu bar is indicated by the menu name being shown in 3-D.

Menu conventions

Each document and application window has its own menu bar. The number and type of menus it contains depends on the type of window or program in question. Most of the items in a menu are commands. But they can also be properties to be assigned to text or images, for example *bold face* or *centered*.

Features of menu items

Not all the items in a menu result in immediate execution of the command it contains. With some items, the menu is closed again apparently without any changes, others open submenus or display a dialog window. What happens after a menu option is selected may be predicted by configuration of the menu items.

Pull-down menu

Thus, for example, the commands marked with a black triangle ▶ open another menu, called *pull-down menu* or *submenu*, in which other commands are listed.

Tick marks

Other properties may be determined from the appearance of the menu items. A tick mark placed in front of a menu item means, for example, that the relative function is active. Tick marks are used when it is possible to activate various commands simultaneously – mostly ones independent of one another –, as in the case of the *View* menu of folders windows with the *Status bar* and the items contained in the *Toolbars* submenu.

Dot

If, on the other hand, you can only select one of the options offered, in front of the corresponding item you will see a black dot ● (example: *View* menu with the view command active, for example *Large Icons*).

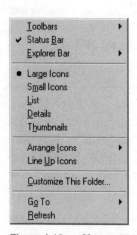

Figure 1.18   Menu conventions

Suspension marks
If behind a menu item there are three suspension marks (...), the command calls up a dialog window in which you are asked to provide further information concerning execution of the command (for example *File/Print...*). Irrespective of the menu conventions, the fastest way of calling a command is by a mouse click. When the pointer is placed on a menu command, the latter is shown with a coloured progress bar.

Alternatives
To select menu items using the keyboard, press Alt and use the keys ↓, ←, → or ↑, until the desired item is selected and then press ↵.

Another possibility is to press the key corresponding to the underlined letter of the required command.

Overview
The overview that follows is a summary of the main menu conventions.

Menu convention	Meaning
New	*Triangle*: Submenu with further commands
Folder Options...	*Suspension marks (...)*: Calls up a dialog window with options
Copy	*Key combination:* Shortcut key combination for the command
Open	*Bold:* Standard command executed with a double click on an object in the zone of the document

Menu convention	Meaning
✔ <u>S</u>tandard Buttons	*Tick mark*: Marks a selected option which can be de-activated by reselecting. Multiple selections are possible
● T<u>h</u>umbnails	*Dot*: Active options, mutually exclusive
<u>P</u>aste	Option *de-activated* or *not available*: The command has been de-activated, and cannot therefore be selected

Use of the dialog windows

Windows Me distinguishes between different types of window. In application windows, programs are run or document windows showing certain items of information are displayed. The folders are also displayed in document windows. *Dialog windows* let you change the characteristics of commands selected in an application or document window. For doing so, the dialog windows contain unique controls described below.

Dialog window

Dialog windows are easy to recognize because they do not have a menu bar. In addition, there is no toolbar or status bar. Dialog windows cannot be resized, they can only be moved or closed. Open dialog windows are overlaid upon other program or document windows: to go back into these windows, you must close the dialog window by clicking on *OK* or *Cancel*.

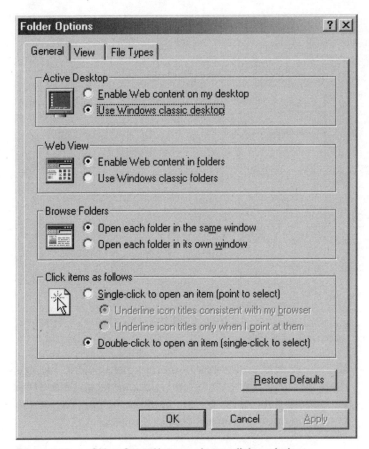

Figure 1.19   *OK* or *Cancel* let you close a dialog window

Suspension marks   The commands that can be executed by *Windows* or by a given program which require parameters to be set, automatically call up a dialog window. This is shown in the menus by the presence of three suspension marks after the command (...).

Figure 1.20   The menu commands followed by suspension
marks open Dialog windows

Tabs

If a command comprises numerous parameters, the options available are grouped into suitable tabs. To activate an options tab, click on the relative name. To set the command options, various checks are used.

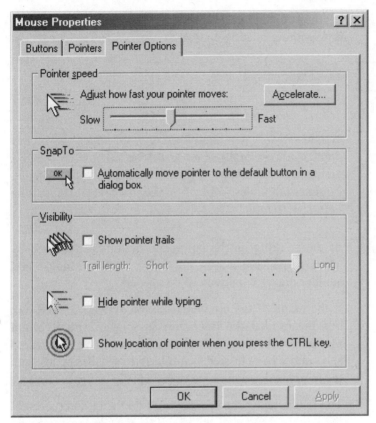

Figure 1.21   Control Panel window with three tabs

Command buttons

The highlighted, rectangular-shape 3-D zones with words inside are called "command buttons". A command button's function depends on the name of the command itself. The most important of these buttons are *OK* and *Cancel*. The *OK* button confirms the changes made in a dialog window and results in execution of a command with its parameters. With *Cancel* changes made are ignored and a dialog window closed. By pressing ⏎ you activate the predefined button, which is recognized by its having a thicker edge. Press [Esc] to close a dialog window without making changes.

Figure 1.22   With [↵] you activate the defined button

 Windows Me has a handy option with which the mouse pointer automatically sets on the default button when a dialog window opens. This function is activated in the *Pointers* tab under *Control Panel/Mouse*. Here select the item *Use Default*.

Suspension marks If the marking on the command buttons is followed by three suspension marks, click on it with the mouse and another dialog window will be opened.

If the name of the command button appears greyed out, this means that the operation associated with it is not available. The button is therefore shown as deselected and cannot be activated – similarly to what happens with menu items that cannot be called up.

The letters underlined in the word on the button represent the key used together with [Alt] to execute the command from the keyboard.

Option buttons

If, in a dialog window, you can only activate one of the options offered, option buttons are used to do this. Deactivated option buttons may be recognized by an empty ball: ⚪ .

If the option button is activated, it is marked by a full ball ⦿ .

The letters underlined in the name of the option indicate the key used together with ⟨Alt⟩ to select the option from the keyboard.

When it is possible to select various options in a group of options, *Windows* uses so-called check boxes inside the Dialog windows.

Check box

These are squares ☐ to the left of the option name. Selected check boxes contain a tick mark ☑ .

To select a check box, click inside the box ☐ or on its description.

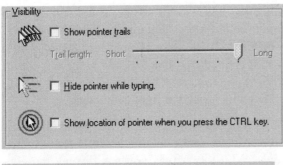

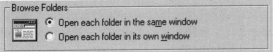

Figure 1.23   Check boxes (above) and option buttons

Text fields

Text boxes let you insert numbers of characters in Dialog windows using the keyboard. Typical insertions are file names, but you may also give indications in inches or centimetres, for a page margin for example Left: 1.25" . In text boxes, the cursor is shown as a blinking vertical line indicating the insertion point.

Setting values

With the ← key, you delete a character to the left of the cursor, and with the Canc key one character at a time to the right of the cursor. If the text fields contain setting values, after these you will sometimes see an up arrow and a down arrow Wait: 14 minutes with which to gradually increase or reduce the value shown.

Drop-down lists

In drop-down lists, the various items can be displayed by clicking on the opening arrow ▼ . Then if you select the item you require with the mouse, the drop-down list is closed and the selected item is displayed in the one-line text field. If the list is a long one, use the scroll bar displayed automatically along the right edge of the list.

Pull-down menus
on several lines

If in a dialog window various list items are displayed in an area, this is called a pull-down menu arranged on several lines or a list. If the desired item is selected with a mouse click, it is displayed in a text box at the top part of the list. If there are numerous list items, the scroll bar appears automatically along the right hand edge.

Scroll bar

A scroll bar ◄ ► scrolls horizontally or vertically and contains a scroll bar box and scroll arrows. With the arrows you can display the contents line by line or column by column. If you click in the free field above and below the scroll bar, then you scroll mostly a page at a time.

Mouse button held down

The scroll bar box can also be moved by holding the mouse button down. From the size of the scroll bar box, you can deduce the relationship between the section represented by the Figure and the items not shown.

Resizing Windows windows

Windows Me makes a distinction between different types of window. The most important ones are *program windows*, which command application programs. Programs that work with documents also dispose of what are called *document windows*. There are various ways of changing the dimensions of a *document window* or of a *program window*.

In this section we shall explain how to perform resizing using the buttons of the title bar.

Figure 1.24   The title bar contains resizing buttons

Before adapting the size of a window, make sure that the window in question is active. In *Windows Me* only a single window at a time is activated; all insertions and commands act exclusively on that window.

Activating document windows and program windows

To select a *document window* or a *program window*, click on a free point of the window or on its title bar – this bar is shown coloured. If the title bar is invisible, click on the window button in the applications bar along the bottom edge of the screen.

Resize buttons

Close button

Dialog windows and message windows do not have re-sizing buttons, as there would not be any point with windows of this type. The *Close* ☒ button on the extreme right of the title bar is always present in all windows. It is used to close the window.

Maximize

Beside it to the left is the *Maximize* ☐ button, with which to enlarge the active window so that it occupies the entire screen.

Restore button

When the window is maximized, the *Maximize* button is replaced by the *Restore* ⧉ button, with which you can restore the maximized window back to its former dimension.

Minimize button

With the *Minimize* ▬ button, an open window is mini-mized to the form of a button of the applications bar at the bottom of the screen. In this way, the window disap-pears off the screen, but the program is not closed.

Minimized windows remain in the background. Click on the button in the applications bar to return the window to its former dimension.

Resizing windows with the mouse

There are various ways of changing the size of a *document window* or a *program window*. This section de-scribes resizing at the edges and in the corners of win-dows.

Window edge and corners

A *document window* and *program window* are always surrounded by an edge. Window width and height can be modified at the edges and in the corners using the mouse: for this purpose, set the mouse pointer along the vertical

edge, for example. The mouse pointer assumes the semblance of a *double arrow* ←→.

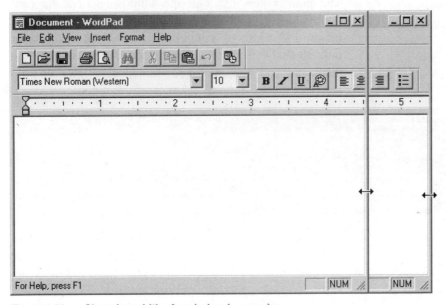

Figure 1.25   Changing width of a window by an edge

"Gripping" the edge

With this shape of pointer, you can "grip" the edge and,
holding the mouse button down, increase or reduce width
of the window by moving the mouse to the right or left.
While you are resizing a window, you are shown the dimensions that it will have depending on what movement
you make. To establish the new dimension for the window, simply release the mouse button.

Changing window height

To change height of the window, set the mouse pointer
on a horizontal edge. The mouse pointer now assumes the
semblance of a vertical *double arrow* ↕. With this shape
of pointer you can "grip" the edge and, holding the mouse
button down, change height of the window.

Changing height and width

To change width and height of a window at the same time, set the pointer on one of the corners of the window. The pointer now assumes the semblance of a diagonal double arrow ↖ or ↙. Holding the mouse button down, height and width of a window can now be changed simultaneously. The new dimensions of the window are displayed and become fixed immediately after you release the mouse button.

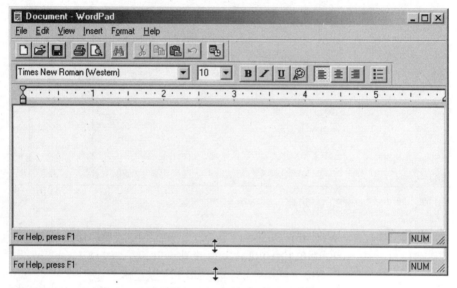

Figure 1.26   Changing height of a window by an edge

Obviously resizing by the corners and edges of a window will not work if the window is maximized. Maximized windows can be reduced by means of the *Restore* 🗗 button.

Closing Windows windows

Windows Me distinguishes between various types of window: a distinction must be made, for example, between document windows and application windows. An application is run in a program window, for example *Wordpad*, *Paint* or *Notepad*. These programs will be described later.

In a document window information is displayed. This may take the form of text in the document window of a word processing program or of files and subfolders. Each open folder in fact belongs to document windows, for example *My computer* and the relative folders windows (double click on the *My computer* icon on the desktop). We will discuss this type of window in the next section.

Closing folders

After exercising a little with folders windows, you will have various document windows open in *Windows*. You will, therefore, at a certain point have to close some of these down.

Closing a document window

In *Windows Me* document windows can be closed via one of the following procedures. You can use:

- The *Close* command in the *File* menu

- The key combination ⌷Alt⌷ + ⌷F4⌷

- The *Close* command in the control menu

- A double-click on the box in the control menu 🗁

- The *Close* button ✖ in the title bar

- The *Close* command from the contextual menu of the folder button/object of a minimized window in the applications bar

All the above methods result in a window being closed. How to close a program window, i.e. the program itself, will be discussed in chapter three "Programs and documents".

Control menu

The control menu can be called up by clicking on the box in the top left hand corner of the title bar of a folder window. In the case of folders, the control menu box is depicted with the icon of an open folders map ▨, in the case of applications with the corresponding program icon.

Changing position of windows and how they are arranged on the desktop

In *Windows* you can open various windows simultaneously, within any preestablished limit. The windows are displayed on various overlapping levels.

Unlike resizing, you can reposition not only program or document windows, but Dialog windows or confirmation messages as well.

Moving a window

A window is always moved on the desktop for the same reason: in *Windows* the screen can never be large enough. Windows are displaced to display windows or information underneath or to get an overview of various applications or information in the windows.

To move any window on your desktop, set the mouse pointer on the title bar. Then displace the window holding the mouse button down. Its new position is shown with a dashed edge. When you release the mouse button, the window is displayed in its new position.

Control menu

The control menu, which may be called up by clicking on the relative box on the left of the title bar, also lets you move a window: click on the command *Move* and move the window using the keys ⌜↑⌟, ⌜↓⌟, ⌜←⌟ or ⌜→⌟ on the keyboard. The *Move* command is not available for maximized windows.

Figure 1.27   Control menu (on left) and contextual menu of the applications bar

Automatic
arrangement

The movement of windows in clearly visible layouts can also be performed in Windows. To automatically arrange all the windows on the desktop, set the pointer in a free area of the applications bar and press the right mouse button. From the contextual menu select the command *Cascade windows*, *Tile windows horizontally* or *Tile windows vertically* to arrange all the windows as you wish.

Automatically interrupting *Windows Me* start-up

After the computer is switched on, the *Windows Me* 32-bit graphic operating system is always started automatically, without having to give any commands. In some cases, however, the starting process may need to be interrupted, for example when wishing to start *Windows* in what is called *Safe mode* to eliminate problems with the current Windows configuration.

45

Interrupting
Windows start-up

To interrupt the automatic start-up of *Windows Me*, follow closely the messages displayed on the monitor after the computer is switched on. After the system components have been initialized, the first messages are displayed, for example the list showing the amount of working memory available, the hard disk installed and recognized, in some cases an overview of all the important system components.

Automatic Startup
Menu

Immediately after display of these system components, the hard disk starts to work and the PC gets ready to start *Windows Me*. If, at this point, you hold down the key ⌨F8, *Windows* does not start and instead the *Microsoft Windows Millenium Startup Menu* shown in Figure 1.28 is displayed.

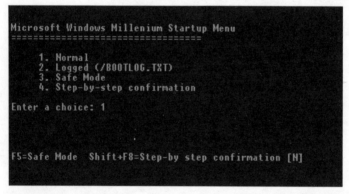

```
Microsoft Windows Millenium Startup Menu
========================================

    1. Normal
    2. Logged (/BOOTLOG.TXT)
    3. Safe Mode
    4. Step-by-step confirmation

Enter a choice: 1



F5=Safe Mode  Shift+F8=Step-by step confirmation [N]
```

Figure 1.28   The automatic Startup Menu after interruption of the *Windows Me* start-up

Calling up the
options

To call up one of the options displayed in the *Microsoft Windows Millenium Startup Menu*, simply key in the number appearing beside the option and confirm with ⌨↵. If you wish to start the normal *Windows* operating mode, i.e. *Normal*, press the key ⌨1 and confirm your choice with ⌨↵.

Normal Mode

After this, *Windows Me* starts in so-called *Normal* mode, in other words the standard way. The other Startup Menu options are described later in this manual.

> If there are problems when you start *Windows Me* or error messages are displayed, interrupt the next startup phase with ⌞F8⌟ and select startup option *2. Logged (\BOOTLOG.TXT)* in the *Windows Millenium Startup Menu.*

File
BOOTLOG.TXT

In this way, *Windows* places in the main hard disk drive a text file called *BOOTLOG.TXT*, in which each single driver is stored with an indication of the outcome of the loading operation. The file *BOOTLOG.TXT* may be copied on to a diskette and opened using any text editor. Skilled operators may identify from this which programs or components have caused the startup problems.

Starting *Windows Me* in Safe mode

In rare cases, problems may arise during automatic loading in *Normal* mode, for example where incorrect hard disk drivers are activated and Windows cannot complete loading correctly.

Causes of the
problems

These problems are caused more often than not by incorrect network or hardware settings. Sometimes it is the programs that cause problems such as these by overwriting important drivers with invalid versions, even if Windows Me has a series of protection mechanisms suitable for preventing most of these problems.

Safe mode

In any case, it is always possible to start *Windows Me* in *Safe mode*. In this case, *Windows* does not perform loading of all the critical drivers and uses a minimum driver configuration, so as to be able to start the system at any rate.

However, in *Safe mode* various extended *Windows functions* will not be available, such as for example multitasking or use of the CD-ROM drive or the video adapter. These functions are not supported, since the sole function of Safe mode is problem solving.

Microsoft Windows
Millenium Startup
Menu

To activate *Safe mode* you will need to restart the computer. Hold key ⌶F8⌶ down during the startup phase in order to display the *Microsoft Windows Millenium Startup Menu*. Then press key ⌶3⌶ and confirm with key ⌶↵⌶ in order to activate the *Safe mode* option.

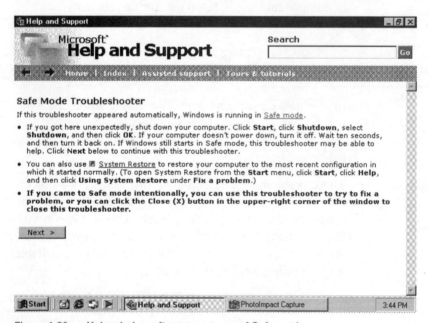

Figure 1.29   Help window after appearance of Safe mode

To avoid conflicts in Safe mode, *Windows Me* uses the VGA standard resolution of 640 x 480 Pixels and 16 colours.

Safe mode

Windows Me automatically opens the *Help and Support* window, essentially a help page, to help eliminate certain Windows problems. This mode is also shown in the corners of the desktop where you will see *Safe mode* marked (Figure 1.31).

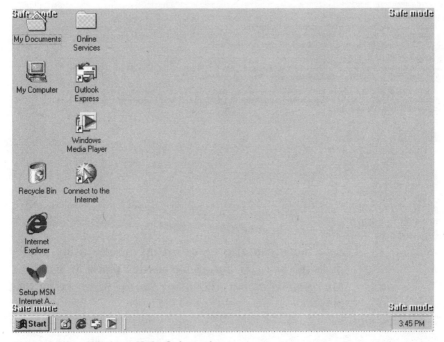

Figure 1.30   *Windows Me* in *Safe mode*

Help and Support

At this point you can try to solve the Windows problem using the help page. Click on *Next* in the *Help and Support* window and answer the office assistant's questions by selecting one of the options offered to you and by

49

clicking on *Next*. Depending on the type of problem in question, the PC offers tips on how to solve the problem.

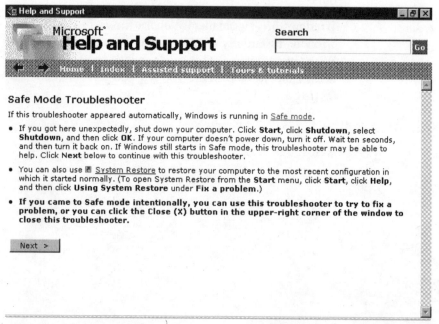

Figure 1.31   Help in *Safe mode*

Key [F5]

Safe mode can also be called up directly using a key: press the key [F5] during the starting phase to avoid the *Microsoft Windows Millenium Startup Menu* being displayed.

Calling the *MS-DOS Prompt* in *Windows Me*

Unlike the earlier versions of Windows 98, *Windows Me* no longer requires the operating system to be started in MS-DOS mode. One exception to this is starting using a Startup disk, which is created on the tab *Startup Disk* in *Control Panel/Add/Remove Programs*. Most of the tasks for which use of MS-DOS is required can be executed in the Windows environment.

Program startup

For this purpose you use the *MS-DOS Prompt* program. To start the program, in *Windows Me* open the *Start* menu and set the pointer on the command *Programs*. Click on *MS-DOS Prompt* in the *Accessories* submenu. What happens next depends on how your system is configured.

MS-DOS Prompt

There are two possibilities: either the *MS-DOS Prompt* window appears in the top left corner of the desktop, or the screen may be blacked out and certain characters appear.

"Window" mode

In both cases, the *MS-DOS Prompt* is started, in the first case in *Window* mode (see Figure 1.32), in the second case in *Full screen* mode. However, both display modes operate in exactly the same way.

Figure 1.32   MS-DOS Prompt in Windows Me

The *MS-DOS Prompt* imitates MS-DOS (*Microsoft Disk Operating System*). At the top left, the version number is displayed, then the system prompt *C:\WINDOWS>_* with the blinking cursor. Bring up the DOS application drive using the MS-DOS command *CD* and run the program with the specific command.

To change from *Full screen* mode of the *MS-DOS Prompt* to *Window* mode or vice versa, press the keys [Alt] + [↵]. To exit from the *MS-DOS Prompt*, type the command *exit* and confirm with [↵] before closing the window.

Setting the *MS-DOS Prompt* properties

According to the manufacturer *Microsoft's* declarations, problem-free starting is possible of almost all the MS-DOS applications from *MS-DOS Prompt* directly in *Windows Me*. And generally this does happen without problems.

Multiple DOS Sessions

In *Windows Me* various DOS sessions may be run simultaneously in parallel in protected areas of the memory. However, simply opening a DOS window does not present any particular difficulties. The difficulties could arise if a DOS application is run even when a single *MS-DOS Prompt* window is open.

Starting difficulties

If problems occur while an MS-DOS program is running, in most cases a corresponding error message is displayed indicating what the likely causes of the problem are, for example *Program does not run in Windows* or *Insufficient memory,* etc.

In these cases, you can configure the MS-DOS Prompt from *MS-DOS Prompt Properties*.

Setting the command line and the working drive

Key combination

For the *MS-DOS Prompt* general configuration, select *window* mode with $\boxed{\text{Alt}}$ + $\boxed{\leftarrow}$ and click on the *Properties* button in the toolbar 🗗.

Command line

In the *Program* tab, you can display the *command line* and the *working drive* of the command line interpreter and in the field *Shortcut keys* you can define a combination of keys with which to call up the *MS-DOS Prompt*.

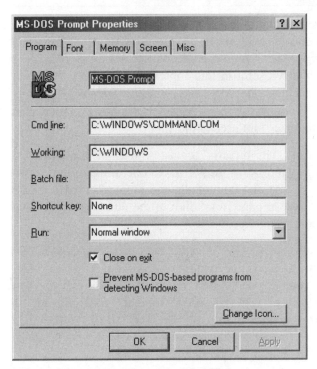

Figure 1.33   *Program* tab of the MS-DOS Prompt

View

In the *Run* box select the desired view for starting the *MS-DOS Prompt*. You can choose between *Normal Window*, *Minimized* or *Maximized* (Full screen). *Maximized* mode is advisable if the programs have performance problems.

File batch

If it is necessary to execute a *batch file* to call up the DOS program, enter the name of the batch file in the appropriate text field. If you tick the *Close on exit* check box, the window is closed automatically when you exit the DOS application.

Setting the character type for *MS-DOS Prompt*

Those wishing to use old versions of DOS applications in *Windows Me* will not be able to do without the *MS-DOS Prompt*. The *Window* mode of the *MS-DOS Prompt* is particularly useful in this context. In this case, *Windows Me* manages the MS-DOS window (almost) like any other *Windows* window. Many users, however, feel that the character font used is too small.

The *Font* tab directly manages size of the *MS-DOS Prompt* window, as the MS-DOS operating system is oriented to text and commands and represents the contents of the screen page in relation to the number of lines and characters on a line.

Font tab

Call up the *MS-DOS Prompt* via *Start/Programs/Accessories* and select the *Window* view. You can select character font in one of two ways: one is through the box *Font* `T 8 x 14 ▾` in the toolbar (generally set on *Auto*), the other is through the *Font* tab of the *MS-DOS Prompt Properties* dialog window, which you bring up using the button *Properties* 🖼.

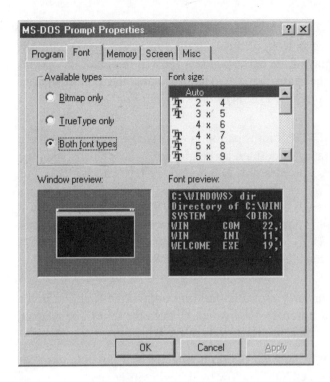

Figure 1.34 The *Font* tab

Font summary box

Open the pull-down menu *Font* in the toolbar and click on the desired font size. *Windows Me* simultaneously changes the size of the *MS-DOS Prompt* window.

On the *Font* tab of the Properties window, on the other hand, you can observe your changes in two preview windows. *Window preview*, on the left, displays the approximate dimensions of the DOS window on the screen, whereas *Font preview*, on the right, shows a preview of the character size. You can select two types of font:

Bitmap and TrueType fonts

On the one hand, there are the fixed *Bitmap* fonts, and on the other the Windows *TrueType* flexible fonts. In the pull-down menu *Font* on the *MS-DOS Prompt* toolbar, the *TrueType* fonts are recognizable by the icon **T** placed in front of them. In the *Properties* dialog window, display of the corresponding fonts in the group of options on the right can be managed using the option buttons *Bitmap only*, *TrueType only* or *Both Font types*.

In MS-DOS information is displayed in text mode. Each character is defined by height and width. This is what the values listed in the *Font* summary box refer to. If in this box for example you have a font of "8 x 14", this means that each character in the *MS-DOS Prompt* is exactly 8 graphic dots high and 14 pixels wide. It is this that gives the DOS window its size. Standard size of *MS-DOS Prompt* characters is 25 lines by 80 characters.

Auto option

Particularly useful is the *Auto* option, the first one in the *Font* summary box, which enables the font to be adapted to the current dimensions of the window.

Only if the *Auto* option is selected is it possible to maximize the DOS window by dragging its edge.

However, reducing the dimensions of the window – even without the Auto option – is not a problem as it is possible to scroll the contents thanks to the scroll bars displayed.

Changing the *MS-DOS Prompt* character font is only possible for DOS programs with graphic features. In other cases, *Full screen* mode is selected automatically.

Changing Properties of the *MS-DOS Prompt* for single DOS applications

To change the Properties of the *MS-DOS Prompt* for single DOS applications, look for the corresponding program file in *Windows Explorer* or in a *My computer* window and open its contextual menu with the right mouse button. Click on the item at the bottom, *Properties*.

Disable Windows detection

In the case of programs for which an error message is displayed because they do not run under *Windows*, tick the check box *Prevent MS-DOS-based programs from detecting Windows* in the *Program* tab in the *Properties* dialog window.

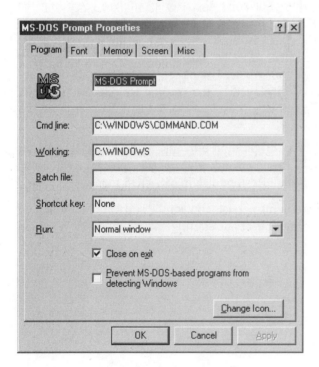

Figure 1.35 *MS-DOS Prompt* Properties

Problem-free use Most DOS applications can be activated without problems simply by changing the options in the other tabs of the *Properties* dialog window. If an insufficient memory message is displayed after you have called up the DOS program, use the *Memory* tab and enter the amount of memory required in Kbyte in the relative fields.

 The MS-DOS applications for which specific *Properties* are changed must be called up by double clicking on the program icon in *Windows Explorer* or in the folders window of *My computer*. It is also possible to insert the icons of a program group in the *Start* menu.

If this does not solve the user's problem regarding the MS-DOS applications, run the *Windows* on-line Help from the *Start* menu. Insert MS-DOS at the top right under *Go* and select *MS-DOS-based Programs Troubleshooter* at the bottom of the list of topics. Follow all other instructions displayed by the On-line Help in the right half of the window.

Starting in *MS-DOS Mode* If all the configuration attempts made in the tabs of the *MS-DOS Prompt* window *Properties* prove in vain, start the PC with a Restore disk in MS-DOS mode.

If the problems persist, contact the software manufacturer for information about starting the program in Windows Me.

Text copy from *MS-DOS Prompt*

For reasons of compatibility with earlier versions of MS-DOS applications, the *MS-DOS Prompt* has been integrated in *Windows Me*. As is known, the *MS-DOS Prompt* may be represented in *Maximized* mode and as a window. In *Window* mode, it is possible to select the window contents with the mouse and bring them into other applications using *Windows* notes.

Text copy

To copy text from an MS-DOS window into *Windows Me*, click on the *Mark* icon on the left in the toolbar of the *MS-DOS Prompt* window.

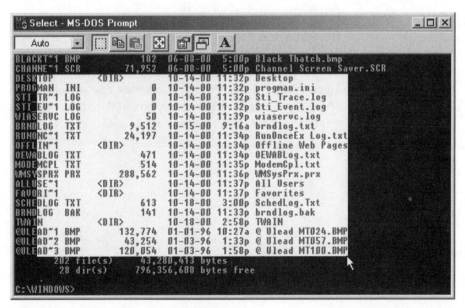

Figure 1.36   Selecting text in a DOS window

Selecting

With the mouse drag a rectangle onto the area of text that you wish to copy. By clicking on the *Copy* button, the text is copied into the notes and may be inserted in other programs using the *Edit* menu.

Paste command

Using the keyboard

This may also be done using the keyboard: move the cursor to the start of the text ⬚ T ⬚ and ⬚ ← ⬚. Then press the key ⬚ ⬚ , hold it down and extend your selection with ⬚ → ⬚ by a character at a time to the right or with ⬚ ↓ ⬚ by a row at a time downwards.

View of the toolbar

To copy the selection, press the key ⬚ ↵ ⬚. At this point what you have copied may be pasted into any point of the MS-DOS or *Windows* windows. If the toolbar of the DOS window is not displayed, select the *Properties* command in the control menu. Move on to the *Screen* tab and tick the check box *Display toolbar* under *Window*. Close the *Properties* window with *OK*.

Quick edit

Recurrent text blocks may be copied from the MS-DOS window by selecting what is known as Quick edit, avoiding the user having to click on the *Select* button. Open the MS-DOS Prompt Properties and select the tab *Misc*. Tick the *QuickEdit* check box in the *Mouse* options group and close the Properties window with *OK*.

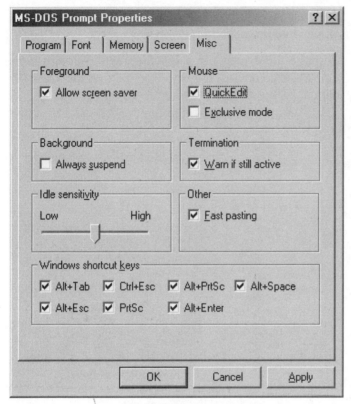

Figure 1.37   Activating the *QuickEdit* option

You cannot insert text into an MS-DOS window or into an MS-DOS-based program if these are on display as full screen. Not all the contents of a DOS window are shown in the *Windows* applications as is the case in the DOS window. To close a DOS window you should click on the *Close* button and confirm the message displayed with *Yes*.

To copy the full window of the *MS-DOS Prompt* as a bitmap into notes, press Alt + Print Screen.

To paste the contents in a *Windows* application, use the *Edit/Paste* command, the keys Ctrl + V or the *Paste* button.

2. Windows Help

This chapter is about the way in which *Windows Me* can help you in your daily work. The function of the general Help to *Windows Me* on the *Start* menu is illustrated in detail. This version of Windows has a new auxiliary system and Web design and has been expanded by the addition of various tours and tutorials. The index and summary functions of the Help are, however, the same as in previous versions of Windows. Since the Internet has been integrated into the Windows environment, you can now access Microsoft's Help and user forums by a series of simple steps.

Calling up *Help and Support*

Do you need a Help to specific functions while you are working with *Windows Me*? This manual contains an introduction to the main functions of *Windows Me*. The operating system also provides a good introduction as it contains many functions.

Windows *Help*

This section explains how to access the *Windows* Help and Support function, known as *Help and Support*. How to use the *Help*'s special functions will be dealt with later on in the manual. You'll be surprised at how much information you can find in the *Help*.

First of all, how do you display the *Windows Help* on the screen? In fact there are several possibilities.

Start/Help

The conventional method is to use the *Start* menu. Open the *Start* menu and click on the heading *Help*. The *Help and Support* window will open immediately. In this window you can select the services of the Help that you require.

Shortcut key

The *Help and Support* window, which is the *Windows Me* Help, can also be displayed using a shortcut key. Just press the F1 key once you are inside the *Windows* environment, for example, in a folder, in *Resources* or in desktop.

Warning: if you call up the Help with the F1 key, close any other applications windows that are open, otherwise the Help concerning those applications will start up. This will be dealt with at the end of this chapter. If the program is reduced to an icon in the applications bar and there is a folder open, start up the *Windows* Help by pressing the F1 key.

You will see the *Help and Support* dialog box displayed in the typical web layout with various hypertext links:

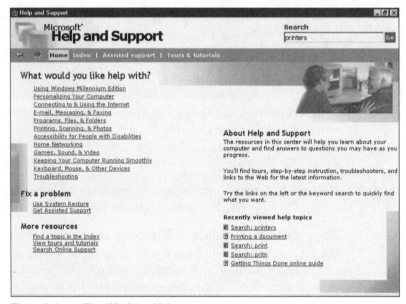

Figure 2.1   The *Windows Help*

"Help" menu

The *Help and Support* dialog box can also be called up through the *Help* menu, which is always present in folders, *Explorer*, and the *Index* button.

Key word *Search*

After calling up the *Windows* Help, the dialog box *Help and Support* is always displayed. The simplest way to access information is similar to an Internet browser. In the upper right corner of the window is the text field *Search*.

Searching for a Help topic text

Once inside, you can look at the content of all the subjects available in the Help. You can limit the number of matching words found through criteria that restrict the search. Consequently, all the entries in the Help will be displayed, as will the troubleshooters, tours and even on-line Helps containing the search word and topics related to the search topic.

Entering a search word

First start up the *Windows Help* with *Start/Help*. Enter the search word or expression in the text box *Search*, at the top of the screen on the right.

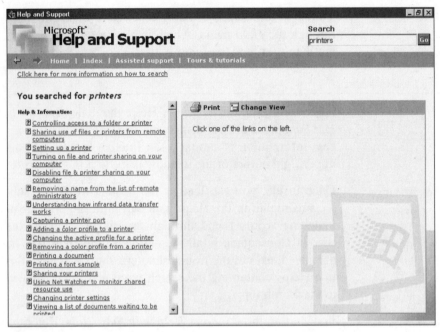

Figure 2.2   Entering a search word

Expression

'Expression' means two or more independent words. Enter the words consecutively, separated by a space. Then press the ⏎ key or click on *Go*.

List of topics

The list of topics is displayed on the left side of the window as soon as the search is over. Try it out with the term *Printers*.

Selecting a topic

Now scroll through the results list and look for an entry containing the information you want. Try selecting the heading *Printing a document*. To display your chosen topic, just click on the heading – the procedure is the same as that used for hypertext links on the World Wide Web.

If you click on the *Back* button (the arrow pointing to the left in the title bar), you will return to the previous window. By clicking repeatedly you will pass backwards through all the steps you have taken.

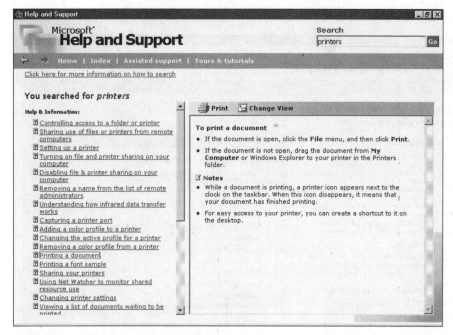

Figure 2.3   Displaying a searched help topic

Display on the right side of the window   Immediately afterwards, the corresponding Help topic will be displayed on the right hand side of the window. In this window there are also troubleshooters that you can click on (at the bottom of the results list). Tours, on the other hand, are displayed in a separate window.

Links to carry the search further   In the list of topics displayed, all the matches found for the search word or expression are selected. Through the links displayed as text extracts underlined in blue you can display other specific information or link up to a Web site. If, in this way, other *Windows* elements are highlighted, simply click on the link and the window will open up, as happens in the case of the Control Panel, for example, so that you can use what you have read immediately.

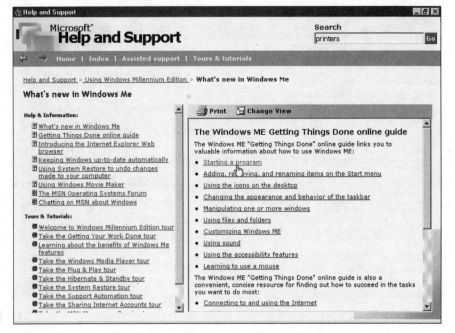

Figure 2.4   Hypertext links can also be recognized by the hand-shaped mouse pointer

In addition, at the bottom of most texts is the link 'Find out more', which leads you to a similar topic or a context menu containing the relevant Help pages on subjects relating to the subject concerned. Select the heading on the menu by clicking on it.

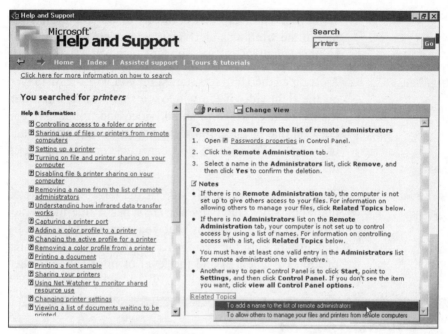

Figure 2.5   The *Find out more* link leads you to texts on subjects relevant to the chosen subject

Close the *Help* by clicking on ⊠.

Windows Help Home Page

When you call up the *Help*, the *Help and Support* window will be displayed. On the page *Type in the keyword to find:* you will see the Windows functions that you want to find out more about subdivided according to subject.

Browse with a simple click

If you choose one of these topics by clicking on it, the subject menu is updated and new links containing specific information on the selected topic will be displayed. Scroll through the hierarchical list of topics in the Help, click on a topic and the information in the Help will be displayed. The Help text is mostly displayed in the right half of the window and, if necessary, other Help windows are displayed.

Help entries

As soon as the Help has started up you will see displayed on the right side of the window a short list of important topics, such as desktop, audio, video and printers. If you click on one of these links, the list on the left of the page is updated. From there you can click onto actual Help texts.

Hierarchical Structure

The headings on the left side of the page are organized hierarchically. The *Windows Help* has a tree-like structure with many branches that you can scroll through by clicking through the various topics. At each click, the list of topics is updated and the level of information is then described in detail.

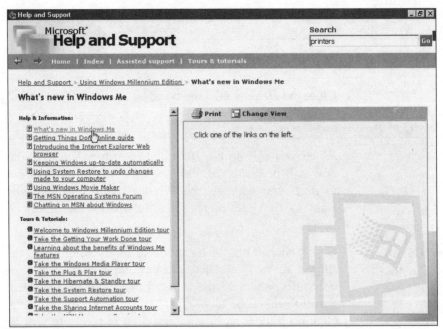

Figure 2.6   Scroll through the Help by topic

Internet-style

hypertext links

In general, the *Windows Help* is used in the same way as an Internet Web site – you can scroll through the topics in the Help through hypertext links underlined in blue.

Links underlined in green refer to a glossary entry. By clicking on this type of link a brief description of the term you clicked on will be displayed in the command description.

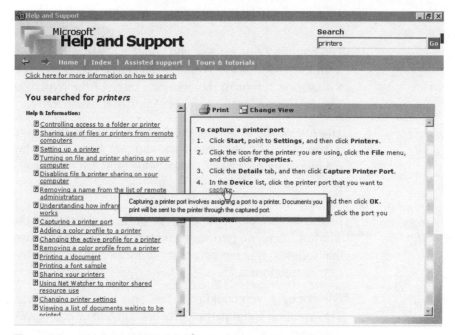

Figure 2.7   Links underlined in green open up a glossary entry

Microsoft has completely abandoned the open and closed book structure, similar to that in folders, used in *Windows 95/98*. However, an overview is provided in the line of text underneath the title bar. Through the topics separated by greater than signs > you will complete the journey you began with hypertext links. Obviously, these page names are other hypertext links. Just click once on one of the names to return to the appropriate point in the hierarchy.

Figure 2.8 Hierarchical structure of the *Windows* Help

The buttons *Forward* ➡ and *Back* ⬅ are well-known from the World Wide Web. By clicking on *Back* ⬅ you will always return to the previous stage of the hypertext link, in effect cancelling the last click of the mouse.

The *Forward* ➡ button, on the other hand, is only used if you have already gone back and you want to display the following page again, namely the topic list or Help information.

How to use the Help text

If a suitable Help topic appears in the right side of the window, there are two ways of managing the information that follows. It is not necessary to memorize the step-by-step instructions.

Printing

For example, you could print the large topics in the Help. This solution is not particularly economical or ecological, but sometimes it is necessary – if you prefer to see the instructions on paper, for instance, or if you want to pass information and advice on to your colleagues.

Click on the *Print* button on the upper border of the information window. At this point the dialog box *Print* will appear, similar to that of Internet Explorer and other programs. Inside the box, select a *printer*, define the print range and decide how many copies to print. Printing will only begin once you click on *OK*.

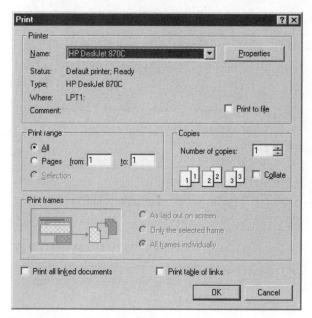

Figure 2.9   *Print* dialog box in the *Windows Help*

Help window display

The second way to use the Help texts involves displaying important information while the operations described are carried out. In this case, a small Help window which shows only the Help text is constantly displayed.

To display the Help window, click on *Change View* on the upper border of the box in which the Help text is displayed.

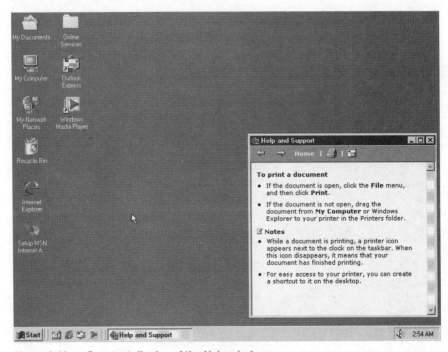

Figure 2.10   Constant display of the Help window

To restore the normal display of the *Help and Support* window, click again on *Change View* 🔲. A search for information can only be carried out with the maximum size window. The reduced window only serves to display the information found.

Supplementary information

Hypertext links that you can click on are not only found in the left page of the index. Sometimes there are also links in the right side of the window, underlined in blue, which refer mainly to supplementary information. Some links automatically open *Windows* system windows (e.g. the Control Panel) or refer to Help texts on similar topics.

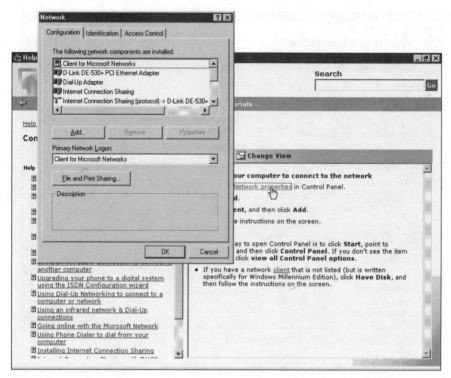

Figure 2.11 Some links open the *Windows* window, like the heading *Network* in the Control Panel

Troubleshooter

The text window changes appearance slightly after calling up a *Troubleshooter*.

In the *Windows Help*, the availability of troubleshooters is rather limited. However, they offer an interesting interactive journey to solving a problem. Enter the word *Troubleshooter* in the *Search* text box to display all the troubleshooters.

First of all, reply to the question displayed by activating the relevant option ○ and clicking on *Next*.

75

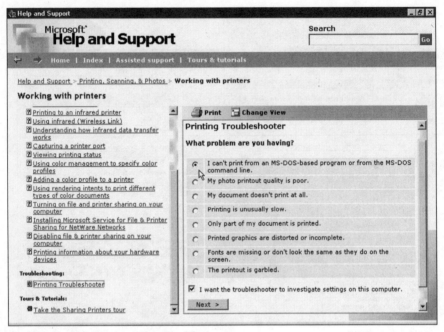

Figure 2.12 A *Windows* Help troubleshooter

Proceed in this way until the correct solution to the problem is displayed.

Program start up link

In some Help topics you can introduce the relevant Help program by clicking on the link *Click here*. The Help can be closed at any time, independently of the window that has been opened, by clicking on *Close* ⊠.

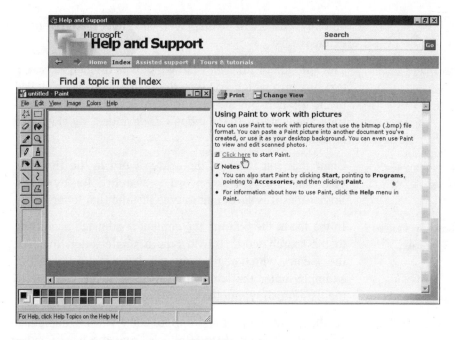

Figure 2.13   Program start up link in a Help topic

Internet link   A few hypertext links are even linked up to the Internet, for example, to Microsoft help pages. To display this information, you will need a correctly-installed Internet link. If that is the case, you will be given access to extensive and updated Help functions.

Windows Help Index

This section describes the alphabetical register of the *Windows Help*, which can be accessed through the *Index* link in the title bar of the *Help and Support* window.

Firstly, call up the *Windows Help* through *Start/Help* and click on the *Index* link. You may need to wait for *Windows Me* to create the search index. Then all the important key words will be displayed one under the other in an extensive list.

Entering a search word

The left side of the *Index* tab window is divided in two: a text box into which you type the search word is displayed in the top half ; at the bottom there is a list of all the entries available in the *Windows Help* index, displayed in alphabetical order.

Entering a key word

Enter the first letter of the search word in the first text box. This way the key word is searched for by letter. Sometimes it is sufficient to type just the first letter.

Entering alphabetical letters

In the list at the bottom, the content is adjusted according to the search word. If you type a single letter, the first index entry which begins with that letter is displayed. For example, enter the letter "p" and look at the changes to the list. Finish typing the word "print".

Selecting a Help entry

At this point the first appropriate entry will be displayed. Select the heading *Print Preview* from the list of index entries and click on the *Display* button on the lower border of the window. Information on printing documents is displayed in the right side of the screen.

Display of Help entries

If you click on the heading *Print* -[search element] from the list in the left page, then again on *Display,* a troubleshooter appears which will help you to find a solution to printing problems. Troubleshooters display a series of contextual possibilities. Choose the appropriate one and click on *Next.* In this way, the problem is identified and the *Windows* Help suggests solutions.

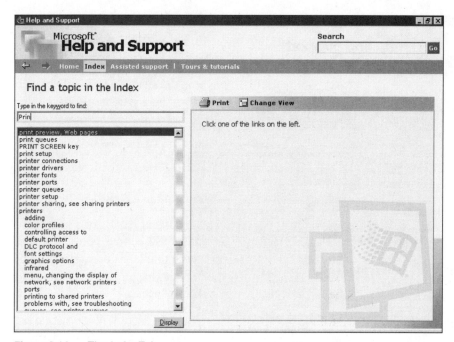

Figure 2.14   The *Index* Tab

Windows Help Assisted support

If you have an Internet link you can request assisted support on a particular function of the Windows Help. By clicking on the link *Assisted Support* in the title bar of the *Help and Support* window, you will be connected to Microsoft support and forums, in which Windows users can swap experiences and work together to find a solution to problems.

Microsoft Support   Click on *Assisted Support* in the title bar. To link up directly to Microsoft support, click on the link *Microsoft Corporation* underneath *Contact Support*. Immediately afterwards, the Microsoft Passport is displayed, through which you access the Microsoft online support field.

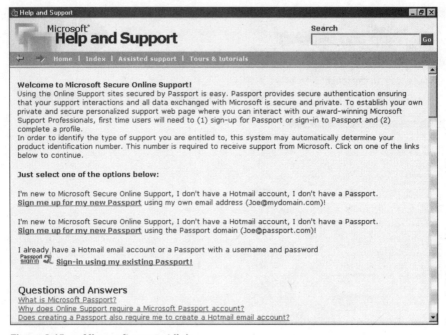

Figure 2.15   Microsoft support link

**MSN technical
support groups**

By clicking on *MSN Computing Central Forums* you automatically open Microsoft Internet Explorer, from which you download the support site.

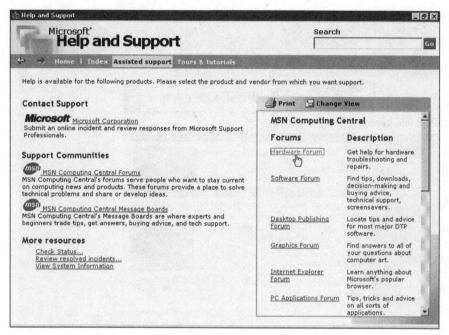

Figure 2.16   Choosing a discussion forum

Here you can find out the latest Windows news, and there is support in the form of forums, dialogue interfaces and even links to download useful programs and tools. However, to access the site you must be familiar with English.

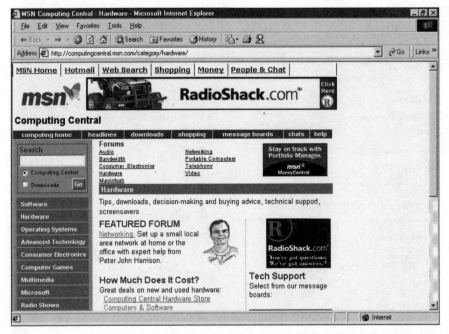

Figure 2.17   *MSN Computing Central* gives information and advice on *Windows Me*

In particular, the *MSN Computing Central* download zone is a point of departure from which to download basic Windows programs. Here you will find the main shareware and freeware programs, ordered by page, which facilitate your daily use of Windows.

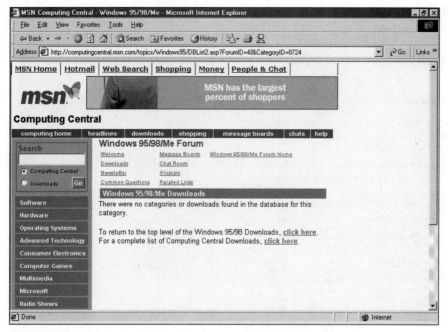

Figure 2.18   Useful downloading tools through *MSN Computing Central*

Windows Help *Tours & Tutorials*

The tours and tutorials are mini foundation courses set out in a clear and comprehensible way in a separate presentation window. After you have started up the Windows Help with *Start/Help*, click on the link *Tours & Tutorials* in the title bar of the *Help and Support* window.

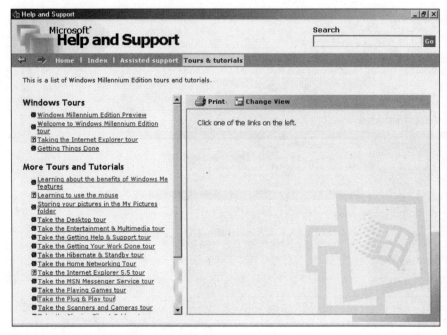

Figure 2.19 List of the tours available in the *Windows Help*

List of tours available

On the left side of the window a list of the tours available appears. Click on one of the headings and the *Windows Millennium Edition Tour* window opens.

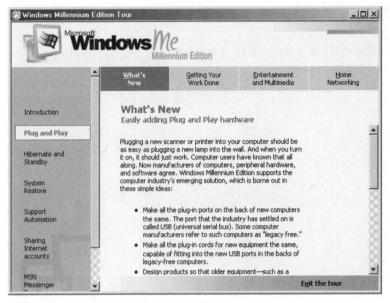

Figure 2.20   *Windows Millennium Edition Tour*

The heading *Learning to use the mouse* is a learning program aimed in particular at beginners who have not yet become familiar with how to use the mouse and pointer. Start up the tutorial by clicking on *Tutorial*. The window *Mouse Tutorial – Microsoft Internet Explorer* will open. Click on *Next* and the basics of mouse use will be explained step-by-step.

Figure 2.21   The *Learning to use the mouse* tour for beginners

The *Windows Millennium Edition Tour*

The *Windows Millennium Edition Tour* is divided into four pages; *What's New, Getting Your Work Done, Entertainment and Multimedia* and *Home Networking*. Click on one of these topics to select it. If you click on one of the subtitles in the left border of the window, information will be displayed in the main part of the window.

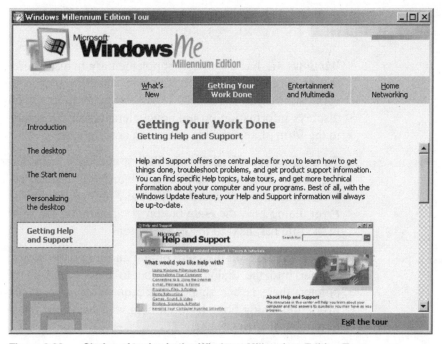

Figure 2.22   Choice of topics in the *Windows Millennium Edition Tour*

If you click on a Tour inside the *Help and Support* window, you will be linked directly to the relevant part of the text. You can scroll through the various pages and titles by clicking in the *Windows Millennium Edition Tour* window.

Exit

Close the *Windows Millennium Edition Tour* by clicking on the *Exit* link in the lower right corner of the window or click on the *Close* button ⊠ in the upper right corner.

Calling up the *Help* for *Windows* elements

Windows Me has a range of supplementary helps. There-fore in almost all dialog boxes, and sometimes even in applications, you can access a special type of Help, which displays information on unknown elements in the screen in the form of appropriate command descriptions.

Opening the dialog box

To try this type of help, you will first need to open a dia-log box. For example, open *Wordpad (Start/Pro-grams/Accessories)* and then choose *File/Print....* In the *Print* dialog box, the *Help* button **?** appears on the right in the title bar, next to the *Close* button.

Help button

Now click once on the *Help* button and move the mouse pointer into the dialog box. Next to the usual type of pointer, there is one shaped like a question mark. Click inside the dialog box you want help with using the ques-tion mark-shaped pointer.

Command Descrip-tion

If there is a help text corresponding to the selected topic, *Windows Me* will display a command description, which is a text explaining the command function or element that you have clicked on. If no information is available, the question mark-shaped pointer disappears. In this case, call up the Help in another part of the dialog box. To clo-se a command description, just click on it.

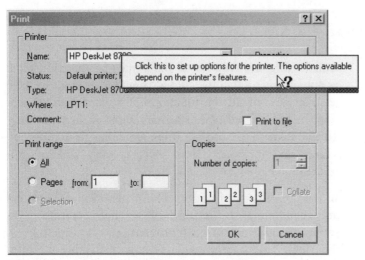

Figure 2.23   Activating the *Help* in a dialog box

What's This?

Another way of displaying the Help to find out about an element on the screen is to click with the right hand mouse button on the area that you want information about. Click on the *What's This?* command in the context menu.

The *What's This?* can also be called up by pressing the ⟨⇧⟩ + ⟨F1⟩ keys. In this case, information is displayed on the element highlighted in the window (the active element). In text boxes, the active element is recognizable by the pointer or by selected text highlighted in a colour. Activated buttons, control panels and other elements are recognizable by a shaded frame. To highlight an element without activating it, click on it, holding the mouse button pressed down, and drag the pointer to an area which is free of elements.

Calling up and using the Help for *Windows* applications

Considering the number of *Windows Me* applications, it is not surprising that even experts find it difficult to have an overview of all the functions of a *Windows* application. In fact, according to statistics, most of them use only 10 per cent of the possibilities available in a program. This is an unnecessary limit because every *Windows* application contains an internal help.

Help

In the present era of multimedia, program manufacturers are abandoning the writing of manuals, preferring to group all information on a program and its functions in the Help. This section explains how to display the relevant applications' Help.

Starting up the application

Before you can display the help to a particular program, you obviously need to start up the program in question. Select *Start/Programs* and click on the relevant program command, or click on the corresponding group of programs and click on the program command.

To try it out, call up the *Windows* text processing program, *Wordpad*. Then press the ⌷F1⌷ key.

Active program window

Be careful: to access the Help, you will need to activate the program window. If the active window is a desktop folder window, the *Windows Help* will be displayed. If a program is reduced to an icon, the ⌷F1⌷ key will not cause the specific application help to start up.

"Help" menu

Nonetheless, the problem of abbreviating keys can be easily resolved: just use the *Help* menu instead. In the *Help* applications menu, you will always find the *Index* command.

Program Help

This command calls up a window of the internal program help, the contents of which are adjusted to suit the active program. The help windows in most programs are divided according to a particular model which is described below, although in some programs tabs may be missing.

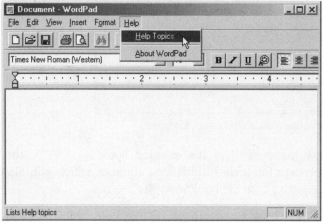

Figure 2.24   Calling up the *Windows* applications Help (in this case, *Wordpad*)

The *Contents* tab of the Help

Expand with just a click

The entries in the drop-down menu in the *Contents* tab can be opened by clicking on the topics 📖 in the left side of the window or by clicking on one of the help entries ❓ . The help text is displayed mainly in the right half of the window, and other help windows are displayed if necessary. To extend the structure further, click on an object, for example, *Working with Documents* in *Wordpad*. Important help pages relating to this topic will be displayed.

Hierarchical structure

This section explains the hierarchical structure of headings in the left window of the *Contents* tab. The help is divided into headings marked with a book icon 📖. The drop-down menu on the left represents the shelf on which you can find the books. To open a book, just click on it.

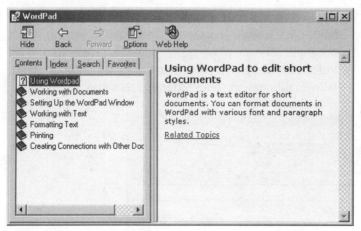

Figure 2.25   Specific program Help (in this case, *Wordpad*)

Book

Now the content of the selected book 📖 will be displayed in the form of chapters, some of which will also be marked with the book icon 📖.

Help entries

In other cases, an open book 📖 may contain the first help entries, which are marked with the question mark icon [?] (see the Wordpad help, Figure 2.26). The chapters of an open book can be displayed by clicking on them.

Internet technique

As a rule, the principle at the basis of this procedure is the same as that used in the structure display folders in *Internet Explorer*. The difference is that, in this case, instead of the work folder icon, the book icon is used and you only need to click once.

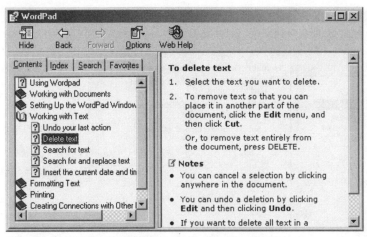

Figure 2.26   Open book/chapter in the *Wordpad* help

Open books

Open books 📖 can be closed with another click to reduce the display in the left window. Use the scroll bar to browse unopened books or help entries. Any help topic marked with a question mark icon ? in the left help window can be displayed in the right window by clicking on the corresponding heading.

Information displayed

Read the information displayed. A tool bar is always displayed. With the buttons on the tool bar you can move inside the help topics.

Moving to another help topic

To move from a displayed topic to a topic described on the left, click on one of the books on the left 📚 or on another help entry ?. With the *Forward* ⇨ and *Back* ⇦ buttons, you can scroll back and forth between Help pages.

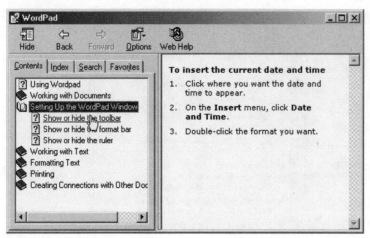

Figure 2.27   Help text display in the right side of the window

Options button

The *Options* button allows you to change the display of the help. You can change to the help on the Web (for this you will need a modem/ISDN and Internet access) or browse back and forth. With the *Print...* command, you can print information relevant to a particular help topic on a correctly installed and connected printer.

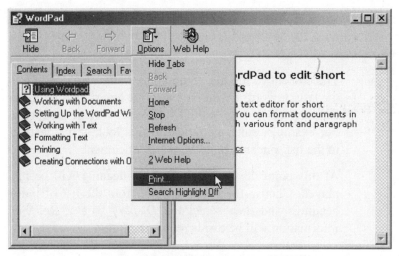

Figure 2.28   *Print...* a help text through the *Options* menu

Further information   To display further information, click on the underlined text extracts in the right window and on the links already mentioned in the *Windows Help* or on the Internet.

The *Index* tab of the Help

This section describes the alphabetical register of the Help, which is called up through the *Index* tab.

Index tab   First of all, call up the help for the application you are using with the F1 key or through *Help / Index*. Make sure that the program window is active, otherwise the *Windows Help* will start up instead.

Entering a search word   The left side of the *Index* tab window is divided in two: a text box in which you type the search word is displayed in the top half; at the bottom there is a list of all the entries available in the help index, displayed in alphabetical order.

Entering a key word

Enter the first letter of the key word in the text box. This way, the key word is searched for by letter. Sometimes it is sufficient to type just the first letter.

Entering alphabetical letters

The content of the list at the bottom adjusts according to the search word. If you type a single letter, the first index heading which begins with that letter will be displayed. For example, enter the letter "d" and look at the changes to the list. Finish typing the word "documents".

Selecting a help heading

At this point the first suitable help heading will be displayed. Choose the heading *Print* from the list of index headings and then select the *Display* button. Relevant information will be displayed on the right.

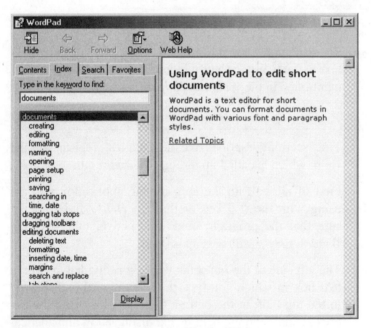

Figure 2.29   The *Index* tab of the *Wordpad* Help

The *Search* tab of the Help

In the *Contents* tab, the help topics are subdivided hierarchically into books; through the *Index* tab, the tab of the help appears in alphabetical order. If you cannot find the appropriate entry in the Contents or the Index, the *Search* tab offers a further possibility.

Searching for a text on a Help topic

Inside *Search* you can look at the content of all the topics available in the Help. The number of matching words found can be limited through criteria that restrict the search. In this way you obtain only those entries which are relevant to the topic and which contain the search word.

Creating an index of compound words

This help function is a small database which searches intelligently for the particular word in the texts available in the help. Type the search word or expression in the text box at the top of the left side of the window.

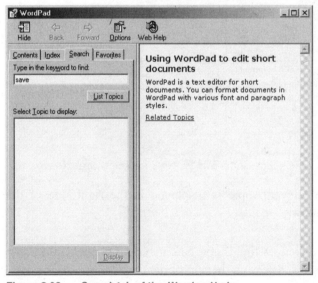

Figure 2.30   *Search* tab of the *Wordpad* help

Expression

Expression means a group of two or more words. Enter the words consecutively, separated by a space. Then click on the *List Topics* button.

List of topics

The list of topics in the drop-down menu at the bottom of the left window of the help is displayed by clicking on the *List Topics* button. Try it out with the word *Save*.

For example, choose the heading *To save changes to a document* in the Wordpad help. Click on *Display* to display the topic.

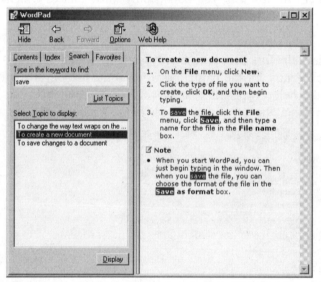

Figure 2.31   Display of a search topic in the help (in this case, the *Wordpad* help)

The relevant topic is displayed in the right side of the window.

To display a topic, you can also double click in the left window, selecting the appropriate topic.

Links to carry the research further

All occurrences of the search word or expression are selected in the displayed topic. Through the links displayed in the form of text extracts underlined in blue you can refine the search further. The read links (that is, the links you have clicked on) are highlighted in grey. The technology used here is that of the World Wide Web, an Internet information service. To close the help, click on ☒.

The *Favorites* tab of the Help

The *Favorites* tab is only available in Microsoft programs. It is comparable to a bookmark which selects and remembers various points in help texts (or in Internet Explorer Web sites), so that they can be accessed more quickly.

Adding to Favorites

The *Favorites* function in the window of Microsoft program helps can memorize a page of program help text. If you find a page of text that you think you will need later, select the *Favorites* tab (in some cases you may need to enlarge the help window slightly) and click on the *Add* button on the lower border of the window.

The page will immediately be bookmarked and the title will appear in the list which takes up most of the space in the left side of the window.

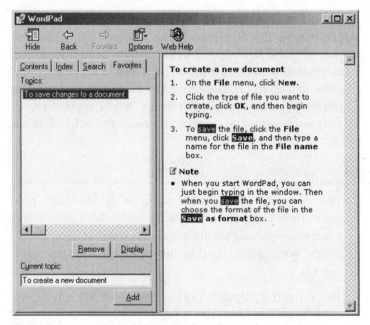

Figure 2.32   Adding a help text to Favorites

Display

To call up Favorites, click on the heading in question and then on the *Display* button. You can also display the content of your Favorites in the right side of the window with a double click.

Remove

If the list becomes too long, you can erase individual headings. To do this, select one of your Favorites by clicking on it and then click on the *Remove* button. Be careful: no confirmation messages are displayed – the entry will be erased from the list immediately.

3. Programs and documents

In this chapter we will focus on programs and files (i.e. the documents created in a program). There are many ways you can access and close applications in *Windows Me*. We will look at these methods first. Then we will go on to look at the various operations associated with saving, loading and organizing documents.

Running Programs

Windows Me is extremely flexible, especially when it comes to running programs. As the saying goes "all roads lead to Rome" and this is certainly true for *Windows Me!*

We will begin by describing the method of accessing applications using the *Start* menu in *Windows Me*. For beginners, this is the easiest way of performing this operation. However, as you begin to gain more and more experience with *Windows Me*, you will see that using the *Start* menu to access a program is actually the longest way of doing this.

Accessing programs from the *Start* menu

The *Start* menu represents the operating area of *Windows Me* and can be accessed by clicking on the *Start* button on the left hand side of the taskbar.

In this menu you will find everything you will ever need in Windows. By using the *Programs* command in the *Start* Menu and clicking on the relevant submenu, you can access any *Windows Me* application via the *Start* menu. To run a program, select *Programs* from the *Start* menu and the relevant cascading menu will open automatically. For example, in the first cascading menu that appears when you click on *Programs*, you can access *Internet Explorer* and *Windows Media Player*.

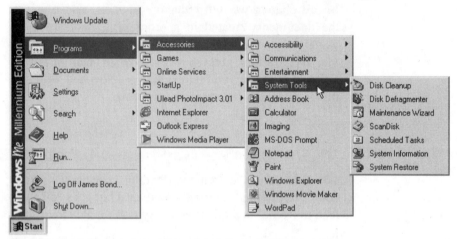

Figure 3.1   Applications in the *Programs* submenus

The other programs, such as *Calculator*, the word-processing application *WordPad* and the graphics application *Paint*, are all grouped under *Accessories*.

Program groups

By positioning the mouse pointer on a program group, you automatically open the submenu. To access a program, simply click on the program desired. For example, to access a word-processing package, all you would need to do is click on *WordPad*.

Menu closes automatically

Each time you access an application the *Start* menu automatically closes down. This is why it is actually the longest way of accessing programs. If, for example, you wanted to access two of the system tools found in *Start/Programs/Accessories/System Tools,* you would have to click on the *Start* menu and follow the whole procedure twice.

The number of items in the *Start* menu will depend, on the one hand, on the number of components you chose to install when installing *Windows* on your system and, on the other hand, on the number of applications that you have installed subsequently.

Alphabetical order The applications in the *Programs* menu are listed alphabetically. Starting at the top of the *Programs* menu and working down, the program groups are listed first - in alphabetical order - and these are followed by the program commands, once again in alphabetical order. The program groups are special folders. Program groups don't contain the program files for the applications themselves, rather they contain a series of links to the position in the computer's memory where those program files are to be found. Applications are grouped under the various program groups according to function or type. Program groups can be renamed, deleted, and even created or "filled" with other program commands.

When you install a new *Windows Me* application, *Windows Me* will automatically create a new entry in the *Start* menu. The majority of applications will create a new program group with its own cascading menu containing all the relevant program commands. If a program you have installed recently doesn't install its own icon(s) in the *Start* menu, you can also do this manually. We will describe how to do this shortly.

There is a whole range of different ways of accessing an application in *Windows Me*. In this section, we will describe how you can access an application in *Windows Me* by using *My Computer* in 🖥 .

My Computer is a special folder in *Windows* where all the directories available in your computer are displayed in the form of icons. Not only are you able to view icons for all the drives of your PC, but *My Computer* also has an icon for the *Control Panel* of your computer.

Accessing programs from the *My Computer* system folder

To access a program, double-click on the *My Computer* icon on the desktop of your computer. In the window which opens, double-click on the icon corresponding to the drive where the program you wish to use has been saved. If the window comes up empty, i.e. if there are no folders and files showing in this drive, click on the instruction *View the entire contents of this drive* on the left hand side of the window to show the files.

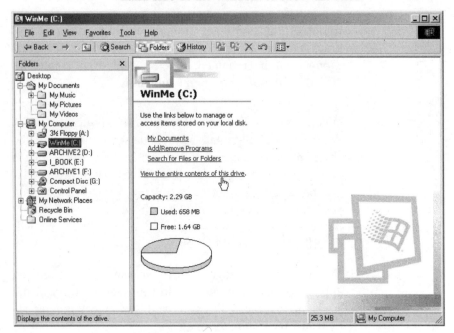

Figure 3.2   Viewing files in *Windows Me*

Next, by double-clicking on the folders to open them, go to the folder that contains the program icon of the program you wish to use.

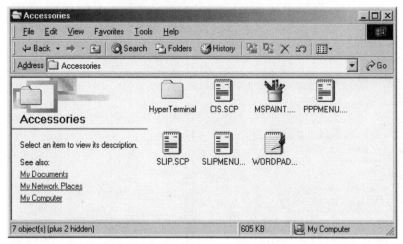

Figure 3.3   *Browsing* in My Computer

Folder where a program is saved

For example let's take a look at the folder *(C:)*, *Programs* and *Accessories*. Inside this folder, for example, are to be found the program files *Paint* (*MSPAINT*) and *WordPad* (*WordPad*).

Double-click

To access an application, simply double-click on the relevant program icon. Alternatively, you can select a folder or a program by single clicking it, and run the application you wish to use by choosing *Open* in the shortcut menu or in the file menu. To use this method, you will need to know the name and the location in the computer's memory (e.g.: *MSPAINT*) of the program file you are trying to access, or of a relevant shortcut.

To configure *My Computer* so that the contents of a folder are shown in a new window when you open that folder, select the *Folder Options...* command in the *Tools* menu, click on the *General* tab, and choose the *Open each folder in its own window* option in the *Browse folders* section. Confirm your choice by clicking on *OK*.

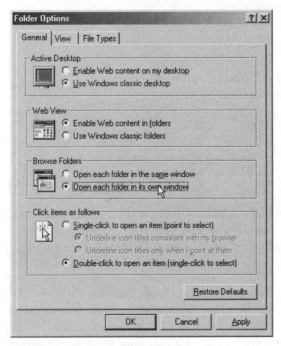

Figure 3.4   Folder Options settings

Accessing programs using *Windows Explorer*

One of the main functions of *Windows Explorer* is to allow you to organize and manage your files in a professional manner. *Windows Explorer* is the only place on your computer where you will be able to see a visual representation of the structure of the drives and folders on your computer. It goes without saying, of course, that this isn't the only function of *Windows Explorer*. It has many other functions besides allowing you to view the structure of the drives and folders on your computer!

Short-cut Menu

Windows Explorer can be accessed by clicking on the *Windows Explorer* icon in the *Program/Accessories* folder of the *Start* menu. A quicker, alternative, method is to use the shortcut menu by right-clicking the Start button on the taskbar and choosing the Explorer command in the shortcut menu.

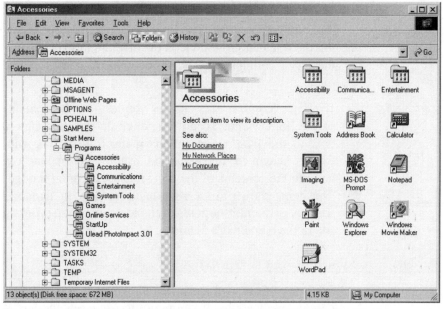

Figure 3.5   Double-clicking on a program icon opens that application for you.

Folder Structure

To run a program using *Windows Explorer* you need to know the name of the file, or of the relevant shortcut, and where it is located in the computer's memory. View the contents of a folder by double-clicking on the plus sign ⊞ next to the folder in the directory and then open the folder that contains the program you wish to use. To view the contents of a folder simply click on that folder's name.

Double Click

To open an application all you need to do is to double-click on the program file shown in the right-hand window. To use the *Calculator*, for example, all you need to do is click on the file *CALC* in the C:\Windows folder. A more simple method is to use the shortcut, as you don't need to know the name of the program file to be able to do this. For example, the shortcuts to open the applications in *Windows* can be found in the folder *C:\Windows\Start Menu\Programs*.

***Open* Command**

Alternatively you can also open an application by selecting the relevant program icon or folder and then choosing the *Open* command in the shortcut menu or in the *File* menu.

Contents of the Start Menu

Windows Explorer also enables you to view the contents of the Start Menu. To do this, click on the plus sign ⊞ next to the *Windows* and *Start* menu folders. The sub-folders shown in the right-hand window correspond exactly to the contents of the *Start* menu. Attention though! The items shown in the right-hand window in *Windows Explorer* are only shortcuts to the location of the program file in the computer's memory.

Accessing programs using the Run command.

Windows Me is extremely flexible when it comes to accessing applications. If you prefer the direct method, or if you have some experience with the old operating system *MS-DOS*, using the Run dialog box, as described in this paragraph, to open an application may be the best solution for you.

Using this method, you not only need to know where the file is stored in your computer's memory you also need to

Specifying the filepath

know the correct filename as well. You will also need to know the syntax used in writing commands. As you can see this method is more suited to people using the old DOS system, which is becoming extinct, than it is for *Windows* users.

Run command

Let's now take a look at the practical procedure. Open the *Start* menu and click on the Run command. This will open the *Run* dialog box. Insert the file-path and the name of the file in the *Open* command line. The example shown in Figure 3.6 will open *Paint*. The full file-name of this application is *MSPAINT.EXE*. The following is the correct syntax to use:

```
Relevant Drive:\path\filename
```

Then press ⏎ or click on *OK*.

Figure 3.6   You have to enter the full path when using the *Run* command

Select the program file

If an error message appears it means that the path or the file in question do not exist. If this happens, click on the *Browse* button and, using the window that will appear, try to find the file in question by looking through the folders stored on the hard-drive. After you have found the file you are looking for, select it and open it by using the *Run* command. Enter the file-path in the *Open* command line in the *Run* dialog box and click on *OK* to confirm that you want to open this application.

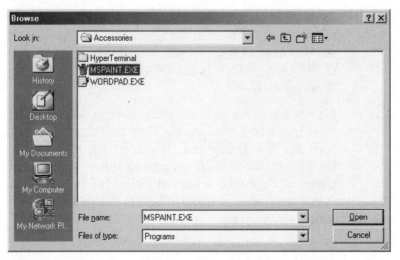

Figure 3.7   Inserting the filename using the *Browse* pop-up window

 To open a file stored in *Windows*, all you need to do is insert the program filename. In our example, this is *MSPAINT*. Windows does the rest for you and will automatically find the file.

Opening programs and documents with Windows Me

If you tend to use only one program to do most of your work, say a word-processing application such as *Word-Pad*, one really practical solution would be to launch that program every time you StartUp windows. *Windows Me* allows you to do this.

The same goes for opening documents that you need to work on a lot, such as a thesis or something similar. In fact, if you launch a document automatically whenever you switch on your computer, you cut out two of the steps you would otherwise have to perform: accessing the program and opening the file

To allow you to do this, *Windows Me* has a special folder where you can store all the items you wish to work on as soon as *Windows* has been started up.

This is called the *StartUp* folder and it is stored in *Programs* in the *Start* menu. If you haven't installed any additional *Windows* applications it is likely that the *StartUp* folder will be empty.

Open the *Start* menu and position the mouse pointer on *Programs/StartUp*. If the folder is empty, the cascading menu will show the status non-activated. If, for example, you have installed the *Microsoft Office* package, the *StartUp* folder will already contain some of the icons for these *Office* applications.

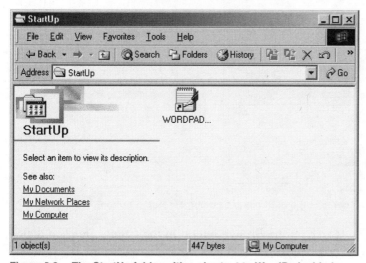

Figure 3.8   The StartUp folder with a shortcut to WordPad added

To automatically launch a program every time you start up Windows, you need to create a shortcut to the program icon in the StartUp folder. This can be done in a whole number of ways.

Let's take a look at the method of adding items to the *Start* menu by using the *Taskbar Properties* window.

Click on the *Start* button and then select *Settings*. Click on *Taskbar and Start Menu* and then click on the *Advanced* tab in the dialog box that appears. Next click on the *Add...* button.

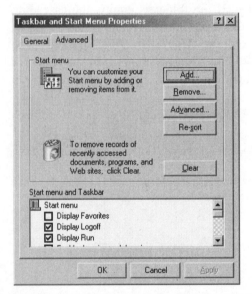

Figure 3.9   Adding items to the Start menu by using the *Add...* button

Create Short-cut dialogue box

Click on the *Browse* button in the *Create Shortcut* dialog box. Here, you will need to know where the file is stored in your computer's memory or the position of a relevant shortcut. Let's try and do this for the word-processing application *WordPad*.

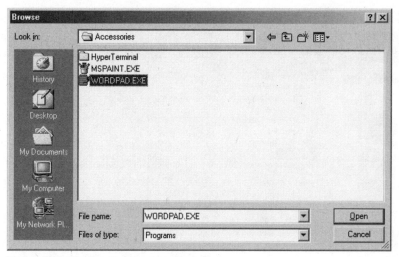

Figure 3.10 Finding the program file-path

The program *WordPad* is called WORDPAD.EXE and is stored in the *C:\Programs\Accessories* folder. If you need to insert an application that was loaded on to your computer at a later date into the *StartUp* folder, you can access this application by using the menu shortcuts in the *Start* menu, which can be found in the folder *C:\Windows\Start Menu\Programs*.

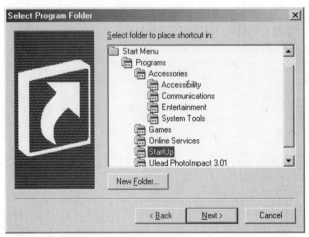

Figure 3.11 Selecting the programs

Select the program file you wish to use and click on the *Open* button. In the *Create Shortcut* dialog box click on the *Next* button and double-click on *StartUp*.

At this point you can specify the name that will appear in the *StartUp* menu, in the *Select a name for the shortcut*. Then click on *Finish*, close the *Taskbar Properties* window by choosing *OK* and check that the item has been added to the Start menu.

These modifications will come into effect the next time you start up your system using Windows. Going back to our example, *WordPad* will be launched, together with *Windows Me,* the next time you start up your system. Only place the most important applications in the StartUp folder to avoid overloading the memory and slowing down your system

Documents in Start-Up

As well as programs, you can also place documents in the *StartUp* folder. In this case, the relevant program will also be launched to allow you to start using the document in question straightaway.

A more convenient method is to copy the shortcuts in the *Start* menu into the *StartUp* folder. For example, you could select *Start/Programs/Accessories* and then select the program you wish to start automatically

Holding down the Ctrl button, drag a copy of the icon you wish to use into the *StartUp* folder in the open *Start* menu. If you don't keep the Ctrl key pressed all you will do is *move* the program icon from one place to another. Shortcuts can be removed from the *Start* menu by using the *Remove* command in the shortcut menu.

Closing applications

Methods

After you have opened an application and worked on your documents, the next thing you need to know is how to close them after saving them. This can be done in the following ways:

- The *Close* command in the *File* menu

- By pressing the key combination Alt + F4

- The *Close* command in the *Control* menu

- By double-clicking the tab in the *Control* menu

- By clicking the Close button on the title bar ✕

- By selecting *Close* from the shortcut menu of the program tab on the taskbar

Save changes message

All of these methods will close the application. If the document hasn't been saved a message will appear on the screen (Figure 3.12) that allows you to perform this function. If you click on *Yes*, the *Save as* dialog box will appear. Clicking on *No* will close the application, whilst clicking on *Cancel* will take you back to the current document.

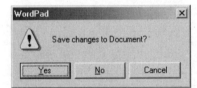

Figure 3.12 Request to save a document that hasn't already been saved

The *Control* menu is activated by single clicking the *Control* menu tab on the left hand side of the title bar in a program window. The icon used to identify the *Control* menu tab is the same as the icon of the program that is being used. If it is a program you are trying to close, the same icon will be used as appears in the *Start* and *Windows Explorer* menus.

Customizing a program icon

Short-cuts

Before going on to explain the procedure, we need to clarify a little bit what we mean by customizing a program icon. The program icons in *Windows Me* are stored in the executable part of an application (file extension EXE) and can only be modified by using special editing programs. When we say "customizing a program icon" we mean customizing the icon of the shortcut that is linked to that program. These are the shortcut icons you can find in the *Start* menu. At a first glance, it might appear that there is no difference between a program icon and a shortcut icon.

Short-cut icon

A shortcut is only a copy of the program icon containing information about where that program is stored in memory and the filename of the program So, for example, the shortcut *Calculator* in the *Start* menu points to the file-name *CALC.EXE* in the *C:\Windows* folder. Behind the shortcut *Paint,* on the other hand, is the program file *MSPAINT.EXE* in the *Programs/Accessories* folder. Shortcut icons can be recognized by the symbol 🔲 found in the bottom left hand corner of the icon.

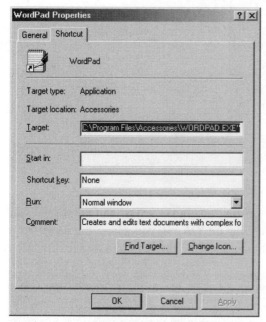

Figure 3.13 The Shortcut dialog box

Below you will find instructions on how to substitute a shortcut icon using *WordPad.* To do this, go to the *Windows/Start Menu/Programs/Accessories* folder. Click on the *WordPad* icon and choose *File/Properties.* This command is also available in the icon's shortcut menu.

Next, choose the *Change icon...* button on the *Shortcut* dialog box. This will bring up the *Change icon* dialog box, which will show the current icon in the *Current icon* field. Below this are shown a number of different icons. Use the scroll bar to review all the icons if necessary.

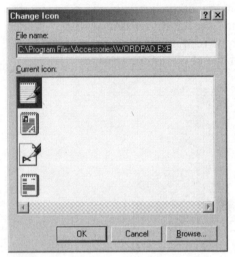

Figure 3.14 Choosing another icon

Choose one of the available icons and confirm your choice by clicking on *OK*. If you close the *Properties* window by clicking on OK, the icon will be substituted.

If there are no icons available in the *Change icon...* dialog box click on *Browse*. In the dialog box that comes up, go to the folder that contains the icon you wish to use or a library of icons and open by choosing the *Open* command.

Opening documents

The flexibility of *Windows Me* isn't limited only to running programs. There are also many options available for opening documents. Let's begin with the simplest method, i.e. opening a document that has already been saved by using the *Start* menu.

Opening documents from the *Start* menu

As well as allowing you to run programs, the *Start* menu also allows you to open documents. In the *Documents* menu, *Windows Me* holds a list of the 15 most recently used documents independently of whichever application was used.

The last 15 documents

The only requirement for *Windows Me* to be able to open the file is that the file extension has already been registered in *Windows Me*. To open one of the last 15 most recently used documents, click on the *Start* button on the *taskbar,* move the mouse pointer to *Documents*, and choose the file you wish to open from the submenu that appears.

Program icon

The icon shown just to the left of the filename is the icon of the application relevant to that document. Click on the name of the file you wish to work with (cf. Figure 3.15). This will launch the application that the file was created in and open the document ready for you to use.

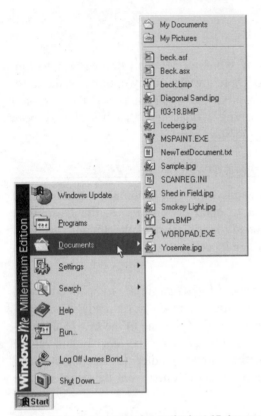

Figure 3.15 *Documents* shows the last 15 documents used

If the document contained in the Documents menu has been saved to another location, *Windows Me* will automatically search through the hard disk until it has found it. If the file is found, *Windows Me* will automatically launch the application and open the file. If *Windows Me* cannot find the file, the following message will appear:

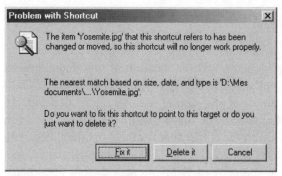

Figure 3.16 *Windows* looks for a similar filename

Alternative

If the name of the file doesn't correspond to the file you are looking for, because the file has been deleted for example, click on the *Delete it* button in the message box. Not clicking on this button will open the wrong file. If it is the file you are looking for, click on *Fix it* to update the settings of the shortcut so that it points to the right file. Let's now look at an alternative method for opening documents.

Organizing and managing

The *Windows Explorer* folder is designed to allow you to organize and manage the directories - and the files they contain- that are stored on your computer. *Windows Explorer* also allows you to access the Control panel. It goes without saying, of course, that the representation of the contents of the drives and folders in your computer isn't the only function of this feature of *Windows*! The following section describes how to open documents stored in *Windows Me* using the *Windows Explorer* feature.

Opening documents using the system folder *My Computer*

My Documents
folder

To open a document using *My Computer*, you need to know the filename and the location of that document, or of a relevant shortcut, in your computer's memory. Double-click on the *My Computer* icon 🖥 on the desktop and then on the icon of the drive that the document has been saved in. Go to the folder that contains the document you want to work on by double-clicking through the folders shown. The majority of *Windows* applications documents are saved by default, for example, in the *C:\My Documents* folder, which can also be opened by double-clicking on the *My Documents* icon on the desktop. A number of new subfolders have been introduced in *Windows Me* where you can also store your images, films, or music files.

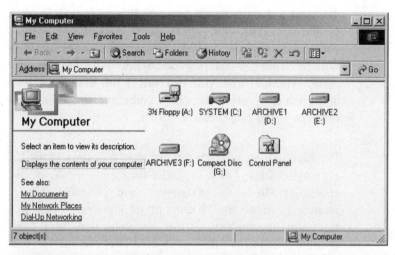

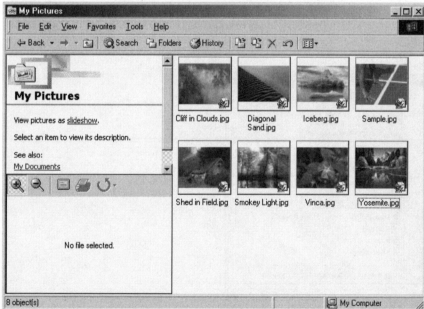

Figure 3.17   An example of the contents of the *My Computer* folder

Double Click

To open a document, all you need to do is double-click on the icon corresponding to the document you wish to use and the application that that document was created in will be launched and the document will automatically open. Alternatively, you can select the document icon and open it by using the *Open* command in the shortcut menu or in the *File* menu.

Double-clicking on a document icon will only work for *registered* files. Only in these files can Windows Me recognize, from the extension, the program that is launched when the document is opened. This will normally happen for all the programs that have been correctly installed. If you double-click on a file that hasn't been registered, the Open with... dialog box will appear. This allows you to choose which program to use to open the file.

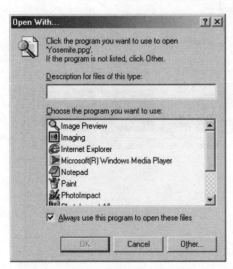

Figure 3.18 The Open With...dialog box for types of non-registered file

Opening documents from *Windows Explorer*

Thanks to its panoramic structure, *Windows Explorer* is designed to allow you to organize and manage your files and folders.

Panoramic structure

Windows Explorer is the only place in your computer where you can have a clear visual representation of the contents of the various drives, folders and subfolders stored on your computer. Of course, that is not to say that that is the only function of *Windows Explorer* as it has many other uses as well. For example, *Windows Explorer* allows you to the open documents of the registered applications.

To do this, you will need to open *Windows Explorer*. This can be done by selecting *Start/Programs/Accessories* and then choosing *Windows Explorer*.

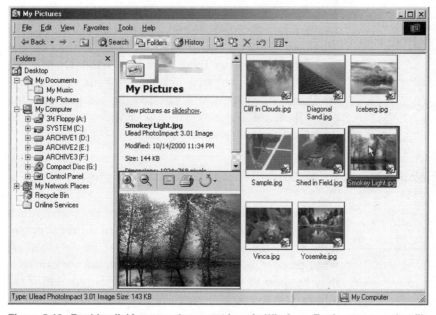

Figure 3.19 Double-clicking on a document icon in Windows Explorer opens that file

Opening a
document

Even when opening a file in *Windows Explorer*, it is still useful to know the filename and its location (or the location of a relevant shortcut) in the computer's memory. Click on the plus sign ⊞ next to the icon for the drive you wish to access and then look through the folders that are stored in this drive, until you come to the one that contains the document you wish to open. This can be done by simply clicking on the name of the desired folder.

Double Click

To open a document all you need to do is double-click on one of the files shown in the right hand window. This will launch the relevant application and open the document in question. Alternatively, you may choose to open the document by selecting the document icon and using the *Open* command in the shortcut menu, or by using the *File* menu.

As before, double-clicking on a document icon in *Windows Explorer* will only work for registered file types. It's only from these files that Windows Me can recognize, from the extension, the program that the files are linked to. If the file is not a registered file type, the *Open With...* dialog box will appear which allows you to open the file using another application.

Opening the documents directly in the application

Windows Me contains a whole range of programs which allow you to perform a whole number of different operations from the most basic to the most complicated. A word-processing package such as *WordPad*, for example, may be used to write letters; the graphics program *Paint* allows you to create your own pictures or to edit simple images. For other functions, such as spreadsheets, presentations, or working with databases you will need to install additional applications.

Documents created in a particular application will be saved a format specific to that application, also known as the *file type*.

Different file types Each application will only allow you to open certain types of file. Generally speaking, this will be the file type used by the application at the moment the document is saved which is given an extension recognized by *Windows Me*.

Extension file The extension file is an abbreviation consisting of three characters. A *Word* document has the extension *DOC*, which stands for *DOCument*, whilst *PAINT* has the extension *BMP*, which stands for *Bitmap*. To open a document created in a specific application, first open the application in question.

Once you have opened the program, select *File* and choose the command *Open*. If the application has a toolbar, it is also possible to click on the open button on the toolbar, which can be identified by the *Open* folder symbol.

The Open dialogue box Whatever application you are in, this will open the *Open* dialog box, as shown in Figure 3.20.

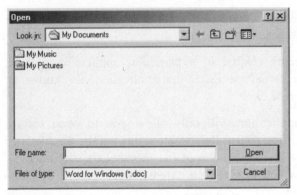

Figure 3.20   The Open dialog box (of *WordPad*)

Some of the elements of the *Open* dialog box are the same for all *Windows Me* applications. First, you will need to use the *Look In* drop-down menu and then choose the drive that your file is saved in.

Next, choose the folder that contains the file you wish to open from the list that appears below. The documents of most applications are saved by default in *My Documents*. Music files, films, and images will all be saved in their respective folders.

Open button

If not all the files are visible, use the scroll bar to scroll along until you find the desired file. Select the icon corresponding to the document you wish to open and click on the *Open* button. The document will now be loaded.

Using the buttons that appear on the top border of the dialog box, it is possible to modify the way the items in the list are shown. Alternatively, you can also move up to the folder on the level above.

Up button

The *Up* button allows you to jump from the folder you are viewing to the next level up. The active folder is shown in the drop-down menu *Save in*.

Views button

The *Views* button ⊞▾ , found at the top right, allows you to change the way the files are listed in the dialog box by choosing either the *Large Icons*, *Small Icons*, *List*, *Details* (provides additional information about the file such as file size and date last saved), and *Thumbnails* option. This is done by clicking on the downward pointing arrow and looking through the little drop-down menu that appears.

The standard type of file of the active application is always indicated in the *file type* drop-down menu in the *Open* dialog box. To view the various file types that that can be opened in the application you are using, all you need to do is open the file type drop-down menu using the drop-down menu arrow. With *All files (*.*)* (or *All Documents*) all of the files saved in the folder will be displayed.

However, you can only open the type of file permitted by the application, the text documents of a video writing program, for example. Modern applications can open many many different types of file, in many cases using special conversion programs to do so.

Overview

The following table shows the standard file types of programs contained in *Windows*:

Windows program	File type	Extension
WordPad	Documents	*DOC/.RTF*
Paint	Bitmap	*BMP*
Internet Explorer	Web Pages	*HTM*
Sound Recorder	Wave Sound	*WAV*

Figure 3.21 The file types of *Windows* applications

Saving documents in an application

Text written with WordPad or images drawn with Paint are saved by these programs in a format specific to each application, in this case appropriate to text or images.

File extension

Each application allows you to save your data only in certain types of file. The computer does this by assigning an extension file, an abbreviation consisting of three characters. A *WordPad* document has the extension *DOC*, which is short for *DOC*ument, whereas Paint has the extension *BMP*, which stands for *Bitmap*.

To save a document in an application using the specific program format, you first need to create the document. For example you could write a letter in *WordPad*.

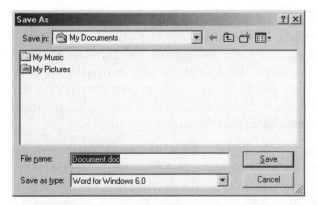

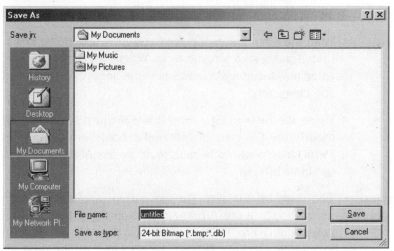

Figure 3.22   The Save as dialog box (top: *WordPad*, bottom: *Paint*)

Activate the program's *File* menu and select *Save*. If the application has a toolbar, it will also be possible to click on the *Save* button.

If the document is being saved for the first time, the *Save As* dialog box will appear, as shown in Figure 3.22. Some of the elements in the *Save As* dialog box are identical for all *Windows Me* applications.

Drive and destination folder

Windows requires four things to save a document from the application you are using. The drive and destination folder, and the name and type of file. To select the drive and destination folder, open the *Save In* drop-down menu and select the drive you wish to save your file to. By double-clicking on the list below that, you can then choose the destination folder.

Up one level

The *Up one level* button ⬆ allows you to jump from the folder you are in currently to the one on the next level up, effectively undoing the last double-click that you made. The current folder is shown in the *Save In* drop-down menu.

Creating a new folder

With the *Create New Folder* button 📁 you create a new folder and assign a name to it. Where it says *File name*, enter the document's name but remember not to exceed 255 characters.

Using the *Files of type* drop-down menu it is possible to modify the file type of the application. For example, in *Paint*, it is possible to determine the number of colours used in a bitmap.

Standard file type

The standard file type for the current application is always shown in the *Files of type* drop-down menu in the *Open* dialog box. The type of files that you can save in this application can be seen by clicking on the arrow of the *Files of type* drop-down menu. With modern applications it is often possible to open many many different types of file. These file types will only be needed where you need to open the document using another application. There are, for example, certain types of files that are independent of any platform and which are valid for the whole operating system, whose purpose is to allow you to transfer data from one computing system to another, rather than trying to find the best format to save the data for the application that it was created in.

What is the difference between *File/Save* and *Save As...*? If the file hasn't already been saved, then both will open the *Save As...* dialog box. If the file has already been saved with a name, *File/Save* will simply update the existing file, whereas *Save As...* will always open the *Save As...* dialog box.

Creating empty documents in *Windows Me*

Generally speaking, a document is saved in the program that it was created in. In *Windows Me*, however, you can also do the opposite. That is, you create an empty document first, then you give it a name, and then you open it with the application associated with the type of file you wish to use. What at first sight may seem illogical is actually an extremely practical alternative to following the *File/New* menu command procedure for the vast majority of programs.

Windows Explorer or My Computer

It is recommended that you save the new document in the position in the computer's memory where you want to have access to it in the future. To do this, open *Windows Explorer* or click on the *My Computer* icon on the desktop. Then go to the folder that you wish to save the new document in.

Make sure you don't select files that already exist. In *Windows Explorer* or the current folder window of *My Computer*, choose the *New* command from the *File* menu.

Shortcut menu

Alternatively, the *New* command may also be found in the shortcut menu. In Windows Explorer the mouse pointer must be positioned in the right hand window to be able to do this.

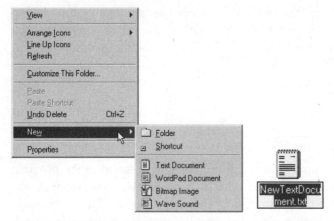

Figure 3.23   The types of file will depend on the applications installed

New **Command**

All the file types available in the system are shown in bold text in the lower part of the *New* command sub-menu. The number and type of files that you can create will depend on how many applications have subsequently been installed on your PC.

Choosing the file type

Click on the file type you wish to create the new document in. To create a document for the notepad, for example, choose *Text Document;* to create a document for *Paint,* choose Bitmap Image; and for text documents in WordPad, choose *WordPad Document*. If, for example, you have installed a word-processing package such as *Word*, you can create a new document using *Microsoft Word Document* instead.

A document icon is added to the current folder with the name *New [file type]*...(as in Figure 3.23, on the right). To name the file, all you have to do is to overtype the name that is highlighted with the name you wish to call the document.

It is important that you leave the three letters of the file extension as they are. Confirm your choice with ⏎ and open the new document by double-clicking on the icon. This will also open the application associated with that file.

Creating a shortcut to a document on your desktop

Shortcuts allow you to rapidly access the programs and documents you use most frequently without first having to go to the folder that that program or document is saved in. If, for example, you save your work in a file called *Timings,* a shortcut to that file, which is contained in the folder C:\My Documents, is created on the desktop so you don't have to go to C:\My Documents every time you want to open it. The actual document *Timings* can be opened at any time simply by double-clicking on the shortcut icon that appears on the desktop.

Note of the position in memory

In this way, you can open the document without first having to open the application it is associated with. A shortcut doesn't alter in any way the position in the computer's memory the document is saved in, it simply contains a note of the name of the file and where it is saved in the computer's memory so that the system will access that file or application every time you click on the shortcut. If you delete a shortcut, it doesn't in any way delete the original document.

Creating a shortcut

In *Windows Me* it is possible to create a shortcut to absolutely anything, for example you can create a shortcut to an application, a folder, a drive, another computer or a printer. To create a shortcut on your desktop, all you need to do is follow a number of simple steps. Select the item you wish to create a shortcut to, either in *Windows Explorer* or in *My Computer,* by clicking on it. For example, select a document or a folder. Then select the *Create Shortcut* command from the shortcut menu or from the *File* menu.

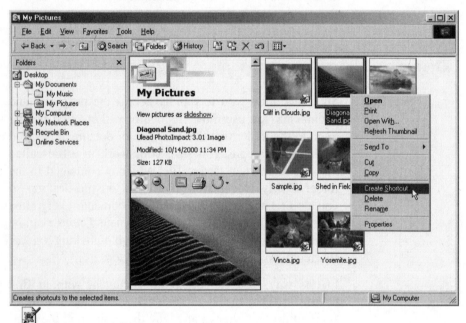

Figure 3.24   Creating a shortcut to a document

The shortcut file created is named *Shortcut to [file name].* The shortcut icon can now be dragged to any point on your computer such as the quick launch bar or the active desktop of the computer. To open the document or application in question, simply double-click the shortcut icon (or single-click on it if it is on the quick launch bar).

It is recommended that you only create shortcuts to the most important, most frequently used, documents on your desktop. If too many icons appear on the desktop it will soon become overloaded and hard to read.

Shortcut icons

Shortcuts can be recognized by the 📌 symbol that appears at the bottom left corner of the icon. If you want to create a link on your desktop to an application you use frequently, it is always necessary to create a shortcut Many applications give you the option to automatically create a shortcut on the desktop when you are installing that application.

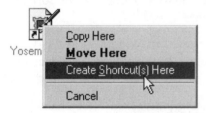

Figure 3.25 Creating a shortcut using the right mouse button

A more rapid way of creating a shortcut is to use the right mouse button. For example, to create a shortcut to Word-Pad, open the *C:\Programs\Accessories* folder in Windows Explorer.

Using the right mouse button, drag the *WORDPAD* icon onto the desktop. Let go of the button and choose the *Create Shortcut(s) Here* command from the shortcut menu.

It is possible to customize any of the shortcut settings (key combinations, icon, description, etc.) by clicking on the shortcut using the right mouse button and choosing *Properties*. To delete a shortcut, all you need to do is drag the icon into the *Recycle Bin* or click on *Delete* in the shortcut menu of the icon itself. The original file or application remains exactly where it is in the relevant folder in the computer's hard disk.

Document icons for Windows applications

Each *Windows* application saves files created in that application in a format specific to it. These specific formats are also known as file types.

Internal file extension

These file types are registered in Windows. In this way, Windows can recognize the application that a document was created in from its file extension.

The file extension normally consists of three characters. A *WordPad* document normally has the extension *DOC*, which stands for *document*, whilst an image in *Paint* has the extension *BMP*, which stands for *Bitmap*.

Document icon

Similarly, *Windows Me* assigns a special document icon to each of the registered files. From this icon the user is able to recognize which application a document belongs to.

Overview

The following table shows the most important document icons of the applications in *Windows*:

Windows application	Document type	Document icon	File Type
Notepad	*Text file*		*.TXT*
WordPad	*WordPad document*		*.DOC*
Paint	*Bitmap*		*.BMP*
Internet Explorer	*HTML document*		*.HTM*
Internet Explorer	*GIF file*		*.GIF*
Multimedia Player	*Wave Sound*		*.WAV*
Multimedia Player	*MP3 music file*		*.MP3*
Multimedia Player	*MIDI sequence*		*.MID*

Document icons for other registered applications

Other document
icons

If you wish to have an overview of the registered file types, select the *Tools/Folder Options...* command in a folder window of your choice, or in *Windows Explorer,* and click on the *File Types* tab.

The *Registered file types* list contains all the document icons and a description of all the registered applications. The descriptions to be found by clicking on the icon can also be viewed in *Windows Explorer* by clicking on the *Views* button.

By clicking on one of the registered file types, further information about the file type appears in *Details for [abbreviation of the extension] extension,* for example the type of application that is launched when you click on an icon in *Windows Explorer.*

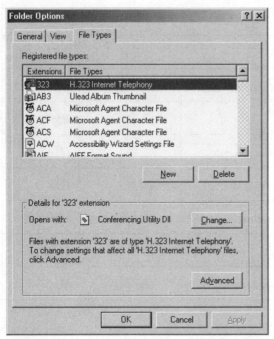

Figure 3.26 The Registered File Types list found in *Tools/Folder Options...*

You can change the icon associated with a given file type in the *Edit File Type* window, which is opened by clicking on the *Advanced* tab in the *Folder Options* dialog box. After you have clicked on the *Advanced* tab, select the *Change icon* button to view the other icons available to you. After you have done this, you may return to the *Edit File Type* window.

Opening a non registered file

Each application will only allow you to open certain types of file. Generally speaking, this will be the file type that the application uses as a default when you save your document. *Windows Me* is able to recognize these file types from the file extension.

Registered file

To open a registered document contained in a folder in *Windows Explorer* or *My Computer,* all you need to do is to click on the icon corresponding to the document or file you wish to use.

Non-registered file type

If, on the other hand, you try to open a document in *Windows Explorer* or *My Computer* that isn't recognized as a registered file type, the *Open With...* dialog box will appear.

Figure 3.27   List of registered applications in the *Open With...* dialog box

Registration

The list shown in the lower part of the dialog box shows all the registered Windows applications.

Open file

Select the name of the application you wish to use from the list and then click on *OK* to open the file. Attention though! If the application is unable to read the file type an error message will appear. The application and the file type must always be compatible otherwise this method will not work.

If you always want to use a certain application to open a file using this procedure, make sure the *Always use this program to open these files* box is ticked. Using the *Other...* button you can search for other programs that aren't contained in this list.

Viewing the contents of a document without using the associated application

To view the contents of a document, the normal procedure is to open the file once you are in the application that that file was created in. A more rapid method is to click on the document icon in *Windows Explorer* or *My Computer*.

Viewing the contents of a document

Windows Me offers a number of methods of viewing the contents of a document. In this way it is possible to view the contents of a bitmap, a Web page or Web graphics file already saved in one of the folders of your computer or in *Windows Explorer*. The operating system, in fact, has an integrated file viewing system *Preview* which allows you to view some of the contents of a file without having to access the application.

Viewing documents in folders and in *Windows Explorer*

To see a preview of a document, find the folder in *Windows Explorer* or *My Computer* that contains the document you wish to view. Then choose the *Thumbnails* command from the *View* menu. In some folders the preview option is already set as default. Using *Thumbnails*, for example, it is possible to preview the images saved by *Windows Me* in the folder *C:\My Documents\My Pictures*.

Thumbnails

When you select the Thumbnails option in a folder, *Windows Explorer* will try to show a preview of the contents of all of the documents stored in that folder. This means that *Windows Me* will recognize, for example, the vast majority of files with *BMP*, *JPG* or *GIF* extensions.

Enlarged Preview

If you select one of these files, *Windows Explorer* will show an enlarged version of the preview. However, this will only happen if the folder window or the window in *Windows Explorer* is large enough to accommodate the enlarged preview.

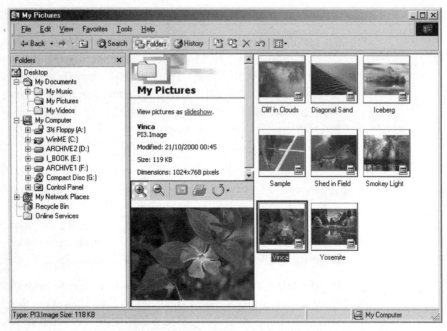

Figure 3.28 Enlarged Preview of the contents of a bitmap in Windows Explorer

File viewer

The *Windows Me* package also contains a separate file viewer capable of reading the format of the most important applications, which enables you to quickly scan the contents of your files.

Using the pocket calculator for calculations

Even though the vast majority of people use their PC to write letters, create drawings and images, play games or surf the internet, computers are also well known for their ability to "compute" or calculate data. Behind the scenes, in fact, your computer is constantly handling columns and columns of incomprehensible data, which is totally unimportant to the average PC user.

However, a number of applications exist that work with numbers and values, such as spreadsheets and databases. In these cases the computing or "calculating" function of the PC becomes self-evident.

Windows
Calculator

This section sets out how to use the simple calculator function in *Windows*.

Programs/
Accessories/
Calculator

To open the *Calculator*, click on the *Start* menu and open the *Programs/Accessories* menu. Next click on Calculator and the pocket Calculator will appear in *Standard* view.

Figure 3.29 The Windows Calculator in *Standard* view

View/
Scientific

To view the enlarged version of the *Calculator*, as shown in Figure 3.30, click on *View/Scientific* in the program menu bar of the *Calculator*. In this way, you will also be able to use the functions for the calculation of curves and angles as well as the more simple calculations.

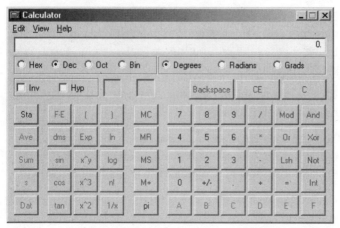

Figure 3.30 The Windows *Calculator* in *Scientific* view

You can use your mouse to use the calculator. All you need to do is click on the buttons of the numbers and the functions of the calculator that you wish to use.

For further information on the function of a specific button, all you need to do is click on it once with the right mouse button and select the shortcut menu item that appears *What's This?*

Keyboard
To speed up the process it is also possible to use the keyboard. The best method is to use the number keys on the keypad, which can be activated by pressing the `Num` key. Key in the numbers you wish to calculate and then, for simple calculations, use the function keys `*`, `+`, `-` and `/`.

The results of a calculation can be copied onto the clipboard via *Edit/Copy* or the key combination `Ctrl` + `C`, and then pasted into the Windows application desired using *Edit/Paste* or the key combination `Ctrl` + `V`.

4. Desktop, taskbar and the *Start* menu

This chapter is about the electronic desk, that is to say the desktop in *Windows Me*, and the relevant commands. You will learn how to personalize the taskbar according to your own needs and how to use it to scroll between the programs on screen. You will also learn how to configure the operating area of *Windows Me*, that is to say the *Start* menu. The user will also learn how to modify the on-screen display and how to insert programs or program groups in the menu and how to delete those that are no longer necessary.

Modifying the view of the taskbar

Together with the *Start* menu which can be called up using the *Start* button, the taskbar is the operating area of *Windows Me*. From this point of view the taskbar is the most important element of the desktop.

Moving the application bar

It could prove rather inconvenient to work on your PC keeping the standard position of the taskbar unchanged at the lower edge of the screen.

Position and width   Obviously the position and other set aspects of the taskbar can be adapted according to your own needs. If you want to have the taskbar displayed in a different position on the screen, click on a free zone of the bar. Then move the bar keeping the mouse button held down. If you move the mouse near enough to one side of the screen you will see a selection frame that represents the new position – like a magnet at the edge of the screen.

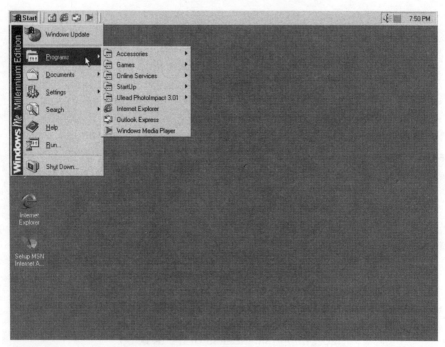

Figure 4.1   The taskbar at the top of the screen

To place the object at the desired point, release the mouse button. From this point onwards the taskbar, the *Start* menu and its sub-menus will be seen in the new position.

Adjusting the height of the taskbar

If there are a lot of open files or programs, the names of the relevant buttons can be difficult to see. In order to see all the buttons you need not do anything other than en-large the taskbar. To do this, point the cursor at the edge

of the taskbar. The cursor will assume the form of a dou-
ble-pointed arrow ⌐.

Keeping the mouse button held down, you can define the
height; a frame will indicate the new height setting. If
you release the mouse button, the buttons on the bar will
be laid out in two lines and the entire bar will be re-
arranged.

Figure 4.2   Adjusting the height of the taskbar (top) and position of the toolbar

Adjusting the size   The width and position of the toolbars in the taskbar can
also be modified.

To adjust the size of the toolbar of the open files or of
active applications, drag the handle of the toolbar ↔ that
is on the left-hand side and then drag it to the left or the
right keeping the mouse button pressed down (Figure
4.2).

Modifying the posi-   If you want to modify the position and the settings of this
tion   toolbar, click on the edge of it and then move it as desired, above, below, in front of or behind the other bars,
for example the quick start bar.

How to view or hide the taskbar

As the most important command element of *Windows
Me*, the taskbar can be configured in other ways. With the
standard configuration the taskbar is always visible.

Settings/taskbar   To configure the display of the taskbar, open the *Start*
menu and point the cursor on the *Settings* item. Click on
Taskbar and Start menu in the sub-menu that appears. In

the *General* tab of the *Taskbar and Start Menu Properties* window a preview of the modifications will appear.

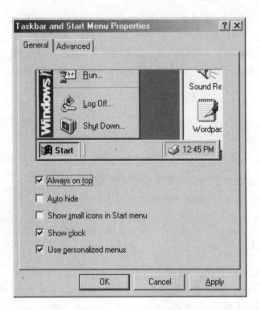

Figure 4.3   Determining whether the taskbar is seen

Always on top   De-activate the *Always on top* box if you want the taskbar to be hidden at the bottom with the window maximized. In this way, there is more space for the program windows. However, in order to move to other applications the program windows must first be reduced to icons, so that you can view the desktop again. For this you can use a special button in the quick-start bar - 📝.

Auto hide   Activate the *Auto hide* box if you want the taskbar to be seen only when you point the cursor at the lower edge of the screen. If you then point the cursor towards the top of the screen the taskbar will automatically disappear again after a brief time.

Always on top and
Auto hide

If you select *Always on top* as well as *Auto hide*, the task-bar will be displayed or hidden by moving the mouse to the bottom of the screen even if the window is enlarged. Confirm with *OK* to have the modifications displayed on the desktop.

To display the clock in the taskbar

Normally, *Windows Me* displays the time with a twenty-four hour clock in the lower right-hand corner of the taskbar: 13:52 . If this does not happen, it could be because the relative option has been de-activated. How to display the time and information about the date will be explained a little further on.

Start / Settings

To configure the taskbar, open the *Start* menu and point the cursor to *Settings*. Click on the *Taskbar and Start Menu* in the sub-menu. The dialog box *Taskbar and Start Menu Properties* will appear.

Show Clock

Select the control box *Show Clock* and confirm your choice by clicking on the *OK* button. The clock will now be (once again) displayed.

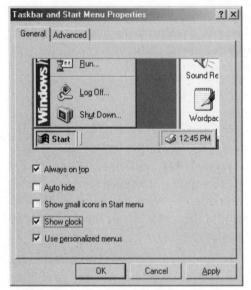

Figure 4.4   To activate and de-activate the clock in the taskbar

Position the cursor over the clock displayed in the taskbar. After a few seconds *Windows Me* will display the date in a command description.

Double-clicking on the clock will display the *Date/Time Properties* window, where you can modify its settings.

Displaying the System Resource Meter in the taskbar

You may ask yourself why your PC is particularly slow or prone to crashing. Perhaps this is due to a particular program because your computer works slower after the program has been started. Some information about the maximum capacity of your system can be viewed using a *Windows Me* integrated program: the System Resource Meter.

Maximum capacity of your system

Using the System Resource Meter you insert in the Taskbar a type of signal that will constantly remind you, clearly and simply, of the maximum capacity of your system.

Accessories/ System Tools

In the *Start* menu position the cursor over the items *Programs/Accessories and System Tools* and then click on the System Resource Meter command in the new menu.

System Resource Meter is not a part of the standard installation of *Windows Me*. To install it, open the control panel, click on *Add/Remove Programs* and select *Windows Setup*. Double-click on *System Tools* from the list to display its accessories. Then select *System Resource Meter* and click on *OK*. The program will then be available in the program group *Programs/Accessories/System Tools* under the item *System Resource Meter*.

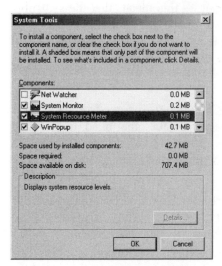

Figure 4.5   Installation of System Resource Meter using Control Panel and the Add/Remove programs tab

The program will first display a single message window in which the fact that *System Resource Meter* is also using resources is communicated. Click on *Don't Display This Message Again*, if you do not want this to be displayed from this point on in *System Resource Meter*.

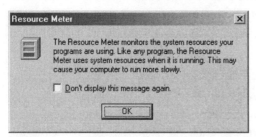

Figure 4.6   Display of System Resource Meter

Green Bar

Confirm with *OK* to insert the System Resource Meter icon next to the clock, in the taskbar. If the bar is green this means that the system is OK.

System highly overloaded

If you see an orange bar this means that the system is highly overloaded. Don't panic! If on the other hand you see a red bar, immediately save all the documents and then re-start *Windows Me*.

The *System Resource Meter* must be opened again every time you start the system. On the other hand, if you copy the *System Resource Meter* icon into *Auto* programs group, it will always be displayed in the taskbar.

To display the correct values as a percentage of the different components of *System resources, User resources* and *GDI resources*, double-click the *System Resource Meter* icon in the taskbar. The following dialog box will be displayed, which can be closed again by clicking on *OK*.

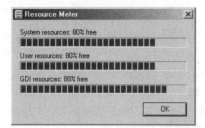

Figure 4.7   The System Resource Meter dialog box

 How to carry out a more accurate control of the maximum system load using *System monitor* is explained in chapter 9 'System Tools. This application is extremely efficient, but evaluating the results of the application is really for professionals only.

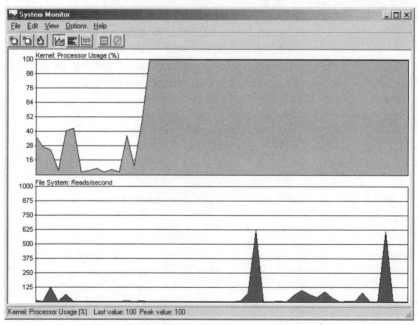

Figure 4.8   More detailed system information from the *System Monitor*

Scrolling through open applications

Much like a real window, the different windows allow you to display different information and to run different programs. Thanks to multitasking, the processing of this data happens at almost the same time.

The active window Insertions can only be made in the active window, that is to say the one shown in colour. De-selected programs remain open but they cannot accept insertions. If a range of applications are open you can scroll between programs if you want to exchange data. The simplest way is to use the taskbar.

Scrolling between active applications using the taskbar

Applications button Each program has a button that contains the name and a description of the document open in the taskbar. The button for the active application is shown as locked, while the other buttons are displayed normally.

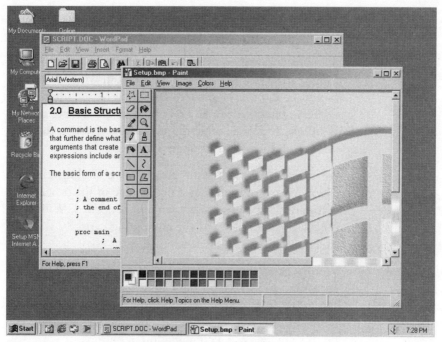

Figure 4.9   Scrolling through different applications

The button in the taskbar   To scroll through the programs, click on the button that corresponds to the desired program. The corresponding window will be open or displayed on top. Now you can work in this *active* window.

Using the contextual menu in the taskbar, all of the windows can be placed side-by-side, one on top of the other, or overlapping. Using the contextual menu in the taskbar it is also possible to adjust the size or the position of the window or to close an application.

Scrolling between open applications using a combination of buttons

The main advantage of *Windows* is that you can run more than one application at a time. For example, you can print a letter from the text processing program while creating a design in *Paint*. The System Resource Meter (mentioned earlier), remains open at the bottom of the screen, as does *Windows Explorer*, which also remains open so that you can search for a file if desired.

Various programs

Windows Me works with preventative multitasking, in which every program uses a percentage of the processor's computing capacity exactly when it is needed. With *Windows 3.1* the division of the computing capacity was carried out with much less flexibility.

Reduced *Task manager*

Various programs are also run at the same time when it is necessary to exchange data between applications. You can move from one application to another if you want to copy information and paste it into another program. To do this you can use a combination of buttons.

Press the ⌊Alt⌋ button and keep it pressed down. Then briefly press the ⌊⇆⌋ button. The reduced Task Manager, that is to say a dialog box containing all the icons of the open files or active applications, will be displayed on the screen. The name of the active application will appear below. The relative program is selected with a blue frame.

Moving to the next program

If you press the ⌊⇆⌋ button again while pressing the ⌊Alt⌋ button, you will move to the icon of the next program of Task Manager. At the same time the program name will be updated. Press the ⌊⇆⌋ button to display the desired application of the Task manager. *Windows* will move to the selected application if you release both of the buttons at the same time.

If you are working with two programs between which you want to carry out an exchange of data, all you need do is press the [Alt] + [⇆] buttons alternately to move from one application to the other.

Modifying the display of the *Start* menu

As has been said, the operative area of *Windows Me* is found in the *Start* menu. The procedure for inserting new items, for deleting existing items and for applying new program groups to this menu is now described. First of all we will look at how to personalize the *Start* menu.

Adjusting size of the *Start* menu icons

If you were expecting to find the same flexibility in the *Start* menu that you found in the *Windows Me* settings, we must first of all warn you that this is not true.

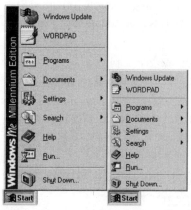

Figure 4.10   Large icons (on the left) and small icons (on the right) in the *Start* menu

Size of icon

The simplest procedure is the modification of the sizes of the icons in the *Start* menu. To do this click on the *Start* button and select *Settings*. In the sub-menu click on the item *Taskbar and Start Menu* and stay on the *General* tab.

Small icons

Select the control box *Show small icons in Start menu* and confirm with *OK*. Examine the modifications in the *Start* menu.

The position of the *Start* menu button depends on the position of the taskbar. If you want to move the button to another position, all you need do is drag the taskbar to another corner of the screen keeping the mouse button pressed down.

Personalizing the *Start* menu

Having installed new applications, the links relative to the program file are automatically loaded into the *Programs* menu, which you can access using the *Start* button.

Inserting new items in the *Start* menu

Applications in the
Start menu

The insertion of links in the *Start/Program* menu can be done by the user. You might want to do this if the automatic method does not work or if you want to personalize the *Start* menu according to your own needs.

In this section you will find out how to insert items in the *Start* menu using the *Properties* window:

Click on the *Start* button and set the cursor on *Settings*. Then click on the *Taskbar and Start Menu* item and go to the *Advanced* tab.

Add...   Now click on the *Add...* button and then on the *Browse* button in the *Create shortcut* dialog box. Now you must know the position in the memory of the necessary program file or the relative link. Let's try to perform this operation using the word processing program *Wordpad* in *Windows Me*

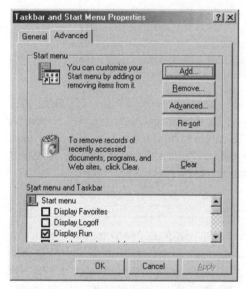

Figure 4.11   Adding new items to the *Start* menu

Program file   The program file for *Wordpad* is called *WORDPAD.EXE* and is stored under *C:\Programs\Accessories*. Look for the program file in the *Browse* dialog box, select it and then click on the *Open* button. When you return to the *Create shortcut* dialog box, click on *Next* and then select the program group that the link is to be inserted in.

161

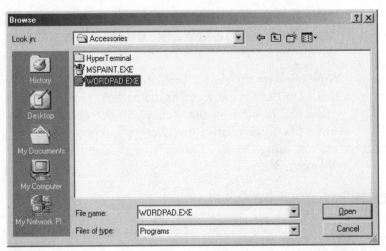

Figure 4.12   Selecting a program to insert in the *Start* menu

Modified program group
Click on *Next* and insert the name in the text field that you want displayed in the program group, for example *Text processing*. Then click on *Finish*. Close the *Properties* window with *OK* and place the new item in the *Start* menu or the chosen program group.

Personalizing the *Start* menu using the *dragging* technique

Using the *Start* menu in *Windows Me* you can start up all the components supplied together with Windows, and also applications that have been installed later. Using the *Programs* menu can be rather inconvenient if you use certain programs very often, above all if you want to register different programs at the same time.

However, as is well known, *Windows Me* is extremely flexible – there are many ways to personalize the *Start* menu. You can do this in the following ways:

first of all you will be told how to copy directly, using the mouse, the links to applications in the *Start* menu. Look for the link or file in *My Computer* that you want to insert in the *Start* menu.

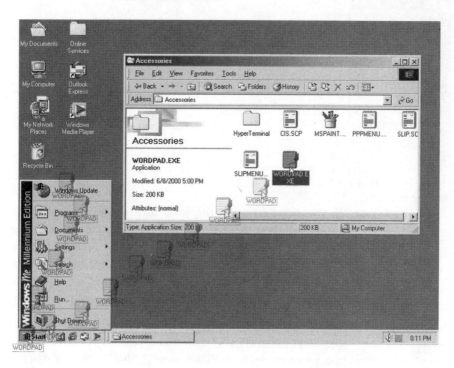

Figure 4.13   Inserting programs in the *Start* menu by dragging

The mouse button pressed down

You can drag the icon of the program that you want by holding the ⌈Ctrl⌉ key pressed down and clicking with the mouse button on the *Start* button in the taskbar. The menu will then be displayed. Then move it slowly to where you want to insert it – *Programs – Accessories* or to another place. *Windows Me* will show the place where it intends to move it to with a black bar.

Copying in the *Start* menu

If you release the mouse button, *Windows Me* will then copy the program or the linking icon into the *Start* menu (see Figure 4.13).

Figure 4.14   New link to *Wordpad* in the *Start* menu

Copying into a pro-
gram group

If you want to copy the icon in a determined program group, all you need do is position the cursor over the item. The corresponding menu will be opened after a brief time. A black bar will once again indicate the new insertion point. Releasing the mouse button will copy the program or the linking icon in the desired program group.

Dragging instead of
copying

At this point the copied program can be called up from the *Start* menu. If you do not keep the key pressed down, the program icons will be *moved*, that is to say deleted from the original program group and inserted in the *Start* menu.

Personalizing the *Start* menu in *Windows Explorer*

Overloading

Computer magazines and publicity and collections of programs now offer an enormous amount of programs or games on CD that are free or very cheap. Some of these applications find the path where they have to be stored very quickly, and are installed almost automatically.

This means that the *Programs* menu is literally overloaded with program groups or application icons. After a while you will notice that the *Programs* menu is not displayed in full on the screen.

Sorting by topic

If all of the programs that are installed on your computer are necessary, you should seriously consider re-arranging them and re-ordering them in single program groups in the *Start* menu.

Simple links

The preceding sections on the personalization of the *Start* menu are particularly useful when it comes to an extended personalization of the *Start* menu. There now follows an explanation of a simple way of personalizing the *Start* menu according to your own needs, using *Windows Explorer*.

The program groups and the links in the *Start* menu are nothing but normal links to a certain area of the hard disk. By 'link' we mean a file that contains only information about the position and name of a program file in the memory. Since these links and the *Start* menu in *Windows Me* are files true and proper they can be displayed in *Windows Explorer*.

Hierarchy of the
Start menu

To have the hierarchy of the *Start* menu displayed you must first extend the *Start* menu display to the left of the *Windows Explorer* by clicking on ⊞ before the *My Computer* item and then repeat this procedure for the directory icon (*C:*) of the first hard disk.

Then highlight the contents of the *Windows* window and extend the display of the stored program group *Initial menu* to the lower level.

To find this position on the hard disk more quickly, right-click with the mouse button on the *Start* button on the taskbar, and then select *Windows Explorer*. A *Windows Explorer* window with the *Start* menu already opened should then appear.

165

Click again on the + sign before the *Programs* item. All the program groups in the *Start* menu should now be visible on the left of the *Windows Explorer* window.

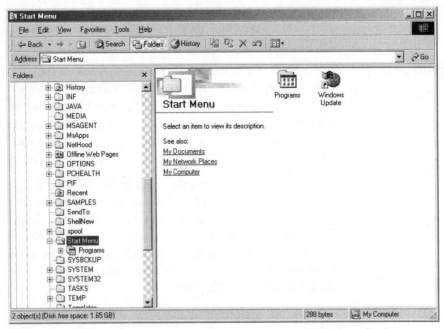

Figure 4.15   Displaying and personalizing the *Start Menu* in *Windows Explorer*

Select a program group from the left hand side in order to see what the contents are.

To create new program groups you can use *File/New* and *Folder*. You can give a new name to program groups that already exist using *File/Rename*, after having selected them with the mouse.

Deleting program groups

Groups of programs that are no longer necessary or empty can be selected and deleted with ⌊Canc⌋ or by using *File/Delete*. Doing this will delete only the links, not the actual program files

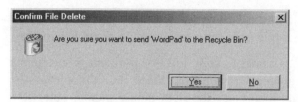

Confirm File Delete   x

Are you sure you want to send 'WordPad' to the Recycle Bin?

          Yes   No

Figure 4.16   Message window for the deletion of a link

Reconfiguring the
Start menu

If you want to reconfigure the *Start* menu you must simply copy and move the program groups. You are advised
to create new program groups first, sorted by topic, for
example *Image processing* and *Internet Programs*. Select
the corresponding program group.

Moving program
groups

To move entire program groups with the mouse, proceed
as follows: keeping the mouse button held down, drag the
folder in question to the new position in the list of folders
on the left of the window.

If you want to move various program groups all in one
go, you can use the multiple selection option, that works
only in the right-hand field. To use multiple selection use
the Ctrl key or the ⬦ key together with the mouse.

To move program groups with a combination of keys,
press down the Ctrl + X keys after you have selected
the program group.

Then click on the folder where you want to move the
program group to, and press Ctrl + V at the insertion
point. If a program group contains links to the start of
programs, these will also be copied.

Copying program
groups

To create copies of program groups use the Ctrl + C
keys. To move or copy program groups using the *Edit*
menu, select *Copy* or *Cut* in the *Edit* menu. Highlight the
program group that you intend to copy. Select the *Paste*

command in the *Edit* menu. Similarly you can also copy or move single *links* from one program group to another.

Copying links

It is also possible to copy links or program groups using contextual menu commands. Place the cursor over the object and then press the right mouse button. Select the *Cut or Copy* command in the contextual menu. Then highlight the program group in which you want to create the link or program group. Position the mouse over a free point and then click with the right mouse button. Select the *Paste* in the contextual menu.

Dragging method

If the links or program groups that you want to move are displayed in the right-hand window of *Windows Explorer* and the program group that you want to move them to is in the left-hand window, the simplest way to move them is by copying them by *dragging* them as described at the beginning of this chapter. To do this place the cursor over the link or the program group and then drag it to the desired program group. Then release the mouse button. To make copies press the Ctrl button as well.

Right mouse button

Alternatively you can copy or move links or program groups by using the right mouse button and *dragging*. To do this place the cursor over the link or the program group and drag it with the right mouse button to the drive or program group that you want to move it to. Release the mouse button, and then select the *Move* command from the contextual menu that appears. To create copies select *Copy* in the contextual menu or press the Ctrl key while it is being moved.

Deleting items from the *Start* menu

Deleting items

Considering the amount of information, programs or games that are available on CD-ROM or the Internet, the *Start* menu will, sooner or later, be overloaded with program groups or links. When you tidy up your hard disk by deleting programs or games that you no longer use, in many cases the program groups or the links are not deleted. The problem is then to delete useless items from the *Start* menu.

Choose the *Settings* command in the *Start* menu and then click on the *Taskbar and Start Menu* in the cascading menu. Then choose the *Advanced* tab in the *Properties* window. Then click on the *Remove...* button.

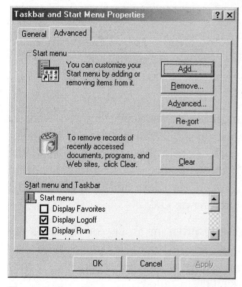

Figure 4.17   *Removing* items from the *Start* menu

Remove
Shortcuts/Folders

In the dialog box *Remove Shortcuts/Folders*, the *Start* menu structure will be displayed, similar to the left side of the *Windows Explorer* window. Extend the structure by clicking on the + symbol before the items in order to display the item that you want to delete.

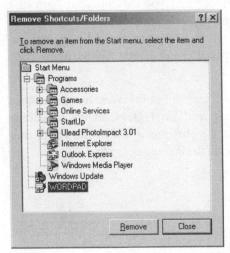

Figure 4.18   Removing unwanted Shortcuts or folders

Removing

Select the program group or shortcuts that you want to delete and then click on the *Remove* button. The dialog box will remain open. Repeat this procedure for all the program groups or shortcuts that you want to delete. End the operation by clicking on *Close* and then confirm the modifications by clicking on *OK*.

With this method only program groups or shortcuts are deleted. The folders and the data relevant to these programs and shortcuts must be deleted separately, if they have not already been de-installed.

There is a quicker and simpler way to delete unwanted items from the *Start* menu. Open the *Start* menu, highlight the item and then press the *right* mouse button. Choose the *Remove* command and then confirm this with *Yes*.

Removing the contents of the *Documents* menu

You can also open documents using the *Start* menu. In the *Documents* menu *Windows Me* keeps a list of the last 15 documents that you used, independently of the application linked to them. This will only happen if you have already registered the file extensions of the programs installed in *Windows Me*. This list of documents is produced to allow rapid access to the documents themselves, and you can also scroll through them or modify them. Select the *Start/Documents* menu and then the file that you want – the corresponding program is opened automatically.

Start / Settings

It is possible to clean up the list of documents in the *Start* menu whenever you want to. To do this select *Start/Settings/Taskbar and Start Menu* and then go to the *Advanced* tab.

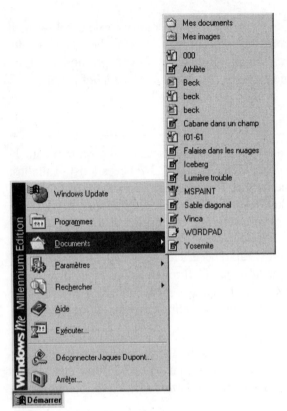

Figure 4.19   Displaying the last 15 documents used

Remove...

Click on the *Remove...* button to delete the list of the last 15 files used. When this is done *Windows Me* will also "forget" the last programs and web sites used.

After you have completed deleting, the *Remove* button is no longer available. Close the *Taskbar and Start Menu Properties* with *OK*. Obviously this deletes the items list, not the actual files that are on hard disk.

Figure 4.20   **Deleting all of the items from the *Documents* menu**

Modifying the *Start* menu display

Using the *Start* menu you can call all the *Windows* functions, start programs and open documents. Beginners, who will not have to install many other programs at first, will find the organisation of *Windows* and the functions of *Windows* very easy to get used to by using the *Start* menu.

If the *Programs* menu contains different programs or a much-changed menu structure, searching for a particular application inside it will be difficult to carry out because a very long list may be displayed that can extend itself over the entire screen.

**Repeated starting
of programs**

This becomes particularly obvious if you call up programs repeatedly. For example, if you want to check for errors on the hard disk by using *ScanDisk* and correct fragmented files using *Disk Defragmenter*, you will have to open the *Start/Programs/Accessories* and *System Tools* menus twice.

Displaying the *Start* menu as a program group window

The *Start* menu can also be displayed as a window of folders with a clearer structure. To do this, set the cursor on the *Start* button and click the right mouse button. Select the *Open* command from the contextual menu.

**Program group
window**

In this way you open the *Start menu* program group or folders window. Inside this window the *Programs* icon at least will be displayed.

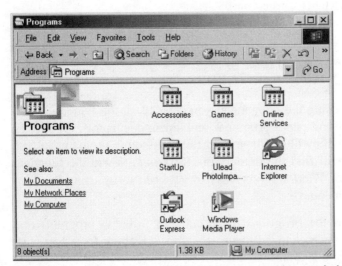

Figure 4.21   The *Start* menu displayed as a program group window

Double click the *Programs* icon or select it and then activate the *Open* command in the contextual menu or the *File* menu. Immediately after this the *Start menu* window will be updated and the contents of the *Programs* program group will appear

To display the contents of recently opened folders in a new window select the *Folder Options...* command in the *Tools* menu. From the *General* tab select the *Open each folder in its own window* in *Browse folders* and then confirm the change with *OK*.

Program group icons

Program group icons are identical to those found in the *Start* menu with which you open sub-menus. Instead of opening the sub-menu with a single click of the mouse, open it with a double-click. Starting an application found in a program group is also performed only by double-clicking.

The organizational structure of the program group window corresponds exactly to the structure of the *Start* menu, but it is limited to the *Programs* menu and relative sub-menus. Those who have already used *Windows 3.x* will find this display easy to use, since it is the same as that used for program groups in *Program Manager*.

This type of display will be particularly useful if you want to call up different programs from a (considerably modified) sub-menu of the *Start* menu. After this you can then keep the window of this program group open for as long as you want.

There is another advantage: if you close *Windows* with program group windows open, the windows will be automatically opened the next time the computer is started.

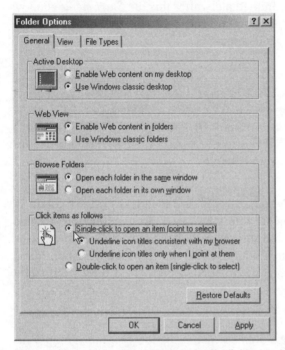

Figure 4.22   Alternating between single-clicking and double-clicking

If you are not good at double-clicking, and you prefer to use the single-click, as you normally do when surfing the Internet, in multi-media presentations and in games, you can eliminate the double-click from Windows. In this case you simply touch the objects with the mouse to open them. To start or open programs or files all you need do is click once with the mouse. However, be careful – you will need time to get used to this technique. If you inadvertently give a double-click, the operation will be performed twice.

Select the command *Folder Options...* from the *Tools* menu in *Windows Explorer*. On the *General* tab, select the option *Single-click to open an item (point to select)* in the area *Click items as follows*. Confirm the change with *OK*.

5. *My Computer* and *Windows Explorer*

This chapter describes two data organization and management applications for *Windows Me*. It explains how to find folders on the hard disk using the *My Computer* system folder and *Windows Explorer*, how to change the view and sorting criteria and how to copy, move and delete files. It also deals with topics related to the creation and naming of new folders and the preparation of floppy disks for data storage.

Working with *My Computer*

The *My Computer* folder is used to organize and manage drives. Due to its strongly object-oriented structure, this folder is extremely easy to use and is particularly suited to the needs of beginners. To open My Computer, simply double click on the *My Computer* icon on the desktop.

Displaying the Contents of the Drive in *My Computer*

Drive objects

The number of drive objects present in the folder depends on the system configuration. Each drive has its own specific icon. *My Computer* also provides access to the *Control Panel* folder.

Browsing

To browse through the contents of a drive, select the icon of the desired drive and then the *Open* command from the shortcut menu or the *File* menu. A quicker method is to double click on the icon of the drive.

If, when you have double clicked for the first time on a drive, for example, C:, a blank window is displayed, the display of files must be activated. Click on *Displays the contents of your computer* on the left pane of the window.

At this point, *Windows Me* shows all the folders on the top level of this drive; the name of the drive browsed is always displayed on the title bar of the window.

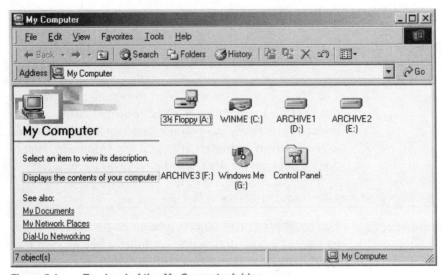

Figure 5.1   Top level of the *My Computer* folder

Drive letter

Each type of drive (floppy drive, hard disk, CD-ROM or network drive) has its own icon. Its name is also displayed and, in the case of hard disks, may be changed using the *Rename* command on the shortcut menu. The letter that identifies the drive in MS-DOS is shown in brackets – the letter *(A:)* represents the first floppy disk drive, and the letter *(C:)* represents the first hard disk.

Difficulties with
double clicking

If, at the beginning, you have trouble double clicking to look for folder, select a folder and then press ⏎. To open the folder you can use the *Open* command on the shortcut menu or the *File* menu. Another alternative is represented by the method illustrated in the following section.

Users who surf regularly on the Internet and are therefore not used to double clicking may activate a special feature of *Windows Me*. Having done this, all operations normally performed by double clicking will be executed by means of a single click of the mouse button; objects will be selected simply by pointing at their icons.

Select the *Folder Options...* command from the *Tools* menu. On the *General* tab, enable the *Single click to open an item* option in *Click items as follows* and then confirm by clicking on *OK*.

Be careful, however, from now on the double-click to select function will no longer be recognized. If you double click on an object, it will be opened or started twice.

Finding Folders with *My Computer*

Normally, users learning to use *Windows Me* prefer to use *My Computer* to view the contents of drives and folders. This is most likely due to the fact that its strongly object-oriented structure typical of *Windows*, makes working with this folder very easy.

Opening *My*
**Computer*

To open *My Computer*, double click on the *My Computer* icon on the desktop. The number of objects displayed in the folder depends on the system configuration. Each drive has its own specific icon.

My Computer also provides quick access to the *Control Panel* folder which is used to set up the *Windows* system to suit your needs or install and set up new devices. The *Control Panel* will be described in greater detail in a subsequent chapter.

To browse through the folders, first of all open the relevant drive. To do this, double click on the drive icon, for example, on *(C:)*.

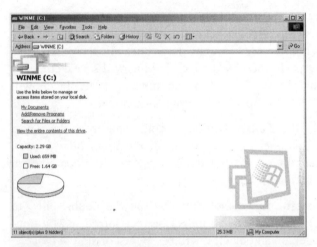

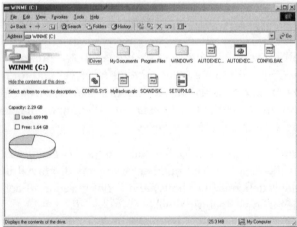

Figure 5.2   To view all files, click on *View the entire contents of the drive*

Folder searched for · At this point, *Windows Me* displays the contents of the top level of the hard disk in the same window. The name of the drive or folder searched for appears on the title bar of the window.

Opening the folder · To open a folder in the window, double click on the name of the folder in question etc. If all the files and all the folders do not fit into the window at the same time, use the scroll bars or change the view from the *View* menu (further details will be provided later).

Having displayed the tool bar, click on the *Up* 🔼 button to move one folder level up. Alternatively, you can skip straight to the desired folder by typing its path into the *address bar*. If you open the *address bar* list using the drop-down arrow in the folder browsed, the hierarchy of the current object is displayed. By selecting items, you can switch to other drives or folders on a higher level. A given path may also be typed on the keyboard at this point.

Changing the View of the *My Computer* Window

The strongly object-oriented structure of *Windows Me* may seem strange to some users, particularly those who are switching from *MS-DOS* (*Microsoft Disk Operating System*), which is character and command-oriented, to the *Windows Me* graphic operating system.

Changing the view · This is particularly evident when you are working with *My Computer*. All folders browsed using *My Computer* are displayed by default in the same window. In this way, it is difficult to identify the hierarchy and copy and move their contents. This disadvantage of *My Computer* is particularly evident for file structures with a large number of branches. If this is the case, *Windows Explorer* is the best tool for handling and organizing data. On the other hand, however, you do not necessarily have to use *My Computer* in its standard configuration.

Customized window

The view of the folders browsed may, for example, be modified so that the contents of newly browsed folders may be shown in special windows. There is however the disadvantage that a large number of folder windows creates confusion.

View / Folder Options

To change the view, select the *Folder Options* command from the *Tools* menu inside any folder,. On the *General* tab, enable the *Open each folder in its own window* option under *Browse Folders* and confirm by clicking on *OK*.

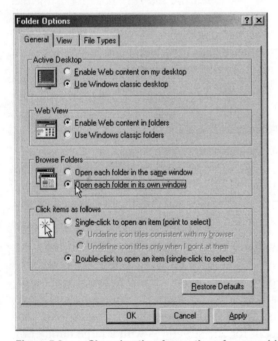

Figure 5.3   Changing the view options for *searching for folders*

From this moment on, the contents of each newly browsed folder will appear in its own window. This setting is global and applies to each new window opened in *My Computer*.

By clicking on the *Up* 🖭 button, you can move up one level – also in this case a new folder window will appear if the old one has already been closed. Alternatively, by using the *address bar* you can move directly to other folders.

Changing the View in *My Computer* and Folder Windows

Large icons

In an object-oriented graphic interface operating system like *Windows Me* all the elements of a computer, that is the directories and folders and the contents of the folders, in the form of files or documents, etc., are represented by means of icons. This gives the major advantage that all *Windows* operations may be performed with the mouse. To view the objects in the folders, *Windows*, by default, uses large icons including the name of the object.

View/ Large Icons

View Menu

On the *View* menu, this standard view is called *Large Icons*. The view may be set in several different ways. Start by opening the *View* menu and check that the *Large Icons* item is market with a bullet. The standard setting is well suited to displaying the contents of folders and, due to its clarity, is particularly suitable for beginners.

Figure 5.4   The *View/Large Icons* view

With the *View/Large Icons* view (Figure 5.4), only a limited number of icons will however fit in the window. When the folder contains a large number of items, scroll bars that may be used to view those that cannot be seen on the screen are automatically displayed.

The *Large Icons* view may also be activated using the tool bar of document windows. The size and appearance of the icons depend on the *View/Tool Bars/Customize....* setting, The available settings are shown at the bottom of the dialog box beside *Text Options* and *Icon Options*.

Figure 5.5   Different views of the Standard tool bar

 If the Standard buttons are not visible in the windows, they may be activated from the View menu. Select the Standard tool bar buttons from the submenu

View button   To set the large icons view, click on the *View* button on the tool bar 🔲 and click on the *Large Icons* command.

View/Small Icons

Select the *Small Icons* command from the *View* menu to view the contents of the window with small icons. The items will first be displayed alongside one another and then vertically. The *Small Icons* view may also be activated by selecting a button on the tool bar. Click on the *View* button 🔲 and then on the *Small Icons* command.

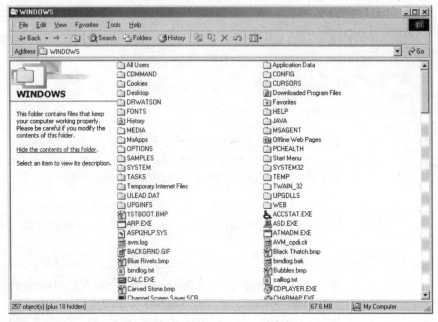

Figure 5.6   The *View/Small Icons* view

View/List

If you select the *List* command from the *View* menu, you will obtain a view that is very similar to the *Small Icons* view. In this view, *Windows Me* shows all the objects arranged in a list one above another. This is why small icons are used.

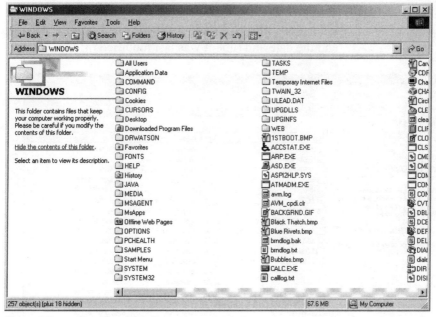

Figure 5.7 The *View/List* view

If the window is too small for all the items on the list to fit into it, a second or third column is automatically created.

The *List* setting may' also be activated by pressing the *View* button ▦▾ on the tool bar and selecting the *List* command.

View/Details

If the view is activated using the *View/Details* command, the contents of the folders are displayed in the form of a list with detailed information about the files. Even if there is not enough space for all items in the window, this list is not divided into more than one column.

Size, type and date indications

Together with the icons, which appear small in this view, indications are given about the *size* and *type* of the file and the date and time it was last modified (*Modified*).

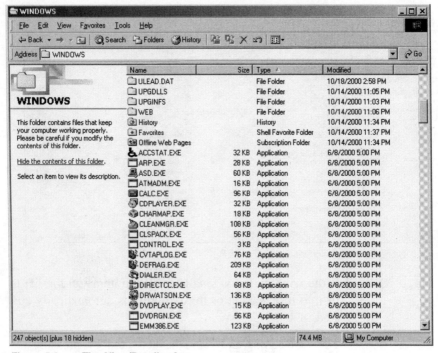

Figure 5.8 The *View/Details view*

Parts that do not fit in the details list window may be reached using the scroll bar.

The *Details* setting may also be activated by clicking on the *View* button on the tool bar and the *Details* item.

View/Thumbnails

The *Thumbnails* view is only useful for folders containing photographs or pictures. In addition to the icon and the name of the file, *Windows Me* shows a thumbnail (small preview) of each picture file, for example in the previously created folder *C:\My Documents\My Pictures*. It may take several seconds to open a folder of this type in that the thumbnails have to be loaded.

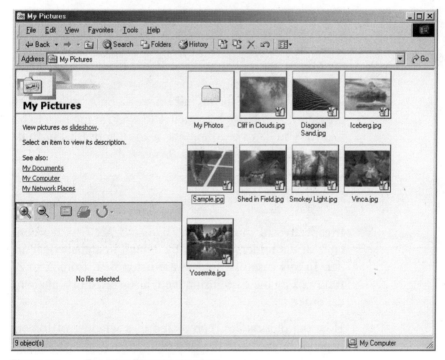

Figure 5.9   The *View/Thumbnails view*

The commands on the *View* menu normally have to be selected separately for each individual document window but you may decide to change this: set the view of the current folder as you please and select the *Folder Options...* command from the *Tools* menu. On the *View* tab, select the *Like Current Folder* button under *Folder Views*. Once you have confirmed by clicking on *OK*, all the folders will be displayed like the current folder from this moment on.

For folders only containing a few objects, the *Large Icons* view is ideal. For folders containing a large number of objects, the *List* view is recommended. For all other folders, we recommend the use of the *Details* view, which provides a lot of information about all the files present. If you have the patience to wait for pictures to be loaded, you can view thumbnails of picture files in folders by selecting the *Thumbnails* view.

Changing the Sort Order in My Computer or Folders

Irrespective of the view set, *Windows Me* lists the contents of the folders browsed by default in alphabetical order. In this case, the folders are listed first, from A to Z, followed by the files inside them also sorted in alphabetical order.

How the objects are represented in a window of folders depends however on the view selected.

In the *Large Icons* view, the objects are shown in a folder from the top left-hand corner to the bottom right-hand corner: for example, the icon of the folder whose first letter is the closest to the first letter of the alphabet appears in the top left-hand corner.

Alphabetical order   The second folder in alphabetical order appears to its right, etc. After the folders have been sorted by their names, the files they contain are sorted on the basis of the same criteria.

There are some exceptions, such as system folders or objects like *My Documents*, *My Computer* or *Internet Explorer* (for example, on the desktop), which are always displayed at the top in this view.

The icons are arranged in the same way on the *Small Icons* and *Thumbnails* views. In the *List* view, the contents of the folders are shown vertically according to their names: the folders first and then the file objects.

Second column   For small folder windows containing a large number of objects, a second column is created automatically to contain the continuation of the list.

View *Details*   Only the *Details* view shows a list of all the objects in the folder arranged in a single column and sorted in alphabetical order.

The sorting criteria in *Windows Me* may be set individually for each folder: to do this, select the *Arrange Icons* command from the *View* menu or the shortcut menu (in the latter case, there must not be any objects selected).

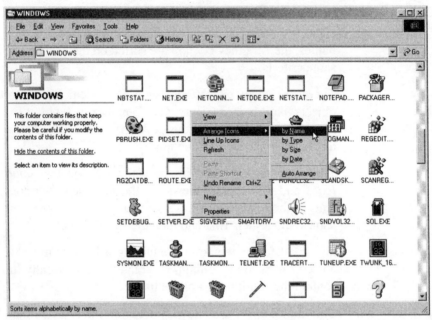

Figure 5.10   The standard configuration: objects sorted *By name*

Setting the Sorting Criteria

The drop-down menu contains the following commands for sorting the contents of folders: *By Name*, *By Type*, *By Size*, *By Date* and *Auto Arrange*. The *Auto Arrange* command – whose name is self-explanatory – will be discussed in greater detail at the end of the chapter.

By Name

The *View/Arrange Icons/By Name* command represents the standard configuration of *Windows*. The folder icons are arranged in alphabetical order. In this case, the folders are displayed first and then the files.

By Type

The *View/Arrange Icons/By Type* command sorts the objects inside the folder according to the type of file. The subfolders are also sorted in the same way.

194

Figure 5.11   Contents of folders sorted *By Type*

This command is useful if you are searching the folder window in question for specific types of files, such as *bitmap* files, listed one above another in the *List* or *Details* views. The files are always sorted on the basis of the description of the type of file, which appears under *Type* in the *Details* view.

By Size

The *View/Arrange Icons/By Size* command sorts the objects inside the folder according to the size of the file. Folders appear first followed by the files sorted by their size. Small files are always listed before large files irrespective of the name or type of file. For this reason, empty folders or folders that do not contain files are always indicated at the top of the list.

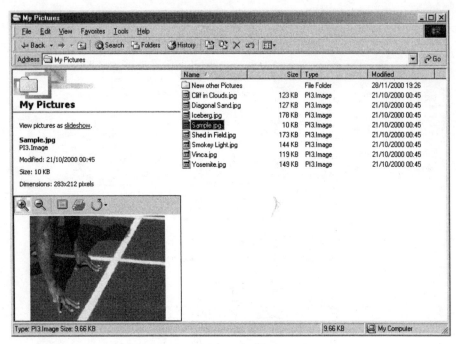

Figure 5.12 Sorting the contents of folders *By Size*

File size

The size of a folder or file may even be 0 KBytes. This command should only be used if you want to browse the folders for files of a known size.

By date

The *View/Arrange Icons/By Date* command sorts the contents of folders according to the date on which it was last modified. In this case, folders are listed first sorted by their date, followed by the files, also sorted according to the date on which they were last modified. The *By Date* sorting criteria puts old files before new ones irrespective of the file name or file type.

Windows Me recognizes three types of date: *Created, Modified* and *Accessed. Created* describes the date on which an object was created.

Modified describes the date on which an object was last modified with respect to the *Created* version.

Accessed indicates the date on which the file was opened for the last time without being saved.

All lists of files sorted in alphabetical order (including the list sorted by the *file types*) or by their *size* may also be viewed in reverse order in *Windows Explorer*. This can be done simply by clicking the mouse button on the title of the column in question.

Working with *Windows Explorer*

Now you will have a better knowledge of the desktop. The word "desktop" gives a very accurate definition of the function performed by the main *Windows* screen in that it is used to do any kind of job in a virtual environment.

Desktop

While to write a letter you would normally need a pen and a piece of paper, to do this on a computer, you have to start a word processor program. The letters written, for example, may be placed in the first drawer of the desk, and people who are particularly tidy will also use a special folder. In the same way, people who would put a memo on the desktop may use the *Windows* desktop for text files.

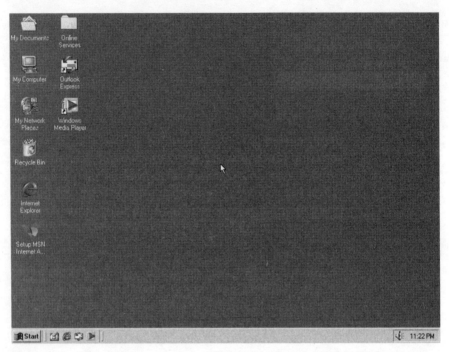

Figure 5.13   The *Windows* screen is called desktop because that is the function it performs

Hierarchy

When this example is applied to the computer environment, the letter written using the word processor program is saved on the hard disk inside a specific folder. This comparison could be carried forward virtually to infinity. What is to be underlined is the importance of a system that lies at the basis of everything. Computers also need a system of this kind. To ensure that procedures are carried out on the basis of the desired criteria, a well-organized structure must be created.

Viewing the Organizational Structure of *Windows Me* in *Windows Explorer*

To browse through the hierarchy of *Windows*, the best method is to use *Windows Explorer*. This application shows all the *Windows Me* objects in a hierarchy in a window split into two panes.

Clarity

The hierarchy shown in *Windows Explorer* has a branched structure like the one used in MS-DOS or Norton Commander. *Windows Explorer* may be used to handle and organize the entire structure in a clearer way than can be done with the window-based method adopted by *My Computer*. The *Windows Explorer* view is particularly suited to expert *Windows* users who save their data in an orderly way on the hard disk in different folders and structures of folders.

Windows Explorer Command

First of all, run *Windows Explorer*, for example, by selecting *Start/Programs/Accessories* and the *Windows Explorer* command. A quicker method is to select the *Windows Explorer* command from the shortcut menu of the *Start* button.

The application window of *Windows Explorer* is split into two panes: the left pane shows the entire structure while the right pane shows the contents of the browsed folder.

Consider the items shown in the left pane of the *Windows Explorer* window.

Hierarchy with levels of the same importance

The *desktop* is always at the top of the hierarchy. If this item is not visible, drag the scroll bar of the left pane of the window to the top. Below it are the *My Documents* folder (probably already open), the *My Computer* folder and the *Recycle Bin*. If you are connected to a network, the *Network Resources* item will also be present.

Then click on the plus sign ⊞ next to the *My Computer* item. As you will see, *Windows Me* shows the available data storage units, that is, the drives or directories, as single objects with a hierarchy of the same type.

The number of drive icons represented depends on the PC. Modern PC's have at least one floppy drive, one hard disk and one CD-ROM drive.

Meaning of drives

The following icons correspond to these drives, whose functions are explained by their names and descriptions:

- *31/2 floppy (A:),* drive for 3.5 inch floppy disks

- *5 1/4 floppy (B:)* drive for 5.25 inch floppy disks

- *[C:\] [name]* hard disk

- *[D:\] [name]* or *[number]* CD drive

- *[letter:\] [name]* network drive

Drive letter

In the description of drives, note that the *31/2 floppy* item indicates that it is a drive for 3.5 inch floppy disks. If there is only one floppy disk drive, it is always identified by the letter *(A:).* This name was adopted for compatibility with *MS-DOS.*

The *5 1/4 floppy* item is used by *Windows* to identify *drives for* 5.25 inch floppy disks. The second floppy disk drive is assigned the letter *(B:).*

Hard disk and CD-ROM drives

The other drives are classified starting from the letter *C:,* which normally corresponds to the first hard disk. This is followed by the other hard disks or hard disk partitions and, finally, by the CD-ROM or rewritable CD drives. For example, in a system with a hard disk and a CD-

ROM drive, the letters *C:* (hard disk) and *D:* (CD-ROM) are used.

Names of data
storage units

You will sometimes find strange names for data storage units. In some cases, the hard disk is identified by a number while in others you may find the name of hard disk manufacturers, such as *SEAGATE, MAXTOR* or *CONNER* etc. The procedure for changing the name of the hard disk is described in chapter 9 "System Tools ".

The name indicated for the CD-ROM drive corresponds to the name of the CD inserted. It is also identified by a wide range of names, which may vary from *CD Audio* to encrypted numbers.

Top Level

The level of the hierarchy immediately below the directories is represented by the folders saved on the top level. If you want to see these folders, click on the plus sign beside the drive icon ⊞▣. In this way *Windows Explorer* will expand the view. At this point, the plus sign is replaced by a minus sign ⊟▣.

Levels of hierarchy

In this way, you will be able to see the structure of the drive. To disable this view, simply click on the negative sign: this will "close" the directory.

The view of the structure list includes other folder icons after the plus sign ⊞▢, containing other subfolders.

Control Panel

On the same level as the directories in *Windows Me* there is the special system folder called *Control Panel*, which is used to make all technical settings for the components installed on the PC and its software.

If you open the *Control Panel* folder by clicking on the plus sign, other system folders will be displayed:

Using the *Scheduled Tasks* program you can automatize maintenance and adjustment procedures for all data storage drives.

Scanners and Cameras is a folder for special hardware devices where flatbed scanners, cameras or Web cameras may be installed.

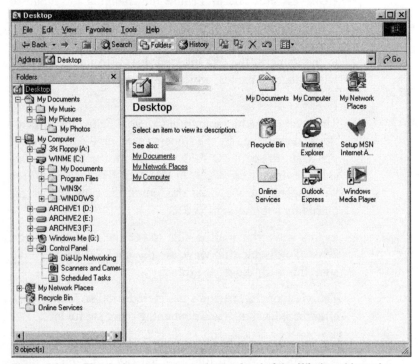

Figure 5.14   The desktop represents the top level of the *Windows* hierarchy

Dial-up networking   If you also have a *modem network* required for access to the Internet, the *Dial-Up Networking* folder will be displayed as an integral part of the Control Panel.

The hierarchy of the desktop and its objects is displayed by vertical lines traced down the left edge of the window.

Objects

The view of the structure in the left pane of the window enables the hierarchy of a *Windows* PC to be recognized with ease.

At the top is the *desktop*, which provides easy access to the *My Documents* folder and the *My Computer* drives. Files and folders may of course be placed on the *desktop*. They are placed at a corresponding point of the hierarchy: folders are set in parallel to *My Documents* and *My Computer*. Files saved on the *desktop* may be viewed in the right pane of the window by clicking on the *desktop*.

Differences with respect to *My Computer*

The difference between *My Computer* and *Windows Explorer* lies in the view of the hierarchy. Using the *My Computer* folder, you can scroll through the entire structure of drives by clicking in a single window, while in *Windows Explorer* all the desired structures may be opened and viewed simply by clicking the mouse button.

Viewing the Structure of Drives and Folders in *Windows Explorer*

Windows Explorer is without doubt the most important application of *Windows Me* in that it is used to handle data. Only in *Windows Explorer* do you get an effective view of the organization of the files and structures of the folders on the data storage drives.

In *Windows Explorer* the objects are represented in a different way from *My Computer*, which may be used to perform the same operations. The most important difference is that in *Windows Explorer* the view of the structure of the folders remains in the left pane of the window.

Viewing the
Hierarchy

Viewing folders in a tree-structured hierarchy is the only way of working efficiently with branched structures of folders. In this way, the folders may be handled and organized in a clearer way than can be done using the *My Computer* window. The *Windows Explorer* view is particularly suitable for expert *Windows* users with an complex hierarchy of drives and folders.

Working in *Windows Explorer* is not as hard as it may seem: first of all, run *Windows Explorer*, for example, by selecting *Start/Programs/Accessories* and then the *Windows Explorer* command. The quickest way is to select the *Windows Explorer* command from the shortcut menu of the *Start* button.

Window split into
two

The application window of *Windows Explorer* is split into two panes: the left pane of the window contains the structure of the folder and the right pane contains the contents of the browsed folder.

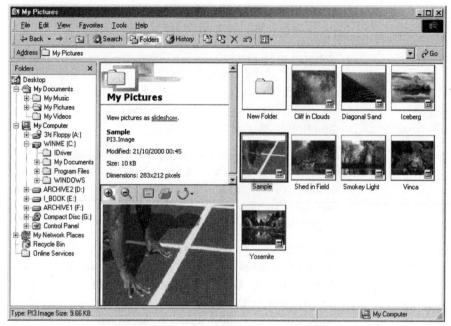

Figure 5.15   *Windows Explorer* window divided into two: the structure appears in the left pane and the contents appear in the right pane

View/Details

The standard configuration of the view in the right pane is the *View/Large Icons* setting for most folders. This view may be changed using the *View* menu. The ideal view is *Details*, which may also be set using the *View* button ⊞▾ on the tool bar and the *Details* command.

Hierarchy of folders

In the work area of *Windows Explorer*, divided into two, you can view the hierarchy of drives and folders on the computer in the left pane of the window. Special icons are used for expanding or reducing the view:

Structure of folders

The most important command element is a small plus sign ⊞ situated beside the drive or folder icons: when you see a drive icon ⊞▭ with a plus sign, you will know that this drive contains folders. To view the folder structure in the left pane of the *Windows Explorer* window, click on the plus sign. At this point, the plus sign will be replaced by a minus sign 🖵⊟.

Plus sign

The plus sign means that the drive structure is displayed. The view of the structure list now includes folder icons with other plus signs ⊞⃞, which lead to other subfolders. To browse the folder, simply click on the corresponding icon of the plus sign.

Minus sign

The plus sign will again be replaced by a minus sign. A folder icon with a minus sign ⊟⃞ indicates that the structure of this folder has already been expanded. To reduce the structure indicator again, click on the minus sign in question.

The folders ⃞ without a plus or minus sign do not contain any other subfolder. Files may however be saved in these folders. By clicking on the plus or minus sign of the structure window, you simply modify the degree of detail with which the window is displayed.

Searching for Folders with *Windows Explorer*

When working with *Windows Explorer* you must watch the two panes of the application window carefully. The files saved in the folders may be viewed exclusively in the right pane of the window. Any subfolders present may also be viewed in the left pane of the window.

Beginners will need a little time to get used to the special icons used in the left pane of the *Windows Explorer* window. First of all, display the folder whose contents you wish to view. The following icons are used to do this:

Folder icons with a plus sign

Folder icons with a plus sign ⊞⃞ contain other subfolders that may be accessed by clicking on the plus sign. At this point, the plus sign is replaced by the minus sign ⊟⃞.

**Folder icons
without a sign**

If the left pane contains folder icons ⌐◻ without a plus or minus sign, this means that these folders do not contain any subfolders. Files may however be saved in these folders.

By clicking on the plus or minus sign, you can open and close folders and there is no limit to the number of folders that may be kept open.

Figure 5.16   Viewing the contents of the *Windows* folder in the right pane of the window

**Selecting the name
of the folder**

If you want to search for a folder and view its contents in the right pane, click on the name of the folder in question. The folders browsed, that is, those displayed in the right pane of the window, may be identified by the open folder icon ◻.

The name of the folder is highlighted and displayed in the *address bar* | Address ☐ WINDOWS ▼ | ⊘ Go | . The address bar may be displayed or hidden using the *View* menu and the *Tool Bars* command.

If you view the tool bar by selecting *View/Tool Bars* and the *Standard* buttons, you can move up one level by pressing the *Up* button 🖳. By typing the path into the *address bar* you can move directly to other drives or folders.

Alternatives

To open or close folders, you do not necessarily have to select the plus or minus sign. The same result may be obtained by double clicking on the name of the folder. Even if a folder is opened by double clicking in the right pane of the window, the list of folders is updated in the left pane, in other words, the next level of folders is opened.

Changing the View in *Windows Explorer*

The right pane of the *Windows Explorer* window contains the objects – files and subfolders – inside the browsed folder. This section describes the various viewing options.

Normal

To view the contents of the folders browsed, *Windows Explorer* uses, for most folders, a view with large icons in the right pane of the window. On the *View* menu, this type of view is called *Large Icons*. An exception is represented, for example, by the *My Documents/My Pictures* folder - in this case, the standard configuration is *View/Thumbnails*. The view in the window may however be modified.

View/Large Icons

First of all, open the *View* menu and check that the *Large Icons* command is marked with a bullet. This standard view is not suitable for viewing the contents of the *Windows Explorer* folders as this program is used for managing and organizing files, so more information than simply the name and icon of the object will certainly be required.

Scroll Bars

Using *View/Large Icons* (Figure 5.17), only a limited number of icons will fit in the *Windows Explorer* window. If the contents of the folders are expanded, scroll bars are automatically displayed to provide access to areas that cannot be seen in the window.

Large Icons **View**

The *Large Icons* view may also be activated using the tool bar of *Windows Explorer* (*View/Tool Bars/Standard buttons*). To change the view, click on the *View* button ⊞▾ on the tool bar and the *Large Icons* command.

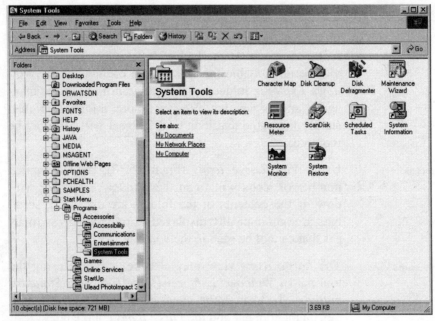

Figure 5.17   The *View/ Large Icons* standard view

View/Small Icons

If you select the *Small Icons* command on the *View* menu, the contents of the window will be displayed with small icons. The items are set first side by side and then one above another.

View button

The *Small Icons* view may also be selected using a button on the *tool bar*. Click on the *View* button 🔳▾ on the *tool bar* and the *Small Icons* command.

View/List

If you select the *List* command on the *View* menu you will get a view that is similar to the *Small Icons* view. In this mode, *Windows Explorer* displays all the objects first in the form of a list arranged vertically and then in columns set side by side.

The *List* view may also be set using the *View* button and the *List* command.

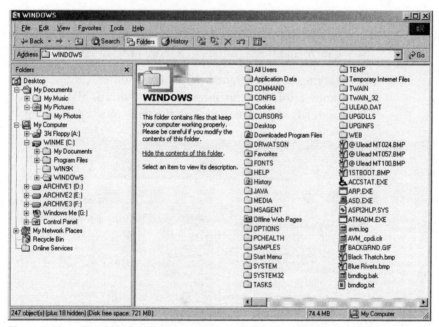

Figure 5.18 The *List* view in the right pane of *Windows Explorer*

View/Details

If the view is activated using the *View/Details* command, the contents of the folder are presented in the form of a list with one column only. Even if there is not enough space in the window, this list is not divided into columns – a scroll bar will appear instead. Together with the icons, which appear small in this view, indications are given as to the *size* and *type* of the file and the date and time the last modification was made (*Modified*).

Recommended view

Details is a view that is recommended above all for *Windows Explorer*. Supplementary information helps to organize and manage files in a more orderly fashion.

Saving the chosen view

Having set the *Details* view (or another view) in *Windows Explorer*, the information is saved. *Windows Explorer* is always started with the view most recently set.

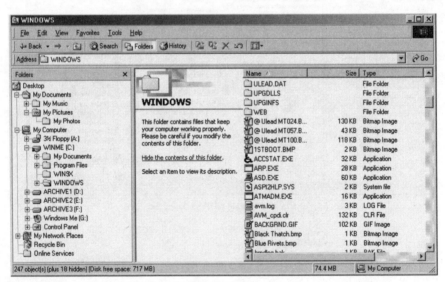

Figure 5.19   *Windows Explorer* in *Details* view

Scroll Bar

On the list displayed with details, you can use the scroll bar to reach the areas not shown on the screen. The *Details* setting may also be activated by pressing the *View* button ▦▾ and selecting the *Details* command.

View/Thumbnails

View for picture files

The *Thumbnails* view option is useful for folders containing pictures or photos. For each picture file, a thumbnail of the picture will appear beside the icon together with the name of the file. It takes several seconds to load the thumbnails however; more time and patience is therefore required to browse through folders containing picture files than for the other views.

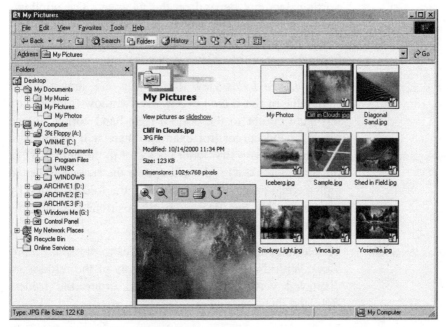

Figure 5.20   *View/Thumbnails* for picture files

The commands on the *View* menu must be selected separately for all the *Windows Explorer* windows opened at the same time. All the *View* commands are present on the shortcut menu viewed by clicking the right mouse button on the *View* submenu.

Changing the Sort Order in *Windows Explorer*

This section describes how to change the sort order of the browsed folders in the right pane of the *Windows Explorer* window. By default, the objects are sorted in alphabetical order.

Sorting does not depend on the view set. The windows always show first the folders present from A to Z, followed by the files, also sorted in alphabetical order. The *arrangement* of the objects depends on the view set.

Large Icons view

In the *Large Icons* view, the objects are shown in the right pane of the *Windows Explorer* window from the top left-hand corner to the bottom right-hand corner. In the top left-hand corner, for example, there will be the icon of a folder whose first letter is closest to the letter "A" of the alphabet. To its right will appear the second folder in alphabetical order, etc. Not only are the folders sorted by their name, but the file objects are positioned in the same sort order.

Small Icons view

This arrangement of icons also applies to the *Small Icons* view. With the *List* view, the contents of the folders are displayed vertically in alphabetical order: the folders first, and then the files.

Details view

If you are working in a reduced window of *Windows Explorer* and with a large number of objects in the window, in the *List* view, a second column containing the continuation of the list from the bottom of the first column, etc. will automatically be displayed. Only with the *Details* view a list of all objects in the browsed folder is created with one column only in alphabetical order.

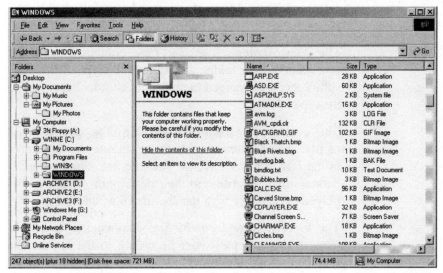

Figure 5.21   Sorting of *Windows Explorer* icons by their names (standard configuration)

Thumbnails view

The sort order of the *Thumbnails* view corresponds to that of the *Large Icons*: first the folders in alphabetical order, then the files – arranged on lines one above another.

Arrange Icons
command

The sorting criteria of the right pane of the *Windows Explorer* window may be set separately for each *Windows Explorer* window opened: to do this, use the *Arrange Icons* command on the *View* menu or the shortcut menu of the right pane of the window (no object must be selected). The submenu contains the *By Name, By Type, By Size, By Date* and *Auto Arrange* commands. The *Auto Arrange* command will be discussed at the end of the chapter.

215

By Name

The *View/Arrange Icons/By Name* command is the standard configuration of *Windows Explorer*. When it is set, the icons of the folder browsed in the right pane of the *Windows Explorer* window will be arranged in alphabetical order. The folders are displayed first followed by the file objects.

By Type

The *View/Arrange Icons/By Type* command sorts the objects inside the folder according to the type of file. Any subfolders are arranged in alphabetical order according to the type of file.

This command is useful for searching for specific types of file, such as *Bitmaps*, which are set one above another in the *List* or *Details* views. The files are sorted in alphabetical order according to their description, which is displayed exclusively with the *Details* view, under *Type*.

By Size

The *View/Arrange Icons/By Size* command sorts the objects in the selected folder according to the size of the file. First of all, the folders are listed followed by the file objects sorted according to the size of the file.

With the *By Size* sorting criteria, small files are always listed before large ones, irrespective of the file name or file type. Use this command if you want to search for a folder on the basis of files of a known size.

By Date

The *View/Arrange Icons/Per data* command sorts the contents of the folders browsed in the right pane of the *Windows Explorer* window according to the date it was last modified. In this case, the folders are sorted according to the date, then the file objects also arranged on the basis of the date they were modified. The *By Date* sorting criteria lists old files before new ones irrespective of the file name and file type.

Windows Me recognizes three types of date: *Created,* *Modified* and *Accessed*. *Created* describes the date on which an object was created. *Modified* describes the date on which an object was last modified with respect to the *Created* version. *Accessed* indicates the date on which the file was opened for the last time without being saved.

Selecting Objects

The following section assumes that you are working with the standard configuration of the folders, in which objects are activated by double clicking on them.

Before selecting a command or performing an operation with an object in *Windows Me*, you must select it.

You should now no longer have difficulty in choosing – that is, selecting single objects. In the relevant window, click once on the object (for example, a file or a folder).

Selecting Several Objects at the Same Time

Rules

A more useful tool for daily tasks is multiple selection, that is, the simultaneous selection of more than one file or folder. To make this selection, it is not enough to click on the files concerned in sequence as each time you click, the last selection made is disabled. If you want to select more than one file or folder at the same time, bear the following rules in mind:

- Multiple selections may only be made inside one window

- In *Windows Explorer* multiple selections may only be made in the right pane of the window

To select several files at the same time in *My Computer*, *Windows Explorer* or any document window, several methods may be used: you can use the mouse and keyboard together or use the mouse only and the menu commands.

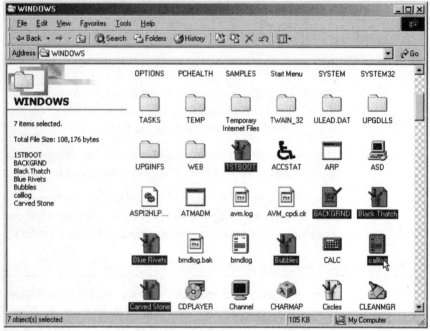

Figure 5.22   Non-adjacent multiple selections using the $\boxed{\text{Ctrl}}$ key

Mouse and keyboard

First of all, we shall discuss the combined use of the mouse and keyboard: select the first file by clicking on it with the mouse. Press the $\boxed{\text{Ctrl}}$ key and, holding it pressed, click on the other objects one by one. At this point, you can release the $\boxed{\text{Ctrl}}$ key. In this way, several objects may be selected irrespective of the order in which they are displayed.

Selecting rows or columns

If the *List* or *Details* view has been set, the objects set above one another or displayed on a row or column may be selected at the same time, first by clicking on the first object on the list, then by holding the ⬦ key pressed and by clicking on the last item on the list.

⬦ key pressed

When the ⬦ key is held pressed, the objects between the two files on which you have clicked will be selected. This method may also be used with the *Large Icons* view, but the effect, in this case, will not be so clear. The Ctrl and ⬦ keys may even be used together.

Selection box

A quick and convenient way of selecting the objects set beside one another is to use the mouse selection box: to do this, place the pointer close to the first object to be selected, press the left mouse button and drag the mouse in the desired direction. A *selection box* will be displayed (see Figure 5.23). If the frame of the selection touches an object or the name of the object, it will automatically be selected. Having selected all the desired objects, release the mouse button.

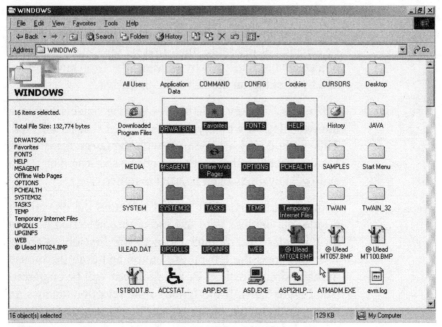

Figure 5.23   Selecting objects using the mouse selection box

If you do not intend to use double clicks to open folders in *My Computer* and want to open the folders by clicking once only – this function may be set under *Tools/Folder Options...*, *General* tab, by enabling the *Single click to open an item (point to select)* option in *Click items as follows* – objects are selected in a different way:

To make the selection, simply point at the desired objects or folders. The selected objects are automatically highlighted with a colour. Alternatively, you can set the function that underlines selected objects using *Tools/Folder Options...*, so that the view is clearer. All other methods of selection (Ctrl and ⇧ etc.) work in the same way as described above.

Selecting objects using menu commands

Let's now examine how to select objects using menu commands: if you intend to select all the objects in a folder or the *Windows Explorer* window, select the *Select All* command on the *Edit* menu.

To select all the objects in the browsed folder, you can also use the ⌈Ctrl⌋ + ⌈5⌋ key combination, which corresponds to the *Edit/Select All.* command.

The *Edit* menu includes the *Invert Selection* command. This may be used, for example, to select 49 objects out of 52 - a procedure that would require a long time if a single click were to be used. To do this, first of all select the three objects that are not required holding the ⌈Ctrl⌋ key pressed. Then select *Edit/Invert Selection*, and all unselected objects will be selected.

Selecting objects from keyboard

In case you prefer to use the keyboard instead of the mouse, we shall explain how to select objects from the keyboard: move to the first object using the ⌈←⌋, ⌈→⌋, ⌈↑⌋ or ⌈↓⌋ keys. Press the ⌈◇⌋ key and move using the ⌈←⌋, ⌈→⌋, ⌈↑⌋ or ⌈↓⌋ keys to the neighbouring objects to include them in the selection.

Scroll bar

If you want to select objects that cannot be seen in the window, you can access them using the scroll bar, taking care not to click in the field of the window because otherwise the previously made selection will be lost.

Information about the status bar

Irrespective of the method of selection used, you should always keep an eye on the status bar or the area between the folder and the list of files. It contains information about the number of objects selected (on the left) and the size of the objects selected.

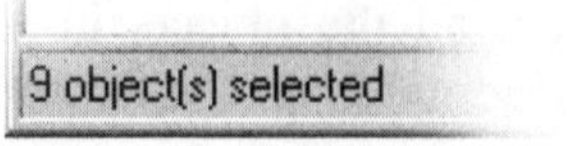

9 object(s) selected

Figure 5.24   Number of objects selected on the status bar

Copying and Dragging Files

Data organization and management represent the most important maintenance operations to be performed on a computer. Normally, files are copied or moved, for example, to improve the organization of data in the documents filed. In *Windows Me*, to copy or drag objects, several methods may be used. First of all, we shall describe how to copy or move files using the *drag and drop* method.

Copying and Moving Files Using the Drag and Drop Method

To copy or move files you must use the Windows applications that display the actual data structure on the hard disk and in folders. The *Start* menu only shows the links and program groups, the actual data is stored elsewhere. To copy and move folders, *My Computer* or *Windows Explorer* should always be used.

Selecting the folder   Irrespective of the method used to copy or move files, first of all you must move to the desired drive or folder:

In *My Computer*, switch to the desired folder by double clicking on the hard disk drive icon and scroll through the hierarchy of folders by double clicking from one to another.

In *Windows Explorer*, expand the list of folders in the left pane of the window by clicking on the plus sign of the

My Computer item and then, if necessary, repeat this step for the hard disk drive icon.

Switch to other folders by clicking on the plus sign and selecting the folder containing the desired files. If you want to copy several files at a time, you can make multiple selections in the right pane.

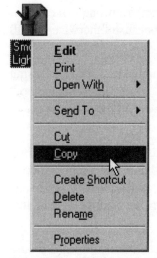

Figure 5.25   Copying an object using the shortcut menu

Select first

First of all select the objects. To do this, click on the icon of a file. To make multiple selections, use the [Ctrl] or [⬦] key.

Copy

Point at the source folder and the target folder in its own window. On the folder list of *Windows Explorer* open the source structure and the target structure. Otherwise open a second *Windows Explorer* window.

Press the [Ctrl] key

To make a copy using the *drag and drop* method, point at the files selected. Then press the [Ctrl] key and hold it down. Drag the file (files) to the target drive or folder in the other window (in *Windows Explorer* to another folder

223

on the list of folders). Release the mouse button first and then the ⌈Ctrl⌉ key. If you copy a file from one drive or partition to another one, you do not have to press the ⌈Ctrl⌉ key. The small icon of the plus sign ⊞ will be displayed automatically on the mouse pointer.

Move

To move an object using the *drag and drop* method, simply drag the files and drop them in the target folder in the other window. To move an object from one drive to another, hold down the ⌈⇧⌉ key, because otherwise, it will be copied instead.

Right mouse button

Another way of copying or moving the files is by using the right mouse button and the *drag and drop* method. First of all, copy it: to do this, move to the selected file to be copied.

Copying objects with the right mouse button

Using the right mouse button, drag the objects and drop them in the target drive or folder in the other window. First release the mouse button and then the ⌈Ctrl⌉ key. Select the *Copy* command from the shortcut menu that appears on the display.

Moving objects with the right mouse button

To move objects, drag the objects with the right mouse button and drop them in the target folder. At this point, release the button and select the *Move* command on the shortcut menu that appears on the display.

Copying and Moving Files from the Keyboard

Below is an explanation of how to copy or move files using key combinations. To do this, use *My Computer* or *Windows Explorer*.

Irrespective of the method used, first of all select the drive or folder containing the files to be copied or moved. Point at the folder containing the desired files. In *My Computer*, move to the desired folder by double clicking on the hard disk icon and then double clicking on the work folder icon.

Structure   In *Windows Explorer*, expand the structure in the left pane of the window by clicking on the plus sign ⊞ beside the *My Computer* item and repeat this operation, if appropriate, for the hard disk drive icon. By clicking on the plus signs, move to other folders and select the folder containing the files to be copied or moved. If you want to copy several files at a time., you can make multiple selections in the right pane of the window.

Multiple selections   First of all, select the objects. To do this, click on the icon of a file. To make multiple selections, use the ⌜Ctrl⌟ or ⌜⇧⌟ key.

Key Combinations   Having selected the objects in the source folder, press the ⌜Ctrl⌟ + ⌜C⌟ keys to copy or ⌜Ctrl⌟ + ⌜X⌟ to cut, that is, to move them. Move to the target folder and paste the data (on the clipboard) by pressing ⌜Ctrl⌟ + ⌜V⌟. If the files to be pasted are large, a dialog box indicating the progress of the operation will be displayed.

Copying and Moving Files from the *Edit* Menu

My Computer or   This section describes how to copy or move files using
Windows Explorer   the commands on the *Edit* menu – called the *Clipboard*. To do this, use *My Computer* or *Windows Explorer*. First of all move to the drive or folder containing the files to be copied or moved.

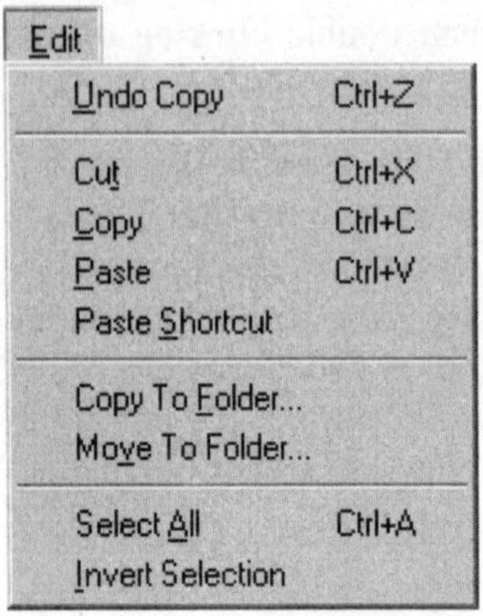

Edit	
Undo Copy	Ctrl+Z
Cut	Ctrl+X
Copy	Ctrl+C
Paste	Ctrl+V
Paste Shortcut	
Copy To Folder...	
Move To Folder...	
Select All	Ctrl+A
Invert Selection	

Figure 5.26   The *Edit* menu with the clipboard commands

Display the source folder. In *My Computer* double click on the hard disk drive icon and then double click on the folder icons.

Structure

In *Windows Explorer*, expand the structure in the left pane of the window by clicking on the plus sign ⊞ beside the *My Computer* item and repeat this operation, if appropriate, for the hard disk drive icon. Move to other folders by clicking on the plus signs and select the folder containing the files.

Multiple selections

If you want to copy or move several files at once, you can make multiple selections in the right pane of the window. First you must select the objects. Click the left mouse button on the icon of a file.

Second window of

Windows Explorer

To make multiple selections, use the ⌨Ctrl key or the ⌨⇧ key. At this point, the source folder and the target folder must be visible in separate windows. In *Windows Explorer*, to open the target folder on the corresponding list, simply click on the plus signs.

Edit / Copy

Select the *Copy* command from the *Edit* menu. To move the object, use the *Cut* command. View the folder or drive where the copy of the folder is to be created. Select the *Paste* command from the *Edit* menu.

Edit / Cut

Files may also be copied or moved using the shortcut menu: point at the relevant file and click the right mouse button: select the *Copy/Cut* command from the shortcut menu.

Edit / Paste

View the folder or drive in which the copy of the folder is to be created. Select a free point with the mouse and click the right mouse button. Select the *Paste* command from the shortcut menu that appears.

When the *Cut* command is selected, the original file is deleted and copied to the *Clipboard*. When the *Paste* command is selected, the copy is transferred to the new target.

If you have chosen to disable the double click to open folders in *My Computer* and folders are opened by clicking once only, objects are selected when the mouse pointer touches them.

Copying and Moving Files Using Buttons

In *Windows Me* you can also copy or move and paste the selected objects using two buttons on the *tool bar* of the folders or the *tool bar* of *Windows Explorer*.

To make the copy, select the *Copy* button 🖺 having selected the objects. If you want to move an object, select the *Move* button 🖺. In both cases, a dialog box appears and the target folder may be opened and selected by opening the structure of the folders using the plus sign icons ⊞.

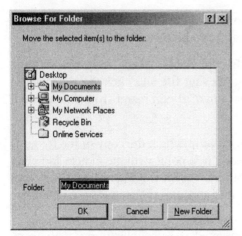

Figure 5.27   Selecting the folder to which objects are to be moved

Organization of Folders in *My Computer* or in *Windows Explorer*

In *Windows Me* folders are also called "directories", a term familiar to users who have worked in MS-DOS. This term is intended to mean a special container whose function is to collect one or more files so as to create an organized structure on the hard disk. Folders are created for installing applications or are used for saving data.

Managing files

A folder may contain other folders which are called "subfolders". To work correctly in Windows, folders are to be used so as to divide the files into topics as they are created and to create a simple and clear structure on the hard disk. For example, single folders are created for documents created using the word processor program, which may in turn be divided into subfolders, for example, for commercial and private procedures, etc.

The same procedure may be adopted with folders of drawings, graphs or data bases. Once *Windows Me* has been installed, the following folders are present on the hard disk: *My Documents, My Pictures, My Music* and, having started the *Windows Movie Maker, My Videos*.

Creating and Naming New Folders

Actual data structure

To create new folders, you must use *Windows* applications that show the actual structure of the data on the hard disk. The *Start* menu only shows links and program groups, the folders with their actual contents are stored at a different location. To create new folders, use *My Computer* or *Windows Explorer*.

Move to the drive or folder where you want to create a new (sub)folder. For personal files, it is convenient to use the *My Documents* folder, which is situated on the top level of the hard disk (*C:*).

My Computer

In *My Computer* 🖥, move to this folder by double clicking on the hard disk drive icon and then on the *My Documents* folder. There is a special icon 📁 on the desktop which opens the *My Documents* folder when double clicked.

Windows Explorer

In *Windows Explorer* the *My Documents* folder is already open when you start the program by selecting *Start/Programs/Accessories*.

Figure 5.28   Creating folders from the *My Documents* folder

File/New   At this point, select the *My Documents* folder. Then choose the *New* command from the *File* menu. The *New* command may alternatively be activated from the short-cut menu. In this case, there must not be any objects selected and, in *Windows Explorer,* the mouse pointer must be inside the right pane of the window.

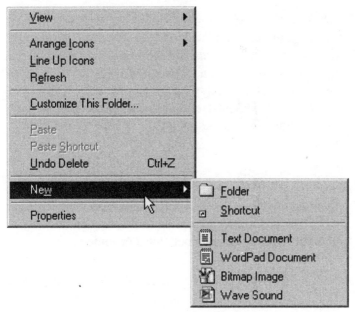

Figure 5.29   Creating a new folder

From the *New* menu, click on the *Folder* item. A new folder icon containing the words *New folder* will be created in the active folder and will be highlighted ready to be overwritten.

Overwriting the name

Assign the desired name by writing it over the one displayed, for example *Texts*. If you confirm by pressing ⏎, the new folder will be displayed as a subfolder of the active folder.

Other folders may be created in the same way. When creating subfolders, make sure that they are created in the desired folder.

All documents created in the future using a word processor program may be placed tidily inside a single structure of folders. To do this, use the *Save as...* command in the application program and select the desired target drive and folder in the structure of folders from the drop-down menus. To calculate tables or make presentations, etc., create other folders to arrange the files in an orderly fashion.

Renaming Files and Folders

In *Windows Me*, files and folders may be renamed with ease. The procedures described in this section are only to be used for user-created documents or folders.

Never change the name of a folder created by a program or the name of an application file. If this is done, it may not be possible to start the program, error messages may be displayed or the program may be aborted due to missing files.

Exception: links

An exception is represented by links on the *Start* menu under *Programs*. In this case, you can change the name as you please, as the link only contains information about the original memory location, not the actual program or document data.

Selecting a single object

There are several ways of naming objects: first of all, select the object in question. To do this, use *My Computer* or *Windows Explorer*. You can only select one object at a time. Then select the *Rename* command from the *File* menu or the shortcut menu (see Figure 5.30). The name of the object will be selected. Overwrite the old name and press ⏎. Press the Esc key if you wish to abort the procedure.

If the folder is opened in WWW mode, by clicking once only (*Tools/Folder Options...*), to rename an object you must always use the shortcut menu method described above.

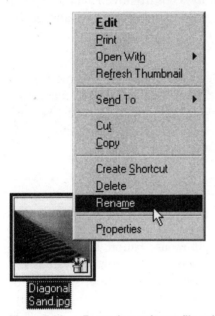

Figure 5.30   Renaming a picture file using the shortcut menu

Overwriting the name

If you use the classical double click, you can also select an object in other ways. To do this, wait for about a second and click once on the name of the file. When you do this the name will be selected. Overwrite the current name with up to 255 characters and confirm by pressing ⏎ but be careful: if you click too quickly the second time, the operation will be considered as a double click and the file will be opened.

If the *Tools/Folder Options.../View* function has been used to activate file extensions for the names of the files saved (*Hide file extensions for known file types* disabled), when you rename the file you must leave the extension unchanged – separated by a dot from the name of the file otherwise the file becomes unusable as the name of the type of file is lost.

If an invalid file name is specified, an error message is displayed indicating the presence of illegal characters. Confirm the message indicating the illegal characters by clicking on *OK* and repeat the renaming operation. To restore its original name, press ⌊Esc⌋.

Copying Folders

The procedure for copying folders is the same as the one used for copying files. You can use the method of dragging with the left or right mouse button, the right mouse button, the *Edit* menu or the *shortcut menu* as well as key combinations. This section provides a brief summary of all operations – in particular, those concerning the copying of folders –.

Actual structure of data

To copy folders in which files are to be saved, you must use a *Windows* program that is capable of modifying the actual structure of the data on the hard disk. The *Start* menu only shows links and program groups, the data is actually stored at a different location on the hard disk. To make a copy of folders, you should therefore use *My Computer* or *Windows Explorer*.

Selecting the drive

Irrespective of the copying method used, first of all move to the drive containing the folder to be copied or view the corresponding folder. In *My Computer* 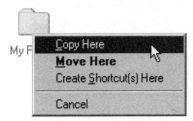 move to the desired folder by double clicking on the hard disk drive icon and then on the folder icons.

Selecting the folder   In *Windows Explorer*, expand the structure in the left pane of the window by clicking on the plus sign ⊞ beside the *My Computer* item and, if appropriate, repeat this operation for the hard disk drive icon. Then select the folder to be copied.

If you want to copy several subfolders at a time, you can make multiple selections in the right pane of the window. If you use a single click to open folders, select the objects using a selection box. For a description of the multiple selection procedure, see the corresponding section earlier in this chapter.

My F | Copy Here
      | **Move Here**
      | Create Shortcut(s) Here
      | Cancel

Figure 5.31   Copying folders using the shortcut menu

Copying the folder   Before copying a folder, it must already have been selected. To do this, click on its icon. To make multiple selections, use the Ctrl or ⇧ key. To copy the folder with a key combination, press the Ctrl + C keys. Then point at the folder or the drive in which the copy of the folder is to be created. Press Ctrl + V in the position where it is to be inserted.

The files are copied   If a folder contains files, they will be copied, too. During
too   this operation, a dialog box showing the progress of the copying operation will be displayed.

To copy the folder using the *Edit* menu, select the *Copy* command from the *Edit* menu. Then display the folder or drive in which the copy of the folder is to be created. At this point, select *Edit/Paste*.

Shortcut menu commands

Folders may also be copied using the commands on the shortcut menu: point at the desired folder and click the right mouse button. Select the *Copy* command from the shortcut menu. Display the folder or drive in which the copy of the folder is to be created. Select a free point and click the right mouse button. Select the *Paste* command from the shortcut menu.

Drag and drop method

If the folder to be copied is visible in a window and the target folder or drive appears in another window (in *Windows Explorer,* it may be the structure/contents box or a second window of *Windows Explorer*), the folders may also be copied using the *drag and drop* method. To do this, move to the selected folder or folders. Press the Ctrl key and hold it down. Drag the folder to the target drive or folder. First release the mouse button and then the Ctrl key.

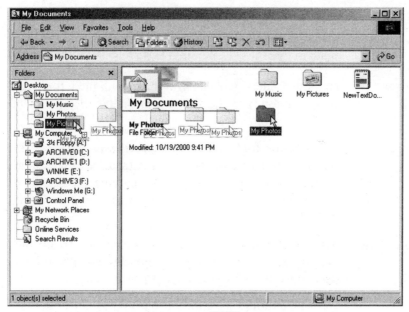

Figure 5.32   Copying a folder with the `Ctrl` **key pressed**

Copying folders
with the right
mouse button

Alternatively, you can copy folders with the right mouse button and the *drag and drop* method. To do this, move to the selected folder or folders. With the right mouse button pressed, drag the folder to the target drive or folder in the other window. Release the mouse button and select the *Copy* command from the shortcut menu that appears.

Moving Folders

In *Windows Me,* folders may be moved to another position in the same way as file objects.

Be careful, however: only use this procedure with your own folders.

If a folder created by a program is moved, the application will probably not be started when selected from the *Start* menu in that the files required to do this no longer exist.

Drag and drop

To move folders, you can *drag* them with the left or right mouse button, use the *Edit* menu or the *shortcut menu* and key combinations.

My Computer* or *Windows Explorer

To move the folders use *My Computer* or *Windows Explorer* to be aware of the actual structure of the data on the hard disk. Irrespective of the moving method used, first move to the relevant drive or display the desired folder.

Selecting a folder

Before moving a folder you must select it. To do this, click on its icon. If you use a single click to open folders, select the objects by pointing at them.

To make multiple selections, use the Ctrl key or the ⬦ key. To cut the folders from the keyboard, press the Ctrl + X keys. Display the folder or drive to which the folder is to be moved. Press Ctrl + V in the position where it is to be inserted. If a folder contains files, they will also be moved. A dialog box that shows the progress of the operation will appear on the display.

Edit/Cut

To move the folder from the menu, select *Edit/Cut*. Display the folder or drive where you wish to create the folder. Select the *Paste* command from the *Edit* menu.

Help menu

Folders may also be moved using the commands on the shortcut menu: point at a folder and click the right mouse button. Select the *Cut* command from the shortcut menu. Display the folder or drive in which you want to place the folder. Point at a free point and click the right mouse button. Select the *Paste* command from the shortcut menu.

Windows Explorer   If the folder to be moved can be seen in a window and the target folder and drive appear in another window (in *Windows Explorer* it may also be the structure/contents box or a second window of *Windows Explorer*), the folders may also be moved using the *drag and drop* method. To do this, point at the selected folder. Drag and drop it in the target drive or folder in the other window.

Right mouse button   Alternatively, folders may also be moved with the right mouse button and the *drag and drop* method. To do this, point at the selected folder. Then drag the folder with the right mouse button pressed and drop it in the target drive or folder in the other window.

Move command   At this point, release the mouse button. Select *Move* from the shortcut menu that appears.

When the *Cut* command is selected, the original folder is deleted and copied to the Clipboard. When *Paste* is selected, the copy is pasted in the new position.

The procedure for deleting files or folders is described in detail in Chapter 6 "Recycle Bin".

Preparing Floppy Disks for Data Storage

Before data may be stored on a floppy disk, the disk must be formatted. During the formatting process, the structure of the data storage disk is organized in the form of tracks and sectors, necessary for the operating system to store data in such a way that it may be read subsequently. Most floppy disks are sold already formatted but it is useful to be familiar with the formatting procedure.

1.44 Mbytes

The only floppy disks currently available on the market are 3.5 inch disks with a storage capacity of 1.44 Mbytes. The types of disk used previously, such as the 5.25 inch floppy disk, are not described here.

Formatting Floppy Disks

3.5 inch floppy drive (A:)

To format a disk you must use *My Computer* or *Windows Explorer*. The formatting method is exactly the same in both cases. Select the icon of the drive in which the disk to be formatted is inserted, in *Windows Explorer* or in *My Computer*. This is normally the *3 1/2 floppy (A:)* item.

Storage capacity

Select the *Format...* command from the *File* menu or the shortcut menu. On the *Capacity* drop-down menu, set the type of floppy disk used. For 3.5 inch, HD (*High Density*) disks, it is always *1,44 MB*, only for the old 3.5 inch, DD (*Double Density*) disks is the *720 KB* item chosen – a case that is unlikely to arise with modern PC's and floppy disks. If the floppy disk has not yet been formatted, select the *Full* option in *Format type*. If you want to clear the data from a floppy disk by formatting it, simply select the *Quick (erase)* option.

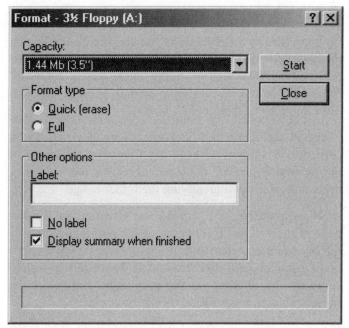

Figure 5.33   Preparing floppy disks for data storage

Naming the disk   Click in the *Label* text box and enter a name for the floppy disk consisting of no more than 11 characters, without spaces.

Starting the   Start the formatting process by clicking on *Start*. The
formatting process   dialog box at the bottom shows the progress bars that indicate the formatting status. At the end, a detailed report will be displayed if the *Display summary when finished* option has been enabled. Click on *Close* and close the formatting window by selecting *Close*.

Bear in mind that the formatting process may be carried out on floppy disks, not on the hard disk. In fact, if you were to format your hard disk you would lose all the data stored on it.

Copying Data to a Floppy Disk

To copy files to a floppy disk, you can use all the known methods provided by *My Computer* or *Windows Explorer* for copying objects. For floppy disk drives, however, *Windows Me* has a specific command. First of all open *My Computer* or *Windows Explorer*.

My Computer

Move to the drive or folder containing the files to be copied to the floppy disk. In *My Computer* 🖳, move to the desired folder by double clicking on the hard disk drive icon and subsequently on the folder icons.

Windows Explorer

In *Windows Explorer*, expand the structure in the left pane of the window by clicking on the plus sign ⊞ beside the *My Computer* item and, if appropriate, repeat this operation for the hard disk drive icon. Move to the desired subfolder by clicking on the plus signs and select the folder containing the file or files to be copied.

Selecting the files

If you want to copy several files to the floppy disk at the same time, multiple selections may be made in the right pane of the *Windows Explorer* window or the folder window. Before making the copy, you must select the objects. To do this, click on the icon of a file. To make multiple selections, use the ⌜Ctrl⌝ or ⌜⬦⌝ key.

Figure 5.34   Activating the *Send To* command

Send To command

To copy files to a floppy disk, select the *Send To* command from the *File* menu or the shortcut menu. Click on the floppy disk drive item on the submenu, for example *3 ½ Floppy (A:)*. If the files are large, a dialog box will appears indicating the progress of the copy operation and the time required to complete it.

Arranging Icons Automatically

The objects in the browsed folders are normally sorted on the basis of criteria such as *Name*, *Type*, *Size* or *Date*. The meaning of these commands was described earlier in this chapter. This section explains how to automatically rearrange the icons moved in folders in *Windows Explorer* or on the desktop.

Icons moved

While you are working in *Windows Me* it often happens

243

that one or more icons in a folder window or on the desktop are moved unintentionally, for example, because you haven't learnt to double click properly or because you inadvertently make mistakes in handling files or folders.

Auto Arrange

If this is the case, windows may appear untidily cluttered and it may become impossible to manually return the icons moved to their original position.

To correctly arrange the icons moved in any folder, select the *Arrange Icons* command on the *View* menu or the shortcut menu. On the submenu that appears, select the *Auto Arrange* item. At this point the icons will be shown in the correct order. This procedure works in the same way in *Windows Explorer* and on the desktop.

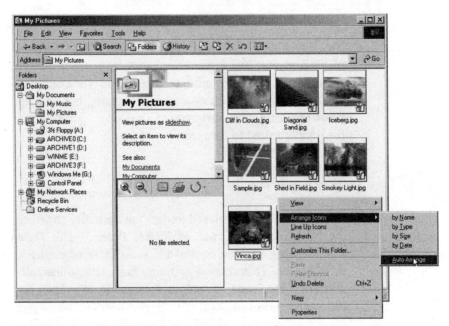

Figure 5.35   Activating the *Auto Arrange* command

Auto Arrange

If, at this point, you try to move an icon by holding the mouse button pressed, all icons are arranged automatically once the mouse is released. The arrangement is also performed after the size of the window has been changed. The *Auto Arrange* command must be activated separately for each open window!

The *Auto Arrange* command is present on the *Arrange Icons* drop-down menu only if the *Large Icons*, *Small Icons* or *Thumbnails* view is selected.

Displaying All Types of Files

Windows Me tries, where possible, to make your job on the computer easier. It is for this reason that the graphic operating system has such a strongly object-oriented structure. Nearly every integral part of *Windows Me* can be viewed and handled as an object, performing almost all operations with the mouse.

Hidden file extension

By default, *Windows Me* shows the contents of the folders browsed without the file extension normally used in MS-DOS. In addition, hidden system files, virtual drivers and program libraries are not shown. This is to prevent mistakes made above all by beginners and to stop important *Windows* files being inadvertently deleted, even though *Windows Me* has security mechanisms that are easy to use to ensure that the system will work even when operating errors are made by the user.

Auto Save

In this way, there is no real need to use the file extension as *Windows* recognizes all files whose applications were stored automatically on installation and can associate them with the single program. Expert users will however require more information about the system. For this reason, you can change the view for all folders or for *Windows Explorer* only.

Folder Options
command

Select the *Folder Options...* command from the *Tools* menu in any folder. Choose the *View* tab. Press the *Show hidden files and folders* option button in *Hidden files and folders* also to show hidden system files, virtual drivers and program libraries.

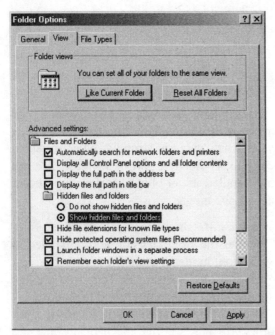

Figure 5.36   The displaying of files is set on the *View* tab

Hidden MS-DOS
extension

Disable the *Hide file extensions for known file types* check box if you want to see the extension at the end of the file name. The extension enables you to determine the program in which a file was created without having to guess the type of document according to the type of icon appearing before the file name. Confirm changes by pressing *OK*.

If you choose to display the extension of all files, take care not to delete the three letters of the extension in *My Computer* and in *Windows Explorer*. If, for example, you delete the extension when you rename a file, *Windows* forgets which program is associated with the document.

Showing the Full MS-DOS Path on the Title Bar

The strongly object-oriented structure of *Windows Me* may seem strange to some users, particularly those who have switched from the *MS-DOS* (*Microsoft Disk Operating System*) operating system, which is character and command oriented, to the *Windows Me* graphic operating system, especially if the standard configurations of *My Computer* are left unchanged.

Current folder name

All folders browsed through using *My Computer* are shown inside a specific window. The name of the current folder always appears on the title bar of the window. This enables you to have a clear picture of the structure of folders even when you are browsing through folder structures with a large number of branches.

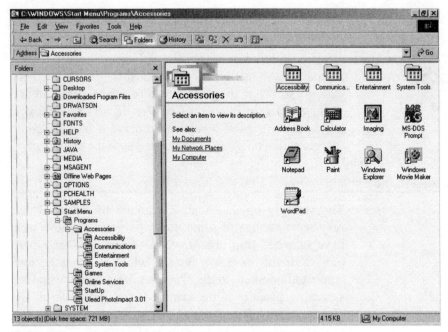

Figure 5.37   Folder window with the full path on the title bar

Displaying the full path

If you presume, but are not sure, that the *System Tools* folder is located under *C:\Windows\ Start Menu\Programs\Accessories*, you can check by looking at the path indication given on the title bar of each folder inside it using My Computer.

Setting the view

To change the view, select the *Folder Options...* command on the *Tools* menu in any folder. Then move to the *View* tab. Select the *Display the full path in title bar* check box and confirm by clicking on the *OK* button.

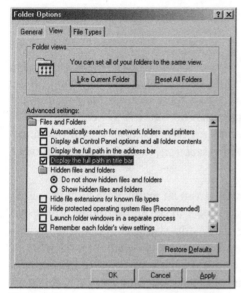

Figure 5.38   Activating the path display

From this moment on, the path where each browsed folder is stored is displayed in full using the classical *MS-DOS* method on the title bar. The setting applies to all folders and also to *Windows Explorer*.

As well as on the title bar, the full path of the current folder may also be displayed in the *address bar* of *Windows Explorer* – which is like the address bar of Internet Explorer, familiar to those who surf on the Internet. To do this, select the *Display the full path in the address bar* on the *View* tab of the *Folder Options* window.

Write-Protecting Files

Windows Me has several mechanisms for preventing users from deleting a file by replacing it with another having the same name. These measures are not required for system files in that a new, complex system, called *PC Health* is activated to prevent damage to the operating system. The following section explains how to protect your own files.

Message box   If you try to save a file from an application with the name of a file that already exists in the same folder, a message appears indicating that a file with this name already exists. You will then be requested whether you wish to overwrite the file or not. If you click on *No*, the *Save As* dialog box appears so that you can assign a different name to the file. If you click on *Yes*, the existing file will be overwritten.

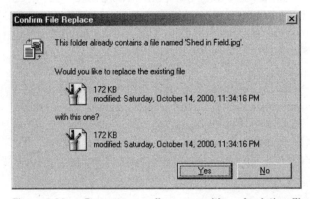

Figure 5.39   Prompt to confirm overwriting of existing files

Safety confirmation   The same procedure is carried out when you try to create or rename a file or folder with a name that has already been used for another one. Also in this case, confirmation messages or messages that prevent existing objects from being overwritten are displayed.

Read-only protection   In *Windows Me* a supplementary protective measure may be set by assigning a file or folder the *read-only* attribute.

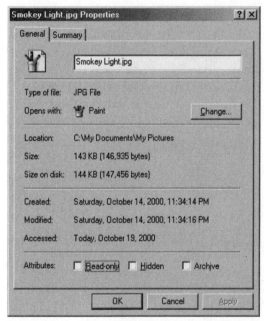

Figure 5.40   Activating the *Read-only* file attribute

Point at the file or folder in *My Computer* or *Windows Explorer* and select the desired object. Select the *Properties* command from the *File* menu or the shortcut menu.

Read-only protection   In the Properties window, activate the *Read-only* check box in *Attributes* and confirm by pressing *OK*.

251

If you try to save a write-protected file, an error message will be displayed and has to be confirmed by pressing the *OK* button. The *Save As* dialog box will then be displayed again so that you can save the file under another name.

To cancel a read-only protection feature, disable the corresponding file attribute in the *Properties* window.

6. The *Recycle Bin*

This chapter describes how to delete files and folders and the safety feature called the *Recycle Bin*. This is where deleted items are handled, the contents of the *recycle bin* may be viewed and any files deleted accidentally may be recovered.

Deleting Files and Folders

In *Windows Me*, any items that are no longer required may be removed from their location on the disk. A list of the available keyboard commands and menus is provided at the start of this chapter.

Warning

Before deleting files or folders, some precautions should be taken. Do not delete files as a trial, even if you know how the *Recycle Bin* works. Remove one file or folder at a time.

If you accidentally remove a folder required by the program, it will no longer be possible to run the application from the *Start* menu as the corresponding files have been removed. If single program files are removed, you will find that some program functions may no longer be performed, or an error message is displayed.

Actual structure of data

Deleting items from the *Start* menu has no particular effect – this menu shows exclusively the links (rather than the program files themselves) and program groups (rather than folders), as the actual programs and data are stored in a completely different location on the hard disk.

My Computer or Windows Explorer

If a link (which may be identified by the icon 🔁) is removed, the original item remains stored on the data storage unit. To delete folders, you can use *My Computer* or *Windows Explorer*. Irrespective of the method used, first of all, move to the drive on which the folder you want to remove is located, or display the folder containing the item or items to be removed.

Deleting Items with the ⌈Del⌋ Key

Selecting the item

To delete the files in question, you must select them first. You can make multiple selections of selected files and folders at the same time. The quickest way of deleting them is by pressing the (Del) key. Having done this, a message will appear prompting you to confirm your intention to send the file *[name]* to the *Recycle Bin*.

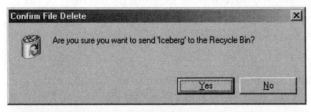

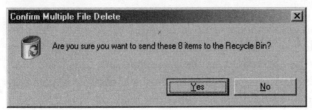

Figure 6.1   Confirming the deletion of single (above) and multiple files

Confirmation
message

If you click on *Yes*, the item will be deleted. *No* aborts the deletion process. If a multiple selection is made, the confirmation message will be different (see Figure 6.1, below). *Windows Me* does not present the names of the items to be deleted.

Deleting Items Using the *File/Delete command*

File/Delete

Instead of using the ⌈Del⌋ key, you can delete the items selected by opening the *File* menu and selecting the *Delete* command. The *Delete* command is also on the shortcut menu of the selected items.

The *Windows Me Recycle Bin* is a special system folder in which deleted items are placed. If the properties of the *Recycle Bin* are not modified, the deleted items remain on the hard disk. In fact, they are simply removed from their original folder.

The protection against accidental deletion represented by the *Recycle Bin* is only valid for the hard disk, not for floppy disks! When an item is deleted from a floppy disk, it cannot be recovered.

Deleting Items by *Dragging* Them

Items that are no longer needed may also be deleted using the mouse. To delete files or folders with the mouse in *Windows Me*, point at the corresponding drive or folder in *My Computer* or *Windows Explorer*.

Dragging items into the *Recycle Bin*

Then select the item and drag it on top of the *Recycle Bin* icon. When you reach the correct point, the *Recycle Bin* icon will be selected. In this way, you can delete several items at the same time: select the items to be deleted using a selection box or with the ⌈Ctrl⌋ or ⌈⇧⌋ key pressed, and drag the selected items on top of the *Recycle Bin* icon 🗑.

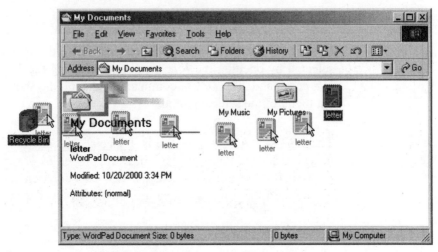

Figure 6.2   Dragging files into the *Recycle Bin*

If the properties of the *Recycle Bin* have not been modified, the items deleted remain on the hard disk. They are
simply removed from their original folder.

Protecting against
accidental deletion
We are talking about the hard disk because the protection
provided by the *Recycle Bin* only applies to the hard disk,
not to floppy disks! If an item is deleted from a floppy
disk, it will be deleted immediately and irreversibly –
once confirmation has been given.

On the contrary, files or folders deleted from the hard
disk are not removed from this data storage unit. *Windows Me* simply moves the items to a special folder
called *Recycle Bin*. This procedure is not based on an ar-
bitrary decision made by a programmer, but a system
rule: the *Recycle Bin* is a protective measure against the
loss of data caused by the accidental or hasty deletion of
files.

Recycle Bin Recycle Bin

Figure 6.3   *Recycle Bin* empty (on left) and full

If you happen to delete a file or folder that you haven't finished with, you must look for these items in the *Recycle Bin*. You can tell that there are items in the *Recycle Bin* by looking at the icon: if the Recycle Bin icon appears full, this means that it has items in it (Figure 6.3, on right).

Immediate and irreversible deletion

If, instead of sending items to the *Recycle Bin*, you want to delete them irreversibly, hold the ⟨◇⟩ key pressed while dragging them on top of the *Recycle Bin* icon. The items are deleted immediately and cannot subsequently be retrieved.

***Delete* button**

An alternative to moving files to the *Recycle Bin* is to use the *Delete* button ✕ (without *icon caption*) or on the tool bar of folders or *Windows Explorer*. Also in this case, you will be prompted to confirm deletion by clicking on the *Yes* button.

Viewing the *Recycle Bin* and a List of Deleted Items

The files inside the Recycle Bin have not yet been deleted irreversibly; they have simply been moved from their original folders to a different system folder.

Protecting against data loss

The *Recycle Bin* prevents data loss caused by the accidental deletion of files.

If you inadvertently delete a file or folder that you still need, look for these items in the *Recycle Bin*.

To view the contents of the *Recycle Bin*, double click on the *Recycle Bin* icon on the desktop or select the *Recycle Bin* icon and press ⏎.

Recycle Bin folder

The *Recycle Bin* folder is displayed. According to the view selected, all deleted items will appear as *Large icons/Small icons*, a *List* or *Details* (see Figure 6.4).

Deleted data

Select *View/Details* to display under *Original Location* the original folder from which the file was removed. The *date* it was *deleted* is also displayed.

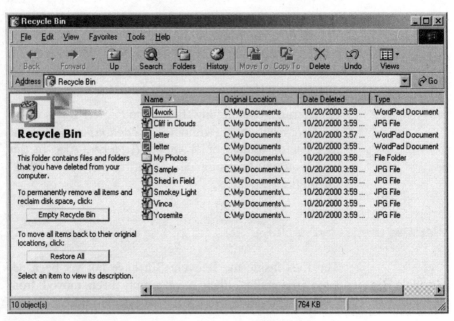

Figure 6.4   Contents of the *Recycle Bin* in the *Details* view

Emptying the *Recycle Bin*

Windows Me simply sends deleted items to a special folder called the *Recycle Bin*. In this way, the *Recycle Bin* prevents data loss caused by the accidental deletion of files.

At this point, it should be explained how to irreversibly delete files you are sure you no longer need. There are several ways of doing this. The safest way is using the *Recycle Bin* itself: double click on the *Recycle Bin* icon on the desktop to view its contents.

File/Delete

According to the view selected, all items are displayed as *Large icons/Small icons*, a *List* or *Details*. Select the files in the *Recycle Bin* that you wish to delete irreversibly, and then select *File/Delete* or press the ⌐Del⌐ key. If you confirm deletion by pressing the *Yes* button, the items will be removed.

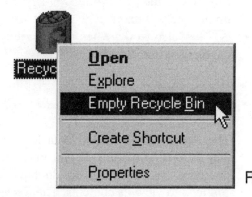

Figure 6.5   *Emptying the recycle bin* and appearance of the icon when the operation has been performed

Empty recycle bin
command

Did you find that procedure too complicated? To remove all items from the *Recycle Bin*, select the *Empty Recycle Bin* command on the *File* menu or the shortcut menu.

Confirm deletion in this case by selecting the *Yes* button. The items will be permanently deleted.

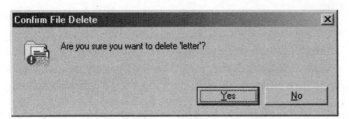

Figure 6.6   Prompt for confirmation of deletion of items

You can select the *Empty Recycle Bin* command on the shortcut menu of the *Recycle Bin* icon even without opening the folder. The items may be moved more quickly by *dragging* and *dropping* them into the *Recycle Bin*. If you then press the ⟨◇⟩ key, they will be deleted immediately without any request for confirmation. The ⟨◇⟩ key also works when deleting items using the shortcut menu or the ⟨Del⟩ key.

Restoring Deleted Items from the *Recycle Bin*

The *Recycle Bin* prevents data loss caused by the accidental deletion of files. If you inadvertently delete a file or folder that you still need, double click on the *Recycle Bin* icon to view its contents. The *Recycle Bin* is also present in *Windows Explorer*; in this case, simply click on it to view its contents in the right-hand box of the window.

If the double click to open folders in *My Computer* has been disabled in *View/Folder Options*, open the *Recycle Bin* by clicking on it once. In this case, all you have to do to select an item is to point at it.

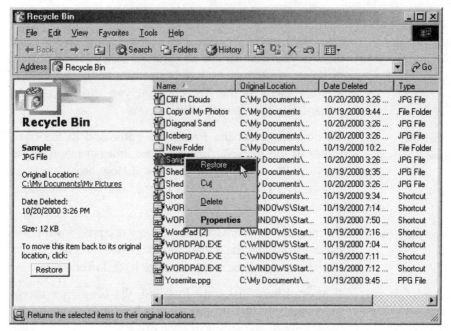

Figure 6.7   Restoring selected items from the *Recycle Bin*

View / Details   Select the *Details* command on the *View* menu, if the contents of the *Recycle Bin* are not already displayed in this form. In the *Original Location* column you can check the folder from which the file was removed. The display also includes the *date* it was *deleted,* the *type* and the *size* of the file.

File / Restore   At this point, select the items you deleted by accident. To undo the deletion, select *File/Restore*.

261

The *Restore* command is also present on the shortcut menu. The items are taken from the *Recycle Bin* and returned to the original folder from which they were deleted.

Changing the Properties of the *Recycle Bin*

More memory space

Files sent to the *Recycle Bin* occupy space on the hard disk. If you want to use this storage space for other data or delete items you no longer need immediately without sending them to the *Recycle Bin*, you can change the properties of the *Recycle Bin*.

Properties command

To do this, select the *Properties* command in the open folder of the *Recycle Bin* or on the shortcut menu of the *Recycle Bin* icon to display the dialog box shown in Figure 6.8. The command is only available on the shortcut menu of the *Recycle Bin* icon.

Reserved memory

To increase or decrease the memory reserved for the *Recycle Bin*, drag the cursor from *10%* to higher values (more storage space is reserved for it) or lower values.

If several hard disks are installed, the *Configure drives independently* option may be used to make the settings separately on the sheets of each drive.

Confirmation message

If you do not want the confirmation message to be displayed prior to deletion, disable the *Display delete confirmation dialog* check box.

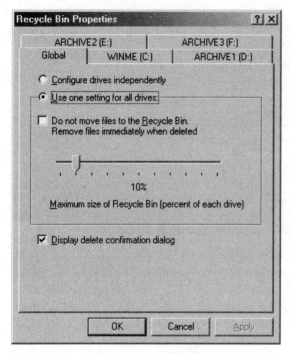

Figure 6.8   Setting the properties of the *Recycle Bin*

Disabling the   To completely disable the *recycle bin* restore function,
Recycle Bin   enable the *Do not move files to the Recycle Bin. Remove
files immediately when deleted* check box. Then confirm
the changes by clicking on the *OK* button.

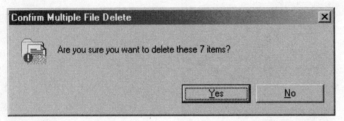

Figure 6.9   If the restore function is disabled, the Recycle Bin no longer serves any purpose.

Warning: from this moment on, all items will be deleted *immediately*. As a result, the prompt displayed for confirmation of deletion is also different.

7. Windows Search Functions

It sometimes happens that the file you need just isn't in the location you had expected. The hotlines of computer customer service centers are buzzing with inquiries sounding like this: "I just had that file...and now it's gone – how can that happen?" Well, it can't really happen – a file which has been saved almost never disappears.

Searching for files What usually happens is you didn't look closely enough at the folder which was displayed in the *Save as...* dialogue box, and the document ended up in the wrong folder. In this case, all you need to do run a search for the missing file.

Searching for files and folders

Windows Me has a powerful search function which can help you solve the problem described above. Open the *Start* menu and point to the *Search* command. Depending on the configuration of your computer, you will see the following options:

- *For files or folders... (finds files/folders on the PC)*

- *In the Internet... (loads Internet Explorer for an on-line search)*

- *Persons... (Addresses from the Outlook address book)*

Files and folders - searching by name

Search for:

All files

To search for files and folders on your computer, you need to use the command *Search / For Files and Folders.... Windows Me* then opens the dialogue box, *Search results*. On the left side of the window, you enter information for the search. The results of the search will apear on the right side of the window.

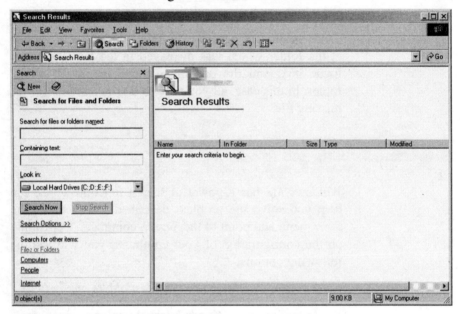

Figure 7.1   Searching for files and folders

Textbox *Search for*

files or folders

named

If you know the file name, enter it in the text box at the top. (*Search for files or folders named:*). Upper and lower case are not important here. If you want to use exact spelling and capitalization, click on *Search options >>* underneath the *Search now* button. Then, click on *Advanced options* and select *Case sensitive*.

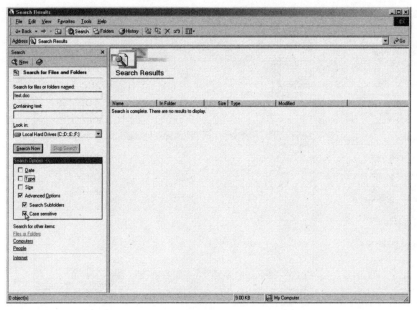

Figure 7.2   Case sensitive search option

Instead of entering the entire file name, you can just enter a part of it, but the results will be more extensive if many similar file names exist.

*Searching
subfolders*

Check to see whether the checkbox *Search subfolders* is checked. If not, only the folders in the highest level of the specified drive will be searched. You will find this checkbox under *Advanced options* >>.

Search now button

To begin the search, click on the *Search now* button. *Windows Me* searches all folders and displays the result in the right side of the window.

If no files or folders are found, the search results window will not contain any entries *(Search is complete. There are no results to display)*. In the status list, you will see the message *0 file(s) found*. Run the search again using a different search term.

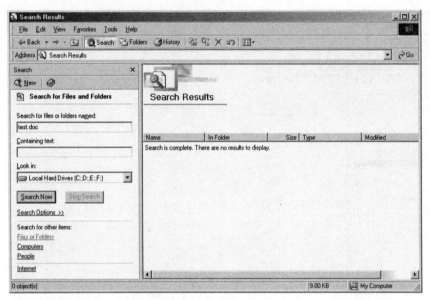

Figure 7.3   The document was not found

Searching for files and folders by location

Multiple drives

The search function normally searches the drive which is displayed in the list box *Look in:* The default setting is *Local drives* which includes all drives installed on the computer, but not CD-ROM drives. If there is more than one drive, you can open the list and have other drives searched. If you want to limit the search to particular drives or folders, click on the last entry, *Browse....*

Browse for folder dialogue box

In the *Browse for folder* dialogue box which appears, mark or expand the display of the desired drive with a click on the plus sign ⊞ before the drive. Expand the tree display for more folders until you see the folder which is to be searched. Mark the folder by clicking on its name and then click on *OK*. In the *Folder:* text box, you will now see the search path, which you can also change with the keyboard. If you want to include subfolders in the search, select the checkbox *Search subfolders* in *Advanced options* >> under *Search options*.

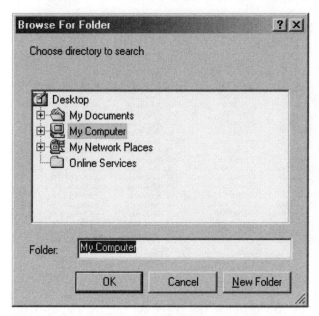

Figure 7.4   Searching specified drives or folders

Starting the search   If you only want to search the folders displayed, deactivate the checkbox. Check the search term in the uppermost text box and begin the search by clicking on *Search now*.

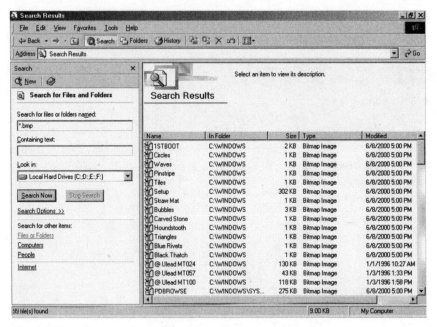

Figure 7.5   The search results

Search results   *Windows Me* searches the specified folders and displays the search results in the dialogue box. If no files or folders are found, the search results window contains no entries *(Search is complete. There are no results to display.* In the status bar, the message appears: *0 files found.* In this case, repeat the search with a new search term.

Stop search button   If the file you are searching for appears in the search results window, you can stop the search at any time by clicking on *Stop search.*

Items in the search results windows are shown in the *Details* view. If this is not the case, you can switch to this display through the *View* menu, or by using the *View* command through context menu.

Other information

In addition to the file name, the search path of the file is displayed under *In folder*. Other information on file size, file type and modification date are displayed. Documents from registered applications can be opened directly through the *Search results* window.

Opening the file which was found

Mark the file and select the *Open* command from the *File* menu or the context menu. You can also do this more quickly by simply double clicking on the icon. The appropriate application is launched and the file is opened.

Using the application, you can now save the file in the desired location. In this case, the "missing" copy will be preserved.

The items in the search results can also be copied or cut by using the commands in the *Edit* menu or context menu and added to the target folder. The target folder should be visible either as a window of *My Computer* or in *Explorer*.

Items can also be moved using *Drag & Drop,* from the search results window into the target folder in *My Computer* or *Explorer*.

Searching for a file by file type

Files can be searched using criteria other than file name and location. For example, you can search for files of a particular file type. This wouldn't be useful if you were searching for a letter, because you would have all text documents on the hard disk displayed. This method would be practical only if you are trying to arrange your files.

Search for file type   It is much more practical to search for file types on multimedia CD-ROMS or on the Setup CD of the Office package for *Windows Me*. These disks often contain hundreds of image, sound and video files which may be stored in hundreds of folders and subfolders. Therefore, it would be nice to be able to display all the images in the search results, in order to find the one you want.

Missing files   Sometimes, when you're saving a file in the *Save As* dialogue box, you don't pay enough attention to the name of the target folder. The document may then end up in a folder other than the one you had intended. Now, you just have to run a search for the missing file.

To launch the search function, open the *Start* menu and point to *Search*. In the submenu, click on *Files and folders...* In the *Search results* window, click on *Search options >>* and select the checkbox *Type*.

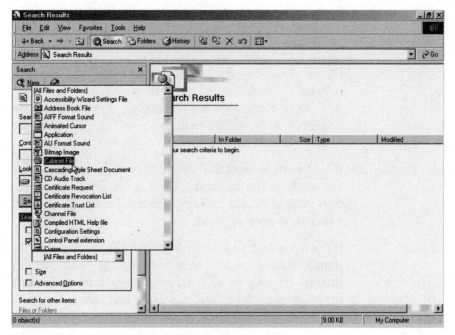

Figure 7.6   Limiting the search to specified file types

Type list

Open the *Type* list and use the scroll bar to find the file type you want. The descriptions in the list correspond to the information which you have seen in the *Folder options* window of *Windows Explorer* (*File types* tab). A file type is selected with a click of the mouse and then appears in the *Type* list box.

Starting the search

To run the search, click on the *Search now* button. *Windows Me* searches all folders and displays the result in the right side of the window. If no files or folders of the specified type are found, the search results window will contain no entries. In this case, you can repeat the search with another drive or file type.

By default, *Windows Me* always searches all local hard drives. If you want to search a CD-ROM drive, select the drive from the *Look in:* list box.

Check to see that the option Search *subfolders* has been selected (*Search options >> / Advanced options*). Otherwise, only the folders on the highest level of the drive displayed in *Look in*: will be searched. To start the search, click on *Search now*.

Limiting the search
If you want to limit the search to specific drives or folders, click on the last entry, *Browse..* in the *Look in:* list box. *Windows Me* always searches using all options which have been selected.

New search
If the file which you are searching for is displayed in the search results window, you can stop the search at any time by clicking on *Stop search*. If you want to define a new search, click on *New,* above the text boxes.

Documents from registered applications can be opened directly through the *Search results* window. Mark the file and select the *Open* command from the *File* menu or the context menu. You can also do this more quickly by simply double clicking on the icon. The appropriate application is launched and the file is opened.

Searching for files and folders by date

Now that you are familiar with searching for files and folders by *Name* and *Location*, you can run searches using these criteria. However, when you don't remember the name of a document, but do remember the date on which it was created, you can limit the search to a particular time period. For example, you might want to search for a letter, of which you have a printed copy with a date.

Searching for a special version

You can also use this option to find a particular version of a file, if the version was defined by a particular modification date.

To launch the search function, open the *Start* menu and point to the *Search* command. In the submenu, click on *For files and folders...* In the search results window, open *Search options >>* with a click of the mouse, and select the *Date* option.

Limiting the time period

If you want to limit the search to a specified period of time, decide in the selection list under *Date,* which date is to be used in the search: the date of the last modification, the date on which the file was created, or the date on which the file was last accessed.

If you know the exact date (example: from the date on a letter), select the option *Between* and enter the starting date in the text box in the format: *DD.MM.YY*. Then, click in the text box below, and enter the end date in the format *DD.MM.YY*.

Date calendar

Alternatively, you can click on the arrow in the date field. Select the desired date from the mini-calendar which appears (see Figure 7.7, below). Change the day by clicking on the date in the calendar, and change the month and year by clicking on the arrows to the left and the right.

Within the last...

If you do not know the exact date, but you do know the month, select the option *Within the last X months* and enter the number of months which are to be searched. If you have modified the document within a specified number of days, use the option *Within the last X days,* and enter the number of days to be searched.

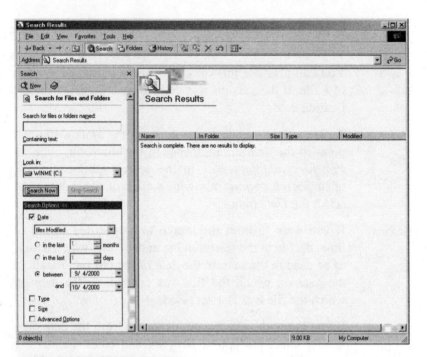

Figure 7.7   Limiting the search to a particular date

Starting the search   To start the search, click on the *Search now* button. *Windows Me* searches all folders and displays the results in the right side of the window. If no files or folders were found within the specified time period, the search results window will not display any entries. Repeat the search with different date settings.

Limit the search date as much as possible. Otherwise, many system and program files may appear in the *Search results* window, since these are modified during each startup or when a program is launched, and therefore would fulfill the search criteria.

Searching another drive

By default, *Windows Me* always searches all local hard drives. If you want to search another drive, change the search path in the *Look in:* list box. Also see that the option *Search subfolders* is selected under *Advanced options*. Otherwise, only the folders in the highest level of the drive displayed in *Look in:* will be searched.

Starting the search

To start the search, click on the *Search now* button. If you want to limit the search to specific folders, click on the last entry, *Browse...* in the *Look in*: list box , and switch to the desired source folder. You can limit the search to a particular file name, which you enter in the first text box.

All search criteria

Windows Me searches using all the settings selected to limit the search. If the file you are searching for appears in the search results window, you can stop the search at any time with a click on *Stop search*. If you want to define a new search, just click on *New* above the text boxes.

Searching for files and folders according to size

You can search for files using criteria other than *Name*, *Location* or *File type*. Sometimes you need to search for files of a particular size, or you want to add size as an additional search criterion.

Minimum and maximum

Don't expect miracles from the search function described below. The file size is limited to a *maximum* and *minimum* in KB. Therefore, it is not possible to search for a file which is exactly 2348 KB. However, this function is useful when you want to find which files are be taking up so much of your hard disk space.

File size

In order to search for a file of a minimum or maximum size, you need to know the approximate size of the file. To launch the search function, select *Start/Search/For files or folders....* Open the *Search options >>* and select the option *Size*.

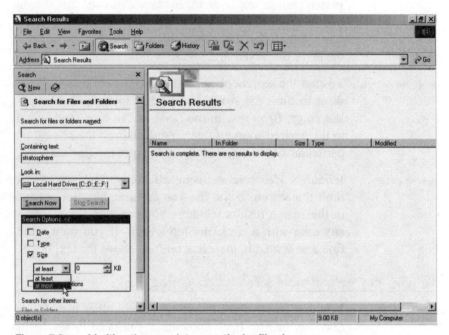

Figure 7.8   Limiting the search to a particular file size

278

Setting size criteria   Select one of the search criteria, *At least* or *At most*. Click in the text box to the right of your selection and enter the file size in KB. You can also use the arrows to set the size.

Starting the search   To start the search, click on the *Search now* button. *Windows Me* will search all selected folders, and list the results in the window on the right. If no files or folders of the selected maximum or minimum size were found, the search results window will not have any entries displayed. Repeat the search using other values.

Searching another drive   By default, *Windows Me* searches first in all local hard drives. If you want to search another drive, select the appropriate entry from the list box *Look in:*. Check to see whether the *Search subfolders* option has been selected. Otherwise, only the folders in the highest level of the drive shown in *Look in:* will be searched. To begin the search, click on the *Search now* button.

Limiting the search   If you want to limit the search to specific folders, select the last entry, *Browse*, from the list box *Look in:* In the dialogue box which appears, you can select the folder to be searched. You can limit the search to a particular file name, which you can enter in the text box at the top.

Windows Me uses all the search criteria which you have set. If you want to define a new search, click on the *New* button above the text boxes ⟨ New ⟩.

Stop search button   If the file you are searching for appears in the search results window, you can stop the search at any time by clicking on the *Stop search* button. You can further limit the search by specifying file size.

Documents from registered applications can be opened directly from the search results window: mark the file and select the command *Open* from the *File* menu or the context menu. You can do this more quickly by double clicking on the icon. The associated application is launched and the document is opened.

Searching folders and files for specific text

Now that you are familiar with searching for files by *Name* and *Location*, you can begin searching with these criteria. If you don't remember the name of an important document, but you do remember a particular passage in the text, you can search for the document which contains that text. For example, you could use this function to search for a letter which contains the word stratosphere.

Containing text... To launch the search function, open the *Start* menu and point to *Search*. In the submenu, click on *For files or folders...*.

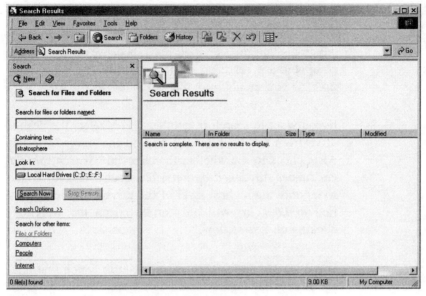

Figure 7.9   Searching for text in documents

Enter the search term in the text box, *Containing text:* Of course, with this option, you can only search files which contain text. A bitmap in which you have used the text tool to make a label cannot be found with this option, because this is not text.

Starting the search   To begin the search, click on the *Search now* button. *Windows Me* searches all folders and displays the results in the right side of the window. If no files or folders containing the specified text were found, the *Search results* window will not contain any entries. In the status bar, the message will appear: *0 file(s) found.* In this case, repeat the search, with another search term in the field *Containing text:*

Sometimes system and program files will appear in the search results window (some of these are simple text files which contain the specified text), because all files in the computer are searched. This operation can take some time, so you should limit the search to specific folders.

Searching another drive

If you want to search in another drive, select the desired drive from the *Look in:* list box on the *Name/Date* tab. Also, check to see whether the checkbox *Search subfolders* (under *Advanced options*) has been checked. Otherwise, only the highest level of the drive or folders specified in *Look in:* will be searched. Run the search by clicking on *Search now*.

Windows Me uses all the search criteria which you have set. If the file you are searching for appears in the results window, you can stop the search at any time by clicking on the *Stop search* button. If you want to define a new search, click on the *New* button above the text boxes .

Documents belonging to registered applications can be opened directly from the search results window. Just mark the file and select the *Open* command from the *File* menu or context menu. This can be done more quickly by double clicking on the icon. The associated application will be launched and the document opened.

Searching for computers in networks

If your *Windows Me* computer is connected to a network, you can use the search function to find other computers in the network. Open the *Start* menu and point to *Search*. In the expanded menu, click on *For files or folders...* The *Search results* window will open. Click on the link for *Computers* near the bottom of the left side of the window.

In the text box *Computer name:* enter the name of the computer or a part of it, and click on the *Search now* button.

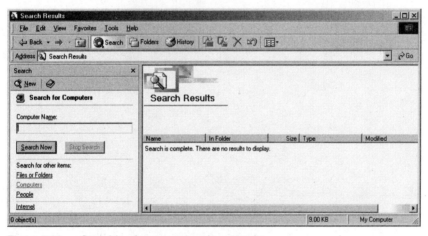

Figure 7.10   Searching for computers in networks

Windows Me searches the network and displays the computers found in the right side of the search results window. If no computers were found, the window contains no entries. In the status bar, a message appears *0 computers found*. In this case, repeat the search with another computer name.

Windows Me offers *an Address book* for storing the telephone numbers, addresses or e-mail addresses of personal and business contacts. This is a part of the e-mail program, *Outlook Express*. Please see Chapter 11 to find out how to search for persons in the address book or for e-mail addresses online.

8. The Control Panel

In this chapter, we will take a detailed look at the *Windows-Me* control panel. You can use this special system folder to customize all components of the computer to suit your requirements. You can also use it to install new components and applications. You will find out how to set up your mouse, the keyboard, or a joystick and how to install new fonts or change the *Windows* display.

Settings / Control Panel

You will also find out how to install new drivers for your graphics card or printer, and how to use the energy-saving features on your PC. To do any of these, you will need to open the control panel. To do this, open the start menu and click on *Settings*. From the expanded menu, select the item *Control Panel*. You can also open the *Control Panel* from *My Computer* 🖥.

Double click

In the *Control Panel,* double click on the appropriate icon. If you have changed the double click to a single click, place the mouse pointer over the desired item and press the mouse button once.

Setting the Properties of the Mouse

You can't really do much under the graphical operating system *Windows Me* without a suitable pointing device. However, even the best mouse has to be customized to suit your needs.

Trackball   In this and in the following sections dealing with the mouse, we will describe how to proceed using a classic mouse. If you have another pointing device such as a *Trackball*, the steps described here are also applicable, and you can proceed as described.

Double click   In the beginning, most users have difficulties with the double-click speed of the mouse. Double clicking means briefly pressing the left mouse button twice in succession. You will need to do this to open folders or to start programs, etc.

Changing the double-click speed of the mouse

In the beginning, if you have difficulties with double clicking, the problem is likely to be that you are not pressing the mouse button rapidly enough. The time between clicks is referred to as the *double-click speed,* and this can be adjusted to suit your needs.

Mouse Properties   Open the *Start* menu and select *Settings*. From the expanded menu, select *Control Panel*. In the *Control Panel* (Figure 8.1) double click on *Mouse* . The *Mouse Properties* dialogue box will appear.

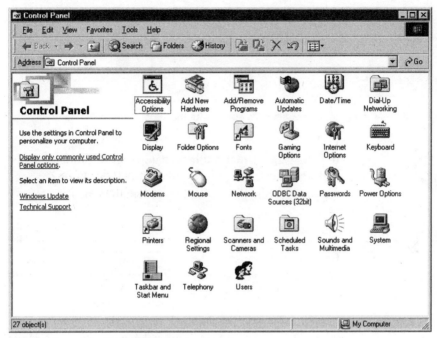

Figure 8.1   The Control Panel

Drag the slide under *double-click speed* in the desired direction, while holding the mouse button pressed (for beginners, move the slide towards *Slow*).

Testing the settings   To test the new settings, double click in the test field on the right side. If you have done the double click correctly, a jack-in-the-box will pop up. Adjust the double-click speed until the jack-in-the-box pops up in the *test field*. Close the dialogue box with *OK*.

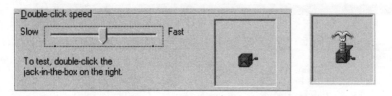

Figure 8.2   Changing the double-click speed with the slide

 If you want to make other changes in the mouse under the other tabs, click *Apply* instead of *OK*. Your changes are saved while the dialogue box remains open.

Setting the mouse button functions

Because the mouse is the most important input device in *Windows Me,* you should ensure that you can work really well with the little electronic rodent.

Left-handers

People who are left-handed have more problems than others in using a mouse. This is because *Windows Me* is set up for right-handed use by default.

Left-handed operations

Of course, it doesn't have to remain that way. You can also set the mouse for left-handed use.

Start / Settings

In the *Start* menu, click on *Settings* and then select *Control Panel* from the expanded menu. In the *Control Panel,* click on the *Mouse* icon.

Tab for *Buttons*

In the *Mouse Properties* dialogue box, click on the Buttons tab. To set the mouse for left-handed use, select the option *Left-handed* under *Button configuration.* Close the dialogue box with a click on *OK.*

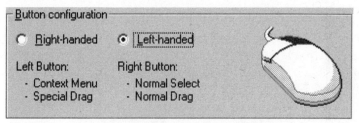

Figure 8.3   Changing the buttons for left-handed use

The new type of mouse with 3 or more buttons and a wheel are supplied with software for customization and programming of the buttons. Some of the applications install these functions in the *Control Panel.*

Working more easily with the mouse

On notebooks which have passive liquid crystal screen displays (LCD display, *DualScan* etc.) it can be difficult to see the mouse pointer and to follow its rapid movement.

Notebook monitors   The problem here is not your eyesight, but rather the slowness of the passive LCD displays. However, *Windows Me* offers a solution to this problem: If you are having difficulty following the mouse pointer in your notebook, open the Start menu, click on *Settings* and select *Control Panel* from the expanded menu. In the *Control Panel,* double click on the *Mouse* icon . In the *Mouse Properties* dialogue box, select *Pointers.*

Displaying pointer trails   Under the *Visibility* options, check *Show pointer trails,* and move your mouse. A little "comet tail" will appear which makes it easier to follow the motion of the pointer.

Pointer speed   If you find the pointer trail too long or too slow, drag the slide next to *Trail length* in the desired direction. Move the mouse again to test the settings. Close the dialogue box with *OK*.

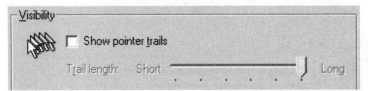

Figure 8.4   Changing the length of the pointer trail

 If you want to make other changes in the mouse settings, click on *Apply* rather than *OK*. Your changes will be saved.

Pointer speed

Under the *Pointer speed* option, you can set the relationship between the movement of the mouse on the mouse pad and the movement of the pointer: If you set the speed on *Slow*, you will need a lot of space for moving the mouse. If it is set at *Fast*, the smallest movement of the mouse causes the maximum movement of the pointer. This makes exact positioning of the mouse more difficult.

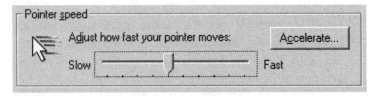

Figure 8.5   Setting the speed of the mouse pointer

Snap to

A special function which is known as *Snap to* makes it easier to use dialogue boxes. Under *Pointers*, select the option *Automatically move pointer to the default button in a dialogue box*. If this is selected, you no longer have to look for the button (this is usually the *OK* button). When a new dialogue box is opened, the mouse pointer automatically jumps to this button, so that in most cases you just need to click on the mouse.

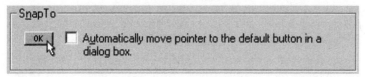

Figure 8.6 Setting automatic positioning of the mouse pointer on the default button

Hiding the mouse pointer

Perhaps you have had this happen: while you are entering text, the pointer lands in a position where it covers the letters. To eliminate this, you can select the option *Hide the pointer while typing.* – after typing, the pointer will appear again as soon as you move the mouse.

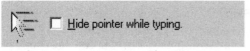

Figure 8.7 Hiding the pointer while typing

Finding the pointer again

If you are working on a large monitor screen, the small mouse pointer can sometimes get completely lost under low contrast. If this function is selected, the loaction of the pointer will be shown when you press the Ctrl key: Under the *Pointers* tab of *Mouse* in the control panel, select *Show location of pointer when you press the CTRL key,* and confirm the setting by clicking on *OK*.

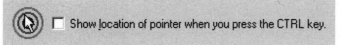

Figure 8.8 Finding the pointer by pressing Ctrl

291

Setting other forms for the pointer

Windows Me responds to each movement of the mouse with a change in the position of the mouse pointer. In addition, when you point to different items, the pointer changes its form automatically. For example, if you point to the edge of a window, the so-called *frame*, the pointer changes to a double-sided arrow ↔, which points to the different directions. If you point to a corner of the window, you will see a diagonal double-sided arrow ↖.

Animated cursors

You can customize the appearance of the pointer or cursor. In the standard installation of *Windows Me,* you can select various cursor sizes – larger cursors are particularly recommended when you are learning to use the mouse. To change the form of the cursor, select *Start/Settings/Control Panel*. Double click on the *Mouse* icon ◗, and the dialogue box *Mouse properties* will appear.

Pointer tab

Click on the *Pointer* tab. Open the combo box *Scheme* by clicking on the arrow, and select an entry. This large list displays all cursor forms contained in the scheme, with their meaning. Using the slide, scroll through the list to see all the cursor forms.

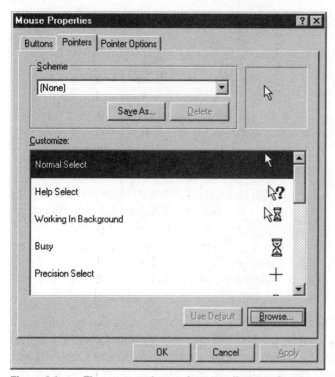

Figure 8.9   The cursor scheme changes all cursor forms

Pointer scheme

The selected cursor scheme changes all cursor forms in *Windows Me*. If you are satisfied with the change, click on *OK*. If you want to change the individual cursor forms, first select the basic scheme from the list.

Browse button

In the list, mark the cursor which is to be changed and click on the *Browse* button. In the *Browse* dialogue box, all cursors available under *Windows Me* are displayed. Click to select the desired cursor form.

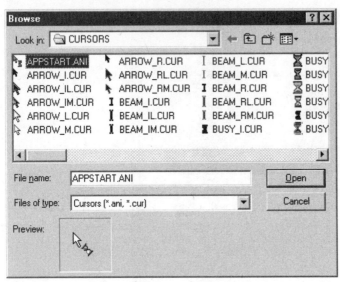

Figure 8.10   Every cursor can be changed

When you confirm the selection with *Open*, the cursor
marked in the list will be used. Repeat these steps for all
cursors which are to be changed. When you are finished,
close the dialogue box with *OK*.

Static *Windows* cursors have the file extension *CUR* and
are found in the folder *C:\Windows\Cursors*. The animated cursors which can be recognized by the file extension *ANI* are particularly interesting.

If you select an animated cursor, you can see a preview
of the cursor motion in the *Browse* dialogue box.

If you have an internet connection, you can find new
cursor schemes in the World Wide Web. You just have to
browse through shareware archives to find cursor
schemes or desktop schemes.

Setting Keyboard Properties

The keyboard is the most important element of the computer for text entry. For this reason, it is particularly important to customize the keyboard to suit your needs. Unfortunately, very few computer users ever consider this point, and they work for the entire life of their computer with the default settings of *Windows Me.*

Keyboard icon

You need to go to the *Control Panel* of *Windows* to configure your keyboard. Click on the *Start* button and select *Settings.* In the expanded menu, click on *Control Panel.* In the *Control Panel* double click on the *Keyboard* icon.

Setting the character repeat of the keyboard

Speed tab

By selecting the *Speed* tab, you can adjust the basic settings to suit your requirements.

Under *Repeat delay,* drag the slide between *Long* and *Short* to set the time after which a character is repeated, when you hold the key pressed.

Increasing the repeat rate

Repeat rate slide

Move the slide between *Long* and *Short* under *Repeat rate* to set the rate at which a character is repeated when you hold a key pressed. Test the settings by clicking in the text box below it, and pressing a key. Confirm the setting with *OK.*

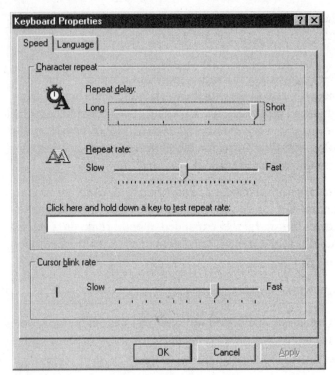

Figure 8.11   Setting the *Repeat delay* and *Repeat rate* of the keyboard

Setting the blink rate for the text cursor

You need to go to the *Control Panel* of *Windows* to configure the blink rate of the text cursor. Select
Start/Settings/Control Panel. In the *Control Panel* click
on the *Keyboard* icon 📖.

Speed tab

Under the *Speed* tab, adjust the basic settings to suit your
needs. Move the slide under *Cursor blink rate* to adjust
the blink interval of the text cursor. The selected cursor
blink rate can be checked in the box to the left of the
slide.

Cursor in texts

Changing the blink rate makes it easier to find the cursor in texts. Confirm your changes with *OK*.

Language settings for the keyboard

The keyboard is the most important medium for text entry. Therefore, there is a different keyboard for almost every language. This has come about partially for historical reasons, and partially because different languages use different characters and symbols.

For example, there are no umlauts on American keyboards; eastern languages have an entirely different set of characters, and Turkish keyboards do not have much in common with German keyboards – other than the number of keys.

Setting keyboard language

In *Windows Me,* the keyboard layout is called *Language.* Go to the *Control Panel* of Window to configure the keyboard language. Click on the *Start* button, point to *Settings* and select *Control Panel* from the expanded menu. In the *Control Panel,* click on the *Keyboard* icon 🔳.

Language tab

Under the *Language* tab, you can set the language, if you need to use the keyboard layout of another language. The language currently in use is shown in the list box under *Language.*

If you want to set a new keyboard layout, click on *Add...,* select the desired language and click on *OK*.

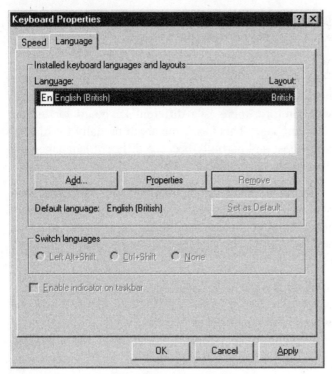

Figure 8.12   Setting the keyboard language

New layout

The new layout is displayed in the *Language* list. Under *Switch languages*, select the shortcut to be used to switch keyboards, and check *Enable indicator on taskbar*. Confirm with *OK*.

If you need to use the keyboard for the new language you have set, either press the key combination which was selected or click on the language indicator in the taskbar. Select the desired language from the menu.

Keyboard and keyboard layout must always be thought of as a double act. Adding the layout of another language can be confusing if you continue to use an English language keyboard. You will have great difficulty in finding the characters of the new language on an English keyboard.

Managing System Fonts

In *Windows Me* there are two different types of system fonts: one is the so-called *Bitmap* fonts, the other is the more useful *TrueType Fonts*.

Bitmap fonts

The *Bitmap* fonts are raster fonts which, for each font size, require a file with the font information for each character. Bitmap fonts, like pixel images, consist of individual dots which when printed out, look like steps Therefore, these are mostly used as screen fonts.

TrueType fonts

TrueType fonts are freely scalable vector fonts for which the mathematical function of the outline is stored in the font file. In *Windows*, fonts of all sized can be created .

The *WYSIWYG* principle

The great advantage of the *TrueType* fonts is that what you see on the screen looks exactly the same when printed out — this is the *WYSIWYG* "what you see is what you get" principle. The quality of *TrueType* fonts is also better than that of bitmap fonts, and it is independent of the font size.

Displaying installed *TrueType* fonts

Fonts folder

To display a list of the fonts installed on your computer, go to the *Control Panel* and click on the *Fonts* icon. In the *Fonts* folder, all installed fonts are displayed as special icons. For scaleable *TrueType* fonts, the double-T icon is used. Bitmap fonts are displayed with the icon: A.

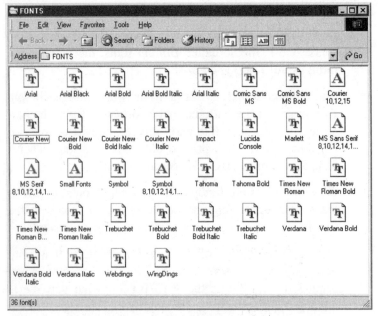

Figure 8.13   Displaying available *Windows* fonts

You can change the display of the *Fonts* folder in the *View* menu, using the usual commands. The *View* command is also available through the context menu of the right mouse button.

Similar fonts

In Figure 8.13 you see the *Large icons* view. When you select the *Details* view, you get additional information on the name of the font file, file size and file date. Later on, we will look at the view called *Display by similarity*. The *List* view is the most practical if there are many fonts installed.

The fonts displayed can be used in all other *Windows* applications. Many applications (e.g. *Microsoft Office 2000* or *CorelDraw!*) install additional *TrueType* fonts.

Sorting fonts by similarity

To display a list of available fonts, go to *Control Panel* and click on the *Fonts* icon.

In the *Fonts* folder, all installed fonts are displayed in the form of special icons. Scaleable *TrueType* fonts are displayed with the double-T icon [T], and bitmap fonts can be recognized by this icon: [A].

Similar fonts

This view can be selected in the *View* menu using the usual commands, and through the context menu using *Display similar fonts*, or by clicking on the button *Similarity* [AB].

This will display a list of all installed fonts which are similar to the selected font displayed in the list box, *List fonts by similarity to:* To change the font to be compared, open the list box *List fonts by similarity to:* and select another font from the list.

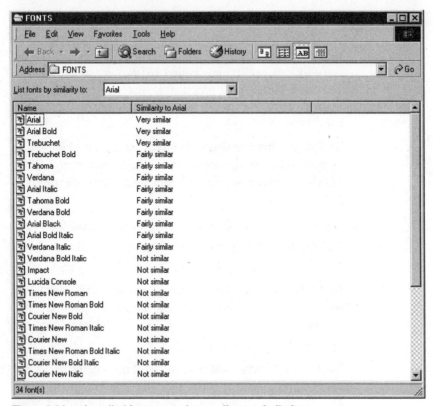

Figure 8.14   Installed fonts sorted according to similarity

Similarity rating

After the font name in the large list, there are ratings such as *Very similar, Fairly similar* and *Not similar*. For example, if you compare the font *Arial* which has no serif to the font *Times New Roman* with serif, you will see the rating: *Not similar*. This view enables users who are not familiar with fonts to get a basic comparison of the fonts.

Printing a sample of installed fonts

Many *Windows* applications contain their own *TrueType* fonts, which are installed during the set-up. The graphics package, *CorelDraw* contains 1000 *TrueType* fonts!

Even in *Microsoft Office* there are some *TrueType* fonts which are automatically installed.

Hundreds of fonts   After some time, you will find that there are hundreds of fonts installed on your computer. At this point, it is difficult even for pros to get an overview of the appearance of the fonts.

For this reason, modern graphics applications give you a preview with a font sample.

No preview   For the applications integrated into *Windows Me* you do not have the advantage of a preview (with the exception of the font preview under *Format* in *Microsoft Word 2000*).

However, *Windows Me* does offer you a sample of the installed fonts, which can be printed out if desired.

***Fonts* icon**   To see a sample, open the *Control Panel* through *Start/Settings* or through *My Computer*. Click on the *Fonts* icon , to open the *Fonts* folder.

A list of all installed fonts is displayed. You can change the display to *Large icons*, etc. through the *View* menu.

Figure 8.15   Displaying or printing a font sample

Font sample

You can easily see a sample of an unknown font by double clicking on the font icon or the font name. Alternatively, for a selected font, you can use the *Open...* command from the *File* menu or context menu.

The font sample with the sample text "The quick brown fox jumps over the lazy dog 1234567890" is displayed in a window. You can enlarge the window or use the scroll bars.

Printing a font sample

By clicking on the *Close* button, you return to the *Fonts* folder. Click on *Print*, if you want to print the sample. The *Print...* command is also available without a font sample in the context menu or in the *File* menu.

Installing new *TrueType* fonts

At the beginning, we spoke about the use of *TrueType* fonts. *TrueType*-Fonts are freely scaleable vector fonts, for which only the mathematical function of the outline needs to be saved in the fonts file. This saves disk space and also allows display of all font sizes without loss of quality.

Many applications contain their own *TrueType* fonts which can be installed in the set-up.

The graphics package *CorelDraw* contains 1000 *TrueType* fonts, and even the *Microsoft Office set-up CD* contains some *TrueType* fonts. If you want to install other fonts, you can theoretically just copy the font files into a special folder on your computer. There is, however, another– official – method for this.

Installing new fonts
For *Windows Me* and its applications to be able to use the new fonts, go to the *Control Panel* from *Start/Settings* or from *My Computer*. Click on the *Fonts* icon 🄰, to open the *Fonts* folder.

Adding fonts
From the *File* menu, select *Install new font....* In the dialogue box *Add fonts...* use the list box *Drives* and *Folders* to change the source drive and folder which contain the new fonts.

Windows Me then reads all fonts available in the browsed folder, and adds them to the *List of fonts*.

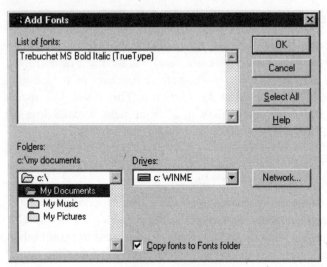

Figure 8.16   Installing new fonts in *Windows Me*

Installation

Mark the desired font(s) (for multiple selection, use the keys ⬆ or Ctrl). Using the *Select all* button, select all files displayed in the *List of fonts*. To install the fonts, press *OK*. Check the contents of the *Fonts* folder for the newly installed fonts.

Please ensure that the option *Copy fonts to Fonts folder* is checked, so that the fonts will be saved in the folder *C:\Windows\Fonts*.

Removing unnecessary *TrueType* fonts

After some time, there will be hundreds of fonts on your computer. Every font file uses up disk space and must be read by the *Windows* start.

Deleting fonts

If you only work with certain fonts, you can delete the unnecessary fonts from your hard disk at any time.

Unnecessary fonts should not be deleted from your computer simply by using *Windows Explorer* or the system folder *My Computer*. There are two reasons for this:

Font file names

For one thing, it is not possible to find a font such as *Futura MD BT* under a file name such as *TT1024M_.TTF*. In addition, the shortcut from this file to the *Fonts* folder should be removed. So that *Windows Me* and its applications will no longer display these fonts, go to the *Control Panel* through *Start/ Settings*.

List view

Click on the *Fonts* icon 🖋, to open the *Fonts* folder. If there are many fonts, change to the *List* view. Select the font(s) to be deleted (for multiple selection use the selection rectangle of the mouse, or the keys ⬆ or Ctrl).

Removal of Fonts

To remove a font, press Del or use the *Delete* command in the *File* menu or context menu. Confirm the deletion with *Yes*, and the fonts will be moved to the *Recycle bin*.

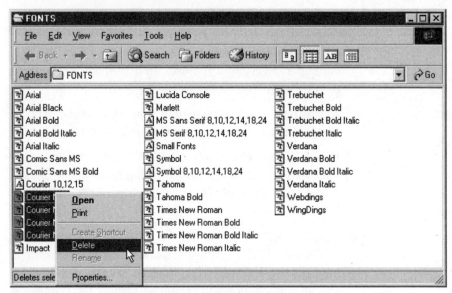

Figure 8.17   Removing unnecessary *TrueType* fonts

To completely delete the fonts from the *Fonts* folder and therefore free up disk space, empty the *Recycle bin*. More information on this can be found in Chapter 6.

Displaying only *TrueType* fonts in applications

Freely scalable

Windows Me uses two different types of fonts: One is the *Bitmap* fonts, and the other is the more useful *TrueType* fonts. *TrueType fonts* are freely scaleable vector fonts for which only the mathematical function of the outline needs to be stored in the fonts file.

Better quality

Windows Me can create fonts in any size from a font file. The greatest advantage of a *TrueType* font 🔠 is that it will be printed out exactly as it appears on the screen (the *WYSIWYG* principle: *What You See Is What You Get*). The quality of the *TrueType* fonts is better than that of

Bitmap fonts, and it is also completely independent of the font size.

Pixel images

Bitmap fonts $\boxed{\text{A}}$ are raster fonts, for which a file with font information for each character must be available for each font size. Like pixel images, *Bitmap* fonts are composed of individual dots which look like steps when printed, and are therefore more suitable for use as screen fonts.

Using only
TrueType fonts

We recommend that you use only the *TrueType* fonts which are more flexible and of better quality. To avoid making mistakes later on, you can limit the display of *Fonts* in the fonts list of various *Windows* applications to *TrueType* fonts. To do this, you need to use the *Control Panel*.

TrueType tab

Select *Start/Settings/Control Panel,* and in the *Control Panel* select the *Fonts* icon $\boxed{\text{A}}$. In the *Fonts* folder, all available fonts are displayed. From the *Extras* menu, select the option *Folder options*, and click on the tab *TrueType*.

Only TrueType
fonts

Check the box, *Display only TrueType fonts*, and confirm with *OK*. Thereafter, *Windows Me* will not display bitmap fonts in any *Windows* applications. Instead, you will only see a list of the installed *TrueType fonts* $\boxed{\text{T}}$ in the fonts lists.

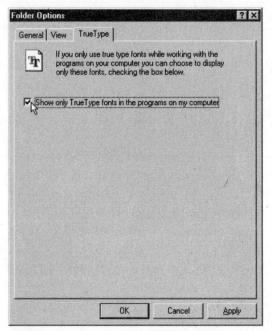

Figure 8.18   Displaying *TrueType* fonts in applications

The changes are only effective after the system is re-started. Confirm the message by pressing *Yes* to restart the system.

Setting the Windows Desktop Display

You've probably already noticed this: The colorful world of *Windows* is even more colorful on the computers of your friends and colleagues. There is probably no other setting which is so strongly influenced by a person's own particular working conditions as the *Windows* desktop.

Changing the *Windows* background color

Scheme list

The *Control Panel*, which you open through *Start/Settings* or *My Computer,* is responsible for the appearance of the screen. Click on the *Display* icon , and select the *Appearance* tab. It is simplest to change all colors at once: To do this, you open the *Scheme* list and select one of the entries shown there.

Figure 8.19   Changing the appearance of *Windows Me*

Item list box

The changes are shown in the upper part of the dialogue box. If you want to keep the settings, click on the *Apply* button. Almost every screen element can also be changed individually. First, select a basic scheme from the *Scheme* list. Then, in the upper area of the dialogue box, click on the item you wish to change. The name of the element is then also displayed in the *Item* list box. You can also select the item directly through the list box. The description of the element gives you a bit of background information, so that you will understand which element is being referred to.

Possible
Settings

The following other settings – depending on the screen element selected – can be made:

■ the *Size* of an element in points

■ the *Color* and *Color 2* (second color) of an element can be selected from a pallette after clicking on *Other...*

■ The *Font*, *Size* and *Color* as well as *Bold* or *Italic* for menus, dialogue boxes, and title bars, etc.

Saving the scheme

After making the desired changes in the elements, click on *Apply*. Some colors can be saved in the *Scheme* list with *Save as....* Enter a unique name and confirm with *OK*. Exit the properties window with *OK* and close the *Control Panel*.

The *Start* menu can be indirectly changed through the display options. By selecting the item *Menu* and changing the *Font* and font *Size*, you can make the items in the *Start* menu larger or smaller. These changes also affect all other *Windows* menus.

Changing the Desktop Background

The default W*indows* desktop background which appears on your screen is blue in color. As you have seen on other computers, you can change this.

Background tab   To change the background, open the *Control Panel* through *Start/Settings*. Click on the *Display* icon 🖳, and select the tab for *Background*.

The small stylized monitor which gives you a preview of your changes displays only a green color at first .

Background picture   If you want to use a background picture, use the scroll bar to browse through the *Background picture* list and select one of the entries shown there.

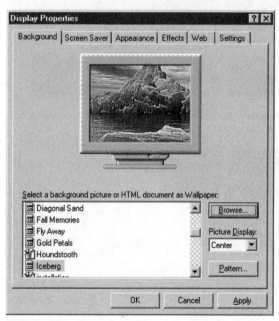

Figure 8.20   **Selecting a background picture for the desktop**

Check the result in the preview. If you only see a small field in the middle, click on the arrow under *Picture display:* and select the entry *Tile*.

Pixel images

Windows Me now creates copies of the bitmaps next to one another in rows. The pixel images are set up in such a way that a homogeneous pattern is created. For larger bitmaps (e.g. *Setup*), you can select the entry *Centered* which displays the background picture surrounded by a border of another color.

Your own backgrounds

You can select your own background in *Bitmap* (*BMP*), *GIF, HTM-* or *JPG format* by clicking on the *Browse...* button.

Figure 8.21   Selection of a background file

Large background pictures can take up a lot of disk space. Therefore, the *Display* list under *Background* also offers the option *Stretch*.

Stretch

Use this option to stretch smaller background pictures so that they will fill the screen even at high resolution. However, with small pictures, the quality may suffer. Confirm your changes with *OK*, and then close the *Control Panel*.

Setting the size of the system fonts

The labels in the title bars, menus, dialogue boxes and messages depend on the settings made under *Control Panel/Display/Appearance*, as well as on the system fonts which the graphics card used for font display. This option can also be set under *Control Panel* and *Display* 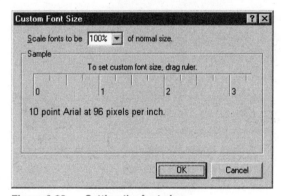, but under a different tab.

List of

font sizes

In the *Control Panel*, click on the *Display* icon and select the *Settings* tab. Click on the *Advanced...* button and then select the *General* tab. From the list of *Font sizes,* you can set the font size used by *Windows* for texts. Settings made under *Advanced...* may result in errors in the display in some applications.

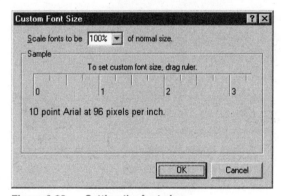

Figure 8.22   Setting the font size

Large and small fonts

In the list of *Font sizes,* you can normally choose between *Large* and *Small fonts.* Click on *Other...,* if you want to make individual settings for the font size.

Preview

To change the font size (Figure 8.22) place the pointer on the ruler and drag it to the left or to the right. The effective percentage is shown in the text field above the ruler. A preview which simulates the enlargement (values above 100 %) or the reduction (values less than 100%) is shown directly over the ruler. Confirm your selection with *OK.*

Restarting Windows

Under *Compatibility,* you can choose whether a restart of *Windows Me* is necessary to change the display. The setting *Restart the computer before applying new color settings* is only necessary with older graphics cards. If your graphics card supports display changes without restarting, select the option *Apply new color settings without restarting.* In this case, when making changes, you only need to confirm the dialogue with click on *OK* and if necessary, confirm the next dialogue with *Yes.*

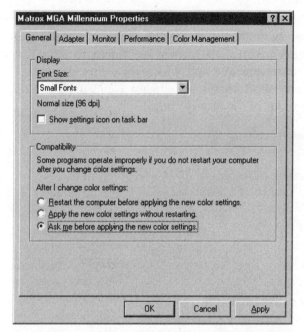

Figure 8.23   Applying new display settings with or without restarting

Setting the icon spacing in folder windows

Whenever you want to organize your desktop or any folders, open the *View* menu or the context menu and select *Line up icons* or *Arrange icons/ Auto arrange*.

Invisible grid

In both cases, *Windows Me* to arranges the icons in the *Large icons* view on an invisible grid. In doing this, different horizontal and vertical spacing is used.

Individual

icon spacing

For some users, the distance between the icons is too large; others dislike the incomplete descriptions ending in three dots (ellipsis). Fortunately, this can be changed. There is a well-hidden function which is responsible for setting the icon spacing:

Open the *Control Panel* with *Start/Settings* or through *My Computer*. Then click on the *Display* icon 🖥, and select the *Appearance* tab. There is a miniature desktop at the top of the dialogue box, which gives a preview of the appearance of all important window elements. The icon spacing is one of the these settings.

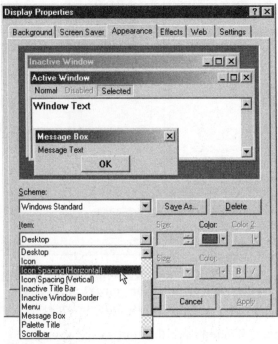

Figure 8.24   Changing icon spacing

Changing the icon spacing

To change the icon spacing, open the *Item* list and scroll through it until you reach the entry *Icon Spacing (Horizontal/Vertical)*. You need to set the icon spacing separately for the horizontal and in the vertical directions.

Horizontal / Vertical   Click on the entry *Icon Spacing (Horizontal/Vertical)* and enter the new spacing in pixels in the adjacent *Size* text box. Check your settings by clicking on Apply. If you want to keep the settings, confirm with *OK*, close the *Control Panel*.

Graphics Card and Screen Settings

The screen resolution in the horizontal and vertical directions is given in pixels. For example, for 640 X 480 pixels, the *Windows*-Desktops is displayed using 640 pixels in the width and 480 pixels in the height. The ratio is taken from the height/width ratio of the monitor. A screen resolution of 1024 X 768 pixels will display two and one half times the amount of information on the screen.

Higher resolution   With a higher resolution, more windows can be arranged next to one another on the desktop. In applications, you will see more of the document.

Figure 8.25   The higher the resolution, the more information can be displayed on the screen

Setting the screen resolution

Reference values

The screen resolution should not be set independently of the size of the monitor. On a 15-inch monitor, you may barely be able to read the titles on the windows/menus, since this monitor has a diagonal of only 38 cm. On a 17-inch monitor, the visible screen area has a 43-cm. diagonal. You can experiment with various screen resolutions, keeping in mind the following reference values:

- 14-inch monitor (34 cm)   640 x 480 pixels

- 15-inch monitor (38 cm)   800 x 600 pixels

- 17-inch monitor (43 cm)   1024 x 768 pixels

- 19-inch monitor (48 cm)   1280 x 1024 pixels

Changing screen resolution

To change the screen resolution, open the *Control Panel* and click on the *Display* icon 🖥. Select the *Settings* **tab**.

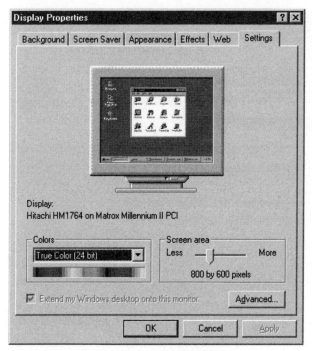

Figure 8.26   Setting the screen resolution

Resolution slide   Drag the slide under *Screen area* to the left or right, until the desired resolution in pixels is displayed (example: *1024 x 768 Pixel*).

Now, click on *OK*. If the color intensity is not changed, you will receive a message as shown at the top of Figure 8.27 which informs you that the resolution has been changed. Confirm the changes with *OK*.

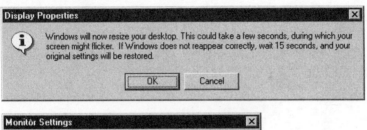

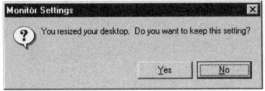

Figure 8.27   Messages before changing the resolution

If *Windows Me* is not able to set the new resolution within 10 to 15 seconds, the old settings will be restored. In this case, confirm the message with *OK* and try another resolution.

Message

If the new resolution can be set, the color depth may be different. If this is this case, you will receive the message at the bottom of Figure 8.27. If you want to keep the new setting, confirm the message with *Yes* within 15 seconds.

When the resolution is changed, sometimes the color depth *(color palette)* is automatically changed. The resolutions available vary with the chip of your graphics card and your monitor, and the color depth depends on the resolution and the memory of the graphics card. Caution: incorrect settings can damage or ruin the monitor! Make sure that the correct and latest driver for the graphics card and the monitor is installed.

Setting the color intensity of the screen display

The *Color depth* is number of colors which can be simultaneously displayed on the monitor, in connection with the screen and graphics card settings. The color depth depends on the performance and the memory of the graphics card as well as on the monitor resolution which is set.

True Color
color depth

For display of the VGA resolution you need about 1 MB of graphics card memory. With this, you can display the *TrueColor* color depth with 16.8 million simultaneously displayed colors. With a resolution of 1024 X 768 pixels, and a 1 MB graphics card memory, you can only display 256 colors. For TrueColor color depth with a resolution of 1024 X 768 pixels, you need 4 MB of graphics card memory. Modern graphics cards usually have about 16 to 32 MB memory, so this isn't usually a problem any more.

Changing the color
depth

To change the color depth, click on the *Display* icon in *Control panel*. In the *Properties* window, click on the *Settings* tab. Open the *Color* list and select the desired item with a click of the mouse. Possible settings are *16 colors, 256 colors, High color (16 Bit)* = 65536 colors, *True Color (24 Bit)* = 16.8 million colors and possibly also *True Color (32 Bit)* = 4 billion colors. The values which are possible depend on your graphics card, and the values which can be set depend on the resolution.

Color palette

If your graphics card cannot display the selected *color palette* in the current resolution, *Windows* automatically lowers the value of the resolution shown under *Screen area*. Confirm with *OK*, and you will be – depending on the settings you made under *Advanced/General/ Compatibility* – asked to restart the computer. The color depth takes effect after you restart the computer. Otherwise respond to the message which appears by clicking on *OK*.

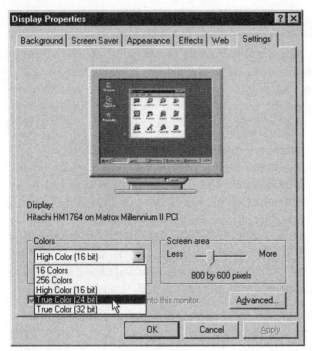

Figure 8.28   Setting other colors

 For a realistic color display you need the TrueColor color depth with 24-bits which can display up to 16.8 million colors simultaneously. With lower settings, you will not obtain such professional results in picture editing. If necessary, you can also use the *High Color (16-bit)* setting, but don't use the *256 colors*.

Installing new graphics card drivers

Next to the processors, the computer components which are the most short-lived are the graphics cards, at least if you always want to have the optimum display speed. Each graphics card has its own graphics card driver, which we will now discuss. If you change the graphics card, you must also change the driver.

Faulty drivers

You must also change the graphics card driver, if the driver causes errors in particular applications or if the screen display is not optimal. Sometimes a newer driver can also greatly improve the performance of the graphics card..

You will find the graphics card driver in the box with the graphics card (or the new PC), on a floppy disk or CD-ROM. If you want to find a newer version of your driver, you should visit the manufacturer's internet website. In the downloads section, look for your graphics card type and download the latest version of the driver.

Display **icon**

If you want to manually change the graphics card driver, open the *Control Panel* with (*Start/Settings* or through *My Computer*). In the *Control Panel,* double click on the *Display* icon 🖥.

Changing the configuration

Click on the *Settings* tab, and press *Advanced....* In the following dialogue box, click on the tab for the *Graphics card*. This displays the installed graphics card driver, manufacturer and version.

Figure 8.29   Current settings of the graphics card

Selecting the model   Click on *Change...*, to start the *Update driver wizard.* Specify whether or not you want the wizard to search for the driver. To search manually, select the option *Specify a location...* and then click on *Next.* In the next step, specify where *Windows* should search for the driver, i.e. on a CD-ROM or in your downloads folder. If you don't want to have the driver detected automatically, select the option *Display a list of drivers in a specific location, so you can select the driver yourself. Windows Me* loads a database with driver information, and in the next step, it displays all compatible drivers which have been installed on your system.

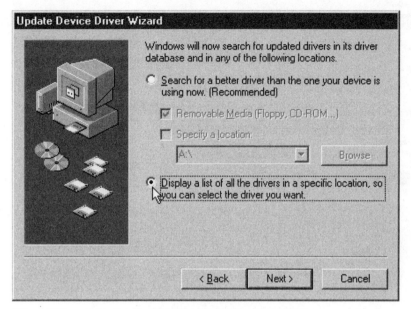

Figure 8.30 Selecting the graphics card driver from a list

To change the driver, select an entry and click on *Next*. You can see a list of all drivers after selecting the option *Show all hardware*.

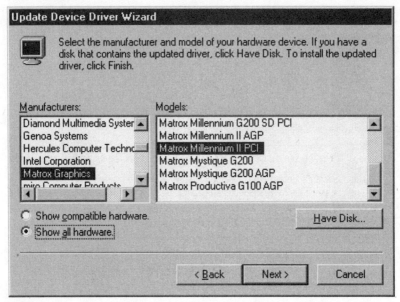

Figure 8.31   Searching for the model and manufacturer of the graphics card

New graphics card

Next, select the *Manufacturer* and the *Model* from the list. If you have a driver update on a manufacturer's disk or on a CD-ROM, click on the *Have disk...* button. In the In the field *Copy manufacturer's files from:* enter the drive and the folder where the information files for the driver are located. Confirm with *OK*.

Browse

Press the *Browse...* button, mark the INF file and confirm with OK. In the *Select* device dialogue box, select the type of your graphics card and confirm with *OK*.

New graphics card driver

The new graphics card driver and information available on it are displayed under the options group *Graphics card*. Confirm all dialogue boxes which are open, to apply your changes.

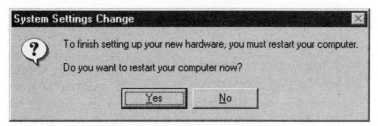

Figure 8.32   Changes take effect after restarting

Restart   You will now see a message requesting you to restart the computer. Click on *Yes*. If the files have not yet been saved, a dialogue will appear in which you can save the files. Check the appearance, the resolution and color depth of *Windows Me* after restarting.

If there are problems with the new driver, you will see a message with the corresponding information. After confirming this, a properties window with *Settings* automatically appears.

Repeat the steps above for selecting another driver.

The *Wizard* automatically detects whether the driver to be installed is really more up to date that the on which is already installed. If necessary, select *Cancel*.

Setting up another monitor type

Correct monitor   For *Plug & Play* monitors, *Windows* automatically detects the manufacturer and model and enters the device data into the *Control Panel*. What do you do when you don't have a *Plug & Play* monitor, or when you have purchased a computer with pre-installed *Windows Me*?

329

Incorrect operating parameters

In this section you will learn why you must install the correct monitor under *Windows Me*, and how to select another model of monitor. Even if there seems to be no problem with your monitor at first glance, you should still read through this section in detail. Incorrect monitor installation can have two consequences: the first is that the monitor can be damaged with incorrect operating parameters, or it can even be ruined.

Refresh rate

The second reason is that in *Windows Me*, the screen refresh rate is set according to the model of the monitor installed. If you have a monitor with lower performance, you will be working with an non-ergonometric refresh rate. This can be recognized by a flickering of the screen which is damaging to the eyes..

Checking the monitor model

To check the monitor model, open the *Control Panel* through *Start/ Settings* and click on the *Display* icon 🖳. Select the *Settings* tab and click on the *Advanced* button. In the next dialogue box, select the *Monitor* tab. The installed monitor and its energy-saving options are displayed. If the name and type of your monitor are displayed, then everything is OK. Just press *Cancel* and *OK,* and close the *Control Panel.*

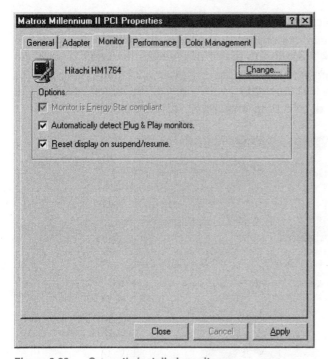

Figure 8.33   Currently installed monitor

| Changing the monitor | If the entry does not correspond to your monitor, click on *Change...*, to start the *Driver update wizard* and click on *Next*. |
| Manual search | For a manual search, select *Specify a location (Advanced)* and then press *Next*. In the next step, select the option *Display a list of drivers in a specific location, so you can select the driver yourself*. In the next step, *Windows Me* displays all compatible drivers which have been installed on your system. |

Manufacturer and model

Select the option *Show all hardware*. In the list of *Manufacturers*, select the brand of your monitor and then look through the list of *Models* for the type. If you find your manufacturer but not the model, select the monitor which is closest to your model. If the manufacturer is not listed, select the first entry *(Standard Monitor types)*.

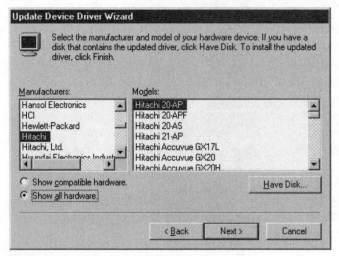

Figure 8.34   Selecting manufacturer and model

Maximum resolution

In the list of *Models*, set the maximum resolution given in the monitor manual, e.g. *Super-VGA 1280 x 1024*. Confirm this with *OK*, and the display will change. If the screen cannot be correctly displayed, repeat the configuration with another model from the list *(Standard monitor types)*.

Have disk... **button**

For a *Plug & Play* monitor, select the Plug & Play entry. Monitor information will be read from the floppy disk or CD when you press *Have disk...*, e.g. when you have downloaded a current driver from the internet. Confirm the *Update driver wizard* with *OK* and close the *Control Panel*.

Setting and displaying a screen saver

In many companies, computers are often left running day and night, even if they are actually in use only for a part of the time. The screen lighting elements of *Windows* can damage the monitor display after some time, if the screen content does not change.

Screen saver

For this reason, screen savers were created, which inactivate the screen display after a set time. This prevents the burn-in of static screen displays. *Windows Me* also contains some screen savers, however the protection of your monitor tube is deactivated by default. To activate a screen saver, go to the *Control Panel* and double click on the *Display* icon. In the *Properties* window, click on the tab for *Screen savers*.

Preview

Open the list of *Screen savers*, and select one of the entries offered there. In the stylized monitor in the upper part of the dialogue box, you can see a preview of the screen saver you have selected.

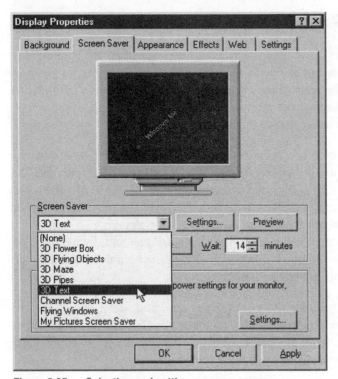

Figure 8.35   Selecting and setting a screen saver

Testing

If you want to see the screen saver in full format, click on the *Test* button. As soon as you move the mouse again, you will return to the *Properties* window.

Waiting time

In the *Wait* field, you can set the time after which your screen saver is activated, when you are not working on the computer.

Settings

Using the *Settings...* button under *Screen saver* you can individually configure a screen saver. When you have made all the settings you need, close the dialogue box with *OK* and exit the *Control Panel*.

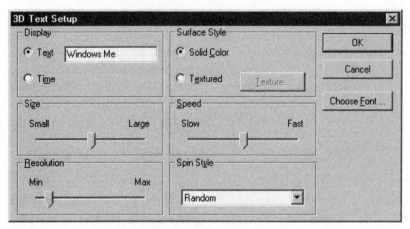

Figure 8.36   Screen saver configuration window

 In place of a screen saver, an energy saving function is activated after the standard installation of Windows. This switches off the monitor after a long period of inactivity. You can find this function in *Power options* under the *Power schemes* tab.

Installing and setting up a printer

To enable *Windows Me* to always print correctly from a multitude of applications, a driver must be installed for the printer. In *Windows Me*, drivers for most printers have already been installed. In any case, you will find the appropriate printer driver packed with you printer, or on the manufacturer's website.

Installing the printer

New printer

New printers can be installed at any time. *Windows Me* copies the necessary driver program which transmits and controls the printing of data. To install a printer, select *Start/Settings/Printers* or go to the control panel and select the *Printers* icon 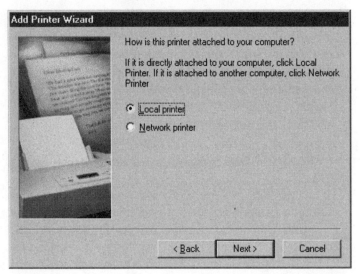. In the *Printers* folder, select the icon for *New printer*, to start the *Add Printer Wizard*. In the start window of the wizard, click on *Next* to continue.

Select
manufacturer

In the second step, you are asked whether the printer is directly connected to your printer. For a stand-alone computer, select *Local printer* and confirm again with *Next*.

Figure 8.37   A *Local printer* is directly connected to your computer

Next, a dialogue box appears where you can select the *Manufacturer* and the model of the printer.

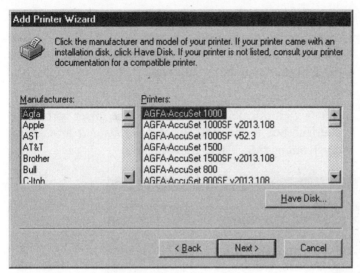

Figure 8.38 *Add printer wizard*

Selecting the model — From the list of *Manufacturers*, select the correct entry. To see the other entries, use the scroll bar or enter the first few letters of the manufacturer's name. In the *Printer* list on the right side, you will see all available models for the selected manufacturer. Select your printer model and confirm with *Next* .

If you don't find your manufacturer and the model in the list, you need to have a floppy disk or CD-ROM from the manufacturer, and you must press the *Have disk...* button.

Most manufacturers also make their printer drivers available for downloading from the internet. Just download the appropriate program archive onto your computer and unzip it. in the In the *Add printer wizard* you can find the new driver by clicking on *Have disk...*

Determining the printer port

In the next step, select *LPT1: Printer port* from the list of *Available ports* and confirm with *Next*. Under *Printer name* you can give your new printer any name you like, or you can accept the default name.

Default printer

If this is your only printer, or if you want to print in preference with this device, click *Yes* in the lower part of the dialogue box to make the printer the *Default printer under Windows Me*. Then, click on *Next*.

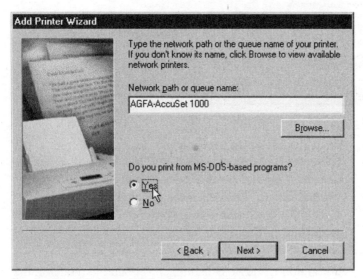

Figure 8.39   Setting the printer as default printer

Now, you can print out a test page. If you want to do this, click on *Yes (recommended)*, wait for the print and answer the question in the dialogue box as to whether or not the printing was satisfactory .

Copying a driver

If you do not want to do a test printing, click on *No* and *Finish. Windows Me* copies the driver into its internal files. Now, the symbol for the printer is displayed in the *Printers* folder.

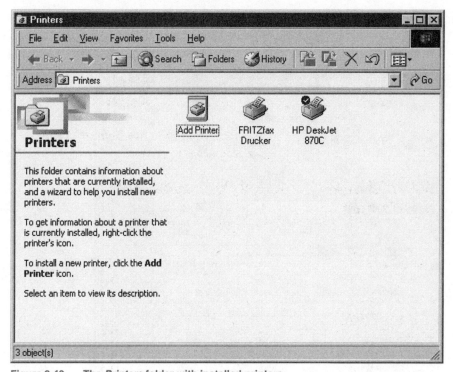

Figure 8.40   The *Printers* folder with installed printers

Setting the printer properties

After the printer has been installed, *Windows Me* uses the default settings of the printer driver. For the printer to function correctly, is useful to customize the properties of the printer driver to suit your needs. You can view and change these settings in the *Printers* folder.

Properties

First, select *Start/Settings/Printers* or open the control panel and select the for *Printers* icon 🖨. Highlight the symbol for your printer. In the *File* menu, click on *Properties*. The settings which can be changed under the various tabs of *Properties of [Printer name]* depend on your

printer model. Click on the different tabs to get an overview of the options which are available.

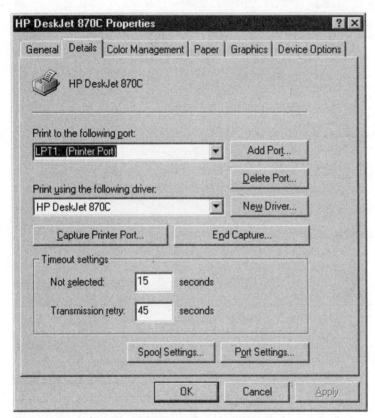

Figure 8.41   Checking the port settings for the printer

Printing a test page   To check that your printer is functioning correctly, select
the *General* tab and then click on *Print test page*. The
Printer port can be seen and changed on the *Details* tab,
in the list *Print to the following port.* You can check the
current driver in the list *Print using the following driver.*

You can get help on an item by clicking on the *Help* icon **?** on the title bar, and then clicking on the item.

Changing the printer properties changes the properties for all documents which you print with this printer. You can change the settings for an individual document by clicking on the *File* menu in the application being used, selecting the entry *Page setup...* and making the appropriate changes in the dialogue box which appears.

Installing a new printer driver

The quality of the printing is directly connected to the performance of the installed printer driver. During installation, if you find the manufacturer and type of your printer in the list boxes, there are usually no problems. However, that may not be the case if you have installed a similar model or if you manufacturer has the current driver on a disk or online.

Changing the printer driver

To change the printer driver, you need to open the *Printers* folder. Select *Start/Settings/ Printer*. Highlight the symbol for the printer you are using.

In the *File* menu, click on *Properties*. Select the *Details* tab and click on the button for *New driver*. Confirm the message which appears with *Yes*.

List of Manufacturers

In the list of *Manufacturers*, mark the appropriate entry. To view the other entries, use the scroll bars or enter the first few letters of the manufacturer's name. In the *Printers* list, you will see all available printer drivers for the selected manufacturer. Select your printer model and confirm with *OK*.

If you do not find the manufacturer and model in the list, you need to have the floppy disk or CD-ROM from the manufacturer. This will be read when you press *Have disk...* Even drivers which have been downloaded from the internet are installed in this manner.

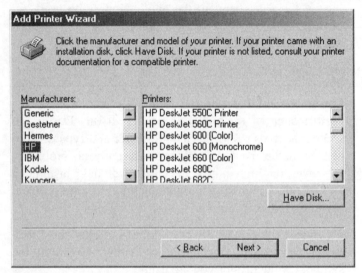

Figure 8.42   Changing drivers for printing

Internet

Select the *Have disk...* button if you have an updated driver on a disk, or if you have downloaded a copy from an online service or the internet into a folder on your hard disk. Enter the location in the text field *Copy manufacturer's files from:* or click on *Browse...*

Source drive and file

Enter the source drive and source file in the text field and confirm with *OK*. Confirm twice with *OK* and select the model of your printer. When you confirm once again, the files will be copied.

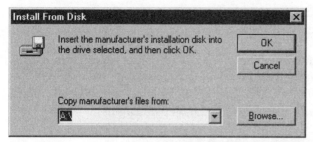

Figure 8.43   Installing a new driver from a disk

Printing a test page   After this, the new driver appears in the text box under *Print using the following driver:* on the *Details* tab. change to the *General* tab and click on the *Print test page* button. If the printing is satisfactory, confirm the properties window with *OK* and close the *Printers* folder.

Setting paper size for the printer

The properties of each printer installed under *Windows Me* can be set in such a way that the settings are used for all *Windows* applications. In this section, we will show you how to set the paper size, paper format and feed for the individual printers. To do this, you need to open the *Printers* folder. This system folder can be opened in the following manner:

- Through the *Start* menu and *Settings/Printers*
- Through the *Control Panel* and the *Printer* icon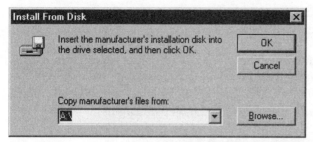

Paper tab   In the *Printers* folder, mark the printer which is to be configured and then select *Properties* from the *File* menu or context menu. Click on the *Paper* tab. The number of options available here will depend on your printer.

List of paper sizes   In the list of *Paper sizes*, click on the entry which corresponds to the size of the paper you will use in the printer. Under *Orientation*, select the either the default *Portrait,* or the *Landscape* orientation. Under *Paper source,* select the tray which holds the paper you have selected.

About button

In addition: The *About* button gives you information about the version of the printer driver being used. The *Unprintable area* button (if available - this depends on the printer!) gives information on the margins.

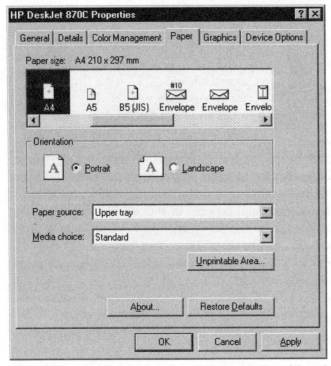

Figure 8.44   The *Paper* tab in the properties window of the printer

If a *Windows* application has its own commands or dialogue boxes for changing the paper size or orientation, the settings made in the properties window of the printer can be overridden. The settings which are used are always those made in the program from which the printing is being done. However, they are only effective for the current document

Setting graphics printing properties for the printer

The graphics properties of every printer installed under *Windows Me* can be set up in such a way that their settings are valid for all *Windows* applications. To change the *Color control,* you need to open the *Printers* folder. This system folder can be opened in the following manner:

■ By selecting the *Start* menu and then *Settings/Printer*

■ Through the *Control Panel* and the *Printers* icon

Graphics tab

In the *Printers* folder, mark the printer to be configured and select *Properties* from the *File* menu or the context menu. Now, click on the *Graphics* tab.

Dithering and intensity

The number of options which are offered depends on the capabilities of your printer. The options group *Dithering*, and the *Intensity* slide are available for *Windows* printer drivers.

Dithering

With most *Windows Me* printer drivers you can select the settings *None, Coarse, Fine, Line art* and *Error diffusion* The *Error diffusion* option gives a very diffused printing result, even with monochrome laser printers. When selecting the numerous options, it is useful to try them out first.

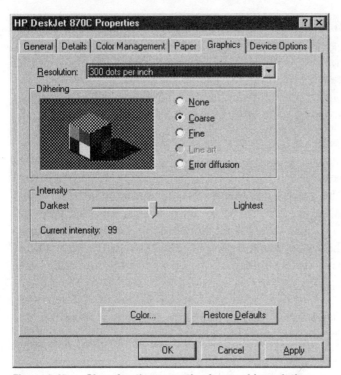

Figure 8.45   Changing the properties for graphics printing

Intensity   ·   The *Intensity* slide is used to control the brightness of the printing. Confirm your changes with *OK* and start printing with another click on *OK*. Here too, it's best to do a test printing and see the results.

    If you have not installed a *Windows Me* printer driver, the properties window may have an entirely different set of tabs available. In this case, you should follow the manufacturer's instructions for printer configuration.

Setting the resolution of the printer

The properties of every printer installed under *Windows Me* can be set in such a way that they are valid for all *Windows* applications. In this section, we will show you how to set the resolution for an individual printer.

Printer resolution

Lowering the resolution of the printer can be useful when only draft printing is needed and the quality of the printing is not important. To change the dpi (dots per inch), you will need the *Printers* folder which you can open through the *Start* menu and *Settings/Printers*.

In the *Printers* folder, mark the entry for the printer which is to be configured, and select *Properties* from the *File* menu or the context menu. Now, click on the *Graphics* tab.

***Resolution* list box**

The number of options offered depends on the capabilities of your printer. The *Resolution* list box is available for all printers.

Dots per inch

In the *Resolution* list box, set the dpi number with which you wish to have all documents printed on the selected printer. The lower the dpi value, the faster the printing will be. Confirm your changes with *OK*.

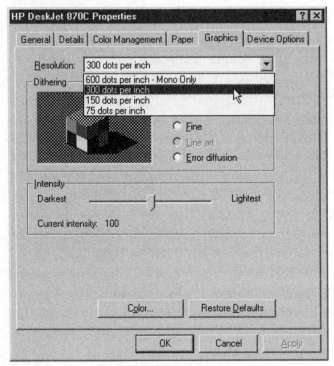

Figure 8.46   Changing the printer resolution

If your *Windows* application has its own commands or dialogue boxes for changing the printer resolution, the settings made in the properties window of the printer will be overridden. The settings which are used are always those which are made in the program from which the printing is being done.

Setting background printing

Windows Me allows you to work with multiple applications in parallel. This is useful for data exchange between different programs and can save a lot of time. For example, you can work on data evaluation in a spreadsheet program while *Windows Me* is printing out an elaborately formatted document from a word-processing program. This is possible through *background printing* in the operating system.

The operation runs automatically

Normally, you have nothing to do with this function: the entire operation runs automatically. However, you can take a look at and change the basic settings for background printing.

Setting the printer separately

To do this, you need to open the *Printers* folder through *Start/Settings/Printers*. The settings for background printing are made separately for each installed printer.

Spool settings

Mark the selected printer and select *Properties* from the *File* menu or context menu. Go to the *Details* tab and click on the *Spool settings*.

Spooling print jobs

By using the default setting *Spool print jobs...*, your print jobs will be temporarily stored on the hard disk, and you can continue working in a (another) program.

Begin printing after last page...

The option *Start printing after last page is spooled* waits until all printing information from the program is stored on the hard disk, before the printing is begun.

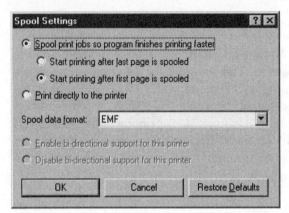

Figure 8.47   Changing the settings for background printing

Start printing after
the first page...

However, this requires quite a lot of memory. With the option *Start printing after first page is spooled,* the printing information is sent to the printer after one page is received. This way, you can immediately can go on working in the active program, and it requires less memory.

Bi-directional
support

With the option *Enable bi-directional support...* you turn on the data exchange between the PC and the printer. Through this communication, printing messages are possible, but it can also lead to transmission problems.

Setting the transmission retry for the printer

Complicated printing jobs, for example from *Microsoft PowerPoint* or *Excel* can put your printer under a lot of stress.

Waiting time

You often have to wait a few minutes just for the preparation of the data. With laser printers it takes even longer until the page is completely written into the printer memory or prepared by the printer. However, an inkjet printer prints line by line.

Problems

Problems can sometimes occur while doing very elaborate printing jobs. Sometimes you receive error messages on the screen which automatically disappear again. At other times, the printing is simply aborted. In this section, we will show you a trick which can solve a few of these printing problems

First, start by opening *Start/Settings/Printers.* In the *Printers* folder, mark the printer which is giving you problems. Select *Properties* from the *File* menu or the context menu and go to the *Details* tab.

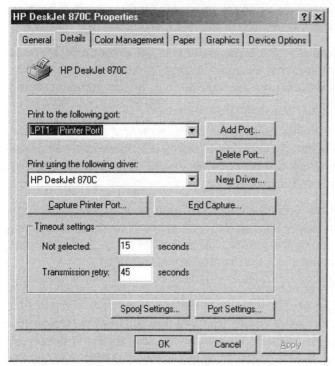

Figure 8.48   Increasing the printer timeout setting

Transmission retry

Under the options group, *Timeout settings,* set the value in the text box *Transmission retry* at 60 to 120 seconds.

This value tells *Windows* how long to wait until the printer is ready, before sending an error message. Confirm your changes by clicking on *OK* and try printing again.

Seeing the print jobs in the print queue

Multitasking

In *Windows Me* you can work simultaneously with several programs. This multitasking is a wonderful thing: You can start a long printing job in one word-processing program and then continue working on another text in a completely different program. This is possible because the *Background* printing is also a multitasking function..

Displaying printing status

Normally you have nothing to do with the background printing, that is, until the page comes out of the printer. However, you can take a look at the current printing status .

To do this, point to the printer icon next to the time in the task bar: a *QuickInfo* of the type *X document(s) in queue* or. *X documents(s) being printed* ... appears and shows the current status.

Printer icon in the taskbar

When your document has been printed, the printer icon no longer appears on the taskbar. You can also double-click on the printer icon in the taskbar to get more information about the documents being printed.

Printer queue

The printer queue of the current printer is displayed with a list of all print jobs. In the printer window, you will find information on the print jobs, the author of the document, etc. In addition, the progress of the printing is displayed, e.g. "4 of 8 pages". You also see the *Starting time* and the *Owner* of the print job.

HP DeskJet 660 (Color)					_ □ ×
Printer Document View Help					
Document Name	Status	Owner	Progress	Started At	
installation.bmp	Printing	VASCO DA GAMA	0 bytes of 1...	00:47:38 22/10/2000	
script.doc		VASCO DA GAMA	24.1 KB	00:47:56 22/10/2000	
2 jobs in queue					

Figure 8.49   Looking at the printer queue

If you want to cancel or interrupt any of the documents you have sent for printing, click on the appropriate document in the printer queue window, and select *Cancel print* from the *Edit* menu. If there are problems with the printer – e.g. if the paper is jammed, select *Printer/Pause printing*, fix the problem and select *Printer/Pause printing* again.

Close the printer queue window with *File/Close* or with the *Close* button in the title bar.

Setting the energy-saving functions

In companies, the computers are often left running day and night. Statistically, the computers are in use only about 5 to 10 percent of the total on-time. For the remaining time, they are uselessly consuming valuable energy - about 250 watts per computer - in addition to the power used to run the monitor and other peripherals such as printers or scanners.

353

Setting the power management for the computer

All modern computers have a software controlled energy-saving mode which can be switched on. This uses only a fraction of the energy otherwise needed. In this mode, processor is powered down and the hard disk is turned off. In this section, we will discuss the energy-saving functions of *Windows Me* .

Energy-saving methods

Another area of use for the energy-saving functions is in notebook computers. For these, the energy-saving functions deal with increasing the battery life and thus the operating time without an electrical connection.

***Power* icon**

The energy-saving functions can only be enabled and configured on PC's which are equipped for it. Also, the energy-saving device in the *BIOS* of the computer must be enabled. If it is, then *Windows Me* installs the application called *Power options* 🔌 in the *Control Panel*. Use this option to set the *power management* in *Windows*.

Power options for desktop PC's

To use the energy saving devices available on your computer, open the dialogue box, *Power option properties,* and under *Power schemes,* select the entry appropriate to your location, e.g. *Home/Office* for desktop computers, or *Portable computer/laptop* for notebooks. The option *Always on* turns off the energy saving devices. The other options available will vary with your computer. The settings for the selected power scheme can be made through the list box in the lower part of the dialogue box: the option *Never* turns off the energy-saving devices. The other entries set the number of minutes after which the hard disk(s) or monitor are turned off.

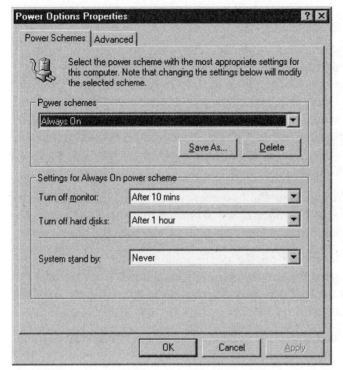

Figure 8.50   Setting the power management for the computer

Set the desired time for the switching off of the monitors and hard disk in the corresponding list. Confirm by clicking on *OK*.

Notebook computer   If you are using a notebook computer, select the *Advanced* tab to see a display of the battery status.

Switching the computer to standby mode

All modern computers have fully automatic software controlled mechanisms for switching them into energy-saving mode, which uses up only a fraction of the usual power. This procedure can be done manually if the command *Standby Mode* is offered in the *Start* menu. This is displayed when *Control Panel/System* is opened and *Advanced Power Management Support* is enabled in *Device Manager / System devices,*.

Standby mode

To put your PC into energy-saving mode, open the dialogue box *Shut Down Windows* from the *Start* menu Select the entry *Stand by,* and do not move the mouse again.

Powering down the processor

Depending on the configuration of the power management, the processor is powered down stepwise and the hard disk is turned off. This saves up to 95 percent of the energy.

Battery life

For notebook computers, use of the energy saving functions results in a considerable increase in the battery life.

To continue working, simply move the mouse or press any key. This brings the computer back to the normal operating mode.

Figure 8.51   Switching the computer into standby mode

You will find the power-savings mechanisms for the monitor in the next section, "Setting energy-saving functions for the monitor". The energy saving devices must be enabled in the *BIOS* of the computer.

Setting energy-saving functions for the monitor

In *Windows Me,* you can protect the tube of your monitor from burn-in by using a screen saver. To do this, you need to follow the steps already described in this chapter. In addition to this, you can put your monitor into standby mode after a specified period of time and later turn it off entirely. This protects the monitor and also saves energy and money.

Energy Star
compliance

In order to activate the energy-saving functions, your monitor should be *Energy Star* compliant. This means that the monitor must have software controls to switch it into standby operation and then shut it off entirely. In addition, your graphics card must support these functions. This is always the case with newer models.

Screen saver tab

Select *Start/Settings* to open the *Control Panel* in the *Control Panel, click on the Display* icon 🖥. In the *Properties* window, select the *Screen saver* tab.

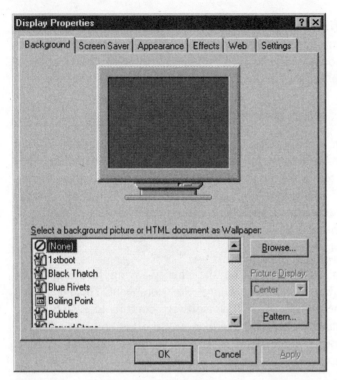

Figure 8.52   Opening *Power Options* through the *Screen saver*

You can activate the *Display* control panel more quickly by right-clicking on an empty spot on the desktop background. From the context menu, select the last entry, *Properties*, to open the *Display Properties* window.

Saving energy   Under *Energy-saving features of monitor,* click on the *Settings...* button. In the *Energy options properties* dialogue box, you can enable and configure the other energy-saving functions.

Monitor tab

These are set through the options on the *Settings* tab (after clicking on the *Advanced...* button on the *Monitor* tab) You can check or enable the functions supported by your monitor.

To set the energy saving mechanisms, go to the *Screen saver* tab.

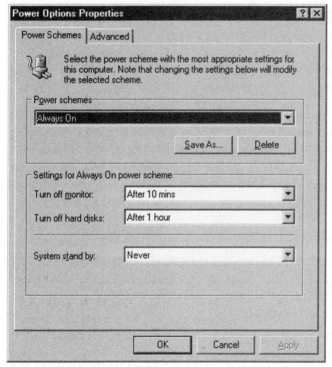

Figure 8.53   Energy saving features which can be activated

Turning off the
monitor after X min.

Under *Energy saving features of monitor,* click on the *Settings....* button. From the list next to *Turn off monitor:,* select a value: *After X minutes.* Confirm by clicking on *OK* and close the *Display Properties* with *OK*, and then close the *Control Panel*.

Installing and setting hardware components

From time to time, most PC users add new equipment to their computers, such as a sound card or video card, a modem or an *ISDN* card. You simply have to inform *Windows Me* that you will be using these new components.

Plug & Play-
hardware

In *Windows Me,* it doesn't matter if you add the hardware before or after installation. If you add *Plug & Play-* hardware, the configuration normally begins as soon as you start up your computer after adding it.

USB hardware

It is particularly easy to work with USB hardware. This port which comes with very new PC's allows you to plug in external devices such as ISDN boxes or monitors, even while the PC is still running. *Windows Me* activates the driver immediately because the device is detected automatically.

Installing hardware components

There is a wizard to help you install hardware: open the *Control Panel* through *Start/Settings/Control Panel,* and click on the *Hardware* icon . The *Add new hardware wizard* is launched.

There is a separate control panel in *Windows Me* for installing scanners and cameras. If you double click on the *Scanners and cameras* icon, a window will open which is similar to the selection of installed printers. When you click on the *Add device* icon, the *Scanner and camera installation wizard* is launched. The steps to be followed basically correspond to those for printer and hardware installation.

Add new hardware wizard

In the first dialogue box of the *Add new hardware wizard*, click on *Next*. In the following window, the detection of Plug & Play enabled hardware begins when you press *Next*. The devices which have been detected are displayed, after which you answer the next step with *Yes (recommended)* and click on *Next*. This process can take a few minutes, if you have already added the new hardware to your PC. Mark the device to be installed and click on *Next*.

System crash

If, during the automatic hardware detection, your computer hangs up or crashes, restart the system and manually select the hardware this time.

Identification

If no devices were detected, you need to give it some help . The next section describes how to select the driver for hardware components without having *Windows* automatically detect the device .

Manual selection

If you select the option *No, select hardware from the list*, you can manually select the components to be installed after clicking on *Next*. Mark the appropriate entry and click again on *Next*. Sometimes, *Windows* displays a list with driver information. In the following dialogue box, you select the new hardware components from the list of *Manufacturer* and *Model*.

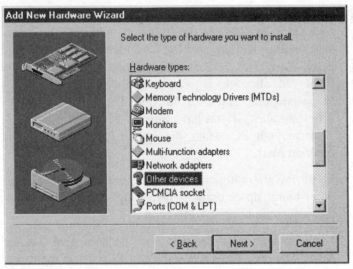

Figure 8.54   Selecting the hardware type manually from the list

Automatic
detection

This dialogue box appears if *Windows Me* does not detect any components during the automatic hardware detection

Driver disk

If the new hardware is not listed, you need the manufacturer's driver disk. The driver information will be read when you click on the *Have disk...* button. Now, click on *Next*. Depending on the component to be installed, you will see other dialogue boxes where you can configure the hardware. Follow the instructions displayed on the screen.

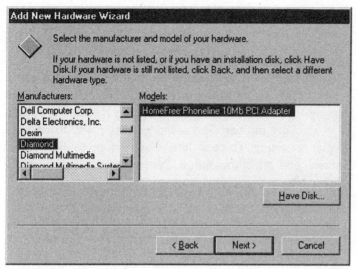

Figure 8.55   Selecting the manufacturer and model of the hardware

Default settings   In the beginning, use the default settings and click on *Next*. The necessary driver will be requested and copied from the *Windows Me* setup CD-ROM or from the manufacturer's disk. If you have an internet connection, you should visit the site of the hardware manufacturer's site to be certain that you are using the latest driver. Please ensure that the drivers are *Windows-Me* compatible – in many cases, drivers for *Windows 98* will also work.

If there are conflicts with previously installed hardware, you will receive a message to that effect. If you click on *Next*, the software for the hardware will be installed, but the device itself will be disabled until the conflict is resolved. The *Add new hardware wizard* closes when you click on *Cancel*.

Hardware conflict
If there is a hardware conflict after installation, you will receive a corresponding message. This usually contains suggestions for eliminating the conflict.

After successful installation of a new hardware component, click on *Finish*. You will now receive a message requesting you to restart the computer. Restart the system by clicking on *Yes*. The component is ready to be used after restarting. To configure it later on, go to the *Control Panel* and select the option, *System* and the *Device Manager* tab.

If the new component has not yet been put into your computer, exit *Windows*, turn off the computer and install the component. Then, you can restart your computer. You should read the following section which describes the checking of resources used by new hardware..

Checking hardware components with the Device Manager

Every computer is composed of different hardware components. In addition to the basic components such as motherboard with processor, boot memory, cache and disk controllers, there are also external storage devices such as hard disks and floppy drives.

According to how it is equipped, it can also have a CD-ROM drive, a graphics card, sound card, video card, scanner card or *SCSI* adapter.

Correct installation
All these devices extend the capabilities of the system. In order to make use of them, the hardware components must be correctly installed and recognized by the system, in addition to having all necessary drivers installed and loaded. Normally, *Windows Me* performs all actions itself during the first installation or performs them automatically when new components and their software are added.

The deficiencies of Plug & Play-technology

Unfortunately, the *Plug & Play* technology doesn't always function as well as the manufacturers promise. However, in the *Control Panel* you can see all the installed hardware components and – if necessary – change the properties of the individual components:

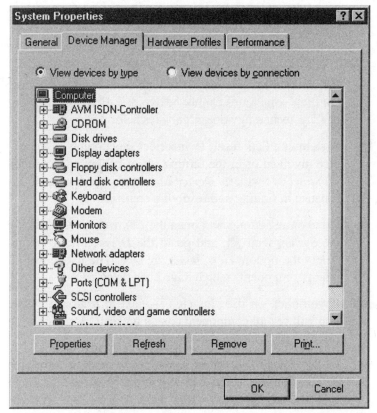

Figure 8.56   Displaying installed hardware components in the *Device Manager*

Device Manager

Open the *Control Panel* through *Start/Settings*. Select *System* 🖥, and go to the *Device Manager* tab. Select the option *View device by type*. The list shows all components detected.

Click on the plus sign ⊞ next to a device group to see all components contained there. A click on the minus sign ⊟ closes the list again.

Properties

To view the details, mark a component and click on *Properties*. In the dialogue box which appears, the status of the device, such as *This device is working properly,* is displayed under the *General* tab.

Eliminating conflicts with the Device Manager

When there are so many hardware components installed, conflicts sometimes cannot be avoided. Here too, the *Plug & Play* technology doesn't always help.

System conflicts result in incorrect functioning of the device involved or in the turning off of certain components. *Windows Me* with its *Device Manager* offer you some assistance in finding and resolving conflicts.

Displaying devices by type

Go to *Start/Settings* and open the *Control Panel*. Click on the *System* icon 🖳, and go to the *Device Manager* tab. Select the option *View device by type*. The list shows all major components which have been detected.

List of components

If you click on the plus sign ⊞ next to a device group, you will see all components listed under it. A click on the minus sign ⊟ closes the list again.

Exclamation point

In the device list, an exclamation point in front of the device, (Figure 8.57), shows you that there is a problem with this component or that there is a conflict with another device .

If you see an "X", this means that the device was disabled because of a conflict.

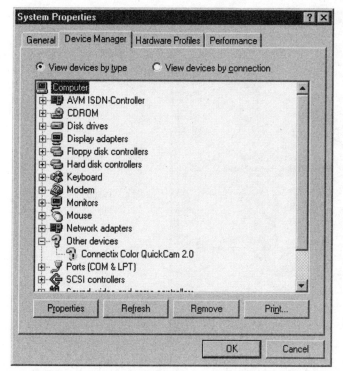

Figure 8.57 Eliminating hardware conflicts in the *Device Manager*

Resolving conflicts   To resolve a conflict, mark the component with the ex-clamation point or red "X" and click on *Properties*. The status of the device is displayed under the General tab in the dialogue box which appears. If there is a problem, you will see a descriptive error message under the options group *Device status* (Figure 8.58).

Other tabs   Now, you need to find the cause of the problem. De-pending on the hardware component, there is another tab in the properties window. Under the *Driver* tab, you can see the list of drivers. You can also display additional in-formation by pressing *Driver file details* or copy a manu-facturer's driver from a disk etc. through *Update driver* .

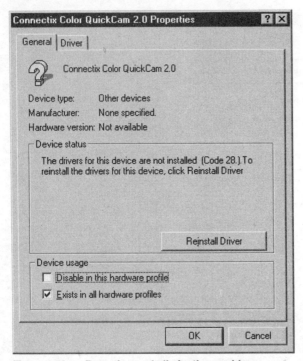

Figure 8.58   Detecting and eliminating problems

Resources tab

On the *Resources* tab, you can manually configure the system resources if you click on the *Change settings* tab. Depending on the hardware, the *DMA* and the *I/O* are also displayed

Automatic setting

If you want to work with these settings, then deactivate the checkbox *Automatic settings*, mark the resource to be changed and click on the *Settings* button.

If no settings are possible, a message to that effect will appear. Otherwise, set another resource in the new dialogue box under *Value*.

In the *Device conflicts* field, you will be given additional information. Confirm your changes and restart the computer if necessary. Check the functioning of the changed components once again in the *Device Manager*.

Caution: If you deactivate the *Automatic settings* checkbox, it is possible that *Windows Me* may no longer be able to configure *Plug & Play* hardware automatically.

Installing software and Windows components

Windows Me is the operating system and graphical inter-face for countless applications. Each program is designed to perform certain tasks, so that you can write your letters with *Microsoft Word*, do calculations and create diagrams in a spreadsheet program such as *Microsoft Excel*, or cre-ate presentations with *Microsoft PowerPoint*.

Copying files onto the hard disk

The list is almost endless. However, there is one thing which all applications in *Windows Me* have in common: Before you can install a program on your computer, you must copy the program files onto the hard disk. Of course, you don't need to do this manually – the setup or installation programs are there to help you do it. In *Win-dows M,e* even running the setup programs is almost child's play.

Installing software

Installation program

To install *Windows Me* programs on your computer, se-lect the *Start* menu and the *Settings* command. Select the entry *Control Panel* from the expanded menu. Double click on the *Add/Remove Programs* icon and select the *Install/Uninstall* tab. Click on the *Install....* button. Put the first program disk or the setup CD-ROM into the corresponding drive and confirm with *Next*. *Windows Me* searches for the setup program and displays the *SETUP* or *INSTALL* file in the command line. Click on *Finish* and the installation program for the application will start. Follow the instructions of the setup program. After installation, the program entry will appear in the list field of the *Install/Uninstall* tab.

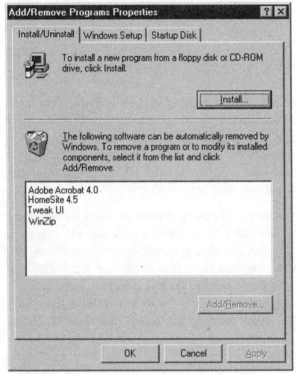

Figure 8.59   Installation of additional applications for *Windows Me*

Removing a program

If you want to remove the program or add components, select the appropriate entry in the list and press the *Add/Remove...* button.

Installing *Windows Me* components

The number of installed Windows components will vary with the type of installation: when you select the option *Standard* or *Minimal*, not all components are installed.

Windows setup

If you find that one of the components described in this book, e.g. a *Windows* accessory is missing, you can install it later with the *Windows* setup.

Add/Remove

programs

From the *Start* menu, select the command *Settings*, and click on the *Control Panel* in the submenu. In the *Control Panel*, click on *Add/remove programs* 🖳. In the *Add/Remove Programs Properties* window, select the *Windows-Setup* tab. Wait while it searches for installed components.

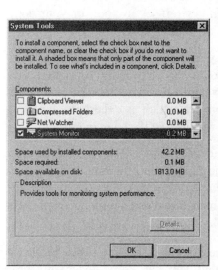
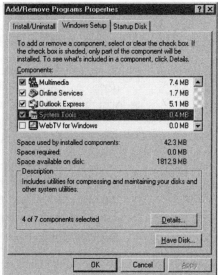

Figure 8.60   **Subsequent installation of *Windows* components**

Components list | Use the scroll bar to view the list of *Components*. Find the component and mark it. Click on the *Details* button if it is available. You will see a list of all programs included under it. Use the scroll bar to look through the details list of *Components*.

Selecting the checkboxes | Select the check box for the necessary application and confirm with *OK*. Repeat this step for any other entries. A partially installed component is displayed with a gray checkbox on the *Windows Setup* tab. Confirm your changes with *OK*. After copying the selected components, close the *Control Panel*.

Creating a startup disk for a system start

Even in *Windows Me*, the most unexpected things can happen. Rarely, *Windows* refuses to boot, or your computer can't be started up at all.

Command line interpreter | In case this happens, you need to have a so-called S*tartup disk*. A startup diskette is a specially formatted disk which contains the system files in addition to a so-called *command line interpreter* which is otherwise found in *Windows Me* only as the *MS-DOS command prompt*.

Starting the computer from a disk | With these files, your computer can be started directly from a disk. With the diagnostic programs contained on the disk, knowledgeable users can also try to find the cause of the error which prevented *Windows* from booting from the hard disk.

Repairing the computer | At the very least, the startup disk allows you to access your computer, so that you can copy documents onto another disk, in case the computer has to be repaired. You should br well prepared for such an event by keeping the startup disk on hand. Ideally, you should have already created such a startup disk during the installation of *Windows Me*.

Control Panel　With *Start/Settings* open the *Control Panel* and click on *Add/Remove Programs* 🖼. Go to the tab *Startup disk*, and click on *Create disk*....

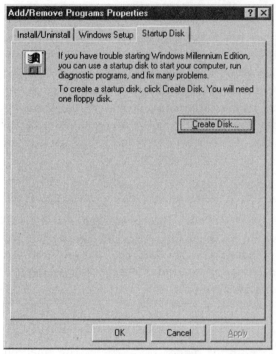

Figure 8.61　**Creating a startup disk for emergencies**

Place a disk in the floppy drive and wait until *Windows Me* has copied all the necessary data onto the disk – the progress is displayed graphically.

Close the *Add/Remove Programs Properties* dialogue box with *OK*, and close the *Control Panel*.

Label the startup disk properly and keep it in a safe place. If there are any startup problems, your computer can be started from this disk

Checking and setting date and time

Programming the chip

Many program functions, such as the display of date and time require a correct system time and system date. Naturally, it is also good to be able to see the correct date and time on your computer. There is a small chip on the motherboard whose information is read by the *Windows Me* operating system. In *Windows Me,* you can program this chip. You do so whenever you change the date or time.

Setting the date and time

Open the *Control Panel* from *Start/Settings*. In this folder, click on the icon for *Date/Time* 🈲, to open the properties window. On the *Date & Time* tab, you can change the date on the calendar and the time in the text boxes underneath the clock.

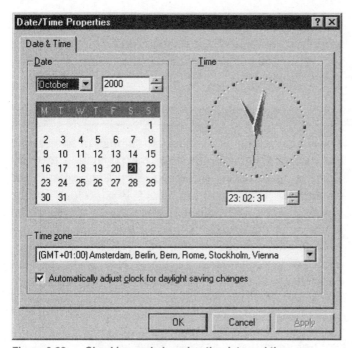

Figure 8.62   Checking and changing the date and time

Setting the date   To set the month, open the corresponding list and click on the current month. To set the year, open the adjacent list and click on the entry for the current year. You set the date by clicking on the date on the calendar. Activate your changes by clicking on *Apply*

Correcting the time   If you want to correct the time, click in the text box underneath the clock for the hour, minutes or seconds. You can use the arrows to increase or decrease the values, or you can type the current time directly into the text fields. Confirm with a click on *OK* and close the *Control Panel*.

The dialogue box *Date/Time Properties* can be opened more quickly by double clicking on the time in the task-bar. When you point to the time in the taskbar, the date is shown as *Quickinfo*.

Automatically adjusting the system clock for summer and winter time

Automatic changeover

The annual setting of the clocks to summer or winter time has caused about two thirds of the population to over-sleep at least once. That's not surprising, since the changeover takes place at about two o'clock in the morning. Then, it's time to change the 15 clocks in the house or in the office. This is a chore which you don't have to worry about on your PC. You can set up *Windows Me* in such a way that the system clock automatically changes over to summer or winter time. To set it in this way, select *Start/Settings/Control Panel*.

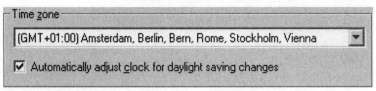

Figure 8.63   Selecting automatic time changeover

In the *Control Panel,* select the icon for *Date/Time*. Then, select the checkbox *Automatically adjust clock for day-light saving changes*. Confirm with *OK*.

 If you are changing your computer to automatic changeover for the first time, you will receive informa-tion about the time change. When you confirm the mes-sage with ⏎, *Windows Me* opens the *Date/Time Prop-erties* dialogue box. Check the system time and close the window with *OK*.

Configuring regional settings

**Number and
currency formats**

Nearly every country has its own way of writing the date and time. When the time in the task bar is 13:52 the 24-hour format is being used. In other cases, the 12-hour format is to be used. It's the same with the date: Americans write the month first, and then the day and the year. Europeans write it with the day first, and then the month and year. The list of differences continues with the various number and currency formats. You can imagine how much work it would entail if you had to change these formats manually for every country. For this reason, *Windows Me* has *Regional Settings*.

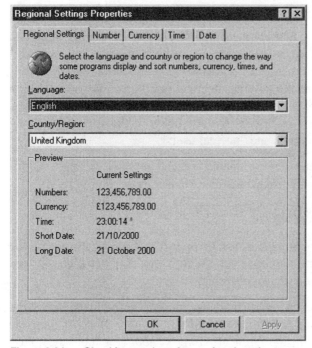

Figure 8.64   Checking or changing regional settings

Regional settings tab

This function can be found in the *Control Panel* (*Start/ Settings*). In the *Control Pane,l* click on the icon for *Regional Settings* 🌐, and a property window appears with five tabs. On the *Regional Settings* tab, select the country whose number, currency, time and date formats you wish to use. For the United States, the entry is *English* and *United States*. Confirm with *OK*, to apply the settings.

The *Regional Settings* tab is particularly useful if you are traveling with your notebook, and want to create documents with the country-specific formats for time, numbers, dates, etc. A click on the country is all that's needed to change all the settings.

Changing the number format in *Windows Me*

Most countries have their own way of writing numbers. Here, we're not referring to the difference between Arabic and Chinese numbers. We're talking about the details such as the comma, decimal point or empty space which can be used to denote thousands, etc. In some countries, there is even a difference between the formats used by accountants and "normal users".

Special number formats

Sometimes you need a special number format, e.g. for foreign correspondence. Thanks to the flexibility of *Windows Me,* you can adjust the number format to suit your needs at any time:

Numbers tab

Select *Start/Settings* to open the *Control Panel.* In the *Control Panel* select the *Regional Settings* icon 🌐, and click on the *Numbers* tab.

In the various list boxes, you can individually select the settings for *Decimal symbols*, *Number of digits after the decimal*, the *Digit grouping symbol* (for thousands, etc.) and more.

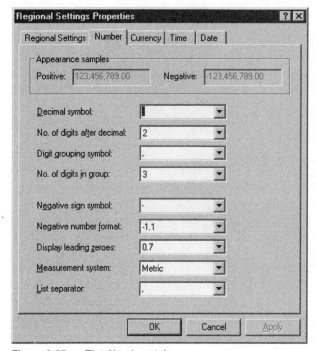

Figure 8.65 The *Numbers* tab

Measurement system tab

Just open the list after the number format which is to be changed, and select one of the available entries. The settings which are available depend on the country selected under *Regional settings*. The *Measurement system* list allows you to choose either the metric system or US measurements (inches instead of centimeters, etc.).

Format for negative numbers

For accounting purposes, it is important to adjust the settings under *Negative sign symbol* and *Negative number format*. When you confirm your changes with *OK*, the settings will be universally applied in *Windows Me*.

If an installed *Windows* has its own program-specific options, commands or dialogue boxes for changing the number formats, the settings of the application are used for the documents created with them. The settings made under the *Numbers* tab are otherwise uniformly used throughout all *Windows Me* components and applications.

Changing the currency format for *Windows Me*

Nearly every country has its own currency format and currency symbols: For example, in the US, the currency format is *US$ 250*; in Germany it is either *250 DM* or *DM 250*.

Universal regional settings

If you want to universally change all regional settings, for example to do all calculations in US Dollars, just use the method shown at the beginning to change the entire *Regional Setting*. Here, we will deal only with the currency format.

Special currency format

In many European countries, you need to use two currency formats: In Germany, you need to use the Euro for correspondence with banks, and the D-Mark for general use. Thanks to the flexibility of *Windows M,e* you can change the currency format at any time to suit your requirements.

Decimal symbols

Open the *Control Panel* through *Start/Settings*. In the *Control Panel,* click on the icon for *Regional Settings* ⬤, and select the *Currency* tab. Using the list boxes, you can individually set the *Decimal symbols,* the *Number of digits after the decimal*, the *Digit grouping symbol* (for thousands, etc.) and the *Number of digits in the group.*

Currency symbols **Open** the list next to the currency format to be changed
list and select one of the available entries. The settings which
are available depend upon the country selected under
Regional Settings. In the list of *currency symbols*, you
can choose between, e.g. *Euros, Dollars,* or *DM.* Or, you
can enter your own symbol, e.g. *Mark.* Just enter the expression you want into the text box.

Format for negative For bookkeeping, it is important to set *the Position of*
numbers *currency* symbol and the *Format for negative numbers.*
Confirm your selection with *OK*, and the settings will be
universally used in *Windows Me.*

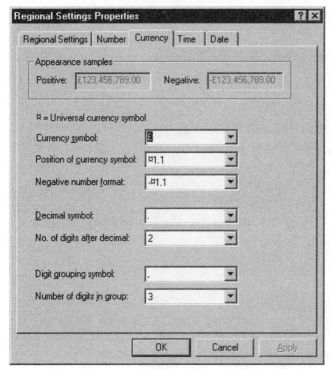

Figure 8.66 Changing currency format in *Windows Me*

If another *Windows* application has its own program-specific options, commands or dialogue boxes for changing the currency format, the settings of the application are always used for the documents created with them. The settings made under *Currency* are otherwise used uniformly throughout *Windows Me* components and applications.

Changing the time format in *Windows Me*

Nearly every country has its own format for date and time. The greatest variation is found in the hours: Americans use a 12-hour clock, whereas central Europe uses a 24-hour clock.

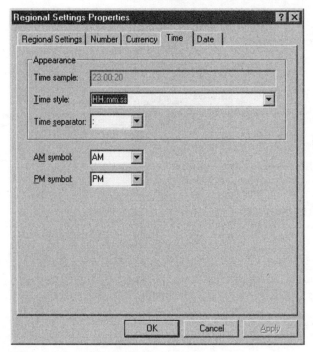

Figure 8.67   Changing the time display in *Windows Me*

Universal regional settings

If you want to change all the regional settings at once, please use the procedure described at the beginning for changing *Regional* Settings. Here, we will deal only with changing the time format.

Special time formats

Sometimes, you need a special time format, e.g. for correspondence with other countries, or for company-specific reasons. This isn't a problem, because you can separately adjust the time format to suit your requirements.

Time tab

Use *Start/Settings* to open the *Control Panel*. In the *Control Panel*, click on the *Regional Settings* icon , and select the tab for *Time*. The display of hours, minutes and seconds can be changed in the list called *Time style* .

Please note the following characters as well as the upper- and lower-case usage:

- *Time in 24-hour format:*
  H or HH (with a leading zero)

- *Time in 12-hour format:*
  h or hh (with a leading zero)

- *Minutes:*
  m or mm (with a leading zero)

- *Seconds:*
  s or ss (with a leading zero)

- *A/P pr AM/PM:*
  x or xx (two letters)

- *Text before/after time:*
  'inside single quotes'

If another installed *Windows* application has program-specific options, commands or dialogue boxes for changing the time format, the settings made in the application are always used for the document created with them.

The settings made under the *Time* tab are otherwise universally used throughout all *Windows Me* components.

Time separators

Under *Time separator,* you can select other separators for hours, seconds and minutes. If available, you can also set the various symbols for morning and afternoon (for the 12-hour format) in *Windows Me*.

Changing the date format in *Windows Me*

Nearly every country has its own format for writing date and time. The most well-known differences are those in the writing of the months. Americans write the month first, and then day and year, whereas in central Europe, the day is written first. Even within a country, different date formats are sometimes used: Friday, 21 April 2000 or 21/4/00.

Date tab

Because *Windows Me* is so flexible, you can change the date format to suit your requirements. Select *Start/Settings* and then open the *Control Panel*. Click on the icon for *Regional Settings* 🌏, and go to the *Date* tab. The options *Short date style* and und *Long date style* allow you to make the two settings independently. In the following, please note the symbols as well as the upper- and lower-case usage:

- *Year:*
  J or JJ (with a leading zero)

- *Day:*
  D or DD (with a leading zero)

■ *Month:*
M or MM (with a leading zero)

■ *Short form with three characters:*
TTT und MMM

■ *Text:*
'inside single quotes'

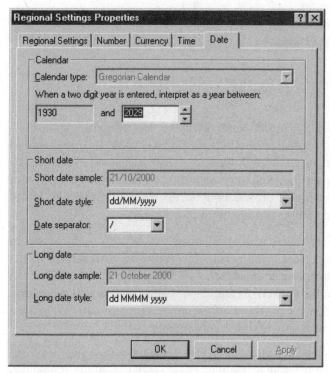

Figure 8.68   Configuring the date format in *Windows Me*

Date separators

Under *Date Separators,* you can select various separators for the day, month and year. Confirm your changes with *OK,* and the settings will be universally used in *Windows Me.*

385

If an installed *Windows* application has its own program-specific options, commands or dialogue boxes for changing the date format, the settings made in the application are used for the documents created with them. Otherwise, the settings made under the *Date* tab are uniformly used throughout all *Windows Me* components and applications. Set the option under *Calendar* to inform *Windows Me* how to interpret a two-digit date display. *Windows Me* can display a period of 99 years spanning two centuries.

Setting a *Windows* password

You can protect your *Windows Me* computer against unauthorized access by using a password. If a password is set, *Windows* will request a *User name* and *Password* after startup. It is very easy to set a password, but the configuring of professional access rights is should be left to the system administrator in a network.

Personal working environment

In this section, we will show you how to use a password to protect your personal working environment, i.e. the content and appearance of the desktop, as well as the configuration of the *Start* menu and program groups. Other users who work on your computer can also protect their own working environments.

Password icon

To set a password, go to *Start/ Settings* and open the *Control Panel*. Double click on the icon for *Passwords* 🐾, and select the *User profiles* tab.

Check the option *Users can customize their preferences and desktop settings...*, and select the appropriate checkbox for user profile settings.

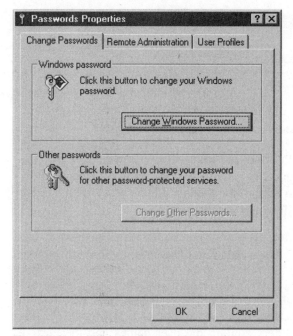

Figure 8.69   Using the *Passwords* tab

**Customized *Start*
menu**

Through *Desktop icons...* settings for desktop icons are made user-specific, and through *Start menu and Program groups...,* the entries in the start menu and program groups can be customized.

When you have made your selections, go to the tab called *Change password,* and click on the *Change Windows password...* button.

Asterisks

Enter your password in the *New password* textbox. Your entry will be shown only with asterisks and must be repeated in the *Confirm new password* textbox. Click on *OK.* If the repeated passwords do not match, you will receive a corresponding error message. Repeat your password entry.

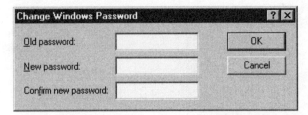

Figure 8.70   Setting a new *Windows* password

Restarting
Windows Me

Confirm the final message with *OK*, and close the *Password Properties* dialogue box. You will now be requested to restart the system. If you reply with *Yes*, the system will restart automatically.

Enter password
dialogue box

After startup, you will be requested to enter your user name and password. Enter the information and confirm with *OK*.

Changes in the *Start* menu – if you have selected this option – are saved in the subfolder *C:\Windows\Profiles*. The subfolders contain the user names and the customized program group structure of the menus.

The password in this form doesn't do very much for real access protection. If you simply close the password dialogue box, the *Windows Me* dialogue box will still appear: You can also delete the suggested user name and log on with another name to get into the system without a password.

Adding and configuring a game controller

Those who like computer games can't manage without a *joystick*. Games such as flight simulators, racing cars and space ships can be best controlled with this input device. If you've tried it with a mouse, you'll understand why.

As with any other device, a *joystick* can also be configured and even calibrated under *Windows Me*. This is possible because you can also run most *MS-DOS* games directly under *Windows Me*.

Game controller
option

If you have a joystick connected to your computer or if your computer has a connection for a joystick (this could also be through the sound card), *Windows Me* displays an icon for *Game controllers* 🎮 in the *Control Panel*.

Properties window

Select *Start/Settings*, and click on *Control Panel*. In the *Control Panel*, select the icon for *Game controllers* 🎮. The properties window for the game controllers appears and displays the status in the upper part of the dialogue box. *Windows Me* allows you to install up to 16 joysticks, which can all be configured independently of one another.

In the *Game controllers* list box, select the desired entry and click on the *Properties* button to configure the model being used.

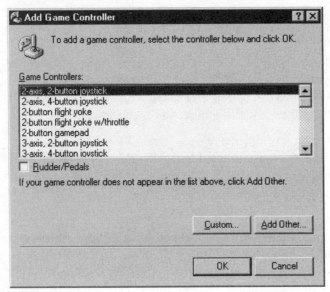

Figure 8.71   Adding game controllers

Installing a game controller

To install a new game controller, click on the *Add....* button. Select the manufacturer and model.

If you do not find the manufacturer in the list select the standard entries such as, *2-axis, 2-button joystick* or *2-button flight yoke*.

Click on *Add...* once again to launch the *Add hardware wizard*. The use of this wizard has already been described in this chapter. The new game controller is ready to use, as soon as the files are copied and the computer has been restarted.

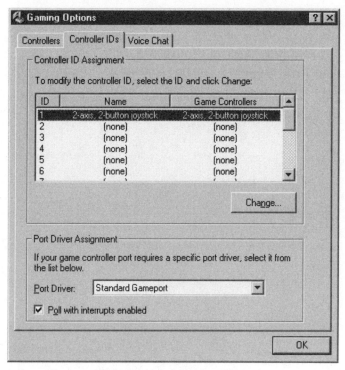

Figure 8.72   Configuring game controllers

In the *Controller ID* tab, you can configure the game controller. For example, you can view and change the controller ID assignment. Confirm any changes with *OK*.

9. System Tools

Everything in this chapter revolves around working with disks: first, you will find out how to check the space on your hard disk and how to change the label of the disk. After that, we will introduce the *System monitor,* an application which monitors the system usage in detail.

ScanDisk and *Defragmentation*

Next, we will show you how to use *ScanDisk* to check your hard disk for possible errors, and how to optimize the data structure with the *Disk Defragmenter,* and how to run both programs automatically with the help of the *Maintenance Wizard.*

Backup and compression

In addition, you will become familiar with *Compressed folders,* with which data on the hard disk can be compressed, archived and sent into the internet. We will also show you where to find the *Microsoft Backup* program and how to use it. You will learn how data can be saved, compared and restored, which backup types are available, and how to customize the program to suit your requirements

Disk space and disk labels

Modern *Windows Me* applications are known for their ability to gobble up disk space. The *Microsoft Office* software package alone uses up to 350 MB for a full installation. Even the *Windows Me* with all its components and help functions can top 300 MB. For this reason, modern hard disks with their gigantic capacity don't seem so huge as they once did.

The 15 GB of a new hard disk will shrink down considerably after a few program installations.

Checking disk space

Therefore, it would be nice if *Windows Me* had a tool with which you could regularly check the amount of space remaining on your hard disk. Well, it has this now, and more than one. However, let us start with the easiest method.

Checking hard disk space

To check the amount of used or free disk space, select the appropriate drive icon. You can do this through *My Computer* or *Explorer.* From the *File* menu, select the *Properties* command. Alternatively, you can select *Properties* from the context menu of the drive's icon.

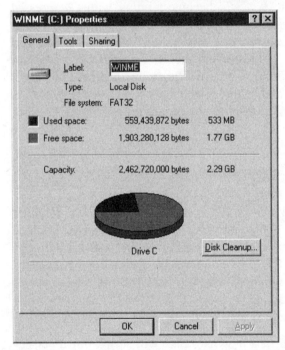

Figure 9.1   Checking disk space on the pie chart

Used space
Free space

In the properties window of the selected drive, you will see all the information you need. In the upper section of the dialogue box, the *Used space* and *Free space* is displayed in *Bytes* and Megabytes (MB) or Gigabytes (GB).

Beneath that, the calculated storage capacity is displayed, i.e. the total size of your hard disk. In addition, you can see the ratio of used to free disk space graphically displayed in the so-called pie chart.

Don't be surprised if the disk capacity shown in the *Properties* dialogue box is smaller than was stated in the brochure or instructions. Dealers like to speak of the unformatted disk space which is most often given in bytes.

You don't necessarily need to open the *Properties* window to see information about the free disk space. *Windows Explorer* and *My Computer* display this information in the status bar at the bottom of the window.

My Computer

In *My Computer*, the free disk space and disk capacity are shown for each marked drive icon. In *Windows Explorer*, the free disk space is shown in brackets. The status bar can be displayed by opening the *View* menu and selecting the command of that name.

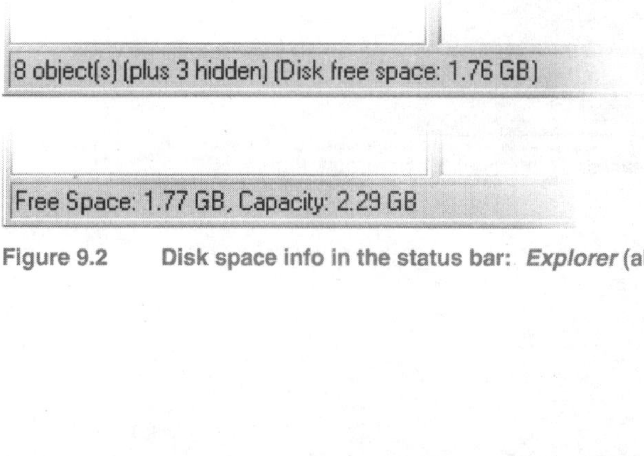

8 object(s) (plus 3 hidden) (Disk free space: 1.76 GB)

Free Space: 1.77 GB, Capacity: 2.29 GB

Figure 9.2 Disk space info in the status bar: *Explorer* (above) and *My Computer*

Explorer

In *Explorer,* you can see the free disk space whenever you mark a folder in a drive. This is very useful when you are working with floppy disks, because you always know how many bytes are still available on the disk.

Units of
measurement

The units of measurement which are used in the status bar (*Bytes, MB, GB*) depends on the type of disk.

Changing the label of the hard disk

You have probably wondered about the unusual labels for the icons for your hard disk. You will see labels such as "Ms_dos6" or "1353_436cky", and also brands such as "Vobis" or "MediaMarkt". These labels can be changed.

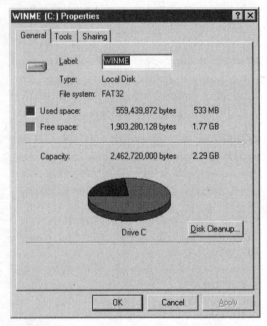

Figure 9.3   Maximum 11 characters allowed for hard disk labels

Properties

To give your hard disk or floppy disk a new label, mark the appropriate drive symbol. You can do this in *My Computer* or in *Explorer*. Next, open the *File* menu and click on *Properties*.

Label textbox

Alternatively, you can select the *Properties* command from the context menu of the drive icon. In the properties window, you will see information about the used and free disk space, as well as the text box, *Label*.

Maximum eleven characters

You can overwrite the default label at any time. This label can contain no more than eleven characters, no empty spaces and no special symbols (* ? % & / : \ /.). In addition, no distinction is made between upper and lower case. Confirm your change with *OK* and *Windows* will change the drive label.

Feel free to simply name your hard disk *HARD_DISK*. If there is more than one hard disk with this name, it will be shown in *My Computer* as *Hard_disk (C:)* or *Hard_disk (D:)*. If you have created one or more partitions on your hard disk, you can add an additional description such as, Windows Me (C:), Programs (D:), Data (E:).

Monitoring system resources with the *System Monitor*

Troubleshooting

At the end of the day, you may notice that the system is running more slowly. Sometimes these performance problems crop up totally unexpectedly. *Windows Me* contains a powerful system program with which the utilization of the system resources can be graphically displayed. Thus, during operation, the system can find the faulty (or performance hungry) program and react accordingly.

System Monitor
program

The system program for checking the resources is known as the *System Monitor* and was originally designed for network use or for monitoring server resources. However, it can be easily installed and used on a stand-alone computer.

Accessories/
System tools

To launch this program, go to the *Start* and then to *Programs/Accessories* and *System tools*. In the submenu, click on *System monitor*

During the standard installation of *Windows Me,* the *System monitor* is not copied onto the hard disk. To install it later, open the *Control* Panel and select *Add/Remove programs.* Click on the *Windows* setup tab and select *Details...* of the component *System tools* and mark the checkbox for *System monitor.* After clicking on *OK,* the program is installed and can be found under *Programs/Accessories/System tools.*

Before the *System monitor* can graphically display the system resource utilization, you must specify which resources are to be monitored.

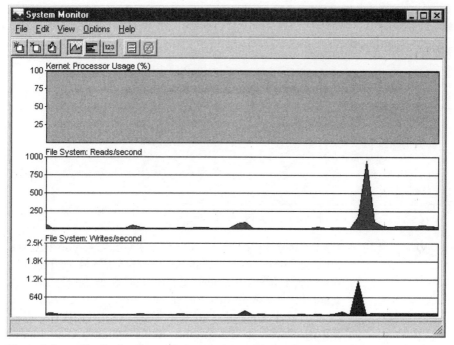

Figure 9.4   Monitoring the system resources with the *System monitor*

Adding a data source   In the *Edit* menu, select *Add item....* In the dialogue box of the same name, mark the desired *Category* at the left. The most interesting and informative are the *File system*, *Kernel* und *Memory Manager*.

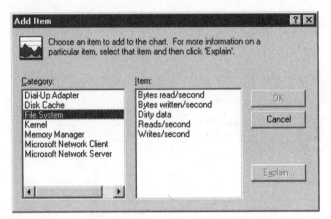

Figure 9.5   Selection of data sources for monitoring

Displaying charts

Under *Item* in the right side of the window, you will see all operations which can be monitored and graphically displayed. Mark the desired item and click on *OK*. If you want other operations to be monitored, select *Edit/Add item...* and confirm with *OK*. Wait until the first values are displayed in the graphs. Items which are no longer needed can be deleted with *Edit/Remove item...*

By selecting *Options/Chart...* you can set the interval for updating the values on the chart. Drag the slide to the desired values in seconds, minutes or hours and confirm with *OK*. A word of caution: even the system monitoring itself uses up system resources.

Checking the processes

To check processes or applications, launch the appropriate application or give the command in the system monitor.

Update interval

Looking at the the update intervals, you can get information on the utilization of resources in the *System monitor*.

Checking drives and correcting errors

Errors can occur again and again when working with data on magnetic media. The causes of the errors can be physical damage to the magnetic surface, as well as incorrectly stored data and file fragments. The latter can occur when you shut down your computer without properly exiting *Windows,* or when a program crashes.

Checking the hard disk for errors with *ScanDisk*

Lost file fragments, cross-linked data, invalid date or time and other disk errors result in less security in one's daily work.

ScanDisk

Windows Me has a system program which can find the most common disk errors and correct them automatically if you wish. If you want to check your hard disk, select *Start/Programs/Accessories/System tools* and click on *ScanDisk* in the submenu. This program is also a part of the *Maintenance Wizard* which also launches the *Defragmenter* to free up disk space.

Drive to be checked

Mark the drive(s) in the field under *Select the drive(s) you want to check...* To make multiple selections, hold the Ctrl key pressed and click on the desired drives one after another.

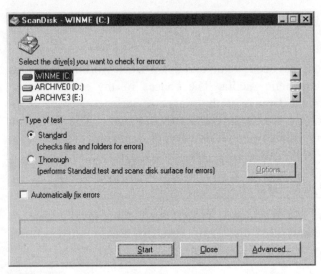

Figure 9.6   Checking disks for errors

Type of test:
Standard

Under *Type of test*, specify whether only files and folders are to be checked for errors. Select the checkbox *Automatically fix errors* to have any existing disk errors automatically fixed by *ScanDisk*.

Starting the scan

Click on the *Start* button to begin the scan. The progress of the scan is shown on a progress monitor bar. After the check is completed, a status report appears with information on the errors which were found and whether they could be corrected.

ScanDisk results

The *ScanDisk results* dialogue box appears. It contains information on the available bytes on the disk which was scanned, the number of folders, the number of hidden files, total disk space, number of allocation units, etc.

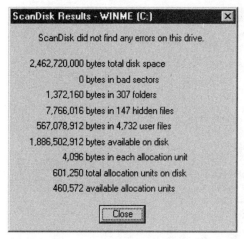

ScanDisk Results - WINME (C:)

ScanDisk did not find any errors on this drive.

2,462,720,000 bytes total disk space
0 bytes in bad sectors
1,372,160 bytes in 307 folders
7,766,016 bytes in 147 hidden files
567,078,912 bytes in 4,732 user files
1,886,502,912 bytes available on disk
4,096 bytes in each allocation unit
601,250 total allocation units on disk
460,572 available allocation units

Close

Figure 9.7   Results of the scan

Using *ScanDisk* regularly

Click on the *Close* button to close the scan results window and exit ScanDisk by clicking on *Close*. You should use *ScanDisk* regularly, at least once a month.

You can use *ScanDisk* together with other system programs, through the *Maintenance Wizard* or *Task scheduler*.

Configuring the *ScanDisk* system program

By default, *ScanDisk* system program finds the most common disk errors automatically and corrects them.

Setting the scanning options

You can control the way in which *ScanDisk* works. To do this, you need to open the *ScanDisk* program. Select *Start/Programs/Accessories/System tools*, and select *ScanDisk* from the submenu.

Selecting the drive

Mark the drive(s) under *Select the drive(s) you want to check...* For multiple selections, hold the Ctrl key pressed and click on the desired drives, one after another.

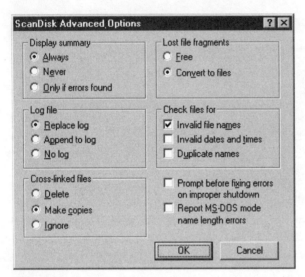

Figure 9.8   Configuring *ScanDisk*

Advanced button

To configure *ScanDisk,* click on the *Advanced....* button.

Under *Display summary,* specify whether the *ScanDisk results* dialogue box should be displayed *Always, Never,* or (the most practical) *Only if errors found*

Setting the logging

In the *Log file* options group, specify whether *ScanDisk* is not to log the results, or if the results are to be logged and saved in the *SCANDISK.LOG* file on *(C:)* drive. If *Append to log* is selected, the information is added at the end of the file.

Cross-linked files

Now, we come to the most important steps in the configuration: Under *Cross-linked files*, specify how *ScanDisk* should proceed with files which are simultaneously using the same allocation unit on the disk. Since you probably can't do anything else with these files, it is best to choose *Delete* here.

Lost file fragments

Under *Lost file fragments,* you must specify how *ScanDisk* is to treat file fragments. These are the remnants of files which might contain data which is still usable, but which normally only take up unnecessary disk space. If you select *Free*, the file fragments are deleted. If you select *Convert to files*, files are created in the root directory with the extension *CHK*, which can be viewed with a suitable editor.

Check files for

In the last options group, *Check files for*, you can have *ScanDisk* check the files for invalid file names or invalid date/time. The *Duplicate* names option can result in incorrect sorting of files as well as errors in archiving programs such as *Microsoft Backup*. Select all the desired options/ checkboxes and confirm with *OK*.

Error messages

If the checkbox *Prompt before fixing errors on improper shutdown,* is selected, *ScanDisk* displays an error message before it corrects an error caused by improper shutdown (such as shutting down from the mains plug). If this checkbox is not selected, *ScanDisk* corrects these errors automatically.

Files with long names

If the option *Report MS-DOS mode name length errors* is selected, files with names which are longer than 66 characters are moved into the root directory. It is best not to select this option, because it is irrelevant under *Windows Me*.

Setting the type of test

Back in the *ScanDisk* window: you can configure the *Type of test*. The *Standard* option checks only files and folders for errors. The option *Thorough* runs the standard test and then subsequently checks the disk surface for physical errors. This procedure can take a long time.

Do not fix errors

Do not select *automatically fix errors*, if you want to receive a message from ScanDisk, asking you how to proceed when there are disk errors.

Starting the scan

Click on the *Start* button to begin the scan. The progress of the scan is displayed on a bar. When the scan is completed, the *ScanDisk results* dialogue box appears. This informs you whether errors were found, and whether or not they could be fixed.

Optimizing the hard disk

If you install the necessary programs one after the other on your computer, and if you save all documents created with the applications, all the data in your computer will be in good order.

However, in practice you delete documents which are no longer needed and eliminate superfluous programs.

Holes in the data structure

This leads to "holes" in the data structure. If you save new documents, or if you install new programs, it can happen that one part of the data is saved in one of these "holes" and another part of the data is stored in another place.

Fragmented files

This is probably not important to you, since you can do nothing about it. However, fragmented storage of data on a disk slows the reading access to the hard disk. This is because the reading head must change its position many times to read the information from a document or a program file

Putting fragmented data in order with the *Defragmenter*

There is a system program in *Windows Me* which – to put it simply – closes these holes. The *Defragmenter* application analyses your hard disk and rewrites all the stored data. Afterwards, the disk is defragmented and works more quickly. This program is also a part of the *Maintenance Wizard* which also launches the *ScanDisk* application and deletes unnecessary data.

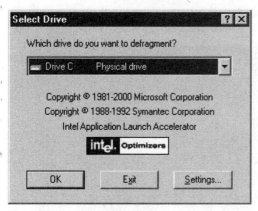

Figure 9.9   **Selecting the drive**

Defragment
command

To start the tuning-up program, select *Start/Programs/Accessories/System tools,* and in the submenu, click on *Disk Defragmenter*. In the dialogue box which appears, select the drive which is to be optimized. When *All hard drives* is selected, all available drives are checked one after the other. *Windows Me* starts the defragmentation after you have selected the drive and clicked on *OK*. The status is displayed on progress monitor bar.

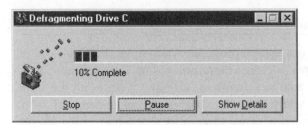

Figure 9.10   Status display during defragmentation

Displaying details   When you click on *Show details,* you display a view in which the reading and writing operations of the individual allocation units are graphically displayed.

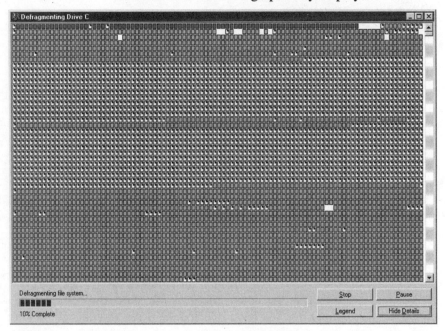

Figure 9.11   The Details view of the defragmentation

If you click on *Legend* a dialogue box appears which explains the meaning of the symbols of various colours. After the defragmentation is complete, click on *Yes* in the message box, to exit the program.

You should not work on your computer during defragmentation, although it is theoretically possible to do so. The defragmenting of large hard disks or compressed drives can take a few hours. You can accelerate the procedures by turning off the details view.

Configuring the Disk Defragmenter program

The *Disk defragmenter* application analyses your hard disk and rewrites all stored data. Subsequently, all data is defragmented and the hard disk can work faster. The *Disk defragmenter* can be customized to suit your requirements.

Selecting the drive

Select *Start/Programs/Accessories/System tools* and click on *Disk defragmenter* in the submenu. In the dialogue box which appears, select the drive to be defragmented.

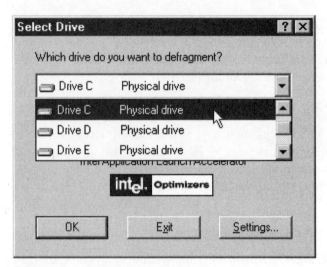

Figure 9.12   Drive selection and *Settings*

Configuring the
defragmentation

The *Settings...* button allows you to adjust the defragmentation method to suit your particular requirements.

Setting the
defragmentation
method

In the options group, *When defragmenting my hard drive:* specify the type of defragmentation you want. The fastest method is to have neither checkbox checked. In this case, the ScanDisk program is not run.

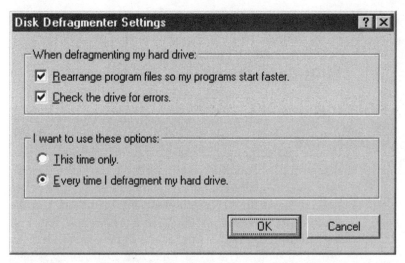

Figure 9.13   Configuring the *Disk Defragmenter* system program

Rearranging the programs

When you select *Rearrange program files so my programs start faster,* all program files are arranged at the beginning of the disk, and all files are arranged in connecting blocks. This makes the startup of applications considerably faster.

Check drives for errors

If you check the checkbox, *Check drives for errors,* the system program ScanDisk is automatically launched before the *Defragmentation.* If there are any errors, the *Defragmentation* is interrupted. In this case, click on *Help* and follow the instructions.

Setting defaults

The remaining options group allows you to specify whether your changes should be applied only to the current operation (*This time only*) or whether the settings should be applied as the defaults (*Every time...*). Make your selection(s) and confirm with *OK.*

Starting the defragmentation

Start the defragmentation by clicking on *OK*. The status of the defragmentation is displayed on a progress monitor bar. When the defragmentation is completed, click on *Yes*, to exit the program.

During the defragmentation, you should not work on your computer, even though it is theoretically possible to do so. The defragmentation of larger hard disks can take a few hours. Therefore, you can have the defragmentation automatically run at a specified time, such as on a holiday or at night. To automate the operation, use the *Maintenance Wizard* or the *Task Scheduler* folder. You will find both programs under the *System tools* program group. If you set a fixed time, the *Defragmenter* and *ScanDisk* will be automatically launched at the correct time. Of course, your computer must be turned on for this to be carried out.

Compressing folders

In the age of total data communication, there are also easy ways to transfer entire program installations or complex data structures to another computer. Instead of having to select files individually and send them by e-mail, there are programs which can collect multiple files and bundle them in a packet using refined compression algorithms which considerably reduce the size of the packet.

ZIP archives

There are many programs for data compression which use the so-called *ZIP* (as in "zipper") *format*.

Say you've just scanned all your vacation photos and saved them in *My Documents/My* pictures and would like to send them to someone. It's easy. Instead of putting each picture into an e-mail, you can package all of them in a ZIP file. The data is compressed and that means less download time. When they arrive on the target computer and are extracted, the recipient gets all of the photos in the same order as they appear on your hard disk.

WinZip

The most well-known compression program is *WinZip*, which can be downloaded free from the internet. However, with *Windows Me* this is no longer necessary. Microsoft has finally integrated the ZIP compression and extraction in to the operating system. The zipping and unzipping of files is a future component of *Windows Explorer* and folder windows.

Compressed folders

The functions for compression and extraction of files and folders are called *Compressed folders* in *Windows Me*.

Compressed folders is not copied onto the hard disk with the standard installation. To use the ZIP feature, open the Control Panel and select *Add/remove programs.* Go to the *Windows setup* tab. You will find the entry *Compressed folders* under the heading *System tools* which you can view by clicking on *Details...* Mark *Compressed folders* and confirm both dialogue boxes with *OK*.

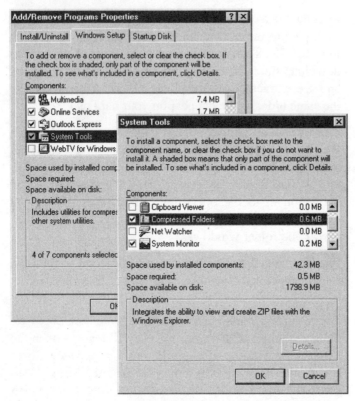

Figure 9.14   Installing *Compressed Folders* through the Windows setup

If the *Compressed folders* feature has been installed on your computer, the functionality of the folders windows and *Windows Explorer* is increased by a few functions:

Extracting *Compressed Folders*

Double clicking on
ZIP files

ZIP files (extnsion .ZIP) have a special type of icon. A double click on the icon opens a new Explorer window. Here, you can see the contents of the ZIP archive and can drag and drop them into other windows. This procedure corresponds to extraction: the original files are extracted onto the hard disk.

Figure 9.15   Contents of a ZIP file after double-clicking on its icon

Extract all...
through the
dialogue box

In the context menu of a ZIP file, you will find in the future, the item *Extract all...* When this is selected, a dialogue box opens, where you enter the path into which the file is to be extracted. If a password was provided for the ZIP archive (see below), you can enter this into the corresponding text box after pressing the *Password* button. Click on *Next* to start the extraction.

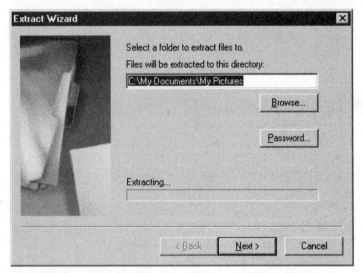

Figure 9.16   The Wizard launched from the context menu of a ZIP file

Creating compressed folders

Send to /
Compressed
folders

The context menus of files and folders in the submenu *Send to* were expanded to include the item *Compressed folders*. If you select this function, all selected items (files and/or folders) will be copied into a ZIP archive. The name of the folder depends on that of the selected items.

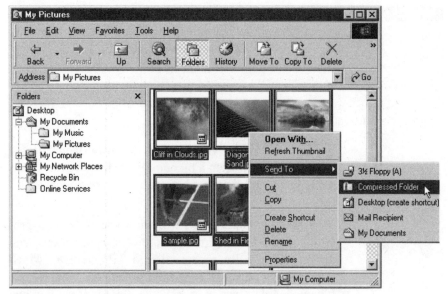

Figure 9.17   Creating a compressed folder through the context menu

ZIP archives in the form of *Compressed folders* are treated exactly like ordinary files. They can be attached to e-mails or removed from the hard disk through the context menu/*Delete*.

ZIP files can also be protected from unauthorized access. You can give any archive a password, without which no one can view a file in the packet. To do this, open the context menu of an already *Compressed folder* and select the item *Encrypt...* In the dialogue box which appears, enter your password twice and click on *OK*.

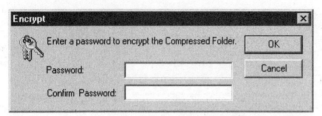

Figure 9.18   Encryption with a password

If you are familiar with *WinZip,* this way of handling a ZIP archive may seem a bit complicated. However, this is really just a question of what you're used to doing.

You also encounter ZIP files when you download programs from the internet. Shareware applications and drivers are usually organized into ZIP archives which require less download time because they are compressed. If you double click on a ZIP file, an *Explorer* window opens from which you can extract the file or use it immediately. The self-extracting ZIP files with the extension .EXE can be opened by double-clicking on them. You just have to enter the name of the folder into which the contents of the archive is to be extracted.

Freeing disk space with disk cleanup

Over the course of time, many unnecessary files collect on your hard disk: the *temporary files.* These originate with software installations or program crashes and take up unnecessary disk space.

Windows Me has a system program which removes files which are no longer needed: the *Disk cleanup.*

Disk cleanup

Select *Start/Programs/Accessories/System tools/Disk cleanup*. Specify the drive which is to be cleaned up and click on *OK*.

Temporary internet files

Wait until you see the calculation of the disk space which will be freed up. The number of options for deletion depends on the configuration of your system. In the *Disk cleanup for...* dialogue box, select the checkbox *Temporary internet files* and *Downloaded program files* if you have internet access, and *Offline web pages* if you have stored internet pages on your computer for offline work. In all cases, read the information displayed under *Description*

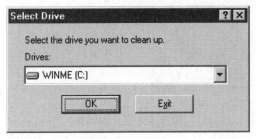

Figure 9.19   Selection of the drive to be checked

If you do not have internet access, you can deselect the checkbox for *Temporary internet files, offline web pages* and *Downloaded program files*.

Temporary files

Select the checkbox next to *Recycle bin*, if you are certain that you will not need the files again. At the very least, you should select the checkbox next to *Temporary files* to remove files which are no longer needed.

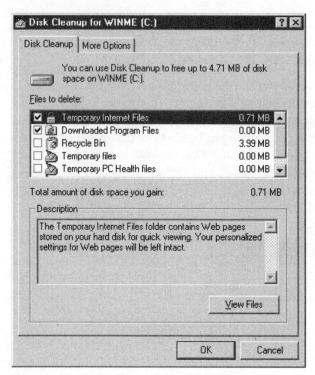

Figure 9.20   Which files are to be deleted?

For *Temporary Windows Setup files*, backup copies of *Windows Me* updates can be deleted (about 50 MB).

Selection of the option, *Temporary PC health files* allows the computer to check the files for general system control. The unnecessary files can be deleted.

With certain options, it is possible to view the contents of the files which can be deleted by pressing a button. Depending on the options selected, the label on this button changes from viewing data to details.... A click on this button usually opens an Explorer window containing the contents in question.

Starting the deletion	Start the deletion by clicking on *OK*, and confirm this with *OK*. If you confirm the message with *OK*, *Windows Me* begins the *Disk cleanup*.

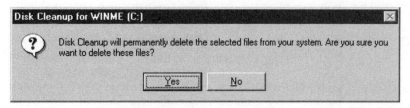

Figure 9.21   Message for confirmation of disk cleanup

The *Disk cleanup* deletes only the specified temporary files, and not unnecessary documents or program files. These temporary files are definitely not needed any longer.

When the temporary internet files and the downloaded files (*ActiveX control items* and *Java* applets from web pages) are deleted, it may take a longer time to access these pages on the WWW. This is because these files must be downloaded all over again.

Backing up data with *Windows Me*

With the *Windows Me* system program *Microsoft Backup*, you can back up data from the hard disk onto magnetic tapes. *Backup* can also back up data onto floppy disks. You can also use *Microsoft Backup* for transferring larger files from one computer to another.

Data security

A regular backup of your data with Microsoft Backup increases the security of the data on your computer. You might not realize this until you have actually lost some data because of a power failure or a defective hard disk!

Microsoft Backup was an optional system component in earlier Windows versions which could be installed with the *Windows Setup*. However, in *Windows Me* it has to be installed later manually. To do this, place the *Windows Me* CD in the CD-ROM drive, and start *Windows Explorer*. Click on the folder named *\ADD-ONS\MS-BACKUP*.

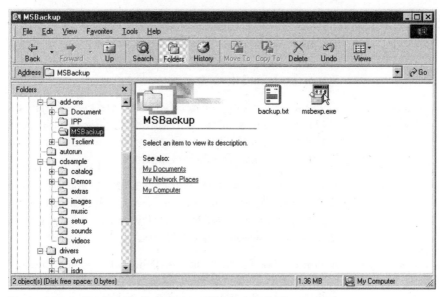

Figure 9.22   Starting the installation of *Microsoft Backup*

Point to the contents of the folder *MSBACKUP* and double click on the file *MSBEXP(.EXE)*.

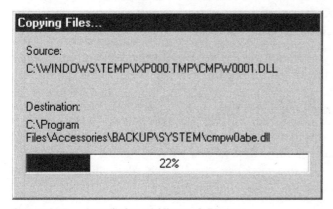

Figure 9.23   Installation of *Microsoft Backup*

423

Backing up data with *Microsoft Backup*

To start backing up data, open *Microsoft Backup*: Open the *Start* menu and point to *Programs/Accessories* and *System tools*, and then click on *Backup*.

Installing the backup device

If you have a backup device (streamer etc.) which has not yet been installed, click on *Yes* when the *Backup* dialogue box appears for the first time, to specify whether the *Add hardware wizard* is to be be launched.

Just follow the instructions for installing a tape drive or a *ZIP* or *JAZ* drive. If the driver is on a driver disk or CD-ROM install the driver for this device by clicking on the *Have disk...* button in the *Add hardware wizard*.

No backup device

If you do not have a backup device and want to do the backup onto a floppy disk, respond to the first message with *No*. Now, you can either use the *Backup wizard* or work with *Backup* in the conventional manner.

With or without wizard?

To open the *Backup wizard,* select the option *Create a new backup job* in the *Backup* dialogue box and click on *OK*. To work without the wizard, click on *Close*. The method is nearly identical.

Backup tab

If you do not use the *Backup wizard,* you will go directly to the *Microsoft Backup* window. Here, select the *Backup* tab, where you can specify the type of data backup to be carried out under *What to back up*.

Using the Wizard

If you use the *Backup Wizard,* select the option *Backup selected files, folders and drives...* under *What to back up*, so that you can specify the files which are to be backed up. Then, click on *Next*.

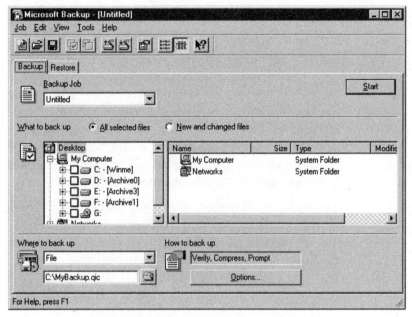

Figure 9.24 The *Backup* program window

Whether or not you use the wizard, you must select the files to be backed up. To do this, use the double window. In the left side of the window, folders and drives are selected by marking the checkboxes.

If you do not want to back up the entire drive, select the items individually.

Backing up the hard disk

You have the following options here: You can select all items of a hard disk by marking the checkboxes: ⊞··☑🖵 C: - [Winme] next to the entry with the name of the disk.

Backing up individual folders

Individual folders or subfolders can be selected by marking the checkbox ☑ next to the folder name in the left side of the window. However, individual files are selected by marking the checkbox next to the item in the right side of the window. To do this, you sometimes need to browse through the whole folder.

The tree view in the left side of the window can – as in *Explorer* – be expanded by clicking on the plus signs ⊞. The contents of the folder are displayed with a click on the folder name in the right side of the window.

What to back up

When you have finished your selection, click on the *Next* button in the *Backup Wizard*. Now, specify *What to back up*.

This functions in exactly the same manner without the wizard. Here, you use the options group *What to back up* in the *Backup* program window. By default, the option *All selected files* is set, so that all marked files are backed up. During the first backup, you must do the backup in this manner. Now, click on the *Next* button.

Backup target

Now, select the target for the backup. In the *Backup Wizard*, open the list *Where to back up* and select the backup device. In the *Backup* program window, you will find this list at the bottom on the left side

No backup device

If you have no backup device, select *File* [File ▾]. To back up onto a floppy disk, click on this button 🖫. The dialogue box shown Figure 9.25 (below) appears.

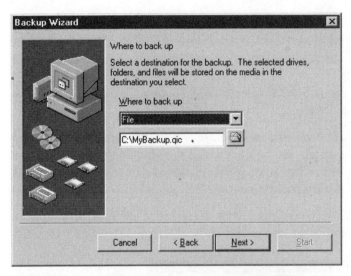

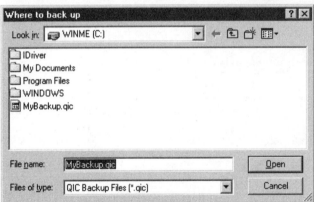

Figure 9.25   Setting the Backup target

Name for the
Backup

Switch to the backup drive through the *Look in:* list; here
it is the floppy drive *A:* In the text box, enter a name for
the backup file. This name should be unique so that you
can later distinguish it from other backups. The file type
is automatically a *QIC Backup file(*.qic).* Confirm by
clicking on *OK*.

Backup options

Using the wizard, click on *Next* and now set the backup options. To set options in the *Backup Wizard,* mark the checkboxes for the desired options: Check the box for *Compare original and backup files...* to compare the backup data with the original data. This increases the reliability.

If *Compress backup data...* is selected, *Microsoft Backup* compresses the data which is written onto the backup device. This saves space on tapes or floppy disks, although it takes more time.

If you are not using the *Wizard,* click on the *Options* button to set the options.

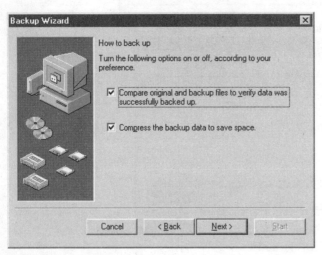

Figure 9.26   Setting the backup options (Wizard)

Naming the backup job

If you are using the *Backup Wizard,* click on *Next.* Enter a name for the backup job in the list box, `Untitled` ▾ to save all backup settings. Without the Wizard, use the list called *Backup job* `Untitled` ▾ in the *Microsoft Backup* window.

Starting the backup

When you press *Start, Backup* begins to back up the data. The progress is graphically displayed in the *Backup* dialogue box. If you are using floppy disks, follow the appropriate instructions for changing the disk.

Operation completed message

If the data was successfully backed up onto the disk, you will see the message *Operation completed.* Confirm with *OK.* Close the status window with *OK* to return to *Backup.*

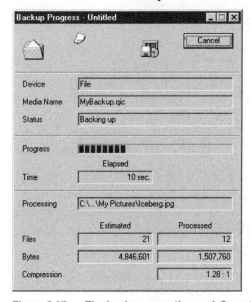

Figure 9.27 · The backup operation and *Operation completed* message (right)

Setting the backup type in *Microsoft Backup*

After the first backup with *Microsoft Backup,* you can change the type of backup, e.g. to back up only data which has been changed. The options of the *Backup* program can be set in detail. However, to set the configuration, you should work directly in the *Backup* program window, rather than with the *Backup Wizard.*

Configuration

Start up *Microsoft Backup*: In the *Start* menu, point to *Programs/Accessories* and *System tools*, and click on the *Backup* command.

In the first *Backup* dialogue box, click on the *Close* button to work without the wizard. In the *Settings* menu of *Microsoft Backup* click on *Options....* Click on the *Backup* tab and press the *Options* button.

Setting the backup type

If you want to set the type of backup, click on the *Type* tab (see Figure 9.28). If you choose the *All selected files* option, a complete backup of the selected files is carried out. This uses up tape or disk capacity and takes a long time, however it must be done once for each backup of selected data. You must begin from the basics, with this backup type.

Backing up selected files

Afterwards, with this type of backup, you can backup only those files which have been changed since the last backup. *Backup* itself evaluates the so-called archive attributes. The backup of selected files can also be additionally configured.

Incremental backup

The option *Only new and changed files* and *Incremental Backu* backs up only those files which have been modified or created since the last complete backup. This method checks whether the "archive attribute" is switched on for each file which is to be backed up – i.e. whether the file has been modified or created since the last backup. Only files meeting those criteria are backed up. This means that unchanged files are not on your backup disk. After this type of backup, the "archive attribute" is again switched off. This ensures that only those files which have been changed since the last *Incremental backup* will be saved.

Quick backup

In practice, this is how it goes: The first time, you do a complete backup with the option *All selected files* and then, you do an *Incremental backup* weekly. Advantage: The backup is faster because the original backup is simply updated. Disadvantage: Restoring is slower since the entire tape must be read.

Differential backup

The option *Only new and changed files* and *Differential Backup* backs up files which have been changed or created since the last backup. The disadvantage of this method is that the changed files are not completely transferred into the backup record of the complete backup. Instead they are transferred weekly onto a new, smaller backup record.

Therefore, over the course of time, you can collect mountains of floppies or tapes ... So to speak, you document your changes from one backup to the next. The backup is slower, but the reading is definitely quicker.

Regular backups

You only need to be concerned about the various backup types when you really want all-around data security. If you backup only particular files such as the texts of a word processing program, then you get a complete backup (*All selected files*) of the selected files each time. It doesn't matter so much which backup type you select. The most important thing is to backup your data at least once a month, and even better, once a week.

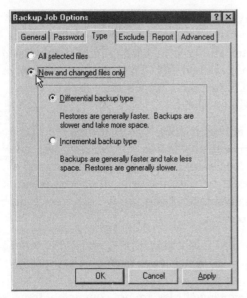

Figure 9.28   Selection of backup type in *Microsoft Backup*

Keep your disks in a safe place and label each disk properly. Note the name of the backup, the backup type and the date.

Select the option *New and changed files only*, if you want to back up only those files which were changed since the last complete backup.

New files

Option

Select the desired type and confirm your choice with *OK*. Select the files to be backed up and the backup target and begin the backup by clicking on *Start*.

Setting backup options in *Microsoft Backup*

With the default settings, *Microsoft Backup* always starts with a backup of all selected file. These are copied onto the backup media in compressed form. To configure the *Data backup* function, open *Microsoft Backup*: in the *Start* menu, point to *Programs/Accessories* and *System tools*, and then click on *Backup*.

Without wizard

In the *Backup* welcome dialogue box, click on *Close* if you do not want to work with the wizard. In *Backup,* click on Options in the *Settings* menu. Go to the Backup tab and click on *Options....*

Options

Normally, *Microsoft Backup* writes the data from the backup in compressed form onto the backup device. This saves disk or tape capacity, but takes longer.

Compressing data

Select the option *Compress data to save time,* to set a faster compression speed. However, it does not work so efficiently.

Saving time

You can save time by deselecting the checkbox *Compare original and backup data...* which uses the comparison function by default during the backup operation to compare original and backup data. This increases the reliability of the backup, but takes longer.

Overwriting the backup media

Select the option *Overwrite the media with this backup*, if you are backing up onto a disk or tape which has already been used and whose contents are no longer needed. For safety reasons, we suggest that you do not use this option.

Password

Under the *Password* tab, you can protect your backup with a password. Mark the checkbox *Protect this backup with a password.*

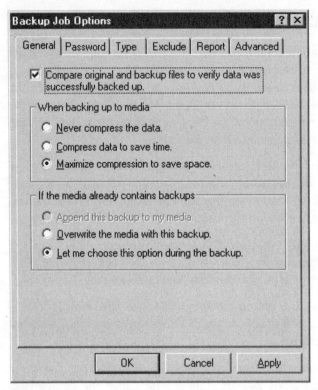

Figure 9.29   Setting options for backing up data

Enter the password twice in identical form (max. 8 characters!) into the text boxes, *Password* and *Confirm
password* and press *Apply*. Only those who have this
password can access the backed up data on the backup
media.

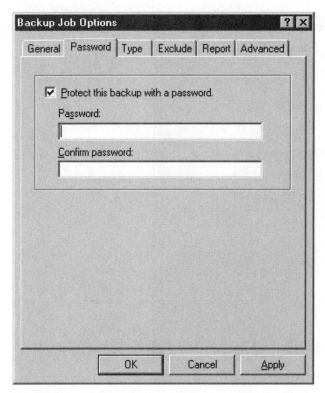

Figure 9.30   Setting password protection for the data backup

Report   Under the *Report* tab, you can specify how *Backup*
                      should react to errors during a backup, and whether the
                      backup can be done unattended.

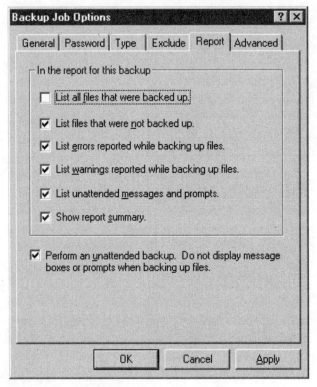

Figure 9.31   Settings for the backup reports

Starting the data
backup

Confirm with *OK*, select the data, the target drive, etc. and start the data backup.

Restoring backed up data with *Microsoft Backup*

With the *Restore* function of *Microsoft Backup* you can restore backed up data from magnetic tapes or floppy disks onto your hard disk.

Transfer of larger files

You can also use *Microsoft Backup* to transfer larger files from one computer to another. To use the restore function, start up *Microsoft Backup*. Select *Start/ Programs/Accessories/System tools*, and then click on *Backup*.

Opening a backup job

In the first dialogue box, select the option *Open an existing backup job* and *OK*. In the *Open backup job* dialogue box, enter the name of an existing backup record and confirm by clicking on *Open*. If *Backup* is already open, select the *Restore* tab

You will receive a message for updating the view, which should be confirmed by clicking on *Yes*. *Backup* now reads the existing backup records and displays the results in the *Select backup records* dialogue box.

Selecting a backup record

Select the name of a backup record and confirm with *OK*. After logging, you will find yourself in the program window of *Microsoft Backup*.

Restore Wizard

As with backup, you can also use a wizard to restore backed up data. To do this, select *Restore Wizard* from the *Tools* menu.

Restoring

Now, select the source of the restoring. Open the list *Restore from* and select your backup device. In the program window of *Backup,* the list is located in the upper right. Select *File* [File ▾]. To restore from floppy disks, also click on the icon: and select the drive and the backup file.

437

Updating the view   You will receive a message about updating the view, which you should confirm with a click on *Yes*. *Backup* reads the available backup records and displays the contents in the *Select backup record* dialogue box. Select the name of the backup record and confirm with *OK*. After logging, you must specify what is to be restored.

What to restore   Even without the wizard, this step takes place in the program window of *Microsoft Backup*. Click on the *Restore* tab. The selection of *What to restore* corresponds visually to the selection procedure in backup. In the left side of the window, mark the folder which contains the appropriate data.

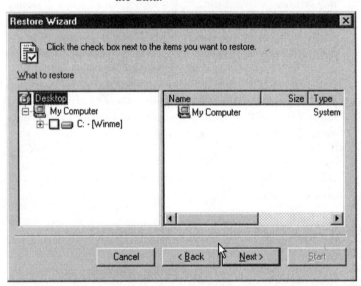

Figure 9.32   Selecting *What to restore* (here, using the wizard)

Tree structure view   To expand the tree structure view, click on the plus sign ⊞ next to the folder name. *Microsoft Backup* lists the original path from which the backup was done. To display the contents of a folder, click on the folder name.

Restoring a backup   Select all items of the backup by marking the checkbox ⊞··☑▭ C: - [Winme] next to the entry with the name on the drive. You can select individual folders or subfolders by marking the checkbox ☑ next to the folder name in the left window.

You can select individual files by marking the checkbox ☑ next to the item in the right window. To do this, you must browse through the folder. The view in the left window can be expanded with the plus sign ⊞. The folder contents is displayed in the right half of the window by clicking on the folder name. Click on *Next*.

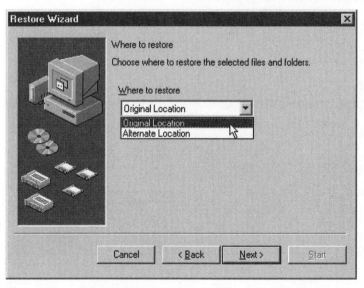

Figure 9.33   Selecting *Where to restore* (here, using the wizard)

Original Location

In the *Restore Wizard,* you can select your restore target. In the program window, use the *Where to restore* list at the bottom left. If you leave this on the default entry *Original location, Backup* will write the data back into the folder from which the backup record was originally taken.

Alternate location

Select the entry *Alternate location,* if you want to restore the data into another folder. The selection of the new target folder is done by clicking on ▣. Confirm with *OK.*

Do not replace

Click on *Next* in the wizard, and specify the type of restore. Select the option *Do not replace files on disk* to avoid overwriting a newer file of the same name as the old version. In the *Backup* program window, you can set this by selecting *Options...* and clicking on the *General* tab.

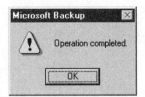

Figure 9.34   The backup data is successfully restored, with message

Restoring the data

Begin restoring by clicking on *Start*. *Backup* will restore the data (see Bild 9.30, left). When using floppy disks, follow the instructions for changing disks.

If the data were successfully restored to the hard disk, you will receive the message *Operation completed* (see Bild 9.30, right), which you confirm with *OK*. Close the status window in order to return to *Microsoft Backup*.

Setting *Restore* options in *Microsoft Backup*

If you launch restore without using the *Restore wizard*, *Microsoft Backup* restores a backup with the default settings in the original folder on the hard disk. If you have backed up data from, e.g. *My Documents*, *Microsoft Backup* restores the data back into this exact location. If the original folder has been deleted, *Microsoft Backup* creates the folder with all subfolders again and restores the backup data to this location.

Customizing

Restore

You can customize *Restore* so that the backup data is written onto other folders in the hard disk.

To configure the *Restore* functions, start *Microsoft Backup*. Point to the *Start* menu and then to *Programs/Accessories* and *System tools*, and then click on *Backup*.

In the first *Backup* dialogue box, click on *Close*. Select the *Restore* tab. Confirm the message for updating the view by clicking on *Yes*.

Selecting the

backup record

Backup reads the available backup records and displays the contents in the *Select backup record* dialogue box. Select one of the existing backup records and confirm with *OK*. After logging, you will return to the *Backup* program window.

Restore target   Open the list of *Where to restore* if you want to restore to another folder. Select the entry *Other folder*. The selection of the target folder is done with the button 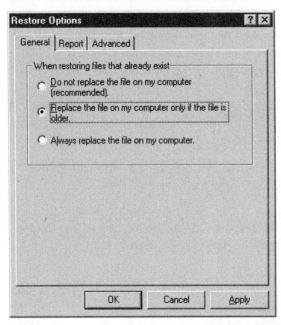.

Specifying the   Open up the tree structure of the desired target drive or
target folder   folder by clicking on the plus sign and mark the target folder by clicking on its name. Confirm with *OK*.

Advanced options   For more options, click on the *Options...* button and select the *General* tab.

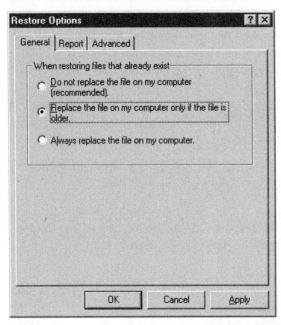

Restore Options   [?] [X]

General | Report | Advanced

When restoring files that already exist
○ Do not replace the file on my computer (recommended).
◉ Replace the file on my computer only if the file is older.
○ Always replace the file on my computer.

[OK]   [Cancel]   [Apply]

Figure 9.35   *General* tab after clicking on the *Options...* button

Select the option *Replace the file on my computer only if the file is older*, if you want *Microsoft Backup* to overwrite older versions with newer ones. By selecting the option *Always replace the file on my computer,* all (even with newer data) will be overwritten with the backup data!

Report

The *Report* tab allows you to specify how *Backup* reacts to an error during restore and whether the operation should proceed unattended – that is, without further user input. Here, it is best to keep the default settings.

Restoring

Confirm your selection of options with *OK*, and start the restore operation with *Start*. *Microsoft Backup* will now restore the backup data.

Operation completed message

With floppy disks, follow the instructions for changing disks. If the data was successfully restored onto the hard disk, you will see the message *Operation completed* (Figure 9.34, right), which you confirm with *OK*. Close the status window with *OK*, to return to *Microsoft Backup*.

The backup and restore wizards can also be launched from the *Backup* window through the *Tools* menu.

10. Multimedia Applications

DVD, Digital TV,
Audio and Games

In this chapter, we will introduce you to the most important multimedia applications which are integrated into *Windows Me*. *Windows Me* is set up for digital video, DVD, assisted digital audio, the latest generation of *Direct-X* games, digital television from the internet and the connection of digital camcorders through *IEEE 1394* (Firewire). *Windows Me* is even equipped with a small program for video editing.

You will learn how to play audio files, apply special effects and make recordings. You will also find out how to play audio files from digital *MIDI* instruments or video clips and music CDs.

Sound card, boxes
and CD drive

Naturally, we must pay attention to the configuration of the necessary drivers and we will show you how to make Windows play certain sounds for particular system events. The requirement for most of these functions is a sound card installed in your computer with speakers and a CD-ROM drive.

Assigning sounds to system events

Would you like to have *Windows* start up to the sound of trumpets, have error messages announced with a crashing sound, and windows open with a gentle "plop"?

Individual sounds

It's really very easy to assign a particular sound to every system event in *Windows Me*. The selected sound will be played each time the event occurs. The requirements for this are a sound card and speakers.

Acoustic signals

To assign sound files to system events, open the *Control Panel* with *Start/Settings/Control Panel* or through *My Computer* 🖳. Select the option *Sounds and Multimedia* and click on the *Sounds* tab. In the list of sound events, mark the *Windows* events to which you would like to assign a particular sound. Open the list of *Names* and select one of the sounds displayed there by clicking on it with the mouse. Use the scroll bars in both list boxes to display the entire list.

Play button

In the list of *Events,* all events to which a sound is assigned are shown with a speaker symbol: ◀€ You can hear the sound assigned to the entry marked by clicking on the *Play* button: ▶ Repeat this step for other events.

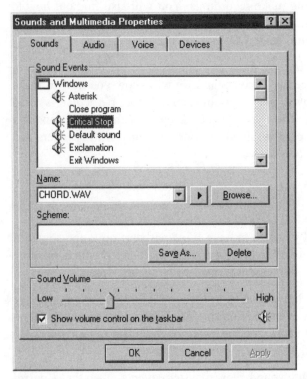

Figure 10.1   Assigning individual sounds to system events

To adjust the volume while playing the system events sounds, click on the speaker icon in the taskbar and pull the slide to the desired position. The files in the *Name* list are located in *C:\Windows\Media*. You can assign your own sounds by clicking on *Browse...*

Installing and setting Windows audio schemes

Audio scheme

A sound can be assigned to every system event under *Windows Me*. The sound is played each time the event occurs. In this section, we will show you how you can assign a *Windows* audio scheme to a selection of system events at one time. An audio scheme contains various sounds which are automatically assigned to certain system events.

The schemes and their sounds usually have a particular theme. Here you will find a diverse selection such as musical instruments, jungle noises or robot sounds.

Acoustic signals

To set up an audio scheme, you need to open the *Control Panel* with *Start/Settings/Control Panel* or through *My Computer* . Select the option *Sounds and Multimedia / Sounds* tab. Open the list of *Schemes*, and select one of the schemes offered there.

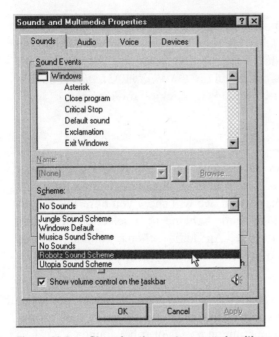

Figure 10.2   Changing the system sounds with an audio scheme

List of *Events*

In the list of *Sound events,* all events to which a sound has been assigned in a scheme are marked with a speaker icon ◀. You can listen to the sound assigned to the marked item by clicking on the *Play* button ▶.

Installing schemes

If only the Windows *Standard* is displayed in the list of Schemes, open the *Start* menu and point to *Settings*, and click on the *Control Panel*. Double click on the icon for *Add/remove programs*.

Windows Setup

Go to the *Properties of Add/remove programs* under the *Windows Setup* tab. In the list of *Components*, select *Multimedia audio schemes*

With the standard installation of *Windows Me* you can only select the standard audio scheme. To install other audio schemes, open the *Control Panel/ Add/remove programs/ Windows Setup*. Select the item *Multimedia* and click on *Details...* Select *Multimedia Audio schemes*. Click twice on *OK*, and other audio schemes will be available in *Sounds and Multimedia*.

Sound databases   Confirm twice with *OK*. The data is copied and you can exit the *Control Panel*. Now you can assign the new sounds through *Control Panel/Sounds and Multimedia*.

To control the volume when playing system event sounds, click on the speaker icon ◀ in the taskbar, and pull the slide to the desired position. If you cannot hear a sound, check to see that the speakers are turned on.

Setting the volume control for playing sounds

Windows Me can play just about any digital sound file. To play or record sound files, you need the special multimedia applications found in the *Accessories* program group. We will speak about these later. Right now, we are dealing with setting the volume for playing sounds and making recordings. All sound applications use the *Windows Me* mixer for this purpose.

Volume control with the *Windows Me* mixer

You will not find the mixer for volume adjustment under this name in *Windows Me*. This program is found under *Start/Programs/ Accessories* and *Entertainment* and then *Volume control*. A window opens (the labels may vary with the installed version), as shown in Figure 10.16.

449

Volume control

You can open the *Volume control* more quickly, as described in the hint. If you want to have fewer slides displayed, select the *Options* menu and click on *Advanced settings.*

Through *Options/Properties,* you can configure the display by selecting or deselecting the corresponding check boxes under *Show the following volume controls.*

Properties

dialogue box

In the *Properties* dialogue box, you specify whether the controls for *Playback* or R*ecording* or for *Other* audio devices are to be displayed.

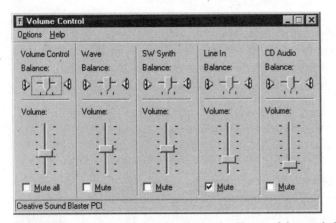
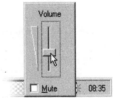

Figure 10.3   Volume control for playback. Above: Advanced view

Volume control

slide

The slide at the far left is used for controlling the basic volume. The volume controls for particular sounds (e.g. *Wave, CD* or *MIDI*) can be adjusted independently of one another with the corresponding slides. The changes take effect immediately.

In the *Control Panel*, (Option *Sounds and Multimedia,* in the *Sounds* tab) select the checkbox *Display volume control in the taskbar,* to be able to adjust the volume by clicking on the speaker icon ◁ 00:53 (Figure 10.3, below). The dialogue box with the slides can be opened by double clicking on this icon ◁.

Setting the properties of multimedia devices

Every modern computer has a soundcard. With this, you can not only set the system sounds or audio CD's, but you can also make recordings by connecting a microphone.

Plug & Play technology

Most soundcards work with *Plug & Play* technology. Normally, you just need to plug the sound card into a slot in the computer, and install the accompanying software. Now, the world of multimedia is available to you through your computer.

Multimedia option

The audio hardware can also be manually configured. In this section, we will describe how to make the basic volume control settings for playback and recording, how to adjust the settings for recording quality, and lastly how to place the speaker icon on your taskbar. Open the *Start* menu and point to *Settings*. In the expanded menu, point to *Control Panel*, and then click on the icon for *Sounds and Multimedia*. Select the *Audio* tab.

Figure 10.4   Specifying preferred playback and recording devices

Playback or
recording devices

From the lists under *Playback* and *Recording*, you can specify the preferred device for the playback of system sounds. In the *Preferred device* list boxes, the active sound card is usually displayed. If your sound card supports multiple sound standards, you can open out the lists where more entries will be displayed.

Only use preferred
devices

If you are using programs which require very specific hardware, specify the required audio hardware under *Preferred device*. For these programs, you can additionally mark the checkbox *Only use preferred devices* in the lower left corner of the window.

452

The basic volume control or the recording level can be set by clicking on the *Volume control* button, or in *Volume control* dialogue box (see later in this chapter).

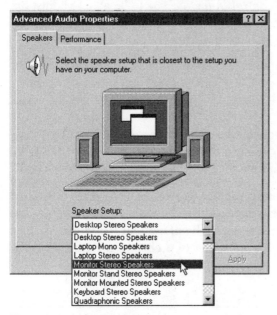

Figure 10.5   Setting the speakers properties

Setting Properties   The *Advanced properties* button allows you to make the basic setting for the playback and recording devices. In the *Advanced audio properties* dialogue box, you can specify the type of *Speakers* connected to your computer (see Figure 10.5). Under the *Performance tab,* you can set the quality of the *Sample rate.* Confirm all changes by clicking on *OK.* You can use *Restore defaults* to return to the basic settings.

The volume control for playback and recording can only be set through the Control Panel, if the audio hardware can be software-controlled. Select the checkbox for *Display volume control in the taskbar* to be able to adjust the volume through the speaker icon [🔊 00:53] . Surround Sound speakers can also be set up for playing films on DVDs.

Playing audio files

If your computer has a soundcard with speakers connected to it, you can play audio files. The so-called *WAV* files are also used for assigning sounds to system events.

Wav files

Perhaps your computer growls like a gorilla when an error message appears, Beethoven's fifth symphony announces the start-up of *Windows* and the windows open and close with the sound of a champagne cork popping. This is only one of the uses for audio files.

Playing of audio files with the *Sound recorder*

To play an audio file which is stored on your computer, you must set up the sound recorder. Select *Start/Programs/Accessories/Entertainment*, and click on *Sound recorder* in the expanded menu.

Integrated sound files

From the *File menu,* select *Open*. By default, the sound recorder opens the folder *C:\Windows\Media*, where the sound files integrated into *Windows Me* are saved. Mark one of the sound files listed there, or switch to another source folder. To load the file, click on *Open*.

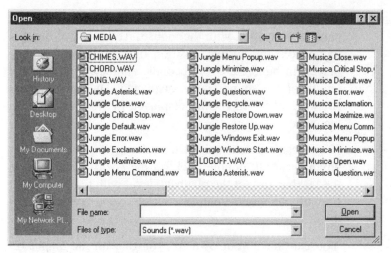

Figure 10.6   The default folder for *Windows Me* sounds

Buttons   When you click on *Play* ▶ the sound file is played. Click on *Stop* ■, to stop the playback. The *Seek to start* ◄◄ button brings you back to the beginning of the sound file, and *Seek to end* ►► brings you to the end of the sound file.

Figure 10.7   Playing *WAV* files

Playback position You can also use the slide ——|—— , to go to a particular position with the mouse. At the left of the dialogue box, the current position of the playback is displayed in hundredths of seconds. At the right, the total length of the sound file is displayed. During playback, sound level is graphically displayed in the black field in the center.

If you can't hear much of the file, or if you can't hear anything at all, double click on the speaker icon ◀꞉ in the taskbar and set the playback level with the *Wave* slide or with the basic volume control. Now, try playing it again.

Record button You can make your own recordings with the *Sound recorder* and a microphone, by clicking on the *Record* button ██●██. You will learn more about this later on in this chapter.

 To control the volume of system event sounds, you can click on the speaker icon ◀꞉ in the taskbar and set the slide to the desired position.

Playing back audio files with the *Windows Media Player*

Windows Me uses the *Windows Media Player* for automatic playback of almost any multimedia files. This is, therefore really a universal playback program which is launched whenever you double click on a multimedia item in *My Computer* or in *Explorer*.

With the *Windows Media Player,* you can play all types of sound files, video clips, *MIDI* sequences or *mp3* files. Select *Start/Programs/Accessories/Entertainment*, and click on the *Windows Media Player* in the expanded menu. You will also find the program in the quick launch menu, with its icon .

Browse icon

From the *File/Open....* menu, select the type of the media file to be played back from the *Files of type:* list. For *WAV* sounds or the *Windows* system sounds, select the entry *Audio file.* Individual tracks from a music CD can be found under CD soundtrack (in the dialogue box, display the contents of the CD-ROM drive).

Figure 10.8 Dialogue box to *Open* multimedia files

C:\Windows\Media folder

Through the list box, go to the source folder. You will find samples of wave sound files in the folder *C:\Windows\Media.* Mark the file and click on *Open.* Confirm the path in the *Open* dialogue box, by clicking on *Open.*

The playback starts automatically. The filename and the current playback status are displayed in the *Windows Media Player* display area.

In the default settings of *Windows Media Player,* you are also visually entertained. The word *Visualizations* means random (or selected in the *View / Visualizations >*) colours and shapes are displayed in the *Media Player* window.

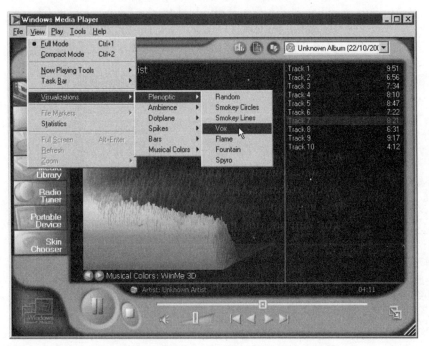

Figure 10.9   Setting colour and shape effects in the *View/Visualizations >* menu

To enjoy the visualizations on a larger screen, select *View / Full screen.*

Those who want to continue working on the computer during the playback can select *Compact mode* from the *View* menu. With this setting, the *Windows Media Player* window is made smaller. On older computers, the visualization takes up an enormous amount of processor time;

if you want to do without the colour and shape effects, deactivate the item *Show visualization* from the *View/Now playing tools* menu.

You can get more visualizations through *Tools / Download visualizations*.

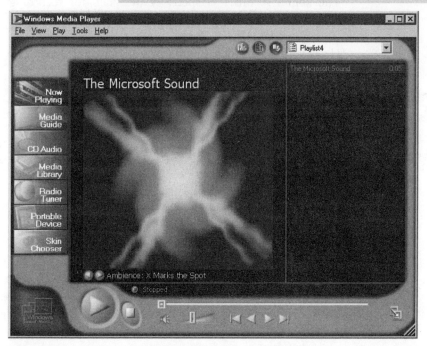

Figure 10.10   Playing sound files with the *Windows Media Player*

Playback buttons   You can control the playback through the *Windows Media Player* with these buttons: To stop the automatic playback, press *Stop* 🔵. Start the playback again with *Play* 🔵. You can pause the playback by pressing *Pause* 🔵.

You can also use the slide to go directly to a particular position with the mouse. You can also use *Forward* 🔵 and *Rewind* 🔵. If there are many titles in the title bar, you can use the buttons ▷| and |◁ to skip forward and backward.

Now, just what is the difference between the *Windows Media Player* and the *Sound Recorder*?

The sound recorder is specially designed for recording WAV files or manipulating them with special effects. The *Windows Media Player* is only used for playback. However, it can play nearly any multimedia item. You can even receive internet radio and video with this program.

When you double click on a sound or video file in *My Computer* or *Windows Explorer* it is automatically played by the *Windows Media Player*. You cannot change or record files with this program. However, the *Windows Media Player* can play all formats known today, even the popular *MP3 files* from the internet.

In addition, the *Windows Media Player* can play video clips (*AVI* and *MPG files, etc.*), *MIDI* sequences (*MID(I)*- files, etc.) as well as *Streaming* data from the web. For more on this, read the following sections

Recording sound files

If your computer has a soundcard and attached microphone, you can produce your own recordings at any time and save them as digital sound files. You can create *WAV* files, which can be inserted as objects in almost all modern *Windows Me* applications. Of course, you can assign them to any system events, too.

Record button

To record sounds with a microphone, open the *Sound recorder* through *Start/Programs/Accessories/ Enter-*

tainment/Sound recorder. Take the microphone in your hand and click on the *Record* button ● .

Stop recording

Speak (or sing) into the microphone. The elapsed time is displayed under *Position* at the left. Click on *Stop* ■ , to stop the recording.

The recording can be played back when you click on the *Play* button ► . The *Seek to start* button ◄◄ brings you back to the start, and *Seek to end* ►► brings you to the end of the recording. You can also use the slide ————⎮———— to go directly to a particular position with the mouse.

Recording level

If you cannot hear much or anything at all of your recording, click on the speaker icon ◀: in the taskbar and set the recording level with *Microphone* or *Line-In* slides, and try recording again.

Figure 10.11   Recording is possible with a soundcard and a microphone

Saving sound files

To save the sound file on a disk, select *File/Save as...* If you want to save the file in the folder with the system sounds, switch to the folder *C:\Windows\Media*. The advantage of this is that you can assign your recordings to system events with *Control Panel/ Sounds* through the *Name* list box. If necessary, select another folder and click on *Save*.

The *Sound recorder* assigns the file extension *WAV* to sound recordings. To change the quality, select *Multimedia* in the *Control Panel*, or the *Change* button in the dialogue box *Save as....* The default format is *PCM*, but other entries are available in the *Format* list.

The sampling rate, and therefore the quality can be set through the *Attributes* list. Next to the values, you will see the disk space used for 1 sec of *WAV* sound.

Effects in sound files

With the *Sound recorder* you can record and play sound files in the *WAV* format, and you can also add effects to them.

The results which can be obtained with this are not really breathtaking, but they are quite sufficient for a first attempt at sound editing with a computer.

Before a sound file can be manipulated, it must be recorded. Otherwise, you can use one of the sound files contained in *Windows Me*.

Setting effects for sound files with the *Sound recorder*

To start the *Sound recorder,* select *Start/Programs/Accessories/Entertainment* and click on *Sound recorder* in the expanded menu.

Create your own recording as described earlier in this chapter or use one of the sounds supplied in *Windows* in *C:\Windows\Media*, by selecting *File/Open.*

Control buttons

The *Play* button ▶ lets you play the sound files. You can stop the playback with *Stop* ■ . The *Seek to start* button ◀◀ brings you back to the beginning of the sound file, and *Seek to end* ▶▶ brings you to the end of the sound file. You can also use the slide ────┃──── to directly reach a particular position with the mouse.

Playback position
At the left of the dialogue box, the current playback position is displayed in hundredths of seconds. The total length of the sound file is displayed at the right. The recording level during playback is shown in the black field in the center.

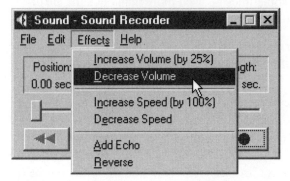

Figure 10.12   The *Effects* menu in the *Sound recorder*

Effects menu
The *Effects* menu is used for the manipulation of an open sound file. All sound effects are applied to the entire length of the file.

■ *Increase volume (by 25%)*
  Increases the volume of the recording by 25 percent. The command can be used more than once, but this quickly causes distortions.

■ *Decrease volume*
  Decreases the volume of the sound file. The command can be used more than once.

■ *Increase speed (by 100%)*
Doubles the playback speed of the sound file. The
command can be used more than once.

■ *Decrease speed*
Decreases the playback speed of the sound file. The
command can be used more than once.

■ *Add echo*
Adds a digital echo to the sound file. The command
must sometimes be used more than once for the effect to be noticeable.

■ *Reverse*
Reverses the playback direction of the sound file.

If you combine many effects, this will decrease the quality of the sound file. Using effeects more than once can
also lead to a loss in quality. You can return to the original state of the *WAV file* by using the *File/Revert* command and confirming with *Yes*. The volume control on
files which have been manipulated can be controlled by
the speaker icon 🔊 in the task bar. Click on the icon and
move the slide to the desired position.

Playing mp3 files

In addition to audio files in *WAV* format, you can also
play the popular *mp3* files with the *Windows Media
Player* program. The *mp3* files are of CD quality, but
take up only 1/10 of the disk space of *WAV* format files.

**Music from the
internet**

Mp3 files are really well suited to distribution over the
internet. One Minute of *mp3* music in CD quality takes
up only 1 MB of disk space. A *WAV* file of the same
quality takes up more than 10 MB disk space.

Browse button

To play *mp3* files, just double click on a file displayed in *Explorer* or in *My Computer*. You can also launch the *Windows Media Player* through *Start/Programs/Accessories/Entertainment* and the entry *Windows Media Player*. Select *File/Open....*

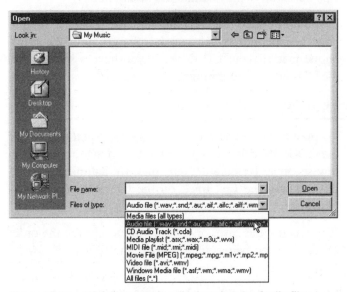

Figure 10.13 MP3 files are also displayed under Audio files

In the *Files of type:* list you can specify the format of the media item to be played: For *mp3* audio files, enter *Audio file.* Now, use the list boxes to go to the source folder which contains the file. In *Windows Me,* there are no samples of mp3 files. However, such files can be found by the thousands in the internet. Select an *mp3* file and click on *Open.* Confirm the path given in the *Open* dialogue box, and click on *Open.*

Playback status

The playback starts automatically. The file name and current playback status are shown in the display area of the *Windows Media Player.*

Playing music CD's

The playing of music CDs is no longer limited to your stereo system. The CD-ROM drive of your computer can also be set up to play audio CDs at any time.

Soundcard and
speakers

If you don't have a sound card and speakers, you need to have headphones which can be plugged into the headphone jack of your CD drive. If you have a sound card, the CDs are played through your speakers.

Playing music CDs with the *Windows Media Player*

AutoPlay

To play a music CD on your computer, open the tray of the CD-ROM drive and place the CD in the drive. Wait a few seconds. By default, *Windows Me* automatically begins to play the first track on the CD. This function is known as *AutoPlay*.

Windows Media
Player program

If this is not the case, or if you want to change the order of the tracks being played, use the *Windows Media Player* program.

Click on the *Start* button and point to *Programs/Accessories/Entertainment*. Click on *Windows Media Player* in the submenu. You can do this more quickly by clicking on the *Windows Media Player* icon ▶ in the quick launch bar.

Tracks and position

In the upper left of the *Windows Media Player* window, the number of the current track is displayed; at the lower right, the position is displayed in seconds.

At the bottom, there are buttons for controlling the audio playback. The buttons are designed to look like the controls on a stereo system

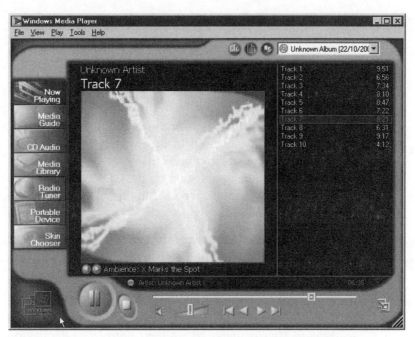

Figure 10.14 Music CDs can be played with the *Windows Media Player*

Control buttons

To pause the playback, press *Pause* ⏸. The *Stop* button ⏹ interrupts the playback, and *Play* ▶ starts it again. When you click on *Next track* ▶| you will get to the next title, *Previous track* |◀ brings you back to the previous title. Press *Fast forward* ▶ to move fast forward, and in the reverse direction with *Rewind* ◀. The title bar in the right side of the window allows you to go to a specific track.

Automatic rewind

In the *Play* menu, you will find *Random play* and automatic replay (*Continuous play*).

In the status bar over the buttons, you will find – if it is available – the title of the track and the current position.

Turning automatic CD playback on and off

In order to play a music CD on a *Windows Me* computer, you only need to open the tray of the CD-ROM drive, insert the CD and close the tray again. *Windows Me* automatically starts playing the CD on the first track.

AutoPlay function

The so-called *AutoPlay* function is useful for beginners, because you do not need to do anything at all. In *Windows Me,* the same function is ussed for CD-ROMs, with the result that the application on the CD is automatically started when you insert the CD. In this case, the function is called *AutoRun*.

Turning off AutoPlay

You may not always want to use the automatic start function. Therefore, you can turn off the automatic playing of the CD.

Device Manager tab

To do this, you need to open the *Control Panel*, which you do through *Start* and *Settings/Control Panel* or through *My Computer* 🖳. In the *Control Panel*, click on the *System* icon and select the *Device Manager* tab. Click on the option *View devices by type*, and look for the entry *CD-ROM* in the list.

Automatic notification

Click on the plus sign next to *CD-ROM*, and mark your CD-ROM drive. Click on *Properties* and go to the *Settings* tab. Under *Options,* deselect the checkbox *Auto insert notification*. Confirm twice with *OK*, and close the *Control Panel*.

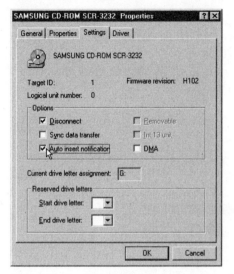

Figure 10.15   This turns off the automatic playback of CDs

Playing video clips

The *Windows Media Player* is used by *Windows Me* to play multimedia items in various formats, e.g. audio files in *WAV* format, *mp3*, *MIDI* sequences (*MID* and *RMI* files) and video files in *AVI* format, etc.

Playing *AVI* video files with the *Windows Media Player*

Windows Me automatically launches the *Windows Media Player* as soon as you double click on an *AVI* video file in *Explorer* or in *My Computer*. Of course, you can also manually open the *Windows Media Player*: Select *Start/Programs/Accessories/Entertainment/   Windows Media Player*. In the quick launch bar, use the icon ▶ for the program to activate it with a single mouse click.

Video files file type   After the program is opened, select *File/Open....* If you
only want to display *AVI video clips,* enter *Video files* in
the *Files of type:* list. Open the folder where the file is located by clicking on the *Look in* button. Mark the desired
file and click on *Open.*

The *Windows Media Player* can also play the *WMV* format which is used in *Windows Me* to save video clips
from the *Windows Movie Maker.*

Figure 10.16   Selection of multimedia file type

The playback begins automatically. To stop the playback,
click on *Stop* 🔵. You can resume the playback with *Play*
🔵. To pause the playback, press the *Pause* 🔵. You can
also use the slide to go directly to a particular position
with the mouse.

On the Setup CD-ROM of *Windows Me*, you will find a sample in the folder *\WINME\TOOLS\PSUTIL\ MEDIATST*. Double click on the file *AVITEST.AVI*, to view the Microsoft test video. In this folder, there are also test files in MP3 and MPEG formats.

Figure 10.17   Playing an *AVI* video clip in compact mode

Playing movie files with the *Windows Media Player*

Video CDs

You can use the *Windows Media Player* to play movie files in the *MPG* or *MPEG* formats. This movie file type is used on video CDs and by many video cards for digitalizing of games or video films. To start the program, click on the *Media Player* icon ▶ in the quick launch bar, or select *Start/ Programs/Accessories/Entertainment* and click on *Windows Media Player* in the submenu.

MPG or MPEG files

The *Windows Media Player* is started automatically, whenever you double click on an MPG or MPEG file in *My Computer* or in *Windows-Explorer*.

Movie file entries

After the program opens, click on *File/Open...* If you only want to display *MPG* film files, select the entry *Video files from the list* Files of type: Open the folder where the video file is located by clicking on *Look in.* Mark the desired file and click on *Open.*

Full screen display

The *Movie* files are controlled in the same manner as the Video files described above. You can use the slide to jump to a particular position directly with the mouse. You can view *MPG* movie files on a full screen display at any time, by selecting *View/ Full screen.*

Figure 10.18   Two designs of the *Windows Media Player*

The appearance of the *Windows Media Player* can be modified in a number of ways. In the *View* menu, you can select (*Standard, Compact, Full screen*), *Visualizations* and *Playback tools* (turn displays on and off).

The *Skin chooser* on the left side of the *Windows Media Player* offers you a list, with which you can change the appearance of the program. Click on one of the designs and use the new layout after clicking on *Apply.*

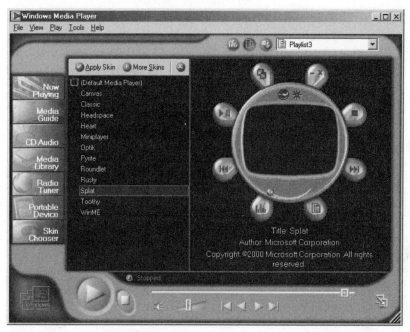

Figure 10.19   You can select various skins for the *Windows Media Player*

Playing *MIDI* files

The *Windows Media Player* is used by *Windows Me* to play a variety of multimedia files. The *Windows Media Player* is launched whenever you double click on a video clip (*AVI* files), an audio file (*WAV* files), an *mp3* file or a MPG movie file in *Windows Explorer* or *My Computer*.

MIDI sequences   The same is also true for *MIDI* sequences (*MID(I) files*) from *MIDI synthesizers*. Select *Start/Programs/ Accessories/Entertainment/Windows Media Player,* or the *Windows Media Player* icon from the quick launch bar.

Browse button

Select *File/Open....* to find the file type of the multimedia object to be played. Select the entry *MIDI-File*. The advantage of this is that only *MIDI* sequences will now be displayed. Use the *Look in* list to find the folder where the *MIDI* file is located. Mark the file you want and click on *Open*.

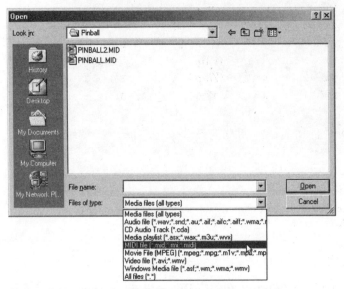

Figure 10.20   Selecting *MIDI* files from the *Open* window

Automatic Start

The playing of *MIDI* sequences is started automatically. To stop the playing, click on *Stop* 🔲. Resume playing with *Play* ▶. Pause the playback by clicking on *Pause* ⏸. You can also use the slide to go directly to a particular position with the mouse.

MIDI sequences of the file format *MID(I)* can be found in large numbers on the internet. The *Pinball* game contains two MIDI files on the hard disk (Folder *\Programs\Plus!\PINBALL*).

Checking and changing the multimedia drivers

Sound or video card

The term "Multimedia" is very often used in connection with computers. This term refers to the integration of various media, i.e. the combination of text, graphics, tables, diagrams, animation, sounds and videos, etc. For the enormous spectrum of multimedia elements, you need additional hardware such as sound and video cards. In addition, your system should have all the necessary multimedia devices, and the associated drivers must be installed. Normally, *Windows* Me takes care of this step automatically at the time of installation.

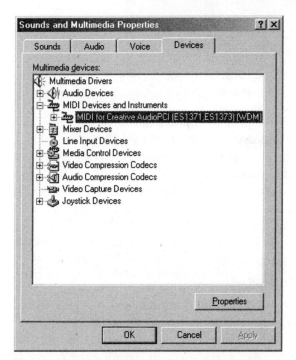

Figure 10.21   Displaying installed multimedia devices

Plug & Play
technology

Unfortunately, *Plug & Play* isn't really as satisfactory as the manufacturers would like you to believe.

Figure 10.22   Checking *Properties* of multimedia drivers

Multimedia option

You can see all installed multimedia devices in the *Control Panel* and you can change the properties of individual components. Select *Start/Settings* to open the *Control Panel*. Double click on the icon for *Sounds and Multimedia*, and select the *Devices* tab. All components which have been detected are displayed in the various lists, such as the sound card under *Audio devices,* any *Cameras* or *Video capture devices* and various software components. Click on the plus sign next to a device group, to see all the devices listed in the group.

Status of the device

In the list, mark any multimedia device which is not functioning or functioning incorrectly and click on *Properties*. In the *Multimedia Properties* dialogue box, the status of the device is shown. If the message *Driver is enabled and active* is displayed, then all is well.

If a driver is disabled or not in use, click on *Settings...* to configure the device or install another driver. The *Remove* button deletes the device from the configuration. When there is a conflict with other hardware, you can turn off a function which is not needed by selecting *Do not map through this device.*

Producing video clips

In *Windows Me*, Microsoft gives amateur filmmakers and producers a new useful tool with which entire video clips can be recorded, edited and composed. *Windows Movie Maker* is a simple but useful application. Although it cannot be compared to professional applications such as *Adobe Premiere,* is quite sufficient for amateur productions.

Projects

The most important elements of the *Windows Movie Maker* are the projects. These projects, which are also independent files, contain a collection of all the audio and video snippets which are put together into a video clip. First, we'll speak about how to collect these snippets using *Movie* Maker.

Launching
Windows Movie
Maker

Start the *Windows Movie Maker* with *Start / Programs / Accessories.* Open the applications window of the *Movie Maker* as well as the *Microsoft Windows Movie Maker Tour.* This separate window explains the most important functions of the *Movie Maker.* The *Demonstration* hyperlink at the end of each text starts up an animation which shows how to use the particular function. Click on *Back to Tour* to end the animation.

Audio/Video recording

Assuming that your audio and video hardware is correctly installed, the transfer of videos onto your hard disk is only a question of a few mouse clicks.

Audio/Video recordings

Select *File / Record....* In the *Record* dialogue box, you will see a preview of the default video device. To receive data from another installed device, click on *Change device....* and select one of the available video and audio devices. The options available in the Video: and Audio: list fields depend on which devices are actually installed.

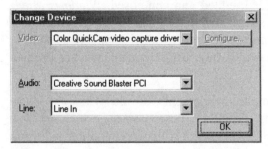

Figure 10.23   Selecting another recording device

End recording

If you are ready to record (e.g. pause play on a video recorder or camera), click on the *Record* button. You can stop recording at any time with a click on *Cancel*.

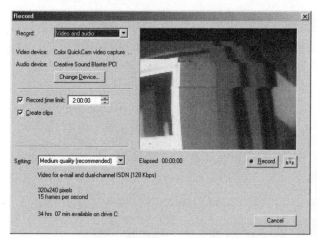

Figure 10.24   Recording window for video (above) and audio (below)

In the *Record* window, you must also specify the quality of the recording (list box: *Settings*). You can see the setting selection underneath the list box.

Saving the
recording

After you have finished recording, the dialogue box *Save Windows Media File* opens automatically. Find the folder to save in (the default setting is My Videos), name your video, and click on *Save*.

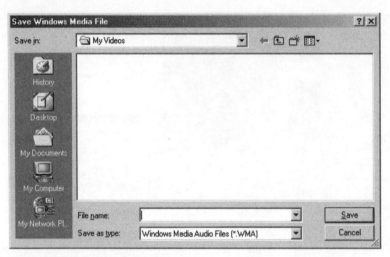

Figure 10.25   Saving a video recording

Audio recordings, e.g. for adding sound or narration to existing video material, are done in another window. Select the menu *View / Time line*, to display the audio track of the future video clip at the bottom of the window. Now you can select the entry *Record narration...* from the *File* menu.

Recording
narration

In the *Record narration* window, the default recording device is shown (for other devices, click on *Change...*). Click on *Record*, and the *Windows Movie Maker* will record the incoming audio data.

Ending and saving
the recording

Stop the recording by clicking on *Cancel*. A dialogue window now opens for saving the WAV file. Look for the appropriate folder, enter a name, and click on *Save*.

Importing Audio/Video

It is simpler to use already existing video clips and video sequences. Even image files (JPEG, GIF, etc.) can be included in the project.

Importing media files

Select *File / Import...* and a dialogue box, *Select the file to import* opens. Select the file to be used and confirm with *Open*. The imported file will now be displayed in the project collection window.

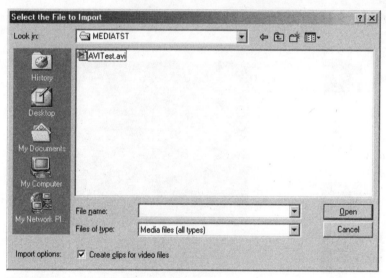

Figure 10.26   Importing audio/video files

Creating video clips

The screen of the *Windows Movie Makers* is divided into four sections:

Windows Movie Maker window

The collection allows direct access to the various (e.g. sorted by topic) groups of files or video segments. In the collection window, you will see the stills or icons of the files contained in the collection. On the right side, there is a mini-*Windows Media Player*, where you can test the data contained in a collection. To do this, use the buttons at the bottom of the preview window, just as you would those on a video recorder or CD player.

The actual area for editing and assembling the video clips is at the bottom of the window. Place the audio or video files along the time line on the audio or video bar.

Figure 10.27   Assembling video segments in sequence

Assembling with Drag and Drop

It's simple to assemble the video clips using Drag and Drop. Just use the mouse to drag the desired video segments from the collection window onto the storyboard or from the time line onto the lower edge of the screen. It makes no difference whether they are audio or video files. You just place the segment where you want it: before, after, or between the already assembled segments. You will notice a type of cursor which shows the position of insertion.

Figure 10.28   Editing the audio track with View / Time line

Positioning
segments

Subsequent positioning of components is also possible with the mouse. Click on the desired video or audio segment and hold the mouse button pressed while you move it to the correct position.

When you click on the label of the time line, you will jump to the corresponding point on the video clip – and the corresponding video image will be displayed in the mini *Media Player* on the right. At this point, an existing video or audio segment can be split into two parts – to shorten the video or to cut out certain scenes.

Splitting segments

Set the marker on the position where the video or audio segment is to be cut. Open the context menu above the segment (take note of the audio and video lines) and select *Split*. This gives you an almost professional editing function.

In order to position the cutting point exactly, you can zoom in on the time line. Select *View / Zoom in*. In the same way, you can also zoom out by selecting *Zoom out*.

Saving and loading projects

If you want to work on a video clip at a later time, you can save the collection of audio and video files in a so-called project.

Saving the project

To save the current project, select *File / Save project as...* and enter the folder and name of the project file into the dialogue box. Then, click on *Save*.

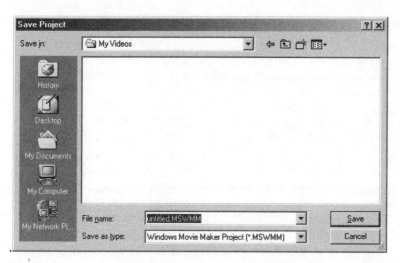

Figure 10.29   Saving a project

Loading a project   To load a project which has been saved previously, select *File / Open Project...*. Find the project in the dialogue box, and click on *Open*. The collection and the collection window will be updated with the new audio and video data. Your previous position appears in the lower area of the window.

Saving complete films

This is the biggest problem with the Windows Movie Maker: Your completed video productions can only be saved in *WMV* format – a media standard which is not yet in common use. However, these files can be viewed with the *Windows Media Player*.

Saving a film   Select *File / Save Film...*. The *Save* Film dialogue box opens, in which you specify the setting for the quality. Next to *Profile*, there is a remark on the quality selected and its main use.

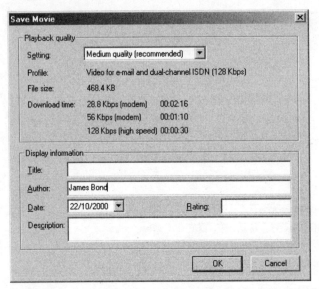

Figure 10.30   Setting the properties of the complete video clip

Information on the video clip   In addition, you can enter information such as *Title*, *Author*, *Date* of creation and a *Description* of the video clip. Click on *OK*, and enter the folder and file name in the next dialogue box. After clicking on *Save*, the video clip will be stored the hard disk and can be played with the *Windows Media Player*.

11. Online Applications

Internet
appearance

This chapter is specially reserved for the most important online applications of *Windows Me*. The user interface of *Windows Me* is already internet-oriented, so that the user sees no difference between data on his hard disk, on the internet, or on his company's intranet.

Internet Explorer

You are already familiar with the Desktop and its ability to display web content such as animation and images. You have probably also noticed the similarity between the folders and the address bar of *Microsoft Internet Explorer 5.5*. However, before you can connect your computer to the big wide world, you have to do a bit of configuration.

Internet Explorer

First, you will learn how to inform the operating system of the presence of a modem, install the hardware needed for online applications, and how to configure the modem. Then we will talk about the *Dial-up network*, an application with which you obtain internet access through *Microsoft Internet Explorer,* the web browser integrated in the operating system.

We will then show you how to use *Internet Explorer*, which is needed to display information from the World Wide Web (WWW).

Phone dialer

After that, we will introduce you to the *Phone dialer* program which you can install on your computer to help you to dial phone numbers.

First, we will go into the technical requirements: without a correctly installed modem or ISDN adapter you can't get onto the internet.

Installing a modem for *Windows Me*

In order to use online services such as *AOL* or *Compu-Serve* and for internet access, you need additional hardware in the form of a modem. The modem changes digital data into analogue pulses which can be transmitted over normal telephone lines. On the receiving end, the modem changes the analogue signals back into computer data. Before you install a modem, you must inform *Windows Me*. If your modem was not automatically detected by *Windows Me* then you should now switch your modem on.

Modem installation

Through *Start/Settings*, open the *Control Panel*. Double click on the *Modems* icon 🖫. This starts the wizard called *Install new modem*.

Add button

If the *Modem Properties* dialogue box appears instead, select the *General* tab and click on *Add...* to launch *Install new modem*. Mark the checkbox for *Don't detect my modem; I will select it from a list*. This allows you to manually configure your modem. Now, click on *Next*.

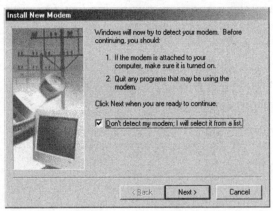

Figure 11.1   Making a manual modem selection

Manufacturer and
Model

In the next dialogue box, select the *Manufacturer* and *model* of your modem from the list fields

If your modem is not in the list, select the entry *Standard modem types* under *Manufacturer*.

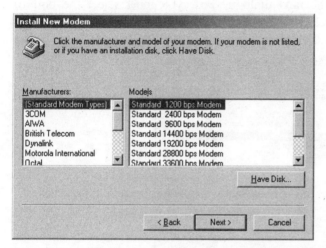

Figure 11.2   Selection of modem manufacturer and model

Transmission
speed

Under *Model*, select the transmission speed of your modem (e.g.: *Standard modem 33600 bps* for a *V.34bis* modem or *Standard modem 56000 bps K56 Flex/X2* for a 56k modem).

With older *V.34* modems, select the entry *Standard modem 28000 bps*; for a *V.90*-Modem with 56.000 bps you will need the appropriate modem driver on a disk from the manufacturer.

V.90 modem

For a *V.90* modem, select either the *Manufacturer* and the *Model* or click on the *Have disk...* button and insert the modem driver on disk or CD-ROM.

Caution: For *Standard modem types* in *Windows Me* you will have to expect some limitations when configuring at a later time.

COM port

In the next dialogue box, you must select the port to which your modem is connected. This means a serial port. Select an entry, e.g. *COM port, (COM1).*

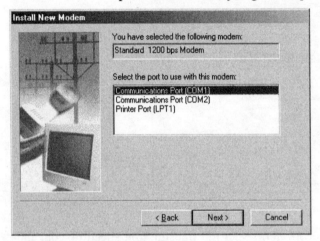

Figure 11.3   Setting the modem port

If you confirm with *Next, Windows Me* installs the necessary modem driver. The next step, *Location,* appears. Enter the required information. The most important is the correct area code. Exit the modem installation by clicking on *Next* and *Finish..*

The dialogue box *Modem Properties* appears. Your modem is now installed and the entry appears in the list.

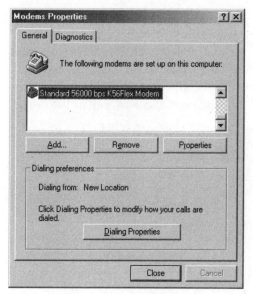

Figure 11.4 The *Properties* window opens after the modem is installed

Plug & Play-
modems

The list of *Modems* displays all installed devices, and the number of the assigned *COM* ports (*COM* stands for *Communications*) appears under *Assigned to*.

Setting modem properties

Modems icon

After installing a modem, the port settings or the maximum speed can be checked and changed. To do this, you need to open the dialogue box, *Modem Properties* through the *Control Panel* and the *Modems* icon 📠. All installed modems are listed in the *Modem Properties* dialogue box.

Setting the port and speed

General tab

Select the entry for the modem whose settings you want to check and click on *Properties*. A dialogue box with two tabs appears. On the *General* tab, you will see information about the *Maximum speed* as well as the *Port*.

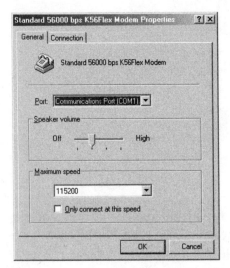

Figure 11.5 Checking the properties of an installed modem

Port list

If the modem is installed on a serial port, open the list of *Ports* and select the correct entry. In the options group *Speaker volume,* you can make settings for the internal speaker in a modem. Drag the slide to the desired position between *Off* and *High*

With standard modem drivers, you may not be able to make the settings described above. For example, the speaker of the *Standard modem types* cannot always be configured. However, the most important connection settings are still available with this modem type.

Maximum speed

One of the most important settings in the properties window is the *Maximum speed*, at the bottom of the dialogue box. This sets the speed between modem and computer. Click on the arrow and mark the entry for the maximum possible data transmission rate of 115,200 bps.

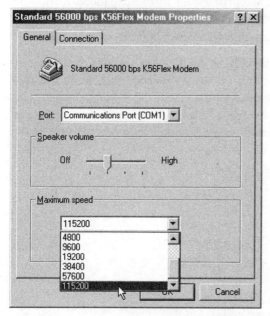

Figure 11.6   Setting the maximum transmission speed between computer and modem

Internal
communication

This setting has nothing to do with the effective data transmission rate of your modem. This only concerns the communication between computer and modem.

Making connection settings for the modem

A modem converts digital data into analogue impulses which can be transmitted over normal telephone lines. On the receiving end, another modem converts the analogue signals back into computer data. How the data is transmitted and checked for errors depends on the type of modem used.

Connection
Settings

Many online applications require a modification of the default connection settings. Select *Start* and *Settings*, and then click on *Control Panel* in the expanded menu. In the *Control Panel*, click on the icon for *Modems* 🖳. In the *Properties* window, all installed modems are listed.

Settings tab

Mark the entry whose connection settings you want to change, and click on the *Properties* button. In the dialogue box which appears, select the *Connection* tab. Under the options group, *Connection preferences*, you can set the number of *Data bits* and *Stop bits* as well as the *Parity*.

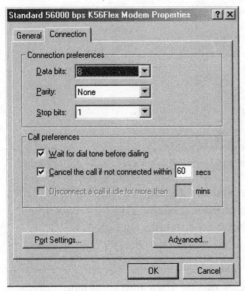

Figure 11.7   Connection settings for the modem

Parity check

In *Windows Me,* the parity check is shown in the *Parity* field, with the options *None, Even, Odd,* and with *Mark* or *Space.* Most online services, mailboxes or internet service providers require the standard configuration of the *Dial-up connection* which is composed of eights data bits, no parity check *(None)* and 1 stop bit.

8,N,1

In online jargon, these settings are often known as *8,N,1,* i.e. eight, none, and 1.

HyperTerminal window

The *Windows Me* default entries are correct for everyday use. However, with some e-mail programs, you may encounter problems. If all other modem settings are correct and you still are not able to connect, or if you only get cryptic characters in the *HyperTerminal* window, incorrect connection settings may be the cause of the problem.

Wait for dial tone

If your modem refuses to dial, deselect the checkbox, *Wait for tone before dialing.* This problem occurs occasionally with modems on extensions or because the modem dials particularly rapidly.

Cancel the call if not connected...

Mark the checkbox *Cancel the call if not connected within [X] seconds,* and enter the time after which the call is to be cancelled by *Windows Me.*

It can help to save money if you select the option *Disconnect a call if idle for more than [X] minutes.* Enter the number of minutes after which the modem is to disconnect if there is no online activity (user input).

You can use the *Add new modem* dialogue to make multiple entries for one modem, each of which has a different name. You can make different settings for each entry. This way, you do not have to change the basic settings every time you are using a special online service which requires different settings

495

Setting error and data flow control for the modem

The way in which the data is transmitted by the modem, the way the data flow is controlled, and whether the data is to be compressed, depends on the purpose for which your modem is used. Many online applications require a modification of the default settings, such as turning off the data compression.

Modems icon

To change the advanced modem properties, select *Start* and *Settings* and click on the *Control Panel*. In the *Control Panel* double click on the *Modems* icon 📠.

Advanced
properties

In the *Properties* window, all installed modems are listed. Mark the entry whose error and data flow control you want to change. Click on the *Properties* button. In the dialogue box which appears, select the *Connection* tab and click on the button *Advanced...*, to open the *Advanced connection settings* dialogue box shown in Figure 11.8.

Internet access

For internet access through *Dial-up networking* and most other online services, select the options *Use flow control* and *Hardware (RTS/CTS)*.

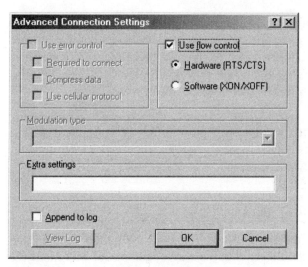

Figure 11.8   Setting advanced properties for the modem

Handshaking

In computer jargon, the communication between your modem and the computer is known as *Handshaking*. The option *Hardware (RTS/CTS)* stores the mutual information between computer and modem, which during transmission automatically stops data flow or allows it to run again, in the hardware of the modem.

The *Software (XON/XOFF)* option is seldom needed. The tasks described above are in this case, controlled by the communications software.

Error control

Much more important are the checkboxes   under *Use error control*. Because most online services work with manufacturer's own error control methods, incorrect settings in this options group can sometimes cause problems. The checkbox *Data compression* turns on the data compression process of the modem. The checkbox *Required to connect* requires the use of this setting.

Use cellular
protocol

If you select *Use cellular* protocol, you specify that the cellular telephone protocol should be used for connections to cellular telephones. The entries are only valid if they are supported by the modem. After you have made your changes, confirm them in the *Advanced connection settings* dialogue box by clicking on *Ok*. Close the dialogue boxes as well as the *Control Panel*.

For internet connections through *Dial-up networking*, you should ask your internet provider which modem options are permitted.

Connection settings for serial ports

COM ports

After modem installation and configuration, nothing more should stand in the way of successful data transmission. However, if you are having connection problems with your computer, or if your high-speed modem reaches only low data transmission rates, you can make use of the suggestions contained in this section. Because your modem is always connected to a serial port, you should take a look at the *Port settings* for the *COM*-ports.

Settings tab

You may have already looked for a direct configuration of the port settings without success. This is because the function is well hidden: Select *Start/Settings* to open the *Control Panel* and then click on the *Modems* icon . In the properties window, click on the *Connection* tab, and click on the *Port settings...* button. A dialogue box will appear for making these settings.

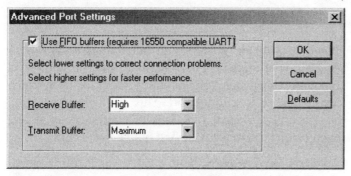

Figure 11.9   Port settings for FIFO buffered serial ports

Using FIFO buffers If you are using a *Pentium I/II/III* computer system, check to see that the checkbox for *Use FIFO buffers...* is selected.

UART chip This refers to the so-called *UART* chip, a communications chip with a buffer in the layout of the port electronics. This chip is also responsible for hardware parity checking. The high connection speeds of the 56,000 modem can only be obtained with this chip. If you have an older PC system, you should definitely read this section.

Transmit buffer list box If you are constantly having connection problems with your modem, and have ruled out problems with the lines and incorrect dialing, set a lower value in the *Transmit buffer* list box and try dialing again.

Receive buffer list box If your high-speed modem is constantly causing you problems in the data transmission rate, and if this is not the fault of the online service, set the highest position *(maximum)* in the *Receive buffer* list box and try the data transfer again.

Testing the serial ports

Windows Me can be helpful in other ways besides configuring your modem. The operating system also offers a function with which you can easily check devices which are connected to a serial port. This will help you to find any incorrect modem functions or configuration errors, even before you make your first online connection.

Diagnosing the ports

To diagnose the ports, you need to open the *Control Panel*. In the *Control Panel* click on the *Modems* icon to display the properties window. Click on the *Diagnostics* tab. All ports and the connected devices are displayed here. Click on the *Driver* tab to see the information on the modem driver displayed in the list.

Details button

Select the *COM* entry, which is displayed next to your modem and click on *Details...*. The modem must be turned on! A message box informs you that data is now being transmitted to the modem. Next, the *Details* dialogue box appears with information which was relayed from the modem and the port. This information is important when using older computers.

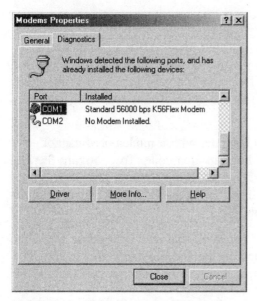

Figure 11.10   Using the modem diagnostics

Ports information

Under *Port information,* you will see information on the interrupt, address and (most important) the type of *UART* chip. If the control chip for the port (*UART*) is given with the name *8250* then no transmission speed higher than 14,400 bps is possible.

UART chip

The *UART* chip (*Universal Asynchronous Transmitter*) is the heart of the serial port and is responsible for creating the necessary signals for the data transmission. The outdated *8250* version of the chip cannot be used with the data transmission rates of modern modems.

UART 16550 chip

Today, it is definitely necessary to have a serial port with the high performance *UART-16550* chip (Standard with all *Pentiums,* and shown in the diagnostics as *NS 16550AN*), which has an integrated buffer (*FIFO,* First In, First Out) and allows data transmission rates of up to 115,200 bps.

Setting the dialing properties for the modem

Extensions

Before you set up your modem for internet access or online services, you should set the *Dialing properties* for your location. These settings are particularly important for modems which are connected to extensions on telephone systems.

Area code is required

Just as with a telephone, with a modem you cannot connect outside without an area code. To configure the *Dialing properties*, select *Start/Settings* and then select *Control Panel* from the expanded menu. Next, click on the *Modems* icon 📞.

Dialing properties dialogue box

In the *Modem Properties* dialogue box, select the *General* tab and click on the *Dialing properties* button. The *Dialing properties* dialogue box shown in Figure 11.11 appears.

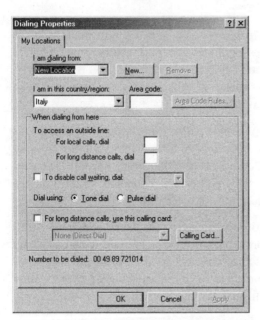

Figure 11.11   Setting dialing properties for the modem

Current location

In this dialogue box, select *New...* under *Location* and enter your location as well as the *Country* and *Area code* You can use the list boxes for this. These entries enable *Windows Me* to distinguish local calls from others, so that it does not use unnecessary area codes and country codes when dialing.

Entering the area code

If your modem is connected to a telephone system extension, enter the number to dial *For local calls* and if necessary, *For long distance calls* in the text boxes under *When dialing from here*.

Locations tab

If you are working on a notebook, you can define various dialing properties for different locations (e.g. office and outside). Click on the *Locations* tab and then press *New...*Click on *OK* and enter the name of a new location. Adjust the dialing properties accordingly. Now, you can select your desired location from the *Location* list, and the dialing properties will be automatically adjusted.

Setting the type of dialing

Dialing properties

Before you begin to use your modem, you must specify whether *Tone or pulse dialing* is to be used for your telephone connection. Select *Start/Settings* and click on *Control Panel*. Double click on the *Modems* .

In the *Modem Properties* dialogue box, press the *Dialing properties* button. The dialogue box shown in Figure 11.12 appears.

Tone or pulse dialing

If these settings are incorrect, it will take unnecessarily long to make a connection. In many countries, two different methods of dialing are used. The old – and in many places, no longer used – method is known as pulse dialing. It can be recognized by the "clacking" noise and longer dialing time.

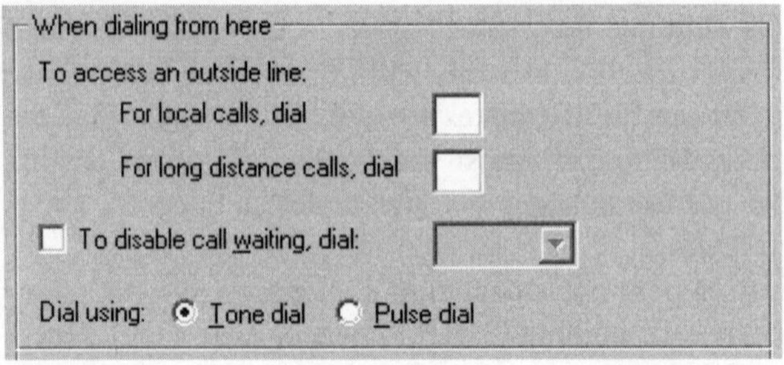

Figure 11.12   Setting tone dialing for the modem

Pulse dialing

If your modem is connected to an older telephone system, you may only be able to connect by using pulse dialing. If so, select the *Pulse dial* option next to *Dial using:*

Tone dialing

If you have modern multiple frequency dialing from a digital exchange, select *Tone dial*. Tone dialing can be recognized by the various high-pitched tones which accompany the dialing.

Changing the type of dialing

If your telephone or fax is still set for *Pulse dialing* you can change it. The information on how to do this is supplied with the telephone or fax machine. Confirm with *OK*, and close the *Modem Properties* dialogue box.

Installing and setting up an *ISDN* adapter

You can also use an *ISDN* adapter as an alternative to a modem for online connections. The requirement for this is a digital *ISDN* connection, because an ISDN adapter cannot be used on an analogue telephone connection .

ISDN network

The digital *ISDN* telephone network (*Integrated Services Digital Network*) is an all-encompassing communications network which combines telephone fax and data transmission in a digital network.

Channel bundling

With *ISDN,* you can reach speeds of up to 64,000 bps (bits per second) through a telephone connection. Because each *ISDN* connection supplies two telephone lines, known as B-channels, data transmission rates of up to 128,000 bps can be reached with the so-called channel bundling. These two telephone connections in the digital network are also available for telephone and faxes.

Two connections

With an *ISDN* connection, you are given two telephone numbers and two connections. This way, you can telephone while you are receiving a fax or while you are on-line in the internet. *ISDN* connections may include the following features:

- *ISDN* connection (2 connections and 3 telephone numbers)

- Maximum 8 *ISDN* end devices per connection

- Data transmission rate per channel: 64,000 bps

- Caller ID for other *ISDN* users

- Call waiting, 3 way conferencing, call forwarding, etc.

ISDN telephones

For telephoning, you need an *ISDN* telephone or a telephone system on which existing analogue end devices such as telephone, fax or modem are operated on the *ISDN* connection. To connect the computer to the digital telephone connection, you need an additional device, the so-called *ISDN* adapter which is most often in the form of an internal *ISDN* card installed in the computer.

External *ISDN*-adapters

For this, you need a free *PCI* or *ISA* slot, depending on the design of the *ISDN* card. In addition, there are external *ISDN* adapters in their own housings, which can be connected to a serial port or a *USB* port on the computer.

Here, we will limit our description to such an external device.

Ideally, the *Windows Me* driver installation begins automatically after connecting the *ISDN* adapter.

Configuring an *ISDN adapter*

Add new hardware
wizard

Most internal *ISDN* adapters are installed with the *Add new hardware wizard* under *Windows Me*. Ideally, this is launched automatically after connecting the device (or after installing an *ISDN* adapter).

If the *Add new hardware* wizard starts automatically after installation of the ISDN adapter, click on *Next* in the first window. Otherwise, open the *Add new hardware wizard* manually through the *Control Panel* and the *Add new hardware* icon 📚. Click once again on *Next* (keep the option *Automatic search for a better driver (Recommended)* checked) to start detection of *Plug & Play* enabled *ISDN* adapters.

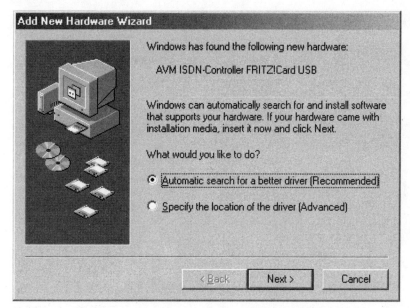

Figure 11.13   Installing an *ISDN adapter* through the Add New Hardware Wizard

Device is not listed   If the driver of the *ISDN* adapter is not automatically installed, select the option *Specify the location of the driver (Advanced)* and click on *Next.* If you want *Windows Me* to search semi-automatically for a driver, leave the option *Search for the best driver (Recommended)* selected, and enter the name of the folder or drive to be searched. At this time, also insert the manufacturer's CD-ROM. With a click on *Next, Windows Me* will give it another try.

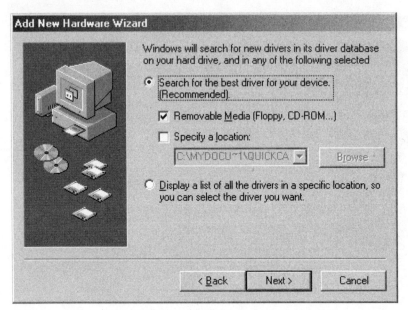

Figure 11.14 *Windows Me* searches semi-automatically for a driver

When you select the option, *Display a list of all the drivers in a specific location, so you can select...* you take complete control of the operation. After clicking on *Next*, look for *Other components* from the list and click on *Next*. In the following step, select the *Have disk...* button and search for the location of the driver. In the next window, select your *ISDN* device and confirm with *Next* and *Finish*.

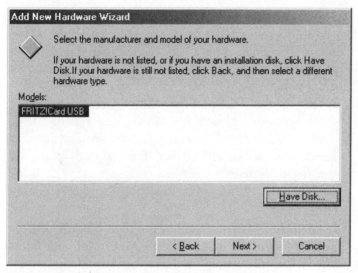

Figure 11.15   Driver on the manufacturer's CD-ROM

Installation of the CAPI communication driver

CAPI driver

With modern *ISDN* drivers, the so-called CAPI driver software is also installed. With older models, you may have to set up the software by hand. This driver is used by *Windows Me* for communication with the *ISDN* adapter. The so-called *CAPI* driver is a standardized driver through which all *ISDN* devices on a computer of various *ISDN* applications can be controlled. Since there is a difference in the hardware between various *ISDN* cards, the card manufacturer must also supply the *CAPI* driver. Install this driver from the disk supplied.

In *Windows Me* you need a *CAPI* driver of the *CAPI 2.0* standard. There are two different versions of *CAPI*, which has nothing to do with how current the version is. They are two different standards for ISDN communication. You need *CAPI 1.1* for *Windows 3.x* and all older

509

16-bit applications. *CAPI 2.0* is needed for all 32-bit *ISDN* programs under *Windows Me.* During the *CAPI* setup, if you can choose between the two standards, select the *CAPI 2.0* or a "dual" *CAPI.* These drivers allow you to use both *CAPI* standards 1.1 and 2.0. With a dual *CAPI* you avoid the problems with different versions of *ISDN* software. Always install the latest version of the needed *CAPI* driver. However, for the first functionality check, use the available driver. You can find updates on the *Euro file transfer* service computer of your *ISDN* card manufacturer.

Launch the *CAPI* installation program according to the instructions in the manual of the *ISDN* card, and follow any further instructions on the screen. For internet access, you just need the *CAPI* communication module. Normally, this driver can be separately installed.

ISDN applications

Sometimes, the setup programs install the *ISDN* applications at the same time as the *CAPI* driver. To be able to use all *ISDN* functions such as fax, answering machine, *Euro file transfer* or integrated modem emulation, you also need the software which comes with the card. However we will not go into these details at this time.

If you only want to use your *ISDN* card to connect to online services or to use the internet, or if you are using only the Windows communications program *Dial-up networking*, you only need the *CAPI* driver to use your *ISDN* card.You need other card-specific applications for using other *ISDN* or card functions such as fax functions, answering machines, *Euro file transfer,* or if you want to use modem emulation.

CAPI configuration

We will now learn how to configure the CAPI driver: the configuration of the various ISDN adapters will vary from manufacturer to manufacturer, although the most important basic settings can be made in a similar manner for all card models. Amongst the most important settings are:

Settings

- Selection of the D-channel protocol

- The options for channel bundling

- The preparation of transmission protocols

- The settings for multiple subscriber numbers

- The settings for end device selection numbers

During installation and configuration, select the correct *D-channel protocol,* which defines the type of *ISDN* data transmission. Instead of the old national protocol 1TR6, select the new *Euro ISDN* protocol *DSS1*. The *DSS1* protocol is necessary for *Euro file transfer*.

Channel bundling

Use all available options for digital data protocol such as *V.110* or *X.75* etc. If necessary, select the options for channel bundling which is also called bundle or *Channel Mapping*. Without the bundling, only one B-channel can be used.. You can only reach data transmission speeds of 128,000 bps with both channels.

Because every *ISDN* connection offers three telephone numbers, you should reserve one of these numbers for the *ISDN* card in your computer, so that it can accept incoming calls and distinguish between these services. One of the numbers can be used for *Euro file transfer*, and another can be used for the *ISDN* computer-fax and your telephone number for the digital answering machine of the *ISDN* card.

Figure 11.16   *Windows Me* uses the standard CAPI driver, version 2.0

Multiple subscriber numbers

The assignment of the *Multiple subscriber numbers (msn)* of your *ISDN* connection is most often done through the *CAPI* configuration (also the *ISDN* configuration). In your configuration application, enter the appropriate numbers for the computer fax, the *Euro file transfer* and the computer answering machine. Often, the call receiver must be separately activated.

End device selection number

You don't need to worry about the *end device selection number* if you are using *Euro ISDN*, because it is no longer used. For older configuration programs which still require the *end device selection number*, you must enter the different *ISDN* services identifications (SI) for each program module.

To simplify the specification of the *end device selection numbers*, you can simply enter a "0", which acts as a so-called *universal call*. This way, the active *ISDN* program module accepts all incoming calls with the appropriate number. The fax program accepts faxes in the same way and the data module allows data transfer via *Euro file transfer*, etc.

The 2-channel transfer with 128 Kbit/sec can be activated later while setting up the *Dial-up networking connection*. If you want to use both *ISDN* channels for internet access, activate the option *Additional device* in the properties window under the *Multilink* tab. Under *ADD*, you can select another B-channel.

Installing and configuring a Dial-up networking

At this point, we welcome back the modem users. All further configurations for internet access are identical for both modem and *ISDN* users.

Checking the installation

To use the internet or other online services under *Windows Me* you need to set up the *Dial-up networking*. Normally, *Windows Me* sets up all necessary components during the installation of the operating system. However, it can't hurt to check whether the *Dial-up networking* is set up on your computer.

To do this, open the *Start* and point to *Programs/Accessories* and *Communication*. In the *Communication* program group, select *Dial-up networking*, and skip the next section.

Web browser

If there is no such entry, you must set up *Windows Me*. To access the various services from the internet, you need additional software. For the WWW, use a web browser such as *Microsoft Internet Explorer,* version 5.5 which is integrated in the *Windows Me* operating system.

Now to install the *Dial-up networking* for internet access under *Windows Me*. Select *Start/Settings*, and click on *Control Panel*.

Double click on *Add/Remove Programs* , and click on the tab *Windows Setup*.

In the list of *Components,* select the entry *Communications*, and click on *Details....* Now mark the checkbox nest to *Dial-up networking*, and confirm with *OK*. After restarting, your *Dial-up networking* will be ready.

513

Figure 11.17   Installing *Dial-up networking* for *Windows Me*

Setting up the *Dial-up* adapter

With *Dial-up networking*, the network driver, *Dial-up adapter* is automatically installed, as well as the internet protocol *TCP/IP*, which you must be individually configured for each dial-up network connection. For a *Dial-up networking connection* to the internet, you need:

- Dial-up networking

- The Dial-up adapter network driver

- The network protocol, TCP/IP

- A Dial-up connection

- Configuration of the internet protocol, TCP/IP

If you plan to have internet access through a service provider such as *CompuServe* or *AOL*, you do not need to do this configuration step. These online services offer a complete package for internet access which enables you to surf the web without the functions described here, which are contained in *Windows Me* (program group *Online services*).

Internet-by-Call providers

Using the following instructions, you will now be able to access the internet through *Dial-up networking* and *Windows Me*. If all of this is too complicated for you, we recommend that you subscribe to a large trans-regional provider such as *CompuServe* or *AOL* who will provide you with an trouble-free total internet package. This will save you the trouble of configuring *Windows Me* for internet access. Many *Internet-by-Call* providers offer similar software and programs which automatically set up and define the *Dial-up connection* for you.

If your internet provider has not given you any software, then you will be working with *Windows Me* and *Dial-up networking*. In addition, internet access through *Dial-up networking* is the more professional method. You will also see that it is not really so complicated, after all. Instead of manual configuration, you can create the connection to the internet with the help of a wizard, as we will explain later.

Installing the *TCP/IP* network protocol

In addition to *Dial-up networking* and *Dial-up Adapter* you need the network protocol, *TCP/IP* for internet access over a *Dial-up connection*. This protocol is automatically installed by *Windows Me*.

Entry

Dial-up Adapter

You need the information in this section only if you have inadvertently deleted the protocol entry from the list of installed components. If you see the entry *TCP/IP* in the list, you can skip this section.

If the *TCP/IP*-protocol is not installed, go to the *Network* dialogue box (*Control Panel/Network* 🖳) and select the *Configuration* tab. Click on *Add...*, and in the *Click on the type of network component you want to install,* select *Protocol*. Now click on *Add....*

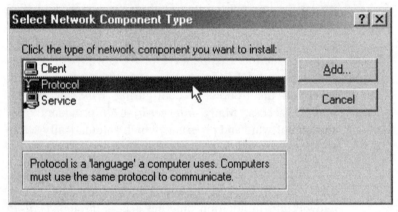

Figure 11.18   Installing a new protocol

From the list of *Manufacturers*, select *Microsoft,* and in the *Network protocols* list, select *TCP/IP*. Then click on *OK*. *Windows Me* installs the protocol and lists it in the *Network* dialogue box.

TCP/IP entries

If needed, use the scroll bar to display the *TCP/IP* entries. If *Windows Me* is installed on a network computer, *TCP/IP* is also installed for the network card.

If you want to make identical *TCP/IP* settings for **all** connection icons through *Dial-up networking,* read how to configure the internet protocol in the next section.

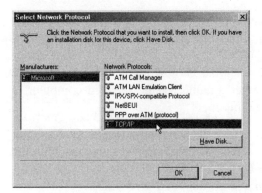

Figure 11.19   Selection of the protocol *TCP/IP* for internet access

Setting up an internet connection with *Dial-up networking*

Now, we arrive at the actual setup of connections for internet access under *Windows Me*. We will describe how to set up *Dial-up networking* for connecting to the internet. This is actually the connection to the server of your internet provider. To do this, the necessary drivers and protocols must be installed.

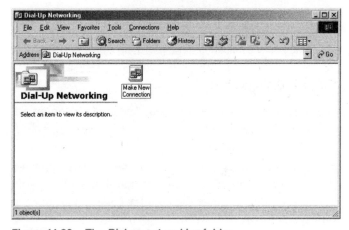

Figure 11.20   The *Dial-up networking* folder

Dial-up networking

To set up access, open the folder *Dial-up networking*. You can open this through *Start/Settings/Dial-up networking*.

Click on the icon *Make a new connection*. In the first dialogue box, enter a name for the selected computer in the textbox, e.g. "Internet".

Selecting an *ISDN* adapter

In the *Select a device* list box, select your modem. For *ISDN* adapters, select either *Miniport* or an entry with the number of the *B-channel*. For a few devices, the appropriate entry can also contain *PPP over ISDN*.

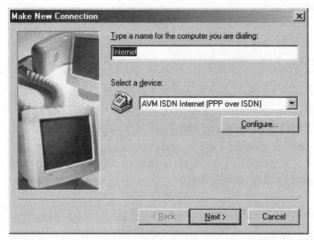

Figure 11.21   Wizard for making a new connection through *Dial-up networking*

When you click on *Configure...* you can switch to the properties window of the modem, and make changes in the modem parameters there.

Entering the telephone number

In the dialogue box, *Make a new connection,* click on *Next*. Enter the telephone number and area code of your service provider. Change the *country code* to that of your country. Confirm with *Next*..

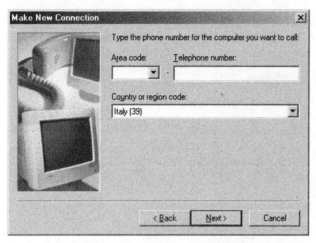

Figure 11.22   Entering the telephone number of the service provider

In the last dialogue box, you can check the name of the new connection. Click on *Finish,* and the wizard will create a new icon with the name you entered, in the *Dial-up networking* folder. Later, a double click on this icon will connect you to the server of your internet provider.

Setting Properties   Before you make the first connection, you must set the properties for the server connection. Point to the icon of the connection you just created. Click with the right mouse button and from the context menu, select *Properties.* Now, select the *Network* tab. If you are using an *Internet-By-Call provider,* deselect all checkboxes under *Advanced options* except for *Enable software compression.* Under *Allowed network protocols* deselect all checkboxes except for *TCP/IP*.

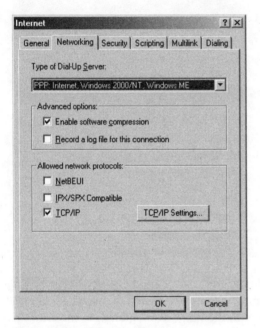

Figure 11.23   The server types tab

TCP/IP settings

Now, independent of your internet service provider, click on *TCP/IP-Settings....* In the dialogue box, *TCP/IP-Settings,* you must enter the *IP address* and/or the address of the DNS server of your internet service provider.

IP Address

Under *TCP/IP-Settings,* mark the option, *Specify an IP Address*, and enter the appropriate *IP address*. Otherwise, you will be given an *IP address* by the server. This is the default setting of *Windows Me.*

Server DNS

If necessary, select the option *Specify name server address,* and in the field *Primary DNS* enter the name of the server in thee form *XXX.XXX.XXX.XXX*, where each "X" is to be replaced by a number. Enter the secondary *DNS* in the corresponding field, etc.

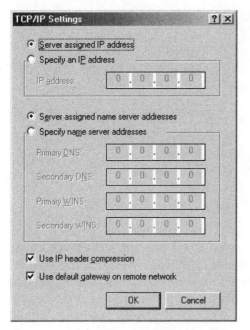

Figure 11.24 Entering the *IP address* of the server

Confirm your settings with *OK*. If no more information is needed, close the dialogue box with *OK*.

Making an internet connection with *Dial-up networking*

You may hardly be able to believe it, but you are now ready to make the first contact with the server of your internet provider. For this, you just need the folder, *Dial-up networking*, and the icon you have just created for the connection.

Double click on the connection icon
In the *Dial-up networking* folder, double click on the connection icon to make a first connection to the internet. The dialogue box, *Connect to* appears.

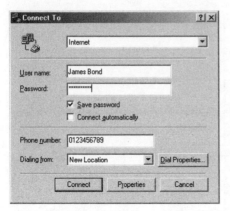

Figure 11.25   The *Connect to dialogue box*

Enter your *User name* and *Password* for internet access through your service provider. With *Internet-by-Call providers,* use the information which has been supplied to you. If necessary, check the phone number at the bottom of the dialogue box and with the *Dial properties...* button, and check the dialing parameters and area code.

Connect button

Click on *Connect* to begin dialing. The dialing status is displayed in a dialogue box (see Figure 11.26).

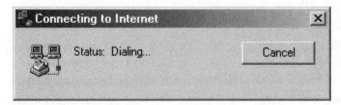

Figure 11.26   Dialing status

With a modem connection, you can hear the dialing and handshake phases. Then there is the network logon with the server of the internet provider. As soon as you are connected, you will receive a message. Confirm with *Close*. If you do not want to have this message displayed each time, select the checkbox option *Do not display this message in the future.*

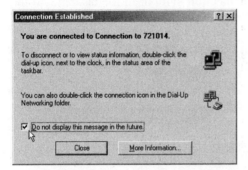

Figure 11.27   Do not display this message in the future

Connected to
dialogue box

When the connection has been made, the dialogue box, *Connect to* becomes an icon in the taskbar, to the left of the time. A double click on this icon opens the dialogue box *Connected to...* which displays the current connection data (see Figure 11.28).

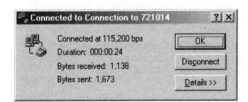

Figure 11.28   You are connected

Microsoft Internet
Explorer

The active connection is displayed in the dialogue box, along with the current data transmission rate and the number of bytes received and sent. Now you can start up the software for accessing the internet such as *Microsoft Internet Explorer,* to display content from the WWW. To do this, click on the *Internet Explorer* icon on the *Windows* desktop. In *Internet Explorer,* the default homepage (*Microsoft Windows Me*) will be displayed.

Disconnecting   There are two ways to disconnect: You can open the dialogue box *Connected to* (Figure 11.30) by double clicking on the connection symbol in the taskbar, to the left of the time. Then, click on *Disconnect*.

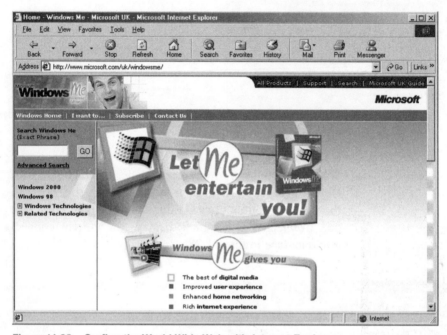

Figure 11.29   Surfing the World Wide Web with *Internet Explorer*

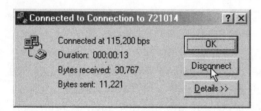

Figure 11.30   Disconnecting through the dialogue box

Context menu

The second way is to right click on the icon and select *Disconnect* (Figure 11.31). The connection is terminated, but *Microsoft Internet Explorer* remains active offline and continues to display the page last visited.

Figure 11.31   Disconnecting through the context menu

Setting up an internet connection with the Internet Connection Wizard

In the previous sections, you have set up a connection to the internet manually, step by step. In this section we will show you how to carry out these same steps with the help of the Internet Connection Wizard.

Figure 11.32   Configuring internet connections with the Internet Connection Wizard

There are several ways to start up the wizard. You can click directly on the *Connection to the internet* icon, or you can select *Start/ Programs/Accessories/Internet tools,* and then click on *Internet Connection Wizard.* In *Internet Explorer* you can select *Tools/Internet options* and go to the *Connections* tab where you click on the *Setup...* button.

Internet connection wizard

Any of these methods will launch the *Internet connection wizard.* In the first dialogue box, the second option specifies that *Windows Me* should set up the internet programs to use an existing internet connection. If you select the first option, you can open a new internet account.

Dial-up Network Connection

At this point, we will only discuss how to work with the connection wizard to set up *Windows Me* internet programs through a *Dial-up Network Connection* which is to be defined: To do this, select the option *I want to set up my internet connection manually...* and click on *Next.*

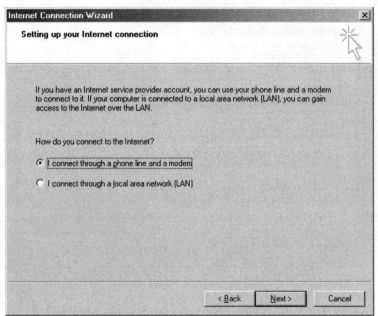

Figure 11.33   Internet connection through a modem or a local network

Modem or LAN

In the second screen of the connection wizard, specify whether the connection to the internet provider will be done through a modem or through a local area network *(LAN)*. Here, we will limit ourselves to the first option *I connect through a phone line and a modem*. Confirm this step with *Next*.

Selecting a modem

In the next step, specify which device will be used to connect to the internet. If you are using a modem, select your modem and click on *Next*.

Selecting an *ISDN* adapter

If you have an *ISDN* adapter, select the entry with the desired B-channel or a *PPP over ISDN* modem. Click on *Next*.

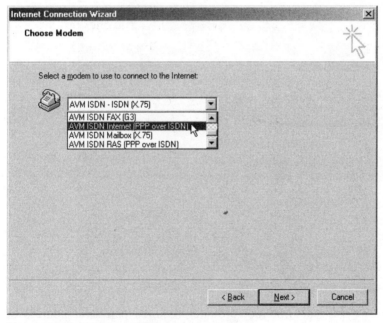

Figure 11.34   Modem or ISDN channel selection

Entering the telephone number

In the next step, enter the information on the internet connection. This corresponds to the procedure for creating a *Dial-up Network Connection*. Enter the number of the internet service provider. You can also use an *Internet-by-Call* provider. You will learn more about that later in this chapter. Enter the correct telephone number under *Telephone number*. Leave the *Area code* empty and only mark the checkbox *Dial using the area code and country code*, if the settings there are required. Click on *Advanced....*

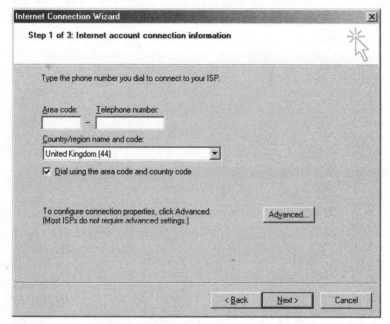

Figure 11.35   Entering the telephone number of the internet service provider

Connection settings

If your internet provider requires particular address or connection settings, you can enter them now:

Under the *Connection* tab you can select the necessary connection type.

Most connections require *Point-to-Point protocol (PPP)*, e.g. all *Internet-by-Call* providers.

Internet connection protocol With so many internet service providers, different connection types are used to specify the connection protocol.

Use the protocol recommended by your service provider.

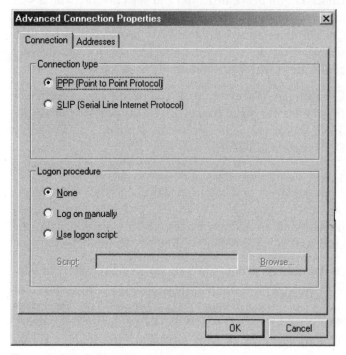

Figure 11.36   Setting the connection type

In the internet, the following connection types are used for modem connections:

- *PPP (Point-To-Point Protocol)*

- *SLIP (Serial Line Internet Protocol)*

- *CSLIP (Compressed Serial Line Internet Protocol)*

The modern protocol, *PPP* is most often used for internet access. This is installed automatically for standard *Dial-up Connections*. Use this protocol for internet access or network connections under *Windows Me*.

Under *Logon procedure,* you can select *None,* which will require you to *Logon manually,* or *Use a logon script.* Certain requests are automatically taken care of by such scripts. You do not need these settings for the internet connections which are commonly used today.

IP address

Click on the *Addresses* tab, if you need to use a particular IP address for your connection. You can set the IP address and/or the addresses of the primary and secondary DNS servers, if needed.

DNS server

Under *Addresses,* select the option *Always use the following address* and enter the address given by your internet service provider. Otherwise, you will automatically be assigned an address by the server (this is usually the case, and it is the default setting of *Windows Me*).

DNS server

address

In the options group, *DNS server address,* select the option *Always use the following address*, and enter the name of the *Primary DNS server* in the form *XXX.XXX.XXX.XXX*, where the Xs are the given numbers. You will receive an error message if the settings are incorrect.

If necessary, enter the name of the secondary *DNS server* in the corresponding field. For example, you would enter the DNS server addresses *145.253.2.11* and *145.253.2.75* for the Internet-by-Call provider *Arcor*.

Confirm you address and connection settings by clicking on *OK*. You will return to the *Internet connection wizard*.

Click on *Next* to confirm the data you have entered for the connection to the server,.

Entering the logon information

In the next step, you enter the logon information, i.e. *User name* and *Password*. If you are using an *Internet-by-Call* provider, use the information supplied to you, and click on *Next*.

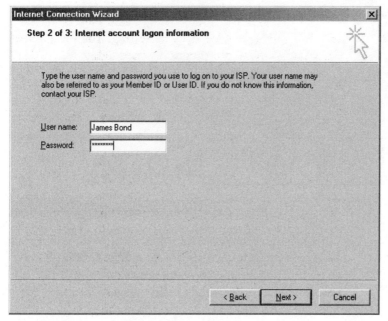

Figure 11.37   Entering the logon information

Name of the connection

In the last step, you can overwrite or add to the name of the connection. Confirm with *Next*, to start the setup of your e-mail account. Select *Yes* if you already have an e-mail address.

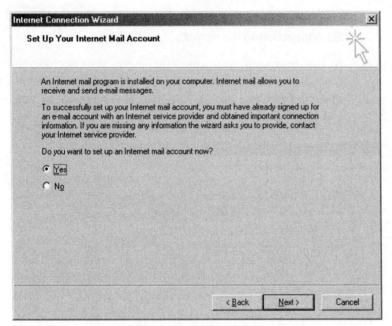

Figure 11.38   *Setting up an internet mail account*

To configure your e-mail account, you need to have an account with an e-mail provider. If you do not yet have an address, click on *NO*. At a later time, we will find out how to manually set up an e-mail account..

If you select *Yes* for the e-mail account, the configuration will be similar to that described in the section, *E-mail account with Outlook Express,* later in this chapter. In all cases, confirm the individual steps of the wizard with *Next*.

Entering the mail server names

All information on an internet e-mail account such as e-mail address and mail server names for incoming and outgoing mail, will be requested step by step. Keep the information supplied by your internet service provider on hand. If you use an *Internet-by-Call* providers, you will be given this information later. Now, click on *Finish* and your internet connection is ready.

Connect button

To make a connection, click on the *Connect* button. The dialing, network logon, and verification of user name and password are shown in the dialogue box. After you are connected, *Microsoft Internet Explorer* is automatically launched

Connection data

In *Internet Explorer,* the default homepage (*Microsoft Windows Me*) or the homepage of the *Internet-by-Call* provider will be displayed. Starting from this page, you can go to any other page in the WWW. You will find out more about navigating the WWW and the use of the web browser program in the next section. The existing connection is now shown as an icon in the systray of the taskbar, to the left of the time. If you point to this icon, the current connection data will be displayed as a *Quick info*. A double click on the icon will display the current connection data.

Working with *Microsoft Internet Explorer*

After setting up a connection icon in *Dial-up Networking,* or after having used the *Internet connection wizard*, you can use an operating system-integrated web browser such as *Microsoft Internet Explorer 5.5* to surf the worldwide information service of the internet, the World Wide Web.

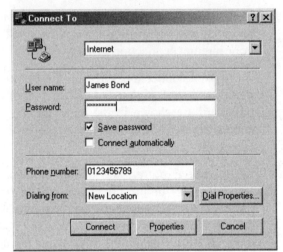

Internet Explorer

Figure 11.39 *Internet Explorer* goes online

Internet Service
Provider

There are several ways to go online with *Internet Ex-plorer.* You can use the internet access software of a data service from your internet service provider, and make a connection through it. Otherwise, you can double click on the icon for a *Dial-up Network Connection* in *Dial-up Networking,* to make an connection by clicking on *Connect.*

As soon as you are connected to the server of the internet provider, you can start up the *Internet Explorer* use the task bar switch to go to the browser if it has already been opened. The default homepage will appear. If you have used the *Internet connection wizard,* double click on the *Internet Explorer* icon on the desktop to display the *Dial-up Connection* dialogue box. When you click on *Connect* the connection is made.

Making a connection

If you click on a button *Windows Me* which contains a link to the internet, *Internet Explorer* starts up automatically and displays the *Dial-up Connection* dialogue box. From here, you can go online by clicking on *Connect*.

World Wide Web

The *World Wide Web,* or *WWW* for short, is the largest information system in the world, and is a part of the internet.. The WWW is the most popular and most frequented internet service. WWW is often used as a synonym for the internet, which is a group of computers connected over the telephone system.

Hypertext technology

Hypertext technology is the basis of the WWW for displaying information in documents. In hypertext, the elements of a document, text and images, function as pointers which refer to other places in the document, or to the content of other documents. These pointers are called *Hyperlinks* or simply *Links,* and are easy to recognize in documents by their color.

Browser

To display the information from the WWW on your screen, you need a *browser* such as *Internet Explorer.* You must use a browser to display information from web servers, i.e. to navigate the web and see or hear the hypermedia documents on your own computer.

Homepage

Now to more practical matters: after you have connected to your service provider through a *Dial-up Network Connection* start the *Internet Explorer* by double clicking on the program icon on the desktop. If you have run the connection wizard, you can activate the icon for *Internet Explorer* at the same time. The web browser opens with the default homepage (*Microsoft Windows Me*), as the opening page is called.

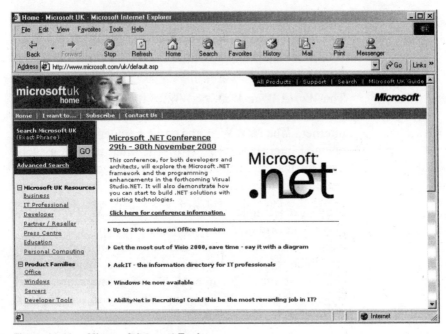

Figure 11.40   *Microsoft Internet Explorer*

Offline

To become familiar with *Internet Explorer* and its controls offline, terminate your online connection to the server of your internet provider, so that you don't accrue unnecessary usage fees.

Figure 11.41   Terminating the connection

Terminating the connection

To terminate the connection, open the *Connected to* dialogue box by double clicking on the connection icon in the taskbar, to the left of the time. Click on the *Disconnect* button.

To disconnect, you can also right-click on the connection icon 💻 and select *Disconnect* from the context menu Figure 11.41). The connection will be terminated, but *Internet Explorer* will remain active offline and will continue to display the website last visited.

The *Internet Explorer* controls

The interface of a web browser is always divided into three sections. At the top, there is the title bar with the title of the current document as well as a menu bar, the *URL* (the web address) is shown in the *Address bar* and there is an animated *Icon* during online use. The middle section is used to display the document you requested. It can be moved up and down with a scroll bar. In the lower area, there is a status bar for information about the connection or the remaining download time. The homepage is a website which is automatically displayed when the browser is launched. You can use also your own page or any other *URL* from the internet.

Title bar

As in every *Windows*-program, there is a title bar in *Internet Explorer* at the top of the program window. In *Internet Explorer,* the title of the document is displayed along with the program name, *Microsoft Internet Explorer.*

URL

The so-called *URL* (*Uniform Resource Locator*) – the address of the website – is found in the *Address bar* as well as in the *Status bar*. *URLs* can also be directly entered into the address bar. If you point to a link, its *URL* is displayed in the status bar.

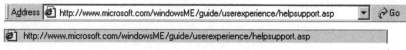

Figure 11.42   The address bar (above) and the status bar

537

Protocol://Service/Serveraddress/Path/Filename.

http://www.

http stands for the transmission protocol, *Hyper Text Transfer Protocol*. *www* stands for World Wide Web. An example of a server address is *microsoft.com*. After that, there is the name of the folder and the file name of the document. The address path never contains empty spaces..

Menu bar

The menu bar is located directly underneath the title bar. Here, you will find the menus available in *Internet Explorer*. Below this is the *Standard buttons* tool bar, used for navigating the web. *Internet Explorer* contains twelve buttons for navigating the WWW.

Figure 11.43   The *Internet Explorer* tool bar with large and small icons

Explorer bars

These buttons give you quick mouse-controlled access to frequently used commands. The table below gives an overview of the function of each button. Buttons shown in gray are not available at the time. To display and hide the tool bar, as well as the *Status bar* and *Explorer bar*, go to the *View* menu. The "grip" is used to move the toolbars or to place them as windows on the screenThe use of the most important buttons in *Internet Explorer* is as follows:

Button	Name	Function
 Back	*Back*	Back to the previously displayed document
 Forward	*Forward*	After having used *Back,* you can return to the document previously displayed
 Stop	*Stop*	Stops the downloading of a page
 Refresh	*Refresh*	Loads the current document again
 Home	*Home*	Return to the default homepage
 Search	*Search*	Searches for web pages in the selected search machine of the WWW
 Favorites	*Favorites*	Allows you to save and quickly open interesting *URLs*
 History	*History*	Divides the window. Previously visited sites are shown on the left
	E-Mail	For writing, reading and sending electronic mail
 Print	*Print*	Prints the current document on the default printer
 Messenger	*Messenger*	Finds friends and acquaintances on the internet

Figure 11.44   The most important buttons in the toolbar

"Secure" Server   The status bar displays information on the loading of the requested document and its address. A lock symbol shows that the server you have reached is "secure". Always look for such secure servers when you are making any data-sensitive transactions (ordering with a credit card, online shopping, home banking, etc.)

Navigating in websites with *Internet Explorer*

Now we take a more practical look at working with *Internet Explorer*. First, you need to connect to the internet. You can online by double clicking on the *Internet Explorer* icon on the desktop. You can also make the *Dial-up Network Connection* first, and then start up *Internet Explorer*. Confirm the *Dial-up Connection* dialogue box, or *Connect to* by clicking on the *Connect* button.

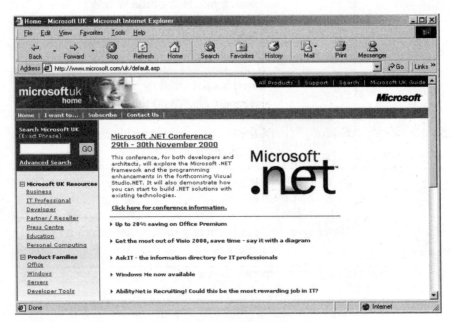

Figure 11.45   Online on the Homepage of *Windows Me*

Dialing status   While the connection is being made, the dialing status is displayed in the dialogue box. After you log on to the network, the default homepage will be displayed:

If you are dialing through an *Internet-by-Call* provider, the homepage of the provider is sometimes displayed, as for example, with *freenet*

Entering web addresses in *Internet Explorer*

To enter a web address (*URL*) click on the *Address bar* of *Internet Explorer*. Overwrite the contents with the full address. If you don't know any *URLs*, enter the following *URL* for Microsoft's English homepage:

▓ *http://www.microsoft.com/uk*

Press the ⏎, to enter the address and start the search for the site. If you are offline when you enter the address, the *Dial-up Connection* dialogue box will appear. Enter your *User name* and *Password*, and click on *Connect*. You will go to the homepage of *Microsoft*. Point to the button for *Windows*, and select the menu item *Support*.

Figure 11.46   Opening a website

Select *File/Open*, and re-enter the *URL* *http://www.microsoft.com/uk* in the text box:

Automatic completion

Take note of the display in the *Address bar*: Press ⏎, as soon as *Internet Explorer* automatically completes the remainder of the address for you. The *Microsoft* home-page is again displayed.

The list box arrows can also be used to open previously visited websites:

History list

Open the *Address bar* by clicking on ▼, and select one of the entries displayed there. *Internet Explorer* displays the pages previously displayed in the current session.

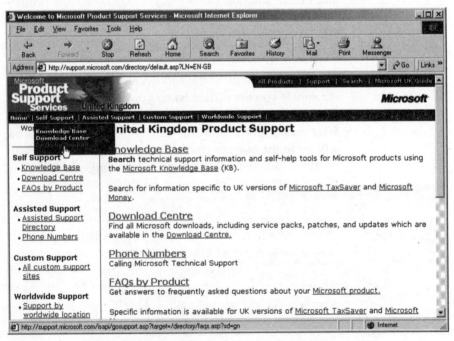

Figure 11.47   Opening the *FAQs* page on the *Microsoft* website

Following links

Point to the *Windows* hyperlink and click on *Support* and then on *FAQ*. Take note of the information displayed in the status bar. You will now find yourself in the *Support section* of *Microsoft*.

Point to one of the underlined texts, the so-called hyperlinks. When you click on a link, a new website is loaded into the browser window.

Back and Forward

To go back to the previous web page, click on the *Back* button. To get back again to the page which you were viewing, click on *Forward*.

Stop button

If the loading of a page takes too long, you can stop it from loading by clicking on *Stop*. Use the *Refresh* button to reload the current page. The *Home* button takes you to the default homepage.

Because web pages are constantly being updated, only a general description of the content can be given in this book. You should take advantage of the possibilities offered by the World Wide Web to obtain the latest drivers and service packs for *Windows Me*. You can also download free graphics, sound files, video sequences as well as icons, games and miscellaneous software onto your computer.

Virus scanner

Please remember that whenever you are online, and particularly when downloading files, there is a risk of getting a virus on your computer. You are always informed of this before you load the data. You should always check downloaded data with a virus scanner.

Working with hyperlinks on websites

Point to the *Microsoft* homepage. If another page is displayed on your browser, enter *http://www.microsoft.com/uk* in the *History* list of the *Address bar*, to go back to the *Microsoft* homepage.

Highlighted text

On the web page now being displayed, you see links in various forms, such as text highlighted in color: An example of this are the *...more* links, which you use to obtain additional information on the articles on the homepage.

Finger

Hyperlinks are called *Links* for short. Move the mouse over various area of the page and watch the shape of the mouse pointer and the display in the status bar. When you move over a link (text which is highlighted or underlined in blue, or perhaps a button or a picture), the mouse pointer changes to a hand.

The *URL* of the linked resource is displayed in the status bar. *Links* can also be hidden behind buttons, pictures or other areas of the screen. Point to the *Office* link, and you will see another menu containing more hyperlinks. When you click on *Support,* you will be taken to the *Support section* for *Microsoft Office* products.

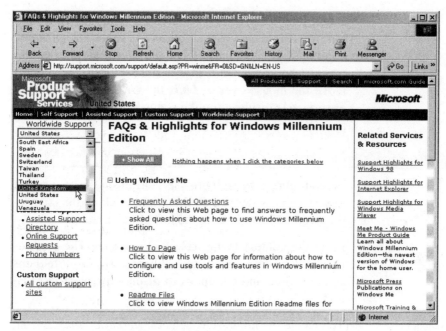

Figure 11.48   Links can also open lists

Using links as menus

Links such as *Support for* open a list. Click on an entry and nothing happens at first. However, once you confirm your product selection with a click on *Go,* the page you requested will be displayed.

Through the *Support* link and the *Support for* list, you go from the *Microsoft*-Homepage to the support websites for accessories, updates or drivers which can be downloaded for free.

Violet links

Internet Explorer shows which links you have already followed by displaying them in another color (*violet* by default).

Clickable Maps

The so-called *clickable maps* are graphics, pictures or photos, as well as lists and tables, which are connected by

545

a link. On the *Microsoft* homepage, you will find such links on the images at the right of the page. The *clickable maps* can be recognized by the fact that the mouse pointer changes when it moves over the item. When you move the mouse over a *Link*, the *URL* of the document or service is displayed in the status bar. To follow a *Link*, press the left mouse button.

Configuring *Internet Explorer*

To configure your web browser, terminate the connection to service provider. To do this, right-click on the connection icon in the taskbar to the left of the time.

From the context menu, select *Disconnect*. The connection will be terminated, but *Internet Explorer* remains active offline and continues to display the page last visited.

Changing the homepage

To change the homepage, select *Internet options....* from the *Tools* menu. Click on the *General* tab. In the *Homepage* options group, you can click on *Use blank* to set *Internet Explorer* to open with an empty page.

Custom homepage

In the *Address* text box, you can enter any address. Please use the correct spelling and enter *http://www.* - otherwise you may get an error message. Confirm with *Apply*.

Figure 11.49   Specifying the homepage of your choice

Homepage

The opening page is called the *Homepage*. It displays the document which is automatically loaded when connected to a web server. You can return to this configurable point of entry by clicking on the *Home* button.

**Your own
Homepage**

Homepages are usually used as graphical displays of a website which give an overview of the resources offered there. Any user can create his own homepage and put it on the web. Almost every internet service provider gives the users a certain amount of space on the server. With the *FrontPage* program contained in *Windows Me,* you can create your own homepage.

In the *Homepage* options group, you can set the default homepage at any time by clicking on *Use default.*

In WWW terminology, a document is referred to as a *Universal Resource Locator.* A *URL* is always in the form:

protocol://Service.Servername/Path/filename, e.g.:
http://www.microsoft.com.

Thus, *www.microsoft.com* is the address, *http://* specifies the transmission protocol, *Hyper Text Transfer Protocol, and www.* stands for the internet service *World Wide Web.* The name of the server is *microsoft.com* is. After that, there is the address path (z. B. */uk*), which may be randomly designated and usually points to a particular document (*index.htm*).

**Setting program
colours**

To set the program colours, select *Tools* and then *Internet options....* click on *General* and then on the *Colors* button. You can open a colour palette for *Text* or *Links* with a click on a color field. Select a color and confirm with *OK.*

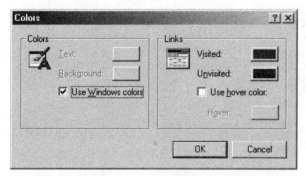

Figure 11.50   Setting colors for *Internet Explorer*

Selecting a font

To set a font, select the *Tools* menu and then *Internet options....* Click on the *General* tab and then on the *Fonts...* button. From the fonts list, select the desired font.

Setting text size

You can set the font size through the *View* menu, by selecting an entry: *Largest, Larger, Medium, Smaller* or *Smallest* from the expanded *Text size* menu.

The font you select in the *General* tab through the *Fonts...* button does not have an effect on the speed of loading pages in *Internet Explorer*. The browser simply converts the *HTML* into the selected font. This is a local process, i.e. it takes place on your computer.

Security settings

Security tab

Select *Tools* and then *Internet options....* to make security settings. Select the *Security* tab. In the upper section, *Zone,* click on the icon of a zone for web content.

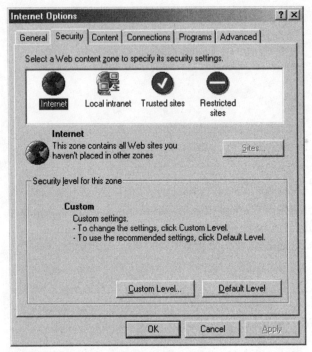

Figure 11.51   Making security settings for *Internet Explorer*

Custom level **button**

By clicking on the *Custom level...* button, experienced users can specify how *Internet Explorer* should react to special active web content, i.e. which programs or data *Internet Explorer* should automatically run or load onto your computer.

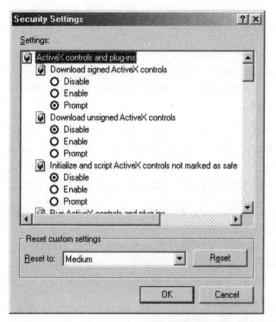

Figure 11.52   Customizing security settings for *Internet Explorer*

ActiveX controls

By default, the transmission of active content is allowed, as well as the downloading of media content. The *ActiveX controls* and *Java Scripts* are used for loading and running smaller programs, animation, sounds and three-dimensional graphics. This improves the appearance, but makes it less secure. Confirm your changes with *OK*.

By clicking on *Reset,* you can restore changed security settings to the original settings, for the security levels displayed under *Reset to.*

Saving and opening interesting websites under *Favorites*

Internet Explorer offers you the *Favorites* function for saving interesting websites. *Favorite* enables you to save the address of websites you've visited and to open them quickly later on.

Displaying interesting sites

Let's give it a try: Load the homepage, e.g. *http://www.Microsoft.com/uk/*. Point to *Windows,* and click on *Support* in the menu. On the support page of *Microsoft,* select the hyperlink *Downloads* from the list.

Add to Favorites

To save the displayed website as a *Favorite*, select the command *Add to favorites...* from the *Favorites* menu or the context menu. Accept or overwrite the suggested name for the Favorite in the Name field, and click on *OK*, to save the current page under *Favorites*.

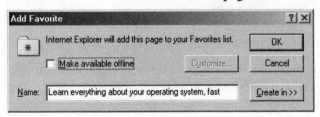

Figure 11.53   Creating *Favorites*

Opening Favorites

Go to other WWW pages and set more *Favorites*. To go to a saved *Favorite*, select it from the automatically updated *Favorites* menu.

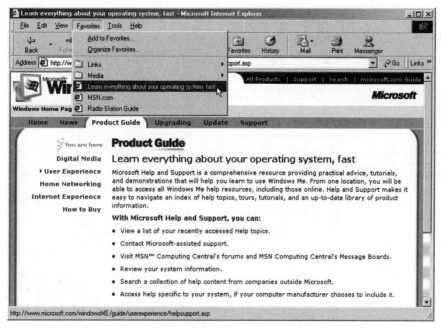

Figure 11.54   Selecting Favorites from the *Favorites* menu

You can alsp click on the *Favorites* button. The *Internet Explorer* window will be divided into two areas: On the left, there is a list of *Favorites* and *Favorites folders*. By default, new *Favorites* are added to the bottom of the list.

Favorites folder

Links

Click on the desired *Favorites* entry on the left side of the *Explorer* window to go to the website. You should also try opening the Favorites folder called *Links*, and try out one of the *Favorites* there.

By default, your new Favorites are always added to the bottom of the Favorites list. You can also put Favorites into existing folders: In the dialogue box, *Add to Favorite,s* click on the button *Create in >>*. Select the target folder from the list and confirm with *OK*.

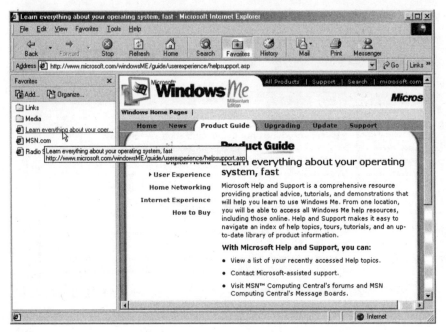

Figure 11.55 Opening a *Favorite*

Favorites saves you the time and trouble entering of frequently used *URL*s, which are often long and difficult to remember. Just click on the *Favorites* button and the double *Internet Explorer* window will appear.

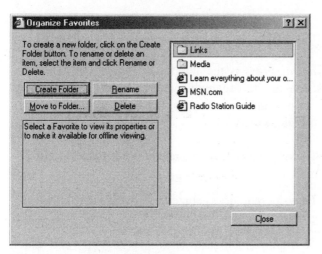

Figure 11.56   Managing Favorites

Favorites menu

When you click on an entry, *Internet Explorer* takes the address from the *Favorites* folder and tries to connect to it. Alternatively, you can also connect to the Favorites directly from the *Favorites* menu.

Favorites can also be changed: To do this, open the *Favorites* menu and select the entry *Organize Favorites*. Open the desired *Favorites* folder and mark the appropriate *favorite* in the list. Use one of the buttons to *Rename, Delete* or *Move to...* Close the window by clicking on *Close*.

Selected Favorotes can be renamed in the *Organize Favorites* dialogue box, by clicking on the name. You just have to overwrite the name entered. To confirm the renaming of a Favorite, click on ⏎.

555

Working with *Microsoft Outlook Express*

Overview

Outlook Express is the *Windows Me* program which assists you in the organizing and general use of data, as well as in communication with others. You can use *Microsoft Outlook Express* to carry out the following tasks:

- To write, read or organize electronic messages (e-mail)

- To write read or organize news from internet newsgroups

- To organize addresses or to save, organize and search for persons and e-mail addresses through the *Address book*

Online access

To use most of these functions, your computer must be a part of a network or have internet access. The e-mail and news functions also require an e-mail account and an internet news account.

Outlook Express
Address book

Outlook Express also sends and receives electronic messages when you are at the office, at home or on the road. Before you open messages, you can preview them , use message ID's and mark messages with an action to be performed later. You can also use *Outlook Express* without internet access. In this case, it serves primarily to organize personal and business address data with the help of the *Address book*. In the address book, you can keep data on personal and business contacts up to date. *Outlook Express* makes it easy to find addresses with its search function.

Starting and using *Microsoft Outlook Express*

In this section, you will become familiar with the *Outlook Express* program window. To do this, open *Microsoft Outlook Express* through one of the following methods:

Desktop
■ Double-click on the *Outlook Express* icon on the desktop

taskbar
■ Click on the *Launch Outlook Express* button in the *Quick launch bar*

■ Select *Start/Programs/Outlook Express*.

Outlook Express

Figure 11.57   The icon for *Outlook Express* on the desktop and in the quick launch bar

Depending on the configuration, *Microsoft Outlook Express* will start with or without further feedback from you. Normally, you will see a program window similar to that shown in Figure 11.58.

If you get a message about working in offline mode, do not change to online use. To familiarize yourself with the e-mail program *Outlook Express* you do not need an online connection.

Outlook Express opens as in Figure 11.58 only when your internet connection is completely set up. If you have not entered the information for your e-mail address or e-mail server, you will receive a request for information from the *Internet connection wizard*. Enter all the data which is required.

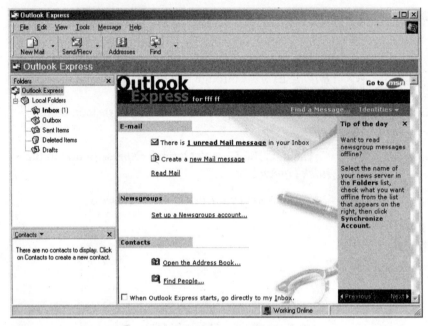

Figure 11.58   The *Microsoft Outlook Express* program window

Selecting a connection, and offline use

With the default settings, *Microsoft Outlook Express* tries to connect to the internet if you are not already online. You will see the message displayed in Figure 11.59.

Offline or Online?

The *Connect to* dialogue box will appear and you can connect to your internet service provider by clicking on *Connect*. If you click on *Work offline*, *Outlook Express* starts up without internet connection.

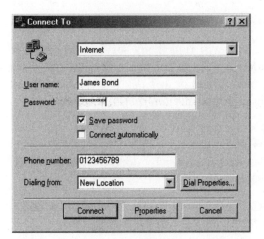

Figure 11.59   **Making an online connection** at the start of *Outlook Express*

Starting offline

If you are in offline mode, you only need to connect to your internet service provider when you want to send e-mails or receive messages and news. To configure the functioning of the program at startup, select *Tools/Options...* and click on the *General* tab.

You should configure your internet connection and e-mail and news services before you open *Microsoft Outlook Express* for the first time. It is easiest to do this through the *Internet connection wizard* which was described earlier.

Your internet service provider will give you all the information necessary for configuring mail and news services. If you are using an *Internet-by-Call*-provider, re-read the information at the beginning of this chapter. The necessary information is shown under *Logon information and e-mail configuration.*.

Setting up an e-mail address in the internet

In the internet, you will find many services which offer free e-mail addresses. Some eof the well known services are *gmx.de*, *hotmail* (*msn*) or *web.de*. You can also obtain an email address through any *Internet-by-Call* provider.

gmx.de

Here, we will show you how to set up a free e-mail address at *gmx.de*. First, you must first connect to the internet. Start up *Internet Explorer* by double clicking on the icon on the desktop.

Click on the *Connect* button in the *Connect to* dialogue box. Enter the following *URL* in the *Address bar*:

```
http://www.gmx.de
```

Filling out the form

Open the list box, *GMX Multilingual* and click on *English* to see the English language pages of *GMX*. Now, click on the hyperlink *Sign up* and fill out the registration form on the on the registration page of *GMX*. Enter all the information requested in this form.

Please use your correct first name, last name and address. Use the lists to select your address or country, if available.

Statistical information

Fill out the statistical information on your date of birth, family status, occupation and computer. You will not be given an e-mail address if you do not enter this information. Click on the *Continue sign up*, and enter the e-mail address of your choice:

```
Firstname.Lastname@gmx.de
```

Figure 11.60   Signing up for an e-mail address with *gmx*

You can also use the international domain names. With some luck, your e-mail address will still be available. The e-mail address cannot contain any empty spaces:

```
Firstname.Lastname@gmx.net
```

Password

It makes no difference which domain you choose, because the *gmx.net* server is always used. Enter a password consisting of at least six characters. If the e-mail address entered by you is still available, it is entered at *GMX*. If not, you will receive a message. Now, try spelling it differently. After you sign up, you will get an e-mail address at *GMX* which can be used anywhere in the world.

561

If you want to open or write your e-mails only through GMX while online, enter your full e-mail address under ID. Then type in your *Password* and click on *Login*. Click on *Inbox* to see any messages which have arrived, or on *New mail* to write your own mail. It is actually easier to work with the *Outlook Express* e-mail program.

Setting up an e-mail account in *Outlook Express*

If you have an e-mail address with another provider which supports the protocols *POP3, IMAP* or *HTTP* you can enter the data for the mail server as requested in *Outlook Express*.

No online
connection

If you want to set up the *Outlook Express* e-mail program for sending and receiving e-mail, you only need to connect to your service provider's mail server when you actually want to send your own messages or download new messages. *Outlook Express* can also be set up to automatically look for new messages whenever *Windows Me* is started up. You can also set up *Outlook Express* to send and check for new mail at specified intervals. Launch *Outlook* Express by clicking in the *Launch Outlook Express* button in the quick launch bar. If you want to remain offline, respond to the message which appears by clicking on the *Work offline* button.

Internet connection
wizard

If you are launching *Outlook Express* for the first time, the *Internet connection wizard* will appear for entering your e-mail address. Enter your name in the way in which it is to appear in the *From* field of your e-mail. Click on *Next*. Select the option *I already have an e-mail address...* and enter the address. Confirm again with *Next*.

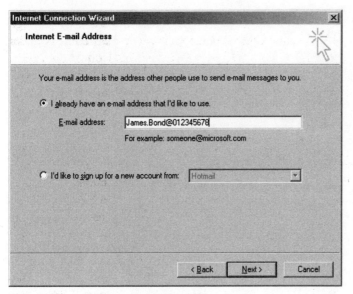

Figure 11.61   Entering the e-mail address

Pop3 server   Enter the name of the mail server of your internet provider. Use the data under *POP 3*, later on in this chapter,
if you are using an *Internet-by-Call* provider.

If you have set up an e-mail address with *gmx.de*, use the
following information:

```
Incoming mail server(pop3):      pop.gmx.net

Outgoing mail server (SMTP):     mail.gmx.net
```

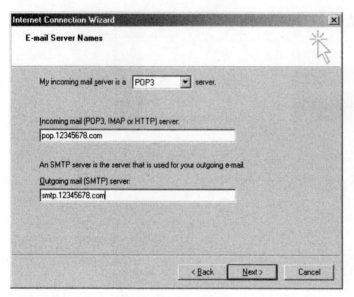

Figure 11.62   Entering mail server information

Account name

Click on *Next*, and enter your account name for logging in to the mail server. With many providers, you must enter the @ sign as well as the domain. At *gmx.de* an account name looks like this:

```
John-Smith@gmx.de
```

If you want, you can enter the *Password*. You can also select the checkbox *Save password*, if you like. However, the saving of passwords on disk is always a security risk. Confirm your next step with *Next* and close the wizard with *Finish*. Now, *Outlook Express* will be loaded.

Defining e-mail accounts

To define more e-mail accounts, select *Tools/Accounts....* in *Outlook Express*. To get an overview of existing e-mail accounts, select the *E-Mail* tab. Here, you can see the accounts for directory services and news.

Directory service or
news accounts

You can view and change marked entries with the *Prop-erties...* button. To set up a new e-mail account, click on *Add...* and select *E-mail*. You can set up accounts for news and directory services through the other entries. This will launch the familiar *Internet connection wizard*.

Enter all information required for the new account. Confirm with *Finish*. Defined e-mail accounts are listed under the *E-Mail* tab. Close the dialogue box by pressing on *Close*.

Organizing electronic messages with *Outlook Express*

Launching *Outlook*
Express

When you use *Outlook Express,* you can have all types of electronic message displayed in one folder. It makes no difference whether you have received them as e-mail from your internet service provider or through online services such as *CompuServe, T-Online* or *AOL*. To launch *Outlook Express* click on the button *Launch Outlook Express* in the *quick launch bar*.

To carry out the first step, you should work offline, i.e. not connected to the internet: To do this, click on the *Work offline* button.

Incoming mail
folder

To check the list of mail which has already arrived, click on *Inbox* icon the left side of the *Outlook Express* window. All existing messages will be displayed on the right side of the window. You can also click on the hyperlink *Read mail* on the right side of the window to go to the *Inbox*.

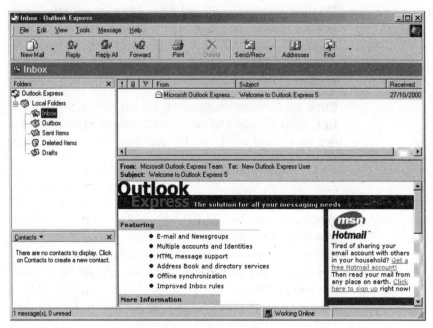

Figure 11.63   Viewing the inbox in *Outlook Express*

Reading messages

This step can also be carried out if you are not connected to the internet, because *Microsoft* has put a sample message in *Outlook*. If you want to read a message, click on the corresponding entry in the right window. *Outlook Express* closes the message in the bottom window.In the upper part of the window, you will see the information on the sender (*From*), the *Date* and the Subject of the message.

Sample message

If necessary, enlarge the *Outlook Express* window, or use the scroll bar to read the message. Every *Windows Me* contains the following sample message:

▓   *Welcome to Outlook Express 5*

Unread messages

On the right side of the window, *Outlook Express* identifies all unread messages with a closed envelope icon. Messages which have been read are identified by an open envelope. You can also sort the contents of in the right window.

Sorting messages

Click on *Subject*, to sort all messages according to subject. Click on *Date* to sort messages according to date of receipt.

Help with *Outlook Express*

Display the existing messages by clicking on the *Outlook Express Team....* Check the sender information in the upper part of the sender information. This message also gives you some help in starting with *Outlook Express*. You can also use the links to go to *Hotmail* where you can get an e-mail address. Through the *veriSign* link, you can apply for a free personal digital ID with which you can identify the sender. Double click on a message if you want to display it in its own window.

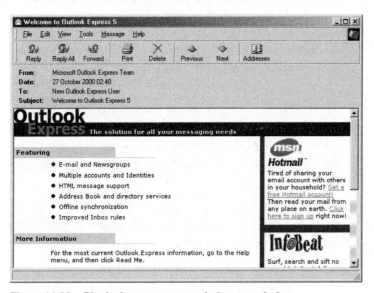

Figure 11.64   Displaying an message in its own window

You can reply to a message by using the icon bar of the messages window, in which the name is displayed in the title bar.

Replying to electronic messages

Reply button

Click on *Reply* to automatically enter the sender information in the reply window *RE:...* Delete the unnecessary quotation of the *Original message*, and enter the text of your reply. Now, click on *Send*.

When using the default settings, *Outlook Express* tries to make a connection to the internet. Confirm the *Connect to* dialogue box by clicking on *Connect*, to send the e-mail immediately.

Outbox folder

In *Outlook Express,* to see the list of messages which are still to be sent, click on the *Outbox* folder in the left *Outlook* window. Here, you will see all messages which have been written but not yet sent. The sending procedure can also be configured so that all messages are manually sent at the same time. Select *Tools/Options....* Under the *Send* tab, deactivate the checkbox *Send messages immediately*, and confirm with a click on *OK*.

To sort the information in the *Inbox* or *Outbox,* click on the title of the column. If you want to view information about thee messages, select *View/Columns...*and mark the column name in the list of columns and click on *Show*.

You can change the sequence of the display with the *Move Up* and *Move Down* buttons. Confirm with *OK*.

Composing e-mails with *Outlook Express*

**New e-mail
message**

You can also use *Outlook Express* to compose and send your own e-mail. Start up *Outlook Express* offline. To write a new e-mail, either select *File/New/ Mail message*, or press [Ctrl]+[N] or click on *New Mail*.

Whe you click on the *New Mail* button, you will see a list of *HTML* models to use as stationery for your e-mail. However, the recipient of the message must have an *HTML* compatible e-mail program such as *Outlook Express* to read the mail.

If the recipient does not have an *HTML* compatible program, you should not use the formatting and the stationery. Otherwise, *Outlook Express* will send the message, but the recipient will receive it as an *HTML* file instead of a text e-mail.

Not all e-mail services can display these formatted messages. It is however, possible with *Internet Mail* which is displayed in a web browser. In text e-mails, you should not use any special characters or special symbols. If you want to send an e-mail as text, select *Tools/Options...* and under the *Send* tab, select the option *Plain text* under *Mail sending format*.

**Entering e-mail
addresses**

In the *New Message* window, enter an e-mail address next to *To:* or click on the *TO:* button to open the *Address book*.

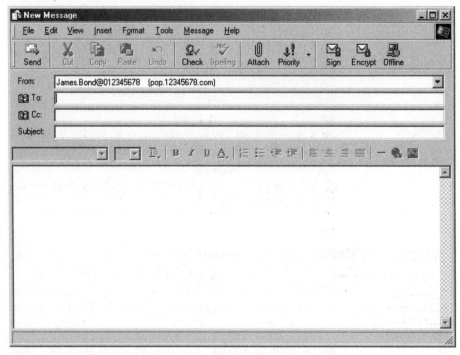

Figure 11.65   *New Message* window for composing an e-mail

Subject

Next to *Cc:* you can enter an e-mail address, to which a copy of the message will be sent. Next to *Subject:* write a brief comment on the contents of the mail. In the lower text field, you can write your message.

Sending e-mail with *Outlook Express*

Send button

To send a mail message, click on *File* and *Send message*. You can also press ⌈Ctrl⌋+⌊S⌋ or the *Send* button to send the e-mail.

Online connection

By default, *Outlook Express* tries to connect to your internet service. Confirm the *Connect to:* dialogue box by pressing *Connect* .

Sent items folder

A copy of the sent message is then saved in the *Sent items* folder.If you have configured *Outlook* through *Tools/Options...* to that the mail is not immediately sent, the e-mail will be placed in the *Outbox* folder. Now, you can compose more e-mails. Click on the *Send/Receive* button *Outlook*. Confirm the connection with the mail server by clicking on *Connect*. Otherwise, the mail will be sent when the next connection is made to the mail server, i.e. when you exit the program or start *Outlook Express,* and confirm with *Yes*.

Attachments

If you want to send files with *Outlook Express*, select *Insert/File attachment...* or press the *Attach* button with the paperclip symbol.

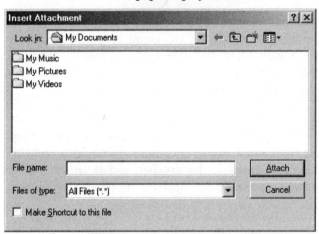

Figure 11.66   Adding a file to an e-mail as an *Attachment*

Inserting an attachment

In the *Insert attachment* dialogue box, mark the folder and click on *Attach*. Always send files as *Attachments*, and do not select the option *Make shortcut to this file*. This way, nothing can go wrong with the sending of the data.

Receiving e-mail with *Outlook Express*

It's really easy to receive mail: Launch *Outlook Express* by clicking on the *Launch Outlook Express* button in the *Quick launch bar*.

Start up *Outlook Express* online, i.e. with a connection to the internet. To male a connection, click on *Connect* in the message which appears at startup.

Send and receive

By default, *Outlook Express* automatically checks the mail server. You can check incoming mail manually by selecting *Tools/Send and receive/Send and receive all*, or by pressing Ctrl+M or by clicking on the *Send/Receive* button.

Inbox
folder

All of these methods check the mail server for all e-mail accounts. The messages are saved in the *Inbox* folder. After downloading the messages, disconnect from the online service and read the e-mail offline by clicking on the *Inbox* folder in the left window.

Incoming mail

You can read the mail you received by selecting the *Inbox* folder in the left window and clicking on the message in the right window. To reply, mark the message and click on the *Reply* button in the icon bar, so that the sender's information automatically appears in the reply window, *RE:....*

Files as
attachments

If incoming mail contains files as attachments, these are shown with a paperclip symbol in the *Inbox* of *Outlook Express*. In the opened message, click on the paperclip button and then on the entry of the file name. In the dialogue box which appears, click on *Open* or *Save*.

Setting up the *Address book*

Address book
application

In *Windows Me*, all addresses, telephone and fax numbers, business contacts or mail addresses can be organized and saved in the *Address book*, and used when needed. You won't find the command for opening the address book in the *Start* menu, because the Address book is actually a component of *Outlook Express*.

Entering addresses in the *Address book*

Microsoft
Office package

The entries in the address book can only be used with other programs besides *Outlook Express*. You can view and use addresses from the address book in the programs of the *Microsoft Office* package, such as *Word*.

Entering new
addresses

To enter addresses in the *Address book*, launch *Outlook Express*. To do this, click on the button *Launch Outlook Express* in the *Quick launch bar*. Start up *Outlook Express* offline. If necessary, click on the *Work offline* button. Click on the *Address book* button in the tool bar or in the *Outlook* window on the right. The address book is still empty.

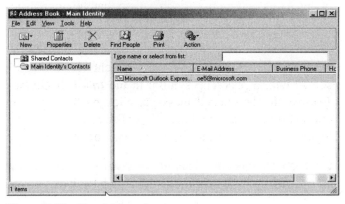

Figure 11.67   The *Address book*

You can add new addresses by selecting *File/ New contact...* or by clicking on *New* and selecting *New contact....*

Personal tab

A dialogue box with many tabs appears. Fill out the fields under the *Name* tab as desired. Enter the first and last name of the recipient in the corresponding fields. Enter the e-mail address and click on *Add*. Use the other tabs to save telephone numbers and addresses. When necessary, import data for digital signatures under the *Digital Ids* tab. Under the various tabs, enter all the information needed for the contact.

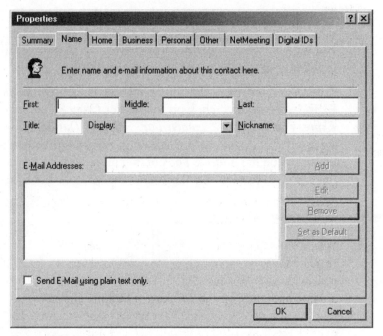

Figure 11.68   Adding new contacts to the *Address book*

Click on *OK* and the dialogue box will close. The new address will now appear in the *Address book* list.

When you are composing a new mail message in the *New message* window, Click on the button next to *To:* or *Cc:* The *Select recipient* dialogue box will appear. Select the name to be entered and click on the *To:* or *CC:* button to enter the name into the corresponding field. If you click on *New contact...*, a new address can be added to the *Address book*. Marked entries can be edited by clicking on *Properties...* Confirm the *Select recipient* dialogue box with *OK*, to use the address in the e-mail.

Organizing addresses in the *Address book*

To organize your addresses, you must start up *Outlook Express*. Open the *Address* book by clicking on the *Address book* button in the tool bar or through the hyperlink *Open address book...* in the *Outlook* window (*Outlook Express* folder). You can also use the key combination $\boxed{\text{Ctrl}}$+$\boxed{\Diamond}$+$\boxed{\text{B}}$.

Details to enter The *Address book* is a simple way to organize postal addresses, fax numbers, telephone numbers and e-mail addresses of people and companies. You can view the details of an address entry by pointing to a selected entry– a *Quick Info* will appear.

File/ Properties When you double click on a contact, mark a name, or select *File/Properties*, the *Properties* dialogue will appear with all available tabs. Alternatively, you can select a name and click on the *Properties* button. The information on the tabs can be changed or supplemented by overwriting any of the entries. The changes are saved with a click on *OK*.

Deleting addresses If you no longer need an address, you can select it and then click on the *Delete* button, or select *File/Delete*. If you confirm with *Yes*, the entry will be deleted from the *Address book*.

Find people button

For many of the entries in the *Address book*, you can also click on the *Find people* button or select *Edit/Find people*....

Finding addresses

To start the search function, use the key combination [Ctrl]+[F]. Enter the desired name or a part of it in the text box and click on the *Find now* button.

Displaying results

In the expanded dialogue box, all matching results will be displayed. If no results are found, you will receive the message "There are no entries in the Address book that match your search criteria". Respond to the message with *OK*, and try again.

You can also search for an e-mail address, street or telephone number. Use the appropriate text boxes in the *Find people* dialogue box.

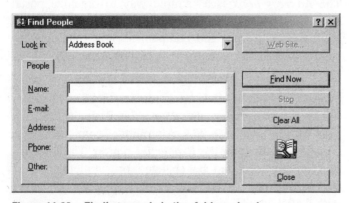

Figure 11.69   Finding people in the *Address book*

Online search

By double clicking on the corresponding entry in the search results window, you can find other information on that person. You can also use the search function to find e-mail addresses in online databases: Open the *Look in:* list and select one of the e-mail databases or directory services.

Online search

Click on *Find now*, and click on *Connect to* to go online, connect to the directory service and conduct a search according to your search criteria.

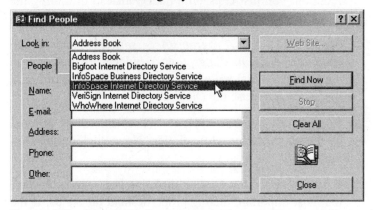

Figure 11.70   Selecting a directory service for an online search for e-mail addresses

The *Phone Dialer*

You can even set up *Windows Me* to dial telephone numbers, if your modem has an appropriate *Voice* function. After you have made the connection you can speak either through the sound card and microphone or another speaking device connected to thee modem. To dial the number, use the *Phone dialer* program of *Windows Me* which looks and functions like a modern push-button telephone.

Dialing telephone numbers with the *Phone dialer*

In this section, we will show you how to dial telephone numbers with the *Phone dialer*. In the next section, we will show an added feature of the function. You will learn how to store telephone numbers for later use. With this function, you just click on a button instead of dialing the entire number

Push-button telephone

Start with *Start/Programs/Accessories/Communication* and click on *Phone dialer,* your *Windows Me* push-button telephone: To dial a number directly, enter the number in the text box. Or use the *Dial* buttons

Separators for phone numbers

You can use symbols such as "-", which will be ignored by the phone dialer while dialing. Now, click on the *Dial* button.

Dialing dialogue box

Windows opens the *Dialing* dialogue box, which displays the most important dialing properties and the status. If the connection cannot be made, you will receive an error message.

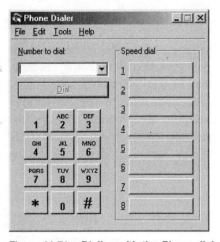

Figure 11.71   Dialing with the *Phone dialer*

After the connection has been made, you can use the *Voice* function of your modem and speak either through the sound card and a microphone or through another speaking device connected to your modem.

Disconnecting

To disconnect, click on the *Hang up* button in the *Dialing* dialogue box. To configure the dialing properties select *Tools/Dialing properties....*

Saving frequently called numbers with the *Phone dialer*

Saving telephone numbers

The *Windows Me Phone dialer* can be set to dial phone numbers directly. The program can also save important numbers which can be used later by clicking on the corresponding button. First, open the *Phone dialer*.

Save button

If you want to save a telephone number to be entered in the speed dial list, select, *Edit/Speed dial...* and click on an empty button. Enter the *Name* and *Number to dial,* for the number you want to save. The name you enter is used to label the corresponding button. Now, click on the *Save* button.

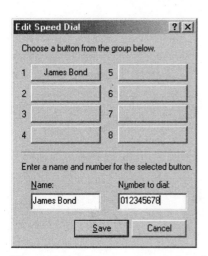

Figure 11.72   Programming numbers for speed dialing

Deleting entries

Use the *Edit speed dial* dialogue box to change numbers which have been saved. When you delete the an entry in the text boxes, the speed dialing button will also be deleted..

Dialing programmed numbers

To direct dial a programmed number, click on a speed dial button. *Windows* opens the *Dial* dialogue box, which displays the most important dialing properties and the status. If the connection cannot be made, you will receive an error message.

Hang up button

To disconnect, select the *Hang up* button in the *Dialing* dialogue box. Close the phone dialer with *File/Exit*.

12. The Drawing Program *Paint*

The *Windows Me* drawing program *Paint* lets you create pixel graphics quickly and easily. To create a drawing, you use basic geometric forms which are gradually transformed into shapes. You can also draw freehand lines or use an airbrush colour spray.

Pixel images

You will learn how to copy move or delete parts of images in *Paint,* how to create coloured images, draw opaque objects and use the zoom function. Other topics in this chapter include how to stretch and skew parts of images, how to rotate and flip them, and how to create your own Windows desktop background picture with *Paint*.

Drawing with *Paint*

This section describes the various drawing options in detail.

Toolbox

Start the drawing program by selecting *Start/ Programs/Accessories* and *Paint*. You will find the drawing implements of *Paint* in the so-called *Toolbox* on the left side of the window.

Quick Info

You can see the function of many of the drawing tools from their names. To view the names, point the mouse to a tool for a few seconds: a *Quick info* will be displayed next to it. .

Selecting drawing tools

To select a drawing tool, just click on its button. *Paint* displays additional information on the function of the tool in the status bar.

If the *Toolbox* is not visible on your screen, display it by selecting the *View* menu.

Figure 12.1　　The Toolbox and Color palette in Paint

Rectangles and ellipses

By clicking on the *Rectangle* ▱ button, you can draw rectangles and squares. The *Ellipse* ◯ button lets you draw ellipses and circles. Other buttons help you to draw a rectangle with rounded corners, lines and arcs as well as polygons. But now, back to drawing with *Paint*.

Drawing

Before you begin to draw, select a tool. Point to the drawing area and press the mouse button. Hold the button pressed and pull the object into the desired size.

Squares and circles

The object is created as soon as you release the mouse button. If you want to draw squares and circles instead of rectangles and ellipses, press the Shift key and hold it pressed while drawing.

Outlines

By default, the tools simply create outlines. To create filled objects with or without outlines, you can make a selection from the *Toolbox Options field*.

582

Toolbox Options field

This field is displayed under the tools, whenever a tool is selected. Mark a tool and select the line width or filling from the *Toolbox Options field* with a click of the mouse.

Drawing straight lines

To draw straight lines use the *Lines* ◥ tool. Mark the tool and click on the desired line width in the *Toolbox Options field*. Set the beginning of the line with a click of the mouse. Pull the line while holding the mouse button pressed. For a horizontal, vertical or 45-degree line, also press ◇.

Drawing free-form lines

You can draw free-form lines with the *Brush* ᴬ. Horizontal or vertical lines can be drawn when you press ◇ in addition. The width of the free-form line can be set in the *Toolbox Options field*.

Drawing curved lines

The *Curve* ᒃ button allows you to draw curved lines. For simple arcs, point to the starting position and click on the mouse. Hold the mouse button pressed and an arc will appear. You can select its form by clicking again in the drawing area.

Polygons

Polygons can be drawn by clicking on *Polygon* ◿. In the *Toolbox Options field,* you can specify whether you want to draw outlines or filled shapes. Click once in the drawing area for the starting point. Now, keep the mouse button pressed.

Closing the polygon

Draw the first line. Then, briefly let go of the mouse button and draw the next line, again keeping the mouse button pressed. Other lines can be drawn by again clicking on the endpoint. To close the polygon, click on the starting point.

Alternatively, this can be done by double clicking in the drawing area. *Paint* will draw a straight line between the cursor position and the starting point. While the polygon is still open, a click on the right mouse button will delete the lines drawn thus far.

Airbrushed free-form lines

Pin-point dots of colour can be applied with the *Airbrush* . Hold the mouse button pressed to draw airbrushed free-form lines. The thickness of the spray can be set in the *Toolbox Options field*. The density of the coloured dots depends on the mouse speed. When the key ⟨Shift⟩ is also pressed, you can draw horizontal or vertical airbrushed lines.

Inserting text

To label parts of the drawing, select *Text* A . When you click on the position of insertion, a text frame and font selection window appear.

Right from the start, you can set the desired size of the text frame. Write your text within this frame. To format it, use the *Text tool bar* (*View* menu).

If you make a mistake while typing, press ⟨←⟩ For multiple lines text, press ⟨↵⟩ at the end of the line.

Bold, italic or underlined

At the right margin of the text frame, *Paint* interrupts the text automatically. You can also set the font style *Bold*, *Italic* or *Underlined* in the *Text tool bar*, while the text frame is still displayed.

> If you click outside of the text frame or if you select a new tool, the text will be fixed and cannot be changed. You can change drawing mistakes with *Edit/Undo*. Save your changes with *File/ Save*. Then you can go back to the saved shape if there is a drawing error.

Setting outline and fill colours with *Paint*

With the defaults settings of *Paint*, you can only create black outlines or black filled objects. If you want to add some colour, use the *Paint Color Palette*

Colour palette

To define colours before drawing, use the *Paint Color palette*. This can be found above the status bar and consists of twenty-eight colours. The field for *foreground/background colors* is located to the left of the color palette.

The field in the foreground displays the current foreground colour. Lines or outlines of geometric shapes are drawn in this colour. This is true for all objects which are drawn with the left mouse button. The field in the background shows the current background colour.

Foreground and
, background
colours

Objects can be drawn or filled with the foreground colour if they were drawn with the right mouse button. To select a colour, just click on the field of the desired colour. If you press the right mouse button, you will set the foreground colour. If you press the left mouse button, the background colour will be selected.

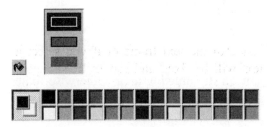

Figure 12.2   *Color fills* (above left), *Toolbox Options field* and *Color palette* (below)

Right mouse button   New colours are immediately pplied to an object. Objects drawn with the left mouse button are always filled with the current background colour, while the outline is drawn in the current background colour. If you draw with the right mouse button, this will change the colour selection, and outline will be filled in the background colour while outlines are drawn in the foreground colour.

Adding colour afterwards

If you want to add colour to objects or to closed line segments at a later time, use the *Color fill* 🔩 button. Click on *Color fill* 🔩, and select the foreground colour from the palette by clicking on the left mouse button.

Color fill

Point to a closed object in the drawing area, and click. The object will be filled with the current colour. To fill objects with the current background colour, set the *Color fill* 🔩 with the right mouse button.

Marking, copying, moving and deleting with *Paint*

Elements which are used more than once in a *Paint* drawing need to be drawn only once. After that, they can be copied as often as necessary.

Position of the drawing

Even the position of the drawing need not be final. Individual elements can be moved at any time to another position within the drawing area. If you have drawn an object, but are not satisfied with it, it can be deleted at any time.

Selecting an object

For all of the steps described, you must select the desired object in advance. The element should ideally be a free-standing element on the drawing area. Otherwise, other components of the picture lying underneath it may be affected.

Selection tool

Paint has two special tools for selection of drawing elements: At the top of the *Toolbox* you will see *Free-form selection* 🔲 and *Selection* 🔲. With these, you can select different types of elements in the picture.

Free-form selection tool

With *Free-form selection* you can select any parts of the picture in the form of a freehand line. Move the mouse around the selected object while holding the mouse button pressed. When you release the button, the line will be closed into a rectangle. However, the selection itself remains as a free-form outline.

Selection tool

When you use *Selection* the areas of the image are selected in a rectangular form. Drawing elements or sections selected with *Free-form selection* or *Selection* are always shown with a dotted outline (see Figure 12.3, left). The selection can now be moved in the *Paint* drawing area, holding the mouse button pressed.

Moving a selection

The moving of an object is done by default with a transparent background. From the *Image* menu, select *Draw opaque* to make the background of the selection opaque and to overlay other objects with the current background colour.

 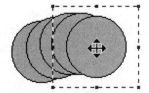

Figure 12.3   Selecting an object (left) and copying with ⌈Ctrl⌉

Deleting an object

Press the ⌈Del⌉ key to delete the object or selected area of the drawing. If the selection is within other drawing objects, you will see an rectangle or free-hand shape which is empty or in the current background colour (default is *white*).

Removing a selection

The selection can be undone by clicking in the drawing area outside the selection rectangle. On the selection rectangle outline, there are always eight gripping points, with which a selection can be stretched or skewed, enlarged or reduced.

Copying objects

Selected objects can be copied onto the *clipboard* with *Edit/Copy* or [Ctrl]+[C]. Alternatively, you can also select *Copy* from the context menu. With *Edit/Insert* or the key combination [Ctrl]+[V], you can copy objects from the clipboard as often as desired into *Paint* or any other Windows application.

Position for insertion

The insertion position in *Paint* is always the upper left corner. The inserted element is always given a selection outline with which it can be can be moved. If you are moving an object and press [Ctrl], you will create a copy of the object, while the original remains unchanged.

Cutting objects

If you select *Cut* in the *Edit* menu or context menu, or if you press [Ctrl]+[X], you can remove an object from *Paint* and put it on the *Clipboard*. From there, it can be copied as often as you like.

If you press the key [Shift] while moving an object, the object will be constantly copied as the mouse moves. This is called *Trail* and creates an interesting "comet tail" on the object.

Opaque drawing or insertion in *Paint*

Elements which have been drawn in *Paint* can be moved to other positions within the drawing area, even onto other parts of the drawing. Elements which are needed more than once in a *Paint* drawing need to be drawn only once, and they can be copied as often as desired.

Transparent mode

The inserted copy can be re-positioned. By default, *Paint* always uses the transparent mode. This way, the background can be seen through the objects being moved.

Opaque drawing

If you are working with a white background and have an inserted object which you want to move over existing white parts of the drawing, then the background can be seen. (see Figure 12.4, right). This is not always desirable. To turn off the transparent mode, select *Draw opaque* from the *Image* menu.

Free-form selection

Select the desired area of the drawing. With the *Free-form selection* ⚟ select any areas of the drawing with a free-form line. While holding the button pressed, move the mouse around the object. When you release the button, the line becomes a rectangle, while the selection itself remains a free-form outline.

Selection tool

With the *Selection* ▱ tool, you can select areas of the image in a rectangular shape, by holding the mouse button pressed. The opaque selection can be moved to the new position (Figure 12.4, left).

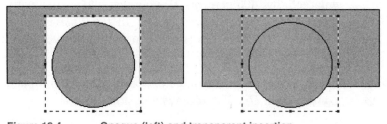

Figure 12.4   Opaque (left) and transparent insertion

Because the *Free-form selection* ⚟ or *Selection* ▱ tools always show the selections surrounded by a rectangle, the pixels which are located within it are also moved with the active background colour.

New background colour

If you change the background colour and move a selection, the original position of the selection is now coloured with the new background colour.

Draw opaque is also has applied to objects inserted from the *clipboard* into *Paint* with *Edit/Insert* or with ⌈Ctrl⌉+⌈V⌉.

Setting the zoom scale in *Paint*

Every object in *Paint* is made up of individual dots. In *Paint,* corrections are made by deleting or painting over.

Crosshair cursor
It is often not really easy to hit the exact start or end point of a new object with the crosshairs. If you want to work accurately, right down to the exact pixel, the only way is to enlarge the picture. In *Paint*, this can be done by zooming, up to 800 percent.

Zoom factor
To enlarge an image, select *Zoom* from the *View* menu. In the expanded menu, you can set the various zoom factors.

Large size
The selection of *Large size* causes the image to be enlarged by 400 percent. If you want to individually control the zoom, select *Custom*. In the *Custom zoom* dialogue box, there are five zoom factors between 100 and 800 percent.

New zoom factor
Click on one of the available options under *Zoom to*, and confirm with *OK*. The zoom is adjusted.

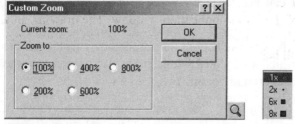

Figure 12.5   Setting the zoom factor and the *Magnifying glass* (below)

You can enlarge the image more quickly by using the *Magnifying glass* 🔍. If you click on this button, a frame appears which marks the area to be enlarged. Click in the frame to enlarge the section. The zoom factor for the magnifying glass can be set in the *Toolbox Options field*.

Editing to the exact pixels

You can edit fine details by enlarging from *600%* (*6 x* on the *magnifying glass* button in the *Toolbox Options field*) to *800%* (*8 x* on the *magnifying glass* button in the *Toolbox Options field*). To edit right down to the exact pixel, use the *Pencil* ✏.

Normal size

Select *View/Zoom* and select *Normal size* in the expanded menu, to return to the 1:1 display. Or, you can click *1 x* on the *magnifying glass* in the *Toolbox Options field*.

Setting picture size in *Paint*

Whenever you open *Paint* with *Start/Programs/Accessories* you are given a new, empty drawing area. You can now draw within the white drawing area. You can enlarge the *Paint program window* with the *Maximize* button, so that it will fill the entire screen.

Drawing area

As you can see, the drawing area still stretches to the edges of the *Paint* application window. The drawing area is actually even larger than it looks, as you can see from the scroll bar.

Unnecessary disk space

If you are drawing a small object, most of the drawing area remains white. So far, no problem. That is, until you save the image. *Paint* saves the entire drawing area, which takes up unnecessary disk space. In addition, you cannot insert a small object surrounded by a large empty white border into another Windows application such as the *Microsoft Office* package.

591

Full insertion size

A *Paint* file is inserted into another application in its full size (along with the white border). You can solve this problem by setting the drawing area of *Paint*. Before beginning to draw, select *Image* and *Attributes...* or press ⌈Ctrl⌉ + ⌈E⌉.

Attributes dialogue box

In the *Attributes* dialogue box, *Paint* displays the current drawing area in centimetres. The units can be changed to *pixels*. The default value corresponds to the resolution with which you are working at the time. For a VGA monitor resolution, this is 640 x 480 pixels, for 1024 x 768 pixels, these are the values which appear in the *Width* and *Height* text fields.

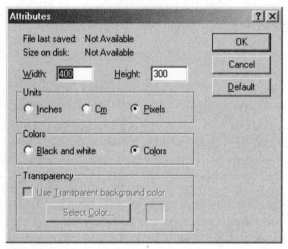

Figure 12.6   Changing the image size with *Image/Attributes...* in *Paint*

Width and Height text boxes

To set the new size in pixels, select *Pixels,* and enter the values in the *Width* and *Height* fields, and confirm with *OK*. If you prefer to make the setting in centimetres, switch to *Cm* under *Units* and enter the new values in centimetres in *Width* and *Height*. Confirm with *OK*.

If you insert an image from the clipboard which is larger than the defined drawing area, you will see a message which must be confirmed with *Yes*. Otherwise, the image will be cropped!

Image effects with *Paint*

Your own drawings, graphics or parts of graphics opened in *Paint* can be rotated, flipped, stretched, compressed or skewed at any time.

Rotating and flipping of images in *Paint*

The rotation of objects or selected area is done in fixed steps of 90, 180 or 270 degrees. When drawing elements or images are flipped, they are turned around an imaginary horizontal or vertical midline.

Selecting areas of the image

Before using *Rotate* or *Flip*, the parts of the image should be selected. Otherwise the commands are applied to the entire image. If only certain elements are to be rotated or flipped, you should select them with either *Free-form selection* 🔲 or *Selection* 🔲 from the *Toolbox*.

Free-form selection

With *Free-form selection,* you mark the desired area of the image with a free-form line. Keeping the mouse button pressed, move the mouse around the object. As soon as you release the button, the line turns into a rectangle. However, the selection itself retains the free-form outline. When you use *Selection,* 🔲 with the mouse button pressed, the area is marked with a rectangular outline.

Rotate
and Flip commands

Now, from the *Image* menu or context menu, select the command *Flip/Rotate....* Alternatively, you can use Ctrl+R. The *Flip and Rotate* dialogue box opens.

Flipping
horizontally or
vertically

To flip an image from left to right, select the option *Flip horizontal* and confirm with a click on *OK*.

If you wish to turn the image upside down, select *Flip vertical* and confirm with a click on *OK*.

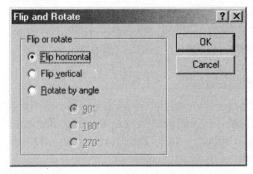

Figure 12.7   **Flipping parts of the image horizontally or vertically**

Fixed angles

If parts of the image or the entire drawing are to be flipped in fixed steps, select *Flip and Rotate....* from the *Image* or context menu, or use Ctrl+D. Select the option *Rotate by angle*, and select one of the angles offered: *90*, *180* or *270* degrees. Confirm with *OK*, to execute the rotation.

Stretching and skewing parts of an image in *Paint*

Stretching or skewing images or parts of an image – your own, or from graphics opened in *Paint* – can be done in freely definable percentage values with respect to the original size. When stretched, an drawing element becomes narrower or taller. When skewed, drawing elements are tipped to the left or the right – or, upwards or downwards.

Stretch and skew

Before you use *Stretch* or *Skew,* you should select the appropriate parts of the image. Otherwise, the command is applied to the entire image.

If only certain parts of the image are to be stretched or skewed, use either *Free-form selection* ⚒ or *Selection* ▢ from the *Toolbox* in advance.

Selection tool

Mark the desired areas of the image in a free-form line, using the *Free-form selection* ⚒ tool. Move the mouse around the object, keeping the mouse button pressed. As soon as you release the button, the free-form line becomes a rectangle, but the selection itself retains a free-form outline. The *Selection* ▢ tool allows you to select areas in a rectangular shape.

Stretch/Skew
command

In the *Image* menu, select *Stretch/*skew or use the key combination ⎡Ctrl⎤+⎡K⎤. The *Stretch and* skew dialogue box will open:

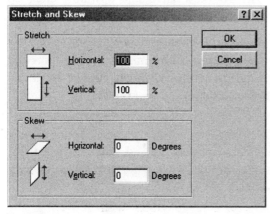

Figure 12.8   Objects can be stretched or skewed

Horizontal option

To widen an image or a part of an image, click in the *Horizontal* text box under *Stretch* and enter the appropriate percentage. Negative values in this field reduce the width. Confirm with *OK*.

Vertical option

If you want to change the height of an image or a part of an image, or it you want to turn the image upside down, click in the V*ertical* text box under *Stretch* and enter the appropriate percentage. Negative values reduce the height correspondingly. Confirm with *OK*.

Skewing images

If an image or part of an image is to be skewed, select Stretch/*Skew*.... from the *Image* menu or context menu. Alternatively, you can use Ctrl+K. The *Stretch and skew* dialogue box opens: To skew an image to the right, select *Horizontal* under *Skew* and enter the appropriate angle in degrees.

Negative values

Negative values skew the image to the left. Confirm by clicking on *OK*. To skew an image upwards, click on *Vertical* under *Skew* and enter the appropriate angle in degrees.

Negative values cause the image to be skewed downwards. Confirm with a click on *OK*, to apply the settings to the selected area.

The selection frame always has eight gripping points. Holding the mousse button pressed, you can use these points to visually stretch or skew a selection, or enlarge or reduce its size.

Opening, saving and printing Paint drawings

With *Paint,* you can create and save your own drawings, and in addition you can also open existing pixel images. The drawings can then be modified and saved again. You can also use a section of the drawing in another program.

Opening drawings with *Paint*

To open a bitmap in *Paint,* select *File* and *Open....* In the *Open* dialogue box, the *Windows* folder is searched for bitmaps by default. This is because *Bitmap* files are selected by default in the list box *Files of type:.*

Bitmap files

If you have no bitmaps of your own, use the scroll bar to display the background pictures saved in the *Windows* folder. *Windows Me* identifies bitmap files with the symbol: 🐾.

***Look in:* list box**

If you have bitmaps, e.g. on CD-ROMs which you want to look at in *Paint*, select the appropriate drive and folder in the *Look in:* list box. Select a bitmap and click on *Open.* You can also load the file by double clicking on it, or by marking it and clicking on ⏎.

Various graphics formats

Bitmaps can be saved in a wide variety of graphics formats. However, *Paint* allows you to open only files in three of the most commonly used formats. Graphics in other formats can be opened with the *Imaging* program. This will be displayed under *Programs/Accessories* after it has been separately installed.

Figure 12.9   Opening bitmap files in *Paint*

Saving a section of a *Paint* image

If you draw a small image with *Paint*, a large part of the drawing area remains white. These white areas are also saved pixel by pixel, because *Paint* saves the entire drawing area.

Unnecessary disk space

This unnecessarily takes up disk space. In a addition, you cannot insert the object saved in this way, e.g. as a logo for a letter created in *WordPad*.

Insert/object command

If you insert such an object with *Insert/Object...* in another program, the *Paint* file will be inserted in its full size, along with the white areas. Therefore, you can define the drawing area in *Paint,* and also use a special method to save sections of images.

Save area

In any position in the *Paint* drawing area, draw the image which you want to save separately. You can also open an existing picture and save a section of it under another name.

Selecting the area

Select the desired area of the image. Use *View/ Zoom /Custom...* or click on *Magnifying glass* 🔍 to enlarge the image and select it to the exact pixel. To save your selection, select *Edit/Copy to....*, switch to the target drive and folder and name the file under *File name*. If needed, specify the colour depth in the list of file types and confirm with *Save*. *Paint* now saves only the selection, without the surrounding areas.

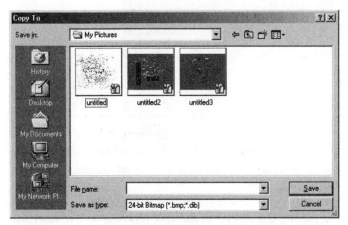

Figure 12.10   Saving selected areas with *Copy to...*

If you want to insert a section from *Paint* into another application, you can also place the selection on the clipboard with *Edit/Copy,* and insert it at the cursor position in the target application with *Edit/Insert*. You can do this without saving.

Saving images with *Paint*

Save as dialogue box

To save your own pictures or modified images with *Paint* select *File* and *Save as*.

In the *Save as* dialogue box, enter a name with a maximum of 255 characters under *File name*.

Capitalization and empty spaces can be used in the name. Now, select the target drive and folder through the list box.

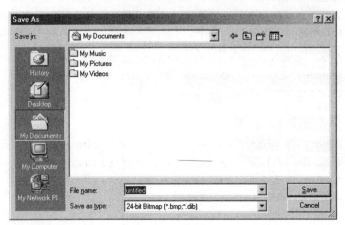

Figure 12.11   Saving *Paint* images as bitmap files

Specifying file type   You only need to specify the file type in the *File type* list box. Using the entries in the *File type* list box, specify the graphics format and the colour depth for the bitmap file: Even with images created without defined colour mixing, you should set *256 ColorBitmap (*.bmp)*.

Number of colours   The use of this number of colours is suitable for most purposes and saves disk space. However, true colour photos which have been opened should be saved as *24-Bit Bitmap (*.bmp)*.

To save an image, click on the *Save* button.

By default. *Paint* saves a bitmap file as a *24-Bit Bitmap* (corresponds to 16.8 million colours), but it can also save in 8-, 4- and 2-Bit, i.e. with 256, 16 or 2 colours (*Monochrome Bitmap*). The number of colours has a direct effect on the disk space used. You can also save *Paint* images in the widely used *TIF* format, by simply entering ".*TIF*" after the file name.

JPEG graphics *(JPG)* and *GIF images* can be displayed in *Internet Explorer* or used in *FrontPage Express* for creating web pages.

If you use *File/ Save* or Ctrl+S to save images again after the first save, you will be saving the image as it has been edited while continuing to work with *Paint*. Saving will overwrite the existing file with the newer version.

Printing your drawings with *Paint*

Printing an image

Drawings which you have created with *Paint* can be printed at any time. The requirement for this is a printer which is connected to your computer under *Windows Me*. You can read more about this in Chapter 8. "Control Panel". To print a file from *Paint* select *File* and *Print*. The procedure for printing is identical in all Windows applications. If more than one printer is connected to your computer, the default displayed in the printer *Name* list box is always that of the *Default printer*.

Selecting the printer

Open the *Name* list box under *Printer*, and select the printer you want to use. A colour printer is recommended for printing from *Paint*.

Setting the print area

You can specify the area of the image to be printed under the options in *Print range*. By default, *All* is selected. This prints the entire drawing area. If you select *Pages*, you must enter the page numbers under *From* and *To*. Unfortunately *Paint* does not offer a preview of the distribution of a large drawing over multiple pages.

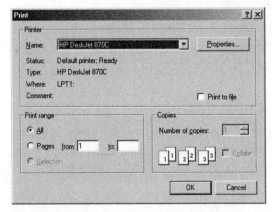

Figure 12.12   The *Print* dialogue box

Setting number of copies

Under *Copies,* enter the number of *Copies* of the drawing to be printed. Select the option *Collate,* if it is available for your printer. Now, begin the print job with *OK*.

Graphics tab

When you print with *Paint*, the settings made under the *Graphics* tab in the properties window of your printer are used. These settings can also be changed in the *Print* dialogue box.

In the *Printer* options group, click on *Properties*. The *Properties of [printer]* will appear. Select the *Graphics* tab, which is similar to that shown in Figure 12.13 for *Windows Me* printer drivers.

Figure 12.13   Changing the properties for graphics printing

If you have not installed a *Windows Me* printer driver, this tab may look completely different. If you have problems with printing, select *Use grid* under *Graphics mode* in the *Graphics* tab.

Color mixing

For most *Windows Me* printer drivers, you can select *None, Coarse, fine, Line art* or *Error diffusion* under *Color mixing*.

Error diffusion

The *Error diffusion* option creates a very diffused printing result, even with monochrome laser printers. It is best to just try out the various printer settings. The *Intensity* slide allows you to set the intensity of the print. Confirm your changes with *OK*, and start the printing with *OK*.

Creating a desktop wallpaper with *Paint*

Any picture which you create with *Paint* can be used as a desktop background picture (wallpaper). You may have already tried out the background pictures supplied. There are some nice motifs, but that's no reason why you shouldn't use a picture you created yourself.

Saving a background picture

Before you set a background picture for the desktop, you can allow your imagination to run wild and create a picture with *Paint*. Click on *Start* and select *Programs/ Accessories/Paint*. Use the tools described in this chapter under "Drawing with *Paint*" to create your own personalized picture.

Setting attributes

If you want to draw a small picture, select *Image/Attributes...* and set the size of the area for drawing.

As a default size for the drawing, *Paint* generally uses the pixel number of your screen resolution e.g. 1024 x 768 pixels. However, *Paint* cannot show the entire screen area at once.

If you want to create a full screen image, don't forget to move to the areas which are not visible, using the scroll bars.

File name

If you have completed the picture, select *File/ Save* to save a copy. Select a folder (e.g. *My documents*), and enter a file name under *File name* and click on *Save*. Now you can save the picture as a background for your desktop.

As background command

Select the command *Set as wallpaper (centered)* from the *File* menu. If you have only created a small picture, select *Set as wallpaper (tiled)*. The tiled effect is only visible if the picture is smaller than the desktop.

Minimize all windows

Right-click on the taskbar and select *Minimize all windows* from the context menu. Check the desktop, which will now display your own *Paint* image as wallpaper. Right-click on the *Paint* button and select *Close* from the context menu.

If you don't like your picture as wallpaper on the desktop, it can be turned off and you can select another default background picture through the *Control Panel* by clicking on *Display* and selecting the *Background* tab.

Working with the *Clipboard*

The *Clipboard* is used for data exchange within and between applications. Under *Windows Me* you can also use the *Clipboard* to copy or move objects between folders. The *Clipboard* is an invisible buffer, whose contents are deleted when the computer is turned off. The *Clipboard* is one of the most important windows functions and is available on every computer.

Clipboard application

The *Copy*, *Cut* and *Move* commands are always available, independent of the type of installation. In this section, we will discuss the *Clipboard Viewer*, with which you can see the contents of the buffer memory.

These windows components are not set up by the *Standard* installation. However, you can change that.

Accessories
program group

Before you follow the further instructions, you should check to see whether the *ClipboardViewer* program is already installed on your computer. Select *Start/Programs* and open the program group *Accessories*. If the *Clipboard* is already set up, you will see its program icon 📋 Clipboard Viewer in the *Accessories/System tools* menu. If this is not the case, proceed as follows:

Installing the *Clipboard Viewer*

Windows setup

Select *Start* and *Settings*, and then click on *Control Panel*. In the *Control Panel,* select the option *Add/remove programs* 🖳. In the *Add/remove programs properties* window, select the *Windows Setup* tab. Wait for the automatic detection.

Using the scroll bar, point to *System Tools* in the *Components* list. Mark it and then click on *Details....*

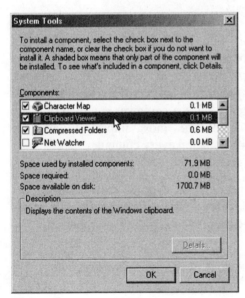

Figure 12.14   Installing the *Clipboard Viewer* application

List of *Components*   Use the scroll bar to move to the bottom of the *Components* list. Mark the checkbox next to *Clipboard Viewer*. Confirm twice with *OK* and the data will be copied. Then, close the *Control Panel*.

Viewing the *Clipboard*

Viewing the
Clipboard

To open the *Clipboard Viewer* program, select *Start/Programs* and open *Accessories/System tools*. Click on 📋 Clipboard Viewer in the *System tools* menu. An empty program window will appear.

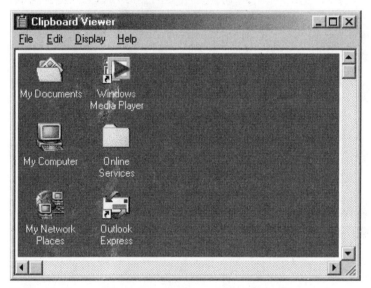

Figure 12.15   Viewing the contents of the *Clipboard*

Bitmap of the
Windows desktop

Press ⌐Print screen¬, to copy the contents of your screen onto the *Clipboard*. In the *Clipboard* program, you will see a bitmap of your Windows desktop. Use ⌐Alt¬+⌐Print screen¬ to create a copy of the active window on the *Windows Me* desktop.

The *Clipboard* can also be used to create copies of folders and files. In the *Clipboard Viewer* program, the path is displayed as text.

13. *WordPad* Word Processor

In this chapter, we will discuss word processing in *Windows Me*. The operating system comes already equipped with its own simple word processing program. The functions offered by *WordPad* are sufficient for the first steps, because the entering of text, control of the cursor and the selection, copying and moving of text is not fundamentally different to that of *Microsoft Word* in the *Microsoft Office* package.

Working with text

In this chapter, we will point out the things which you must be aware of when entering text in a word processing program such as *WordPad*, if you want to work efficiently.

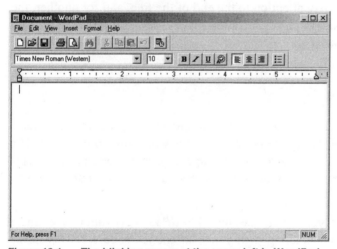

Figure 13.1   The blinking cursor at the upper left in WordPad

After you have opened *WordPad,* you will see the cursor blinking in the upper left corner of the working area. To enter text in *WordPad you* keep away from the "carriage return" (Enter) key. On a computer, this is the ↵ key. Unlike with a typewriter, you should not press the carriage return in *WordPad* at the end of a line. Word processing programs such as *WordPad* have an automatic *line break.*

When one line is full, *WordPad* automatically places the following text on the next line. You enter all of your text without ever having to press ↵.

You only need to press ↵ when you are at the end of a paragraph. *WordPad* organizes text separately into paragraphs. The paragraphs can be kept separate from one another one another, or they can be kept together. Therefore, you should continuously enter all the text belonging to one paragraph. You will quickly realize how easy it is to enter text in this manner. For one thing, you don't need to pay attention to the end of the line, and for another, the paragraph organization makes the word processing much easier

Controlling the cursor

In text fields and in word processing programs, the shape of the mouse pointer changes when you point to text. The pointer blinks in the shape of a short vertical line I This type of cursor is also known as the *text cursor* or *insertion mark.*

If you enter text into *WordPad* Text, another element moves along with your text entry, the cursor. This shows the current text entry position and normally corresponds to the place at which you are entering text at the time. The mouse pointer can be at a totally different position at this time.

The cursor position is most important in text entry or changes made in the text later on. It doesn't matter where your mouse pointer is at the time. The cursor can be positioned in several ways.

Positioning the cursor

The easiest way to position the cursor is with the mouse. Use the mouse to point to the place in the text where you want to place the cursor. Just press the left mouse button and the cursor will start blinking in this place.

To jump to a part of the text which is not visible, use the scroll bars or the ⌨PgUp⌨ and ⌨PgDn⌨ keys. When you have found the place you want, click the mouse button to position the text cursor there. You can now make changes in the text or enter new text in this place.

Selecting text

Before you can use any of the commands in *WordPad*, you must know how to select the correct area of text. Almost all text formatting is applied only to a selected area. If the text is not selected, the formatting is applied to new text. To format an existing document, you must select the text to "inform" *WordPad* which section is to be formatted.

Selecting text

There are several ways to select text.

Selecting with the mouse

To select with the mouse, place the mouse pointer just in front of the first character to be selected. Hold the mouse button pressed and pull the cursor to the right until it is positioned just after the last character to be selected. The selection is marked with a black bar. *WordPad* marks a word automatically if you point with the cursor to any place in the word and move the cursor to the left or right.

If you want to select individual characters, turn off the automatic selection. Select the *View* menu in *WordPad* and click on *Options....* Select the *Options* tab, and deactivate the option *Automatic word selection*. Confirm with *OK*. Now you can select single characters within a word.

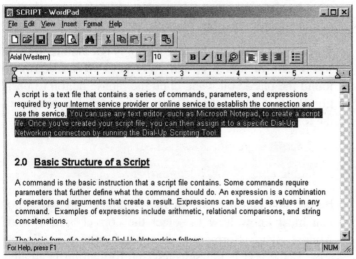

Figure 13.2   Selecting text in WordPad

The automatic selection functions forwards and backwards. You can also use the mouse to easily select whole lines, paragraphs and pages. When the cursor reaches the end of the *WordPad* window, the visible section of the page is automatically moved and scrolled line by line over the screen.

Selecting with mouse and keyboard

To select using a combination of mouse and keyboard, click before the first character to be selected. Now press the ⌈Shift⌋ key, and hold it pressed and click on the last character to be selected. Now release the ⌈Shift⌋ key.

Selection with mouse and keyboard also works with multiple pages. For this, use the scroll bars, to scroll down to the end of the text.

Multiple clicks

If you want to select a word, double click on the word. If you want to select a whole line, place the cursor to the left of the line in the *selection area*.

With the mouse pointer pointing to the right 🡅 , click on the line. Multiple lines can be marked in this way by holding the mouse button pressed.

Double click

A double click in the *selection area* will select the entire paragraph. If you want to extend the selection, press ⌈Shift⌋ and move the mouse up or down, while holding the button pressed.

Selecting with menu commands

The key combination ⌈Ctrl⌋+⌈A⌋ in *WordPad* corresponds to the command *Edit/Select all,* and the entire text will be selected.

Correcting typing mistakes

Correcting
mistakes

It is particularly easy to correct mistakes with a word processing program. The following section explains the options available to you.

If you make a typing mistake while entering text, there are several ways to correct it. We will show you the most important ones. You can then use the one which suits you best.

Deleting a character to the left or right of the cursor

An incorrect character to the left of the cursor can be deleted by pressing [←]. Now, you can enter the correct character.

Correcting typing mistakes

Typing mistakes to the right of the cursor can be deleted by pressing Del. Now, you can enter the new text.

Setting overwrite or insert modes

Replacing longer character strings

To replace longer character strings to the right of the cursor, press Ins. By doing this, you switch from the default insert mode to the overwrite mode.

If you now enter text, each new character replaces the existing character to the right of the cursor. Press Ins again to return to insert mode.

Deleting and overwriting selections

You can select typing mistakes and delete the text with Del. Then you can enter the new text. You can also directly overwrite selected text by simply typing in the new text.

Copy, Cut and Paste

Moving text passages

To move text passages in *WordPad*, use the *clipboard*. Mark the area you want to move. There are several ways to place it on the *clipboard*.

Copying parts of text

Select *Edit/Copy*, to copy selected text onto the *clipboard* without removing the text from its original position. You can also use the *Copy* 🖹 button from the toolbar or the shortcut `Ctrl`+`C`.

Deleting text

If you select *Edit/Copy*, the selected text is removed from the document and copied onto the *clipboard*. You can also use the *Cut* ✄ button from the toolbar or the shortcut `Ctrl`+`X`.

When you copy onto the clipboard, you can insert the text again in the *WordPad* document (or in other applications such as *Microsoft Office*): Position the cursor in the place where the text is to be inserted and select *Edit* and *Paste*.

An alternative

You can also use the *Paste* 🖹 button from the toolbar or the key combination `Ctrl`+`V`.

You can repeat this procedure as many times as you like in the same document or in entirely different documents.

Clipboard

Caution: In the *clipboard*, texts which have been copied or cut can be overwritten by other copies to the clipboard and are deleted when the computer is switched off

Copy. Cut and *Paste* are also available through the context menu of the right mouse button: Select the desired text passage and then press the right mouse button. Select *Copy* or *Cut*. Then, click on the place of insertion, press the right mouse button, and select *Paste* from the context menu.

Formatting text

If you want to write a letter in *WordPad*, the word processing program uses the *Times New Roman* font in the *10 point* size by default.

Of course, you don't have to leave it that way. *WordPad* can be formatted in any available font and any available size.

Setting font and font size

For text which has already been written, select the desired characters, passages or – with `Ctrl`+`A` – the entire text. Use the *Font* command in the *Format* menu of *WordPad* to open the *Font* dialogue box shown in Figure 13.3.

Font/Font size list boxes

The current font and font size are selected from the *Font* and *Size* list boxes. You can see a preview of the font in the *Sample* box. All available fonts are displayed in the *Fonts* list.

TrueType fonts

The scaleable *TrueType* fonts are identified by the symbol Ꜩ next to the font name. Select the new font from the *Font* list by clicking on it. Use the scroll bar to scroll through the list of installed fonts.

Changing font size

To change the font size, enter a new value under *Size,* which is measured in points. Confirm with a click on *OK*.

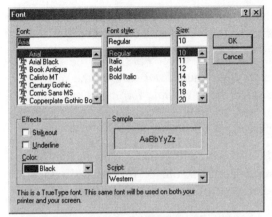

Figure 13.3   The Font dialogue box in WordPad

Font list box

You can format the text more quickly by using the *Font* and *Size* list boxes in the *Format bar*, which can be displayed and hidden through the *View* menu.

Open out the list boxes and select the desired entry. The font size can also be directly typed in and confirmed by pressing ⏎.

Font and font size can also be selected either before or during the text entry and the settings are valid until you make another setting. The *Font* command is also available through the context menu, if you click the right mouse button next to a selected text area.

Bold, italic and underlined text

In the previous section, we showed you how to set the font and font size in *WordPad.* Now you will learn how to apply bold, italic or underlined styles to individual characters or the entire text.

Text attributes

The type styles *Bold, Italic* and *Underlined* are set through *Format / Font...* At the end of the section, you will also see how to change the style using the buttons. If you want to boldface a text passage, select the desired text.

Format / Font

From the *Format* menu, select *Font....* In the *Font* dialogue box, select *Bold* under *Font style.* In the same way, you can also select *Italic or Bold italic* and you can also change boldfaced or italicised passages back into the *Regular* font style.

Preview

In the *Sample* field, you will get a preview of the formatting. You can select *Strikeout* or *Underlined* under *Effects*, by checking one of the available options.

Click on *OK*, to apply the formatting. You can work more quickly with the *Format bar* in *WordPad*.

Figure 13.4   The Format bar in *WordPad*

View /
Format bar

You can display and hide this icon bar with *View/format bar.* For boldface text passages, click on *Bold* **B**, the *Italic* **I** button italicises the characters, and you can put a line underneath the characters by clicking on *Underline* **U**. To do more complicated formatting, use *Format/Font....*

Color list box

The *Color* list box opens out a colour palette with which you can assign a colour to the text. You can open the *Color* list box more quickly through the *Color* button in the *Format bar.*

Setting text alignment

WordPad works like any other word processor with paragraphs. You can create a new paragraph by pressing ⏎. When you are entering text, all lines will be entered in the same paragraph until you press ⏎. You can also create empty lines with ⏎. These empty lines can change the appearance of the text.

Paragraph formatting

The reason for this is that *WordPad* can change the appearance of a paragraph, i.e. the whole text between two lines separated by clicking ⏎, and this is the same for empty sections. You can format or change paragraphs with *alignment, line spacing* or *insertion* of lines.

Paragraph formatting

Every paragraph can be formatted differently in *Word-Pad.* You can use paragraph formatting to set off individual text passages from the others and highlight them. In *WordPad,* paragraph formatting is done by selecting the *Format* menu and *Paragraph,* or through the *Format bar.* If this icon bar is not visible on your screen, open the *View* menu and select *Format bar.*

Write or load (see the end of the chapter) a text in *Word-Pad.* To set the text alignment, position the cursor in the paragraph or select more than one paragraph.

Setting text alignment

Format / Paragraph

Now select *Format/Paragraph....* Open the *Alignment* list box. The entries are *Left, Right* and *Center.* The default entry is always *Left.* Now, do we actually mean by *Alignment*?

The lines of a paragraph are always aligned on the page margins or on the page center. If you want to align the lines of one or more paragraphs on the left margin, select *Left* under *Alignment* in the *Paragraph* dialogue box. Since this is the default entry, you don't usually have to perform this step.

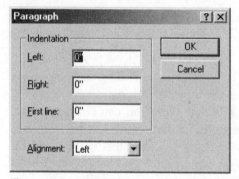

Figure 13.5   The Paragraph dialogue box in WordPad

If you want to align the lines along the right margin, select *Right* under *Alignment* in the *Paragraph* dialogue
box. To align lines along the imaginary midline of the
page, select *Centered* under *Alignment* in the *Paragraph*
dialogue box. The centered alignment is often used for titles; normal text is generally left-aligned. The right alignment is used, e.g. for the date or bill number in documents.

You can apply an *Alignment* more quickly by using the
buttons *Align left* ≡, *Center* ≡ and *Align right* ≡ in the
Format bar. Alternatively, you can select *Paragraph*
from the context menu if the cursor is in the correct paragraph.

Finding and exchanging text

With the *Find* function which is integrated into *WordPad*,
you can quickly find words in a document. If you want to
replace the search term with something else, you can use
the *Replace* function.

Finding text

If you want to find a particular term, individual characters or a group of characters or words in a *WordPad* text, select *Find...* from the *Edit* menu. Alternatively, you can use the *Find* button 🔍 or the keys Ctrl+F.

Find dialogue box

In the *Find* dialogue box, you can enter the search term and configure the search process. When you select the checkbox *Match whole word only*, *WordPad* only searches for the whole word which matches the search term, and ignores parts of words.

Capitalization

When you check the *Match case* checkbox, *WordPad* only searches for words where the case matches that given in the search term.

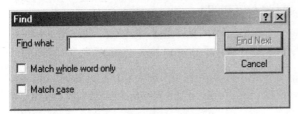

Figure 13.6   The Find dialogue box

Enter the search term in the text box *Find what:* and start the search by clicking on the button *Find next*. *WordPad* will then mark the first match for the search term.

If you click again on *Find next*, the next match will be found. If you close the dialogue box, the search can be started again with *Edit/Find next* or F3.

WordPad always begins searching from the current cursor position or at the beginning of a selection. If the end of the document is reached, the search is automatically continued from the beginning of the text.

In principle, the entire text will always be searched, independent of the position where the search was started. If you have selected a word before you selected the search command, *WordPad* enters this word automatically in the *Find what:* field.

Making changes To make changes in a search term while the *Find* dialogue box is open, just click in the marked area. After the search has ended, you will see a message which is to be confirmed with *OK*. Close the *Find* dialogue box with *Cancel* or with the *Close* ✖ button in the title bar.

Replacing text

If you want to replace certain characters, words or lines and word combinations with something else, select *Replace....* in the *Edit* menu.

The key combination for the *Replace* command is Ctrl+H. The *Replace* dialogue box opens.

Enter the search term in the *Find what:* text box, and enter the replacement term in the *Replace with:* text box.

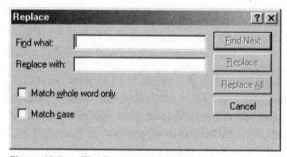

Figure 13.7   The Replace dialogue box

Configuring You can configure the replace function with the check boxes *Match whole word only* and *Match case*. Start the search by clicking on *Find next*. When you click on *Re-*

place, the first match will replaced, and the next match will be automatically found.

Click on *Replace* each time you want to have a match replaced. Select *Replace all,* if you want to have all matches replaced at once. Close the *Replace* dialogue box with a click on *Close* ✕ in the title bar.

Printing, saving and opening documents

In addition to editing the text, you will probably want to print out your document, and perhaps save it on the hard disk.

Printing the document

Print preview

Before you print a document, it can be useful to have a look at the *Print preview* in *WordPad.* Click on *Print preview* ▯ in the toolbar, or you can select *File/ Print preview.* Click on *Print* to open the corresponding dialogue box.

The procedure for printing is identical in all Windows applications. To print a document from a normal view in *WordPad,* select *File* and *Print...,* to open the *Print* dialogue box.

If there is more than one printer attached to your computer, the default printer will be displayed in the *Name:* list box. This is the printer which has been installed as the *Default printer* in the printers folder. Open the *Name:* list box under *Printer,* and select the printer you want to use.

Print range

Options group

By selecting one of the settings under *Print range* you specify which areas of the document are to be printed. The default option is *All,* which prints all pages of the document. Under the *Pages* option, you can enter the page numbers *From:* and *To:*. When this option is used, longer documents can be printed page by page. Selected parts of a document can be printed if you choose the option *Selection*.

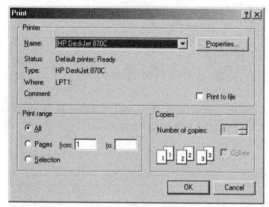

Figure 13.8   The Print dialogue box

Copies
options group

Under *Copies,* you can enter the number of *Copies* to be printed. Select the *Collate* option, if it is available for your printer. Start the print job by clicking on *OK*.

You can print texts with the default settings of the *Print* dialogue box more quickly by pressing the *Print* 🖨 button in the toolbar, which can be displayed through the *View* menu.

Saving documents

If you want to save a document created with *WordPad* on your hard disk for archiving, select *Save* from the *File* menu. If you save a document for the first time – you will recognize this from the title *Document - WordPad* in the title bar – the dialogue box *Save as* opens automatically.

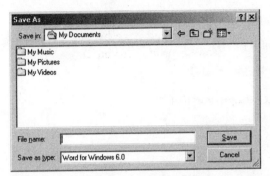

Figure 13.9   The Save as dialogue box

File name text box

The default name appears in the *File name* text box and is highlighted. Overwrite the highlighted text with a valid name of up to 255 characters, including spaces, which is also case-sensitive. From the list box, select the folder into which the file is to be saved. *WordPad* displays the folder which has last been used for saving. Click on the *Save* button to save the text on the hard disk.

Opening documents

To open a text file which has already been saved, select *Open* from the *File* menu. In the *Open* dialogue box, select the source drive or folder where the document has been stored.

Selecting file
names

Under *File name,* enter the name of the desired file or select the file from the list field by clicking on it. Click on *Open*. *WordPad* loads the selected file.

In the *Open* dialogue box, in the *Files of type* list box, there are other text formats listed, in addition to the *Word for Windows 6.0 (*.doc)* format.

Supported formats

WordPad can open documents in the following formats:

■ *Text Documents (*.txt)*

- *Text Documents - MS-DOS-Format (*.txt)*
- *RTF Format (*.rtf)*
- *Windows Write (*.wri)*
- *Unicode Text Documents (*.txt)*

Windows Glossary

.INF File

Setup files with the extension *INF* contain hardware information for the installation of new devices on the computer.

B-Channel

Every *ISDN* connection has two *B-channels* for the transmission of speech or data information.

Background application

An application which runs but is not active. All *background applications* are displayed as buttons in the *taskbar*.

Bits per Second, bps

The measurement of the speed with which a modem can transmit data.

Modern *V.90* Modems can reach speeds of up to 56,000 bit per second (bps).

Clipboard

Temporary storage space, which receives data that is either cut from a document with the *Edit/Cut* command or the *Cut* button, or copied with the *Edit/Copy* command or the *Copy* button. You can insert this data at another position within the document or into another document using the *Edit/Paste* command or the *Paste* button.

Command buttons

Control elements in dialog boxes. A *button* or *command button* is a rectangular box with a label.

Context-Sensitive help

Part of the *Windows* help which gives an explanation about an unknown *Windows* element, such as an item in a dialog box.

Control Panel

Folder containing icons with which all the basic settings for the connected hardware components, like mouse, printer, keyboard, screen, as well as installed software, can be customized.

Defragmenting

Data of a file is not always stored in one location but is often distributed among different sectors of the hard disk. In this case the file is fragmented. A fragmented file slows down the hard disk access.

Desktop

The control center of *Windows*. The desktop is displayed after the startup. It contains standard icons for *My Computer*, the *Recycle Bin* and *Internet Explorer*. Additionally, personal shortcut icons for files and programs can be placed there.

Details

The view that displays information in addition to the file or folder name in *Explorer*, *My Computer*, or in the search function. This view shows the size, type, and the last date of modification of an object.

Device Driver

A small program through which *Windows* communicates with an installed or connected device.

A device will only work after the driver has been installed.

Dial-up Connection

Under *Windows*, a connection with other computers, to a network or to the internet, made through a modem or an *ISDN* connection over the telephone line.

Drag

Moving an element across the screen, by selecting it with the *mouse pointer* and pulling it while holding down the left mouse button. Release the mouse button at the target location. In this way icons can be moved on the *desktop* or within or between folders.

Drag-and-Drop

Method of copying or moving data using the mouse.

DriveSpace

System utility that can compress small drives (up to 850 Mbytes). On a compressed drive, the data is saved in such a way that the disk space required is cut approximately in half.

DVD

Abbreviation for *Digital Video Disc*, an optical data medium which is similar to a CD-ROM.

DVDs can store very large amounts of data and are used for storing films.

Explorer

Program to maintain and organize folders and files. With *Explorer* you can copy and move, delete, create, rename, and create links to files and folders.

HTML

Acronym for *Hyper Text Markup* Language. Programming language for creation of hypertext documents for the WWW, which can be exchanged between different computer platforms.

HyperTerminal

Communications program (*Programs/Accessories/Communication*) which you can use to establish, via a modem, a connection to other computers, a mail box, or an information service.

Internet Protocol, *TCP/IP*

Protocol which is used for the addressing and sending of data in the internet or in the network.

TCP/IP stands for *Transmission Control Protocol/Internet Protocol*.

IP-Address

Internet Protocol address, which is used for identification of a computer in a network or in the internet. It must be unique, e.g. 192.168.17.4.

ISDN Adapter

Device needed for the computer to connect to the digital *ISDN* telephone line with 2 channels, each with a data transmission rate of 64 Kbit/s.

ISDN stands for *Integrated Services Digital Network*.

LAN

A group of computers and devices which are connected to one another in a network through a cable. *LAN* is the acronym for *Local Area Network*.

Local Computer

The computer on which you log in as a user, whose devices and data media you can access.

Local Printer

The printer which is directly connected to a computer.

Maximize

Increasing the size of a window to full screen, which is the maximum size under *Windows*. This process is called *maximizing*.

Menu

Horizontal bar below the *title bar*, which contains the labels of the menus.

Microsoft Backup

Windows Me program to backup files. *Microsoft Backup* is used mostly to backup large amounts of data.

Microsoft Outlook Express

Application to maintain and organize faxes and mail of any kind. *Outlook Express* contains folders for incoming and outgoing mail, as well as for deleted or sent objects.

Minimize

Windows can be minimized using the system menu, a button in the title bar or the shortcut menu. A minimized window is displayed as a button on the taskbar.

My Documents

System folder on the Desktop, which stores user-specific documents, graphics and other files.

In *Windows Me*, the folder is located at the highest level of the boot drive.

If the user management is being used, the file is stored under *Windows/Applications Data/[User name]*.

Modem

Device which transforms digital information from the computer into audio signals, which can be transmitted via telephone lines.

MS-DOS Prompt

Window for entering MS-DOS commands in *Windows Me*.

My Computer

Specific folder to maintain and organize the computer, its disk drives, hard disk(s), CD-ROM drive, connected printer(s) etc. *My Computer* is right below the desktop in the object hierarchy of Windows.

NotePad

Program to open, read, browse and modify unformatted text files. *Windows Me* come with *NotePad* to edit INI files and system files.

Offline

The computer is not connected to the network or the Internet.

Online

The computer is presently connected to the network or to the Internet.

Paint

Graphics program that comes with Windows, which creates and modifies bitmap files.

Phone Dialer

Program which allows you to save and automatically dial phone numbers.

Plug & Play

Standard through which the computer can automatically detect, and configure new devices and install the drivers.

Print Preview

WordPad view, which allows you to check one or more pages of a document before printing. The print preview shows the document exactly as it will be printed.

Printer Sharing

You need to allow sharing of your printer in order for it to be used by other users or computers.

In this case, the printer functions as a network printer.

QuickView

File viewer under *Windows Me*, which allows you to view the contents of files from the search function, *Explorer* or *My Computer* without having to open the program associated with the file.

Recycle Bin

Special folder in which deleted data is stored. Data deleted by the user is temporarily stored here, before being finally deleted.

Resources

IRQ's; DMA channels; I/O ports and *Memory addresses* are called resources and are used by devices.

Information in the internet is also referred to as resources.

Restore

The term *Restore* is used by *Windows* in three different areas. The *Restore* command button in the title bar restores a maximized window to its original size. The *Recycle Bin* will restore previously deleted files with this command. In *Windows Me Microsoft Backup* restores damaged or deleted files from the backed-up data.

ScanDisk

Windows Me system program which you can use under *Windows* to check drives for errors and automatically correct those that are found.

Scroll bar

Window elements at the edge of a window which are always shown if not all the contents of the window can be displayed.

Share Permission

Share permissions allow access to shared resources on ones own computer or on the network.

Shared Folder

Folder on another computer in the network which is shared with other users.

Shortcut

A shortcut establishes a connection to an object, which is saved in another location. You can use shortcuts, for example, to start programs or files directly from the desktop.

StartUp

Program group whose documents and programs are automatically opened when starting *Windows*. The folder can be viewed in the object hierarchy of *Explorer* from *Windows/Start Menu/ Programs/StartUp*.

Startup disk

Since the computer needs an operating system to function, it cannot be used if *Windows Me* is damaged. To be able to start your computer in such a case, you have to make a startup disk, onto which *Windows Me* will copy all the files needed for the Windows startup.

System Menu Icon

The icon in the upper-left corner of the title bar of every window. It contains commands to move, change the size of and close a window.

Target folder

The folder into which you want to copy or move one or more files.

Taskbar

Windows element at the bottom of the desktop. Enables you to switch between different running applications, called 'tasks'. The taskbar displays buttons of running programs.

Universal Serial Bus, USB

External connection to a computer through which up to 127 *USB* devices can be connected, without having to shut down the computer. The devices are automatically detected.

URL

Acronym for *Uniform Resource Locator*, i.e. the internet address which brings you to a web server.

User

A Person with particular user rights on a computer.

V.90 Modem

Modems of the *V*.90 standard which enable data transmission for download at a speed of up to 56,000 bps over analogue telephone lines.

The transmission rate for upload is 33,600 bps.

Virus

A small program which spreads from computer to computer and can cause damage or can cause inconvenience to the user.

Web Server

A computer in the internet which stores information or data and reacts to user requests which are sent over a web browser such as *Microsoft Internet Explorer*.

WordPad

Word processor. You can start it with *Start/Programs/Accessories/WordPad*. *WordPad* contains functions to edit and format text. In addition, it contains a page preview function and the possibility to embed objects from other programs. You can choose in which format *WordPad* should save the documents.

The *WYSIWYG* principle (What You See Is What You Get)

WYSIWYG is the acronym for "*What You See Is What You Get*", which means exactly what it says.

In *Windows,* it means that everything will be printed out exactly as it appears on your monitor screen.

The *WYSIWYG* principle allows you to assess the appearance of texts tables or graphics right on the screen, as long as they were created with *TrueType fonts*.